The Woman's Book of
HOUSEHOLD
MANAGEMENT

*Everything a woman
ought to know...*

The Woman's Book of
HOUSEHOLD MANAGEMENT

Everything a woman ought to know...

FLORENCE JACK

TEMPUS

First published 2007

Tempus Publishing Limited
The Mill, Brimscombe Port,
Stroud, Gloucestershire, GL5 2QG
www.tempus-publishing.com

© Tempus Publishing Ltd

British Library Cataloguing in Publication Data.
A catalogue record for this book is available from the British Library.

ISBN 978 0 7524 4210 5

Typesetting and origination by Tempus Publishing Limited
Printed in Great Britain

CONTENTS

FOREWORD

It is difficult today to imagine a life without the domestic appliances which have freed us from the perpetual grind of housework faced by most women in 1911.

In the first half of the twentieth century women generally had primary responsibility for the household and at that time there were no labour-saving devices to help with the daily chores – no washing machines, vacuum cleaners or dishwashers – and heating was provided by coal fires, which needed to be cleaned of the dirt and dust they produced.

Good housework was a highly valued social ethic of the era and women were dedicated to their house and families, rarely working outside the home. Middle-class families had maids to help with the housework, and this mistress/servant relationship was an important way in which women exerted authority on a daily basis.

Today servants have been replaced by machines; our appliances have reduced household chores to a minimum and opened up our leisure hours – in addition the domestic sphere is no longer specifically the woman's arena. The great interest in recent home programmes such as *How Clean is Your House* and *Perfect Housewife* has reawakened a pride in their abode for both sexes and created an ethos of 'It's cool to have a well run, comfortable and inviting home'.

The Woman's Book of Household Management – the original reference tool in 1911 – gives a nod towards the use of traditional, natural products; indeed *How Clean is Your House* emphasises the use of non-abrasive ingredients such as bicarbonate of soda, lemon and salt.

With information on subjects such as household work, laundry, pets, repairs and food, this comprehensive guide full of practical wisdom was state-of-the-art for its time.

This delightfully illustrated book – still valid today – is one that no house-proud domestic goddess should be without.

Emily Pearce

PREFACE

WE have been asked to address a few words to our readers before the Woman's Book goes to press. Its preparation has been no light task, and we have attempted so much that it is with some reason we fear some omissions and not a few mistakes will be discovered by our critics. But, defects notwithstanding, we are confident that the book is valuable, and we look forward hopefully to new editions being called for, when any suggestions and corrections sent us can be effected.

We have done our best to provide a Reference Book dealing with all subjects of special interest to women. A glance at the Contents will show how varied a list it is. And now that our work is finished and we look back on the book as a whole, thoughts about women's work in general force themselves upon us. Our work would have been mechanically done if they did not.

We have noted the variety of the work undertaken by women. It is matter for congratulation that so many new spheres of usefulness have been opened for women within recent years ; but we look forward to the time when capacity for work will be the only test of competence to undertake it. To have the work well done—that is the end to be aimed at, whether it be done by men or by women.

It is often urged that the limited outlook and training of women in the past have left them insufficiently developed in mental capacity and judgment for certain responsible spheres of work. But it seems to us that, if the test of the educative value of work is the number of faculties it calls into play, woman's work, even in the past—the work of the domestic woman—called forth faculties of the highest order. It has taken months of hard work to write an intelligible book on woman's work. A considerable part of the book is devoted to the ordering of a household, and this portion has not been the easiest to write. In writing it we have discovered afresh that the qualities that are demanded of a field-marshal, and a few not unimportant qualities in addition, are the necessary qualifications of a model wife and mother. Instinct in selecting subordinates, tact in managing them, organising of daily work, financial ability in handling the household budget, the taste that imparts charm to a home—these are not common faculties. But the training of the child makes the highest demand upon a woman. Patience, wisdom, self-sacrifice are called for at every hour of the day. Morally as well as intellectually the domestic woman's life is rich in opportunity.

While, however, we cannot appreciate too highly the value of the work done by the domestic woman, it is absurd to regard that as woman's only sphere. Many have not the opportunity of such a life : many have not the aptitude for it. We have therefore endeavoured to take the widest possible view of Woman's sphere. Everything she can do well, *that* she is entitled to have the opportunity of doing. We hope that the information given in the volume about the various kinds of work now open to women, and the various agencies at work to qualify women for the work they can do, will be found useful ; and we hope, too, that the manner in which we have presented the domestic information may lead to a higher standard of attainment in woman's greatest industry —the home.

F. B. J.
R. S.

LONDON,
April 1911.

SOME OF THE CONTRIBUTORS

MRS. BERNARD MOLE, Principal, St. Mary's Nursery College, Hampstead.

MISS FEDDEN, Principal, St. Martha's College of Housecraft, London.

MISS MAUD COOKES, Head Teacher, Dressmaking and Millinery, National Training School of Cookery, London.

MISS ALICE LEMON, M.R.B.W.A.

MISS MARGARET E. BUCHANAN, Ph. Chem., M.P.S., President of the Association of Women Pharmacists.

MISS K. M. COURTAULD, Principal of Colne Engaine Farm, Earl's Colne, Essex.

MISS N. EDWARDS, President of the Ladies' Poultry Club and Principal of Coaley Poultry Farm, Gloucestershire.

MISS BERTHA LA MOTHE, Teacher of and Lecturer on "Beekeeping."

THE HOUSE

THERE is nothing that requires more careful consideration than the choosing of a house—there are so many points to be studied, so many side issues to remember; yet many people set about selecting what to them must henceforth spell the magic word " home " in the most casual manner, giving never a thought to position, site, aspect, ventilation, sanitary arrangements, or any of the other important matters which are so necessary to ensure the health, comfort, and general well-being of the inmates of a dwelling. It is more often through ignorance, however, than through wilful neglect that the house is chosen in so thoughtless a manner, for the English are proverbially a home-loving nation, and, in spite of all that has been said to the contrary, it is the home life above all others which appeals to the average Englishwoman. In this chapter all the important considerations which should govern (1) the choice of a house, (2) its decoration, and (3) the selection of its furniture, are dealt with in a manner which, it is trusted, will be helpful to many a young housewife, and more especially to those whose choice must in many ways be restricted by the limitations of a slender purse.

First Considerations.—The first point for the would-be householder to consider is what rent can be afforded, or, if she wishes to purchase the house, what sum can be devoted to this purpose. She should be as exact as possible in her calculations before she makes up her mind whether to buy or rent a dwelling. Rates and taxes have to be considered in both cases. The purchase money, it must be remembered, represents money which otherwise invested would have brought in a yearly rate of interest. The loss of this yearly interest must be reckoned as equivalent to annual out-of-pocket expenditure, added to which must be the cost of upkeep and repairs, and those taxes which, in the case of a house let on lease, are paid by the landlord, not to speak of the many other expenses which the ownership of house property involves.

If it is proposed to lease a house there are several points which would increase or decrease the expenditure as the case may be. If it is taken on a repairing lease, the tenant will have to see to all repairs both inside and out. This will amount to not a little expenditure in the course of the year, and therefore repairing leases should be avoided where possible. In London, however, and many other large towns most of the houses are let upon repairing leases. In these circumstances it is more than ever important that the house be in thorough condition and repair before the new tenant takes possession.

In some leases a stipulation is made that the landlord will attend to all outside repairs, whilst a tenant will be held responsible for inside repairs; but the ideal arrangement is undoubtedly that in which the landlord undertakes to do *all* repairs, even though the rent may be a little higher in consequence. There are many important legal points involved in the drawing up of a lease or a deed of purchase (see Law of Landlord and Tenant, p. 379). It is always advisable, therefore, for the would-be householder to secure the service of a good and reliable house agent to act for her in the transaction. She might also find it expedient to consult her lawyer.

A small amount expended upon agent's and lawyer's fees has often been the means of saving large sums of money, and it is worse than folly for the householder without any elementary knowledge of the law in regard to landlord and tenant, or of the intricacies of a contract of sale to hope to cope with the legal technicalities involved in a purchase or lease without any advice. Even if she does possess some knowledge of the law, it is better for her to have expert advice; often flaws are found in leases or agreements which only a trained legal mind can detect, and it is always better to be on the safe side in these matters. (See Agents' Fees, p. 383.)

In regard to the purchase of a house, this may often be done through the medium of a good "Building Society." A Building Society advances to its members loans for the purpose of acquiring houses, or of acquiring land for building purposes. In return for the loan, the house or land so acquired is mortgaged to the Society. When the loan is repaid, the house becomes the absolute property of the member. The fund out of which the Society grants the loans is provided by the subscription of the members themselves.

Locality.—Having calculated to the nearest figure the sum of money she is justified in spending, or the annual amount for rent, rates, and taxes which she can afford to allot out of her yearly income, the householder must consider in what locality she is most likely to obtain a house which will best meet with her requirements. If members of the family have to go into the city daily, then the residence should be one from which the city is of easy access. House rents in towns are higher than in the suburbs, but where a residence in the suburbs is selected, train and omnibus fares will have to be added to the yearly expenditure, so that in the long run the difference may not be so great. Very often in some parts of a town rents will be found to be on a cheaper scale than elsewhere, but this is mostly the case in streets which do not bear the best of reputations; the character of the locality should therefore be well inquired into before deciding to profit by a seeming bargain in the rental of a town house.

Where there is a family of children, it is better as a rule to choose a house in some accessible suburb rather than in a town itself. In the suburbs good roomy houses with gardens can be had at quite moderate rentals. Houses with gardens are rare in town, except at very high rentals, whilst in many towns even a high rental cannot secure the most minute amount of garden space.

A suburb where there is a good train service should be selected, and the house should be as near as possible to the station. This last is of the utmost importance. Some people, whilst being careful to select an easily accessible spot within twenty minutes' train journey of town, choose a residence of about half-an-hour's walk from the station. If they had chosen a home near the station in one of the more remote suburbs, they would have been better off. The time spent in going backwards and forwards would have been the same, and the drawback of the long walk to and from the house in inclement weather would have been avoided.

Many of the smaller towns, it is true, combine the advantages of town and suburban life in that good dwelling-houses may be had with gardens at fairly moderate rentals. These towns, however, are not great centres of activity, and the foregoing remarks must only apply, of course, to those cases where paterfamilias has to earn his livelihood in one of our large towns or cities.

In many cases, it will be argued on behalf of the children, that educational facilities in town are so much greater and cheaper than in the suburbs or in the country. Nowadays, however, good educational establishments are to be found everywhere, and in regard to specialised subjects such as these included in commercial training, many of the large town establishments have opened branches in most parts of the country. Then, again, if the suburb has been selected with due regard to railway facilities, cheap fares, &c., there is nothing easier than to let the young people go into town for their special lessons if necessary. In the selection of a house, educational facilities for the children should never be overlooked, and for this reason it is always better to inquire whether there are good schools in the neighbourhood.

The same argument must prevail if the house is selected in some country place. In many cases, apart from all question of low rental, &c., the love of paterfamilias for the country is so great, that not all the tedium and discomfort of the long train journey twice daily will deter him from pitching his tent "far from the madding crowd." If he is prepared to endure the discomfort, well and good, but the welfare of the children from the point of view of education must be considered, and for this reason he should take care to be near some good educational centre, unless the plan of sending the children to a boarding-school is adopted.

If one decides to pitch one's tent in the country, care should be taken to find out if there are one or two good reliable medical men within easy distance. In case of illness, the fact of having to send two or more miles for medical aid may at times amount to actual calamity. Such risks should therefore be avoided. It is advisable also that the house should not be too far away from a village where food and other commodities can be purchased.

The chief drawback to residence in the country lies in the fact that up-to-date arrangements in regard to sanitation, water supply, and lighting are not always to be found, and although many charms are to be found in life in a country cottage, there are also in many cases disadvantages which will more than counterbalance these charms if great care and discrimination are not exercised in the choice of both locality and dwelling.

House versus Flat.—The comparative merits of houses and flats as places of residence will ever be a debatable subject. There is no doubt, however, that as regards town life, for people of moderate means, flats represent the minimum amount of annual outlay. It is much easier for a woman to regulate her expenditure when she knows that the sums she pays yearly for her flat will cover not only rent, but also rates and taxes. As the latter usually amount to a third of the rental, this is a most important consideration. Then there is an old saying that "a large house is a big thief," and many a weary householder, harassed at the thought of high wages claimed by servants, large sums spent in cleaning and keeping the house in repair, has proved the truth of this old adage.

With a flat expenditure is kept within easy bounds; none of the thousand and one odd expenses are liable to crop up in various unexpected quarters as in the case of a house, and all the rooms being on one floor, one's housework is reduced to a minimum, and the amount spent on servants' wages is correspondingly decreased.

There is also the additional advantage of security, for one feels quite safe when leaving for the annual holiday in locking up the flat and placing the key in the care of the doorkeeper. It can also be locked up during the daytime, when one wishes to go out, without the necessity of leaving any one in charge.

On the other hand, a flat has many disadvantages as compared with a complete dwelling-house. The rooms are small, in many cases dark, the larder and cellar accommodation poor —dress cupboards are generally conspicuous by their absence, and in even the best and most expensive of flats the servant's room, where there is one, is little better than a cupboard in size. Then, again, flats at the lower rentals are always on the top or second top stories of a building or else in the basement. In the case of the luxurious buildings which are let out in flats at high rentals a lift will be provided, but this is seldom the case in regard to the buildings at which flats are let out at moderate rents. In the absence of a lift there will be the weary climb up high flights of stone steps before one can reach one's dwelling, a disadvantage which does much to counterbalance the advantage of the rooms being on one floor. But even with this disadvantage, top floor flats are preferable to flats in the basement in regard to light and ventilation.

In a flat it is impossible to maintain the same degree of privacy as in a house. One's slumbers are apt to be disturbed in the small hours of the morning by the efforts of some conscientious youngster laboriously practising five finger exercises in the flat below, or else a "musical evening" in the flat opposite continued far into the night, though very enjoyable to those whom it may concern, succeeds in robbing you of those precious hours of "beauty sleep" which you prize so highly. In case of contagious illness also the danger of infection is greater, as isolation is more difficult.

On the whole, there are many things to be said for and against flat life; but it may be taken as a general rule that for the young couple beginning housekeeping on strictly limited means, a flat is always best from the point of

view of keeping down expenditure; whilst in the case of a family of young children, flat life is incompatible with comfort owing to the limited space available, and the very fact of all the rooms being on one floor is in these circumstances a positive disadvantage.

Site and Soil.—Absence of damp is of the utmost importance to health, and in this respect a great deal will depend on the soil upon which the house is built. A gravel soil or chalk soil above the water level is best. A clay soil, being non-porous, retains moisture and should be avoided.

On the other hand, the position of the site is an important factor in determining the advantage or disadvantage of the soil upon which it is built. Generally speaking, a house should never stand low: it often happens that a house standing on high ground, although built on clay soil, is dryer than a low-lying dwelling situated in a valley upon gravel soil. Trees are desirable, if not too near the house, as they aid in drying the soil, certain trees such as eucalyptus, plane, and poplar being specially useful.

What is known as "made-up ground" is about the worst soil upon which a house can be built. The word "made" is true in its actual sense, for the ground consists of holes and hollows which have been literally filled up with all sorts of rubbish and refuse to make a foundation. The danger of building on such a soil, which will in many cases be largely composed of organic matter from which noxious gases emanate and force their way upwards, is obvious. Careful inquiry should therefore be made in regard to this important question of soil before selecting a dwelling.

Construction.—The absence of damp will also depend to a great extent upon the construction of the house, proper construction tending to minimise many of the disadvantages of an unsuitable soil. Houses built on clay soil should be well raised above the ground level, and should possess neither cellars nor basements. Houses with basements must be very carefully constructed with the view of preventing the damp from rising up the floor and lower walls. The subsoil should be drained by means of subsoil drain-pipes, which consist of short earthenware pipes laid in trenches several feet below the surface (see p. 4). To prevent dampness rising through the floor of the basement, the floor should be built upon a bed of concrete, whilst to prevent moisture from rising up the lower walls, these should not only be constructed upon a foundation of concrete, but what is known as a "damp course" should be provided. A "damp course" consists of an impervious layer of cement, slate, asphalt, or bitumen, which is placed in the brick-work of the wall above the ground level, but below the floor. Houses with basements should always be separated from the street by an area.

A great deal of the comfort and well-being of the inhabitants of a house will depend upon the plan upon which it is built. Houses with basements always entail work for servants in going up and down stairs between the dining-room and the kitchen. On the other hand, in houses where the kitchen and dining-room are on one floor, care should be taken that the kitchen is not situated in such close proximity to the other rooms as to make the smell of cooking go all over the house. The ideal plan is to have the kitchen and pantry shut off from the rest of the rooms on the first floor by a

one of the upper landings in addition to the bath-room. There should in all cases be a housemaid's pantry on one of the upper landings in which she can keep pails and brushes.

Too much stress cannot be laid upon the necessity of the house being thoroughly dry: for this reason it is never wise to take up residence too soon in a newly-built house, as the walls are usually damp. Fires should be kept burning in all the rooms for as long a period as possible before going into a new house.

A little wall-peeling and discoloration in the case of a new house is almost unavoidable, but

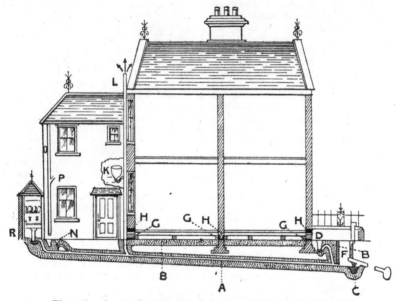

Illustration showing Concrete Foundation of a House with Damp Course and Drainage System.

A. House drain.
B. Concrete foundation.
C. Intercepting trap.
D, N. Gulleys.

F. Dry area.
G, H. Damp proof course.
K. W.C.
L. Soil pipe.

O. Rainwater pipe.
P. Bath waste-water pipe.
R. Sink.

separate little passage and door, the passage running between the kitchen and pantry, the latter being placed at the back of the dining-room, with a hatch, i.e. a small cupboard like an aperture in the wall itself opening from the pantry into the dining-room, through which dishes may be passed to the servant waiting at table. When not in use, this little cupboard can be kept closed and will not be noticeable. A lift from the kitchen to the dining-room where there is a basement is a very great help; but these are as a rule expensive to fit in and are luxuries not within the reach of the many. Plenty of cupboards are also desirable, including a hot-air cupboard for the airing of linen. If the house is a high one, water should be laid on

if, when looking over a house which has been built for some time, the paper is seen to be discoloured, this may be taken as a sure sign of damp, and the house should be avoided. In these cases a musty damp smell will almost invariably be present; a house of this kind cannot possibly be healthy, and residence in damp dwellings is a most prolific cause of all kinds of illness. Many a case of chronic rheu-matism can be traced to residence in a damp house. Care should also be taken to find out if the roof is in good condition, as dampness in the upper rooms may often be traced to some defect in the roof. Though for the purpose of drainage of the soil it is well to have trees near the house, they must not be too near, as in this case they are liable to make it damp. Ivy growing up the walls of the house, though very pretty and decorative in appearance, is also a cause of damp.

Aspect.—A house should also be carefully selected in regard to its aspect. Generally speaking, the front should face south-west or south-east. The front bedrooms and sitting-rooms will in this way catch the morning sun, whilst the back rooms will have the afternoon sun. For this reason it is advisable to have as many bedrooms in the front as possible. The breakfast-room should also have a sunny aspect; where there is no breakfast-room, the dining-room should be in the front of the house in order that the cheering influence of the morning sun may be enjoyed at breakfast, whilst the drawing-room will do well in a position where it receives the sunshine in the afternoon. It is not advisable, as a rule, to choose a house facing due north; the rooms will be dark through absence of sunlight, and the house will be cold, requiring a much greater degree of artificial warmth in winter to make it habitable than in the case of a south-west or south-east aspect.

DRAINAGE

A house should not be purchased nor an agreement for a lease entered into before the purchaser or lessee is satisfied that the drainage system is in thorough order. To make sure of this, it is essential to take independent expert advice upon the subject and to have the premises examined by a sanitary engineer. Failing this, it would be advisable to insist upon a written guarantee from the vendor or landlord that the drains have been recently tested and are in good condition. It is well, however, to always have an independent opinion, therefore the former plan is the better of the two, and by adopting it the intending purchaser or tenant protects himself from becoming saddled with a house where insanitary conditions prevail.

However well a house may be constructed in regard to light and ventilation, if the drainage is wrong, sickness and disease will invariably follow, and a little trouble and expense in investigating this important matter in the first instance will save no end of trouble and expense in the long run.

The most usual system of drainage or disposal of sewage prevailing in towns and almost all but remote country places is that known as the "water-carriage system" by which all the sewage is carried off underground in pipes called drains. The following drain-pipes are to be found in the average house—

The sink pipe for taking away water from the sink; the water pipe for taking away the bath water; the soil pipe (discharging from the water-closets), with its ventilating pipe carried above the roof; the outer drain pipe for carrying off superfluous water.

These pipes all lead to the house drain which, in its turn, is connected with the street sewer. It is not only important that all drains should be properly constructed, but also that they be kept in good condition if the house is to be healthy. To this end they should be regularly examined and all defects put right with the least delay possible.

Good drains should be (1) water-tight; (2) well ventilated; (3) without direct connection between those carrying sewage and those carrying waste from baths, basins, and the like; (4) well flushed.

(1) In order to be water-tight, the drain-pipes are best made of iron, but owing to the expense this involves they are generally made of earthenware. Long iron pipes with lead joints constitute the most water-tight system invented so far. The bed in which the pipes are laid must not be liable to sink, or the joints will give, even although firmly cemented. For this purpose, care must be taken not to sink the original trenches deeper than is necessary, as any filling in with fresh earth promotes consequent sagging.

(2) The ventilation must be very thorough, or sewer gas will find its way into the house in spite of the most careful traps to prevent it.

(3) The waste pipes from baths, &c., should never open directly into the sewer, even although the connection is guarded by a trap. They should pour their water into an open receiver or gully placed outside the house, and the gully should be connected with the sewer. Then if any sewer gas escapes from the gully, it will pass off in the open air without being conducted into the house. In the case of all pipes connection with the sewer must be guarded by a trap. Traps are devised to prevent the escape of sewer gas from the drain into the house. Many of the older traps had the drawback that they allowed filth to accumulate in them. U- or S-shaped traps are the ones now chiefly used. By having it of either shape, whenever the drain is flushed some water is retained in the bent part or trap, which then prevents the passage of gas through this portion of the pipe. The water used to flush the water-closet should not come direct from the chief cistern, but from a special small cistern, the water of which is never used for drinking purposes. By this means, if sewer gas passes into the small cistern, it will be absorbed by the water in it without passing on to the chief water-drinking cistern.

(4) In order that a drain may be well flushed, not only must an ample supply of water pass down it, but the drain must be laid at such an incline that the flow is sufficiently rapid. It must be fairly narrow and as straight as possible for the same reason; and, again, friction must be reduced by making the internal surface

smooth. By these means the accumulation of filth is reduced to a minimum.

Testing the drains is done by plugging the outlet of the suspected drain at the nearest manhole and then filling it with water from the nearest water-closet. If a leak is present, the water soon sinks, and if many leaks are present, it may not be possible to fill the drain at all. Suspected leaks may also be tested by pouring down strong oil of peppermint or assafetida in hot water, whilst a second person in the room below determines whether the odour escapes or not, but this method is not so thorough as the former test, though more easily performed by the householder.

The water-closet must be of such a pattern that it is always clean and efficiently trapped, has no direct connection with the drinking-water cistern, and is flushed by a special cistern of its own which should hold from two to three gallons. The "wash-out" closet and the "valve" closet are two of the best patterns in use at present—a "hopper" closet is commonly used, and it is satisfactory if a short hopper is used, but a long hopper is to be condemned for its lack of cleanliness. What is known as the "pan" closet is an old form of closet which cannot be too strongly condemned. The traps should be furnished with anti-siphonage pipes to prevent them becoming unsealed. In well-built houses water-closets are always separated from the other portion of the house by a small passage, and where there are two or three they are placed on the different landings one above the other. In properly constructed houses all places where water is laid on, such as the bath-room, lavatories, house-maid's sinks, should come one over the other on the various floors.

The Earth System.—In the country, where a sufficient water-supply is not always available for a complete water-borne system of drainage, what is known as the "Earth" system is the most sanitary to adopt. In this system earth is used instead of water in the closet pails, and the contents of the latter are buried at intervals in the garden.

The principle of the earth system is founded on the well-known power possessed by dry earth of deodorising and disinfecting fæcal matter—a given quantity of earth, if applied in detail to *fresh* excrement, destroying all smell and absorbing all noxious vapours. Where sufficient earth is not available, ashes should be used. Moule's earth closets are amongst the best-known sanitary appliances used in connection with this system.

Removal of Refuse.—All the dry refuse of a house which does not come under the designation of "sewage," is removed by dustmen in the employ of the local authorities at regular intervals. The most sanitary dustbins are made of zinc. The dustbin should be kept closed to keep out rain and damp, otherwise the contents will quickly decompose, and noxious odours will be the result. It should not be kept too near the wall of the house, but should be at least six feet away from it. Only dry refuse should be placed in the dustbin. All vegetable matter, such as potato parings, &c., should be burnt if noxious and unsanitary odours are to be avoided. (See Kitchen Refuse, p. 94.)

WATER-SUPPLY

A pure and abundant water-supply is a necessity in every house. Care must be taken, therefore, to find out (1) if the supply is good; (2) if it is constant or intermittent; (3) if the latter, whether the cisterns are adequate for the storage of the water and are in good condition.

In regard to the purity of the water, this should be ascertained by applying to the county or borough analyst for an analysis. The usual fee for this analysis is one guinea. As a rule the water-supply in large towns is pure. When, as in country districts, the water is derived from wells, the utmost precautions should be taken. All well water should be boiled before use, as it is very liable to pollution. If a well is shallow the risk of contamination is often considerable. A well should be deep and have its sides protected by some waterproof material to prevent the surface water from entering it. The best wells are those which are driven through the first impervious stratum so as to tap the one lying below.

Filters are largely used for purifying water, but a number of those in domestic use are not so effective as is generally supposed. Many stop some of the germs, which then flourish in the substance of the filter and infect all subsequent water that passes through. Hence purification of the water by boiling is a much safer method. Among the more reliable filters are the Pasteur-Chamberland and the Berkefeld. In the Pasteur-Chamberland filter the water passes through a thick-walled unglazed earthenware tube, which stops germs. It has been recommended to clean this by brushing the outside with a stiff brush; as, however, the germs are not only outside but probably also distributed through the substance of the porcelain, to be thoroughly cleansed it should be boiled or a new tube substituted. All filters require thorough and constant cleansing if they are to be effective. A dirty filter will do more harm than good.

In most towns there is now what is called a "constant water-supply." The constant supply system renders cisterns for the storage of water unnecessary, excepting in connection with the hot-water supply. Where there is what is known as an "intermittent supply" the water is turned off for a certain time each day. In these circumstances the intending householder should find out if the cisterns are large enough for the adequate storage of the water during those hours in which the supply is cut off, and also if the cisterns are clean and in thoroughly good condition. Cisterns should never under any circumstances be left uncovered, but should be provided with a well-fitting lid. No house should be taken until it has been ascertained that all cisterns have been thoroughly cleaned by the plumber. This cleaning should be repeated at regular intervals. The cisterns should be made of galvanised iron. An overflow pipe should be provided for any overflow of water that might arise; this pipe should discharge into the open air and never into a soil pipe or drain, or pollution of the water by sewage gases is likely to result. Cisterns from which drinking water is drawn should be as far as possible from water-closets and drains. The simple precaution of letting the water run a little before drawing it in the morning for drinking purposes should always be taken, as it should be remembered that the water has been stationary in the pipes all night, and the supply is therefore not so pure as when constantly drawn from during the day.

Hot-Water Supply.—A good hot-water supply is a necessity in every household, and a great deal of the comfort of the house depends upon this supply being adequate to the demands made upon it.

In most houses the water is heated by the kitchen range, at the back of which is a boiler; from this hot water is conveyed to the hot-water tank by means of circulation pipes. The supply of hot water will depend to a great extent upon the efficacy of the kitchen range and the supply system installed. The two best-known systems in this connection are the "tank" and the "cylinder" system. In the first system a tank is supplied for storage of hot water, while a cylinder takes the place of the tank in connection with the second system. Before taking a house, care should be taken to ascertain whether the hot-water system is in thorough working order.

Heating Water by Gas.—There are other methods, however, of securing a hot-water supply independent of the kitchen-range. There has been placed upon the market within recent years an apparatus known as a "Circulator." This is a small boiler heated by gas which can easily be

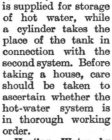

Hot-water Circulator.

connected to the "flow" and "return" pipes from the coal-range boiler, and will then with a quite moderate consumption of gas supply hot water to the circulating tank, either independently of, or in conjunction with, the coal-range boiler, the working of the latter, in the event of the kitchen fire being lighted, being in no way interfered with. These circulators are specially adapted for use in flats, and in villas where the length of the circulating pipes are not abnormal.

In small houses and flats where gas is used exclusively as fuel, many people obtain their supply of water for the bath by installing a geyser in the bath-room for the purpose of heating the bath water, whilst the water for kitchen and other purposes is boiled on the gas stove. Geysers for the purpose can be hired from all the gas companies. The geyser, however, does not give a storage of hot water throughout the house, and does not therefore fully take the place of the range boiler as does the circulator. It is a useful accessory to the bath-room, however, in summer, as hot water for the bath can be obtained by this means independently of the kitchen range.

VENTILATION

A supply of fresh pure air is essential to health, hence it follows that homes should be well ventilated. Good air must be admitted and bad air expelled. Ventilation is the renewal of the air contained in a room. The necessity for such renewal increases with the number of people occupying it, and the number of lights burning in it. Both lights and people alike use up the oxygen of the air and discharge into it a certain amount of carbon-dioxide; but the human breath has a more noxious effect than the flame of an ordinary lamp or gas jet, for it emits a certain quantity of highly poisonous organic matter, and it is chiefly this which vitiates the air and gives it the well-known "stuffy" odour.

Every one is aware that air that has been breathed is warm, and that warm air rises. Many people think that if a room is sufficiently lofty the bad air will all accumulate near the roof and the air near the floor will not be vitiated for many hours. This is a great mistake, for unless some means of letting out the bad air is provided, its warmth will soon become lost and its moisture will condense, causing the bad air to become heavier than the fresh air, when it will sink and mingle with the latter and a vitiated atmosphere will be the result. As a matter of fact, the bad air rarely rises higher than twelve feet before it becomes cool and descends.

Every room, therefore, that is to be adequately ventilated requires both an inlet for good and an outlet for bad air.

To secure the ventilation of a dwelling-room we require no ceiling to be higher than twelve feet, but the windows should reach the ceiling and be open at the top. A fire-place should always be present and the chimney register should never be closed. The window and the chimney are the two readiest means of ventilation.

The ventilation should be arranged so that the fresh air is let in with its current directed upwards, and the bad air let out near the ceiling. It is an error to ventilate the room into the passage by leaving the door open and the window closed. " Windows were made to be opened, doors to be shut." Bedroom windows, especially, should never be altogether closed at the top. Care should be taken that the bed is placed so that the cold air does not beat down upon the sleeper.

The danger of draughts, however, must be reckoned with in many cases, and for delicate

The Hinckes-Bird Method
of Ventilation.

people wide-open windows in winter are not always advisable. In these circumstances a very simple system of ventilation known as the Hinckes-Bird method should be adopted. It consists in raising the lower sash of a window a few inches, and blocking up the opening with a piece of boarding as long as the width of the window and about six inches broad, thus allowing the fresh air to enter the room, but only between the two sashes, and with an upper current.

The proper ventilation of a house will depend to a great extent upon its warming arrangements. Some grates are constructed so that the fire burning in them serves to warm the air before it enters the room. A Galton's grate, for instance, has an air-space behind the chimney communicating below with the outside air and above with the interior of the room, the heat of the chimney being in this way used to warm the incoming air.

A very simple means of ventilating ordinary dwelling-houses is found in what is known as

the "Sheringham Valve," which is a metal guard placed around an aperture in the wall, so arranged as to direct the incoming air upwards and made to work on a hinge so as to show the opening when desired.

A *Tobin's Tube* is a pipe the lower end of which communicates through an opening in the wall with the outside air, whilst the upper end opens into the room about six feet above the floor.

Among other simple aids to ventilation without draught are the following :—

Perforated Bricks, communicating with the room by gratings, which serve to break up the current and thus prevent the draught from being felt.

Boyle's Valve inserted in the chimney near the ceiling. This contrivance consists of an aperture leading into the chimney with two talc flaps, forming a valve, which permits the air of the room to enter the chimney, but prevents the smoke from entering the room.

Louvre Panes, consisting of slips of glass placed obliquely in an oblong opening cut in the window pane. They are commonly used in shop windows that do not open. The Cooper rose ventilator is on the same principle.

LIGHTING

The proper lighting of a house is essential not only from the point of view of the health, but also for the comfort of its inhabitants. A person is more influenced by his or her surroundings than one would think—good temper and cheeriness come naturally amid cheerful surroundings, whereas dark, gloomy, and ill-lighted premises tend to have a most depressing effect upon even the most optimistic of individuals.

Good natural light during the daytime may be secured by a wise choice of aspect (see p. 5). Stained-glass windows should be avoided in living rooms. Many people elect to have the lower sashes of their dining-rooms, for instance, of stained glass. The effect may be imposing, perhaps, but it is certainly not cheerful, and grandeur is dearly bought at the expense of the light and cheeriness of a room. Then, again, creepers should not be allowed to grow over the front of the house in such a way as to over-shadow the windows, nor should the light be shut out by the too close proximity of trees. It must be remembered that plenty of light is essential to our health, and care should be taken therefore to secure it.

Artificial Lighting.—In towns electric light and gas form the chief artificial illuminants. Gas is also supplied in a large number of country places, but where this is not to be had, lamps are generally used. In large country houses, however, air gas is often made from a plant on the premises.

Electric Light as an illuminant has many advantages. It is cleanly, hygienic, and convenient; and if care is taken in regulating its use, the quarterly electric light bill may be kept well within bounds. It is very little trouble to switch off the light when one leaves the room, and if this is done not once in a way, but as a general rule, a substantial saving on the electric light bill is the result. Low candle-power lights should be used in the bedrooms, one or two 7 or 8 candle-power lamps being usually sufficient for each room.

Economy may also be exercised by means of the electric lamps selected. Tantalum and many of the other metallic filament lamps, whilst giving a much brighter light than the ordinary incandescent lamps with carbon filaments, consume much less current than the latter, and are therefore more economical.

In connection with the installation of an electric plant for lighting in country mansions situated in localities where there is no public supply, the initial outlay will necessarily be higher. Where a public supply is available the only expense will be that of wiring the premises and purchasing the necessary fixtures. In most cases the latter may be hired from the electric light company by payment of a fixed sum every year. The cost of electric light varies in different towns. In London it averages from 4d. to 5d. per unit for lighting, whilst for heating purposes the cost is 1d. per unit.

Coal Gas is obtained by the distillation of coal in large chambers or retorts. The distillation proceeds for about four hours under a great heat, and the products are broadly coke, gas, and coal tar. The gas is then cooled, washed with water, and treated with slaked lime to remove impurities.

The large cylindrical vessels so prominent in all gas works are the gas-holders, from which the supply issues to the consumers. These holders rise and sink in a tank of water by their own weight and the upward pressure of the gas inside. The gas is conveyed from the holder by mains and from the mains to the consumer by service pipes.

The use of coal gas as an illuminant is almost universal, and many important improvements in regard to fittings have been made within recent years which have increased its usefulness to a remarkable degree.

Meters are used to measure the gas consumed, and it is important that every householder should know how to read and check the meter. Gas meters are usually lent on hire to the consumer by the gas company. It is important that the supply of gas to the burner should be regulated. This can always be done by means

of a regulator or "governor" on the main pipes or governor burners.

Incandescent Gas.—This is by far the most superior and effective method of gas lighting. It is used in connection with special burners which admit air to be burned with the gas, a most brilliant effect being achieved by the illumination of the white mantle which is used in conjunction with the burner. The burner is usually fitted with a by-pass for lowering and raising the light. By means of this by-pass the gas may be left turned on at the stop-cock, whilst only the faintest flicker of a flame is left on the burner. The Veritas and Welsbach mantles are amongst the best known and most effective to use with incandescent gas.

Amongst the latest improvements in connection with gas lighting may be classed the Pneumatic Gas Switch, by means of which gas can be switched on in the same manner as electric light. With this simple apparatus any number of gas lights can be switched on or off, separately or together. It consists of three parts—a switch, a valve and a coil of small tubing. The switch turns the gas up or down from any position or distance. The valve with by-pass complete screws on to any ordinary gas bracket or chandelier at the burner, which is easily done without tools of any kind, whilst the tube, which is as small and flexible as a bell wire, conducts the air pressure from the switch to the valve, and is attached to the wall or woodwork with small staples supplied with the sets. By touching the switch, air pressure is sent through the fine tube, and the light is thus turned either on or off as desired. One of the special features of the gas switch is the fact that no batteries or chemicals of any kind whatever are required. It is self-contained and requires no further attention when fitted. Another advantage to be found in using this switch lies in the fact that incandescent mantles will be found to last much longer owing to the fact that the gas switches on easily; it does away with the slight explosion which always takes place when a match or taper is applied when lighting the gas in the usual way.

Air Gas.—In large country houses where there is no public gas-supply, air gas is largely used for lighting purposes. This is manufactured from a plant on the premises, and there are many apparatus for the purpose on the market. One of the best apparatus for manufacturing air gas is that sold by Messrs. W. A. S. Benson and Co., Ltd., of 82 and 83 New Bond Street, London, W. It is known as the "Aeos" Gas Apparatus. The light given by "Aeos" gas, whilst being brilliant and pure white, is exceedingly soft and restful. The apparatus is exceedingly simple, as the plant is wholly automatic; it is also absolutely safe to use, being non-explosive.

The price for a 25-light apparatus capable

of supplying 25–26 candle-power burners would be as follows :—

Apparatus	. . . . .	£42 0 0
Pump and Tank	. . . . .	5 10 0
Carriage, including return of empties, about	. . . . .	3 10 0
		£51 0 0

whilst the cost of installing would be about £1 per point. Once the initial cost of installation has been borne this gas proves one of the most economical illuminants it is possible to have.

Electric Light, Gas and Oil Fittings.—A great deal of the beauty of a room depends upon the choice and position of suitable lighting fittings.

In the dining-room there should always be a centre light coming over the dinner-table in addition to any other bracket lights necessary. With electric fittings it is as well to have one or two lamps to the centre light which are switched on by different switches, so that either one or more of the lamps can be lighted at will. A red silk shade over the centre light has a most softening and soothing effect. The metal work is most effective when of antique copper or brass.

In the drawing-room which is lighted by electricity, the centre pendant is of different design, usually consisting of a number of lights, each with separate ornamental glass shades. A high electric standard lamp, with a pretty silk shade of a light colour to tone with the general decorative scheme of the room, gives a very pretty effect, as do small lamps to be placed on mantelpiece, table, or piano as desired.

The hall should be provided with a hanging centre lamp of lantern design, whilst, especially in houses built in the Queen Anne style, a plain old-time iron lantern should be hung outside the porch.

In the billiard-room the lights over the table should have plain green shades. In the library or study a centre light with one or two small metal table standard lamps with soft silk shades should be provided.

In the bedrooms there should always be a light in front of the toilet table and one over the bed, the latter to be turned on by a switch at the side of the bed. Pretty soft silk shades of a light bright colour to tone with the colouring of the room should be used ; pale pink and pale green shades are very effective.

Gas and Oil Lamps.—In regard to gas, where inverted incandescent burners are used, fittings for centre lights and bracket lights may be very similar to those used for electric light, and

Bray's Inverted Burner.

where the " switch on " system is installed, the illusion can be made almost complete.

Many of the disadvantages connected with the use of oil for house lighting can be minimised by means of suitable fittings. Pendant lamps should be used as much as possible. In the hall a lantern lamp is most effective. The dining-room lamp can be provided with a pretty silk shade, or, where it is preferred, a plain white glass shade, and can be carried out in wrought iron metal work or polished brass. (For Care of Lamps, see p. 77.)

Bracket lamps for hanging on walls are also made in many pretty and effective designs.

Warming the House.—The comfort of the house will depend not a little upon the method of artificial heating adopted during the cold season. Warming should always be considered in relation to ventilation as there is a very close connection between the two.

Rooms may be warmed either by open fireplaces, closed stoves (for burning of coal or coke, gas and oil), or by hot-water pipes and radiators.

The old-fashioned open grate will always be popular in English homes. There is something very cheery and comforting about a good bright coal fire that is lacking with closed-in stoves and other methods of heating. It is true it consumes a large amount of fuel for the heat it yields, as most of the heat goes up the chimney, but it makes the chimney a valuable ventilation shaft, which many more economical grates do not. A great deal of the heat-giving capacity of a fire will, of course, depend upon the construction of the grate. The best heating fire-places have the back and sides of brick and not of iron, as brick radiates back the heat, whilst iron lets heat slip through it up the chimney. The back should lean over the fire, not away from it. The slits in the grid that the coal rests on should be narrow so that cinders may not fall through and be wasted. The bars in front of the grate should also be narrow, and the space beneath the fire should be closed up in front by means of an iron shield. Again, the grate should be wider in front than at the back. All these principles of construction are to be found in the grates devised by Pridgin Teale and Lionel Teale ; the Teale system, in fact, has formed the basis of all the latest improvements in fire-grates. Many fire-places are now made almost entirely of glazed briquette, this material covering both the hearth and fire-place surround. This is undoubtedly one of the most artistic as well as one of the most heat-giving styles of grate.

An adjustable canopy is in most cases fitted to the top of modern grates.

Many of the newer types of grate are constructed without the front bars. Of these the Wells fire-grates are perhaps the best known. The " Burkone " patent barless fire is another also of excellent design ; both grates are so constructed as to give the maximum of heat with a mimimum consumption of fuel.

Stoves.—Closed stoves greatly economise fuel at the expense of ventilation. They often give the room a stuffy odour, probably from organic matter in the air being charred by contact with the stove, and also from the fact that hot iron is porous and permits the escape of some of the gaseous products of combustion through it. They also tend to make the atmosphere unpleasantly dry. This latter defect can be remedied to a certain extent, however, by keeping trays of water around the stove. The ventilating stoves specially constructed to admit air by means of pipes or tubes are the best kind to use. Various kinds of fuel are used for burning in these stoves, chief amongst which are coal, coke, and anthracite coal.

The last-named is a slow-burning natural coal which has three times the heating power of ordinary bituminous coal, and is absolutely smokeless. The fuel is very expensive, costing about £2 per ton, but as one fire will last for hours, an anthracite stove will really prove an economy in the long run. It has been calculated that the average cost for fuel for twelve hours continuous burning will not amount to more than 1½d. Anthracite stoves are best fitted in front of fire-places. Where there is no fire-place, it is always necessary that the flue pipe should be carried to a chimney.

Heating by Gas.—The open gas fires, consisting of jets of flame distributed amongst lumps of asbestos and burning in an ordinary grate with

An Anthracite Stove.

the chimney just as open as for a coal fire, form the healthiest method of heating rooms by gas in ordinary dwelling-houses.

The most careful ventilation of the room is necessary when any means of heating by gas is employed. Whenever gas is used as fuel, whether in open fires or stoves, trays of water should be kept near the fire-place or stove to prevent excessive drying of the atmosphere.

The convenience of gas fires as labour-saving

Boudoir Grate.

devices is undoubted, and for bedrooms especially they form an easy and convenient method of warming, the fact that they can be turned off as soon as the room is sufficiently warmed adding not a little to their usefulness. There are some people, however, who, although they quite appreciate the many good points about gas fires, refrain from adopting them from purely sentimental motives, the coal fire representing to them the essence of homeliness and cheeriness. Gas stove manufacturers are quite aware of the existence of this feeling, and are continually inventing new devices calculated to render the gas fire as near as possible in appearance to the coal fire. In a new gas fire-grate sold by Messrs. Davis & Sons, and known as the "Boudoir Grate," an almost perfect imitation of a homely log fire is achieved. In the "Boudoir" fire imitation logs are fitted; and the marked resemblance to the effect of the old-fashioned wood log fire is so great as to almost make the illusion complete. This grate, it is interesting to note, was designed by a woman— Miss Helen Edden, of the Gas Light & Coke Company, London.

Electric Radiators.—Where electric light is laid on in a house the electric radiator stoves make very convenient, cleanly, and useful heating apparatus. They can be switched on and off at will as in the case of electric light. The initial cost is small, very good radiators being procurable for an outlay of 35s. and upwards; but they have the drawback of consuming a great amount of current, and for this reason, unless great care and discrimination are exercised in their use, they are apt to prove expensive.

Oil-Stoves.—Where no other method of heating is available oil-stoves are very useful, but at the same time they have many disadvantages. From the point of view of ventilation they are not hygienic, as they use up a good amount of pure air; and being nearly always used in rooms which contain no fire-place there is no outlet for the fumes which pass into the room and vitiate the atmosphere.

Oil-stoves require constant attention in the way of cleaning and trimming; they have a tendency to smell unpleasantly, and this tendency is particularly marked when their care in either of the above respects is neglected. The prices of these stoves range from three or four shillings to two and a half guineas. Very useful little stoves may be purchased for an outlay of ten to eleven shillings. The more expensive varieties are of course the best. They burn a good deal of oil, however, and for this reason, if burning constantly, the weekly outlay on oil for a stove would represent in many instances more than the outlay on coal for a fire.

Hot-Water Pipes.—This system of heating is mostly restricted to large houses and public buildings and institutions. The heat is diffused by means of hot water circulated through the house by pipes and radiators. The installing of a hot-water system amounts to a considerable sum in the first instance. The disadvantage of this heating arrangement lies in the fact that it is not easy to regulate the temperature, and a stuffy atmosphere is usually the result. Very often in large houses a hot-water system is installed for heating the hall and landings, whilst the rooms are heated with fires in the ordinary way. There is no doubt that many colds and other similar ills may often be attributed to the fact that people are apt to overlook the danger of loitering in a cold and draughty hall after coming out of a warm room. Some method of heating the hall to make it of uniform temperature with the rooms is therefore highly desirable, and no more efficient method than that of a hot-water system could be devised for the purpose.

General Condition of the House.—Before renting or purchasing a house, careful investigation should be also made into the general condition of the premises.

The roofs should be examined by a builder for any defect that might give rise to damp and other similar ills; walls, flooring, and ceilings should be looked into for cracks and other imperfections. Care should be taken to find out that doors fit well, opening and shutting easily, on their hinges; also that locks are in good condition. Windows should be examined to see that cords are good, and that they open both top and bottom; also that they are properly fitted with bolts, and that the shutters (if any) are in working order.

Defects in chimneys should be looked for; these are often indicated by discoloration by smoke of the marble of the mantelpieces. The kitchen range and boiler should be tested, care being taken to find out if a good supply of hot water can be ensured. In some houses it is only after a regular furnace has been blazing in the kitchen grate for some hours that the water begins to show any signs of warmth; this points to some defect in the boiler, and a plumber should at once be called in to put matters right.

If the kitchen fire-place is of an obsolete type, the landlord should be asked to put in a modern range. All pipes should be attended to and put in repair.

Care should be taken to see that the principal rooms are fitted with bells, and if so, whether the latter are in good condition. Needless to say, the house should be thoroughly clean and in every way fit for the occupation of the incoming tenant. The latter must be careful to ascertain that this is the case, and also that it is not infested by rats, mice, beetles, or other vermin of an even more disagreeable kind.

No pains should be spared in attending to all these matters, and seeing that attention is paid to everything that makes for comfort. The landlord who wishes to let a house is a much better-tempered and amenable person than the landlord who has actually " caught " his tenant. Insist on everything being put in order before you take over the premises. If matters are allowed to slide a great deal of future expense will be entailed, more especially where the house is taken upon a " repairing " lease. The need for caution before making a purchase is none the less imperative, or else the purchaser will find that what with the cost of putting the premises into repair in the first instance and the amount expended subsequently upon the general upkeep of the house, he will have made a very bad bargain indeed.

It should be remembered that, excepting in the case of houses let furnished, a landlord is not bound in law to put the premises in a state of repair or even into a habitable condition before the tenantry commences unless he has entered into an agreement to do so with the incoming tenant.

HOUSE DECORATION

Once a house has been taken and all the necessary cleaning and repairs have been duly carried out, the important question of decoration will have to be entered into.

Many women look upon the selection of wallpaper as a tedious task which is best avoided where possible, and leave the entire scheme of papering and decoration to the discretion of the landlord, with very often lamentable results. True, in some instances, the latter may be a man of taste and may take sufficient pride in his property to select papers suitable for the aspect of the various rooms and the purpose for which they are intended. But such a landlord will prove an exception to the general rule. The idea which ranks paramount in the mind of the average landlord is how to save himself expense. In these circumstances it may be taken for granted that if the selection is left to him his choice will be governed by no other consideration that that of his pocket.

The policy of leaving the selection of wall-papers to a landlord is therefore an altogether fallacious one, and should never be adopted. If he has arranged to paper and decorate the premises for the incoming tenant he will be only too pleased for the latter to make his selection, provided however that he keeps within a certain stipulated sum. If the tenant wishes to obtain papers of a better quality than those procurable for the sum allotted, all that he will have to do will be to make up the difference. A landlord will always consent to an arrangement of this kind.

It should be ascertained that the walls are thoroughly dry and clean before the new paper is put on. The practice of pasting a new paper over an old one cannot be too highly condemned from the point of view of cleanliness and sanitation. Care should also be taken that the paper is fixed to the wall with material that does not turn sour; bad size used for this purpose is particularly noxious. A great deal of illness has been traced to the hanging of wall-papers with bad paste or size. The walls of newly-built houses should not be properly papered for six or eight months, as they will not be thoroughly dry before that time. A temporary papering should be provided during this period.

The decorative scheme should be carefully considered both in regard to the shape, size, light, and aspect of the various rooms, and also in regard to the style of furniture which they will contain. Rooms that are furnished according to a special period scheme, for instance, must be papered in conformity with the style of this period. Wall-papers must always act as a suitable background for the furniture of a room both in regard to pattern, style, and colouring, and this fact should never be lost sight of in making a choice. Then, again, the aspect of a room must influence the choice of the colour selected; what are known as warm colours should not be selected for a room with a south or south-east aspect, whilst all " cold " colours should be avoided in the decoration of rooms facing north or north-east. Yellow and red, for instance, are warm colours, whilst blue is what is known as a cold colour. These three colours are known as the " primary " colours.

Any child who has experimented with a box of paints will know that blue and yellow mixed make green, whilst red and blue make purple. The secondary colours so made may be either warm or cold colours according to the proportion in which their primary colours are mixed. In green, for instance, if the blue preponderates over the yellow the result is a " cold " colour ; but many shades of green in which the yellow preponderates will result in an almost warm colour, the warmth of the original yellow being judiciously tempered by the admixture of the cold colour blue. Certain tones of very pale green should always be avoided, because their colour is due to an injurious white pigment containing arsenic. At an inquest held in London a short time ago on the body of a man it was found that his death was due to arsenical poisoning from the cheap green paper on his bedroom wall. Fires in the bedroom had caused the fluff from the paper to be distributed over the room, and as the man was in a weak state of health the poison germs proved fatal.

Just because some greens are dangerous, however, it does not follow that green should be tabooed in house decoration. It is only the cheap pale cold greens which should be shunned. Dark green is one of the most useful colours that can be selected in room decoration, as most other colours tone or contrast well with it. Several delicate greens may also be had which have no injurious ingredients in their composition.

Dadoes and friezes enter largely into the scheme of present-day wall-paper decoration, but their choice must depend upon the size and height of the room. In small low-ceilinged rooms dadoes should never be used, as they only make small rooms look smaller. In regard to friezes, there is a certain difference of opinion amongst furniture experts. Some say that they should not be used at all in low small rooms, whilst others maintain that an unbroken line of wall-paper from floor to ceiling, far from adding to the apparent height of a low room, only serves to diminish it, whilst if the line is broken by means of a narrow frieze, the effect is to make the room more lofty. It may be said as a general rule, however, that the striped self-coloured papers are the best to use in small low-ceilinged rooms, as the stripes tend to give an impression of height. All papers with large patterns should be avoided on the walls of small rooms, although, if judiciously chosen, when used in large lofty rooms they are very effective. Before choosing a wall-paper it is always as well to see it in the piece, and to try the effect of a piece held against the wall before making the final selection.

One important thing to remember in the decoration of rooms is that the various decorations should not match each other in monotonous fashion. The colour scheme is always more effective, for instance, when carpets or table coverings or both form a pleasing contrast to the wall-papers. Where there is a pattern on the wall-paper, let the curtains be of absolutely plain material; never repeat the pattern of a wall-paper in the chintz of curtains or chair coverings.

Ceilings should always be in light tones and cornices should harmonise with the ceiling, whilst all woodwork, including wall skirting, insides of doors, and windows, should be painted in a tint to match the principal tones of the wall-paper—with light delicate papers white woodwork is always suitable. In bedrooms, the designs of which should be always light where possible, light woodwork is also an advantage.

On the whole it may be said that the absolutely plain papers are those which form the most effective background for both pictures and furniture, providing of course that suitable colourings are chosen. Where a number of pictures are to be hung, elaborate designs should never be used. Papers with dull surfaces show off good pictures to the best advantage. Picture rails or mouldings from which the pictures can be hung by means of picture-hooks should be included in the decoration of all the reception rooms. These mouldings not only form an additional ornament to the room, but do away altogether with the necessity of adopting the old-fashioned method of suspending the pictures from large nails in the wall, a method which is certainly not conducive to the long life of the wall-paper.

Picture-hook.

Different Kinds of Papers.—Amongst the most effective of present-day wall-papers may be classed the plain silk fibre papers in uniform tints. These have a softness of surface which is peculiarly pleasing and effective. Pretty friezes in floral and other designs are sold to match these papers.

The most pleasing effects with all plain papers, however, are achieved by means of floral borders, which are not only utilised as friezes, but are carried down the walls at certain intervals to form wide panels. These plain papers with border effects form the most fashionable designs at the present moment. The silk fibre papers may be had from 1s. 6d. per piece, an especially good quality being obtainable for 2s. 6d.

The plain ingrain papers are also very effective; they have a somewhat rougher surface than the silk fibre papers, and may be had from 1s. 6d. per piece.

The moiré papers have a surface resembling the silk after which they are named, and may be had from 1s. 6d. a piece. They are especially effective when thrown into relief by a pretty frieze or border.

Very artistic also are the satin stripe papers.

These are in uniform colourings consisting of satin-like stripes alternating with stripes of a duller surface. Their effect in pink, blue, and all the lighter shades is dainty in the extreme; whilst carried out in alternate stripes of white and silver they make a particularly effective drawing-room decoration, especially when used as a background for seventeenth-century furniture.

Patterned wall-papers, where they are preferred, can be very effective if judiciously selected, but the principle that large and bold designs are only suitable for large lofty rooms should never be lost sight of. Several very pretty designs may be had in the chintz wall-papers. Stencilled papers are much more expensive than the other varieties. They are very handsome in effect, but on the whole are more suitable for the decoration of large public buildings than for that of private houses.

The plain sanitary washable papers are especially useful for nursery decoration when finished with pretty friezes and borders illustrating nursery rhymes, fairy stories, or representing various farmyard animals or any other objects calculated to appeal to the childish mind.

Tiled walls form an ideal decoration for the bath-room, but these are necessarily expensive and beyond the reach of the average purse. A very good substitute for tiles is to be had in the material known as " Emdeca," which consists of an alloy of tin enamelled and is sold at prices ranging from 2s. 4d. the piece ($16\frac{1}{2} \times 22$ inches) and upwards. This, however, would also form a somewhat costly decoration for a bath-room when regarded from the point of view of only a moderately filled purse, but it can be used as a dado, the upper part of the walls being painted with " muraline " or some other washable preparation. Emdeca is also very useful for fixing in sheets at the back of wash-stands and sinks, its appearance being very cleanly and dainty.

Painting and Distemper.—The usefulness of paint in wall decoration must not be overlooked, especially when quite plain walls are required. It does not show damp or dirt in the same degree as plain wall-paper, nor is it liable to fade when exposed to the glare of the sun in a room with a sunny aspect.

Of the various preparations for painting walls " Ripolin " is one of the most satisfactory. The Flat Ripolin has a dull velvety surface which is very soft and pleasing in effect. Ripolin may be had in any colour. It should be finished off where possible with a paper border or frieze, and a dado of lincrusta or other material where the decoration scheme of the room admits of it.

Sanalene is also an excellent paint for wall decoration. Ripolin Gloss and Sanalene Gloss are especially good decorations for nurseries, bath-rooms, larders, kitchens, &c., as they are washable. Both Ripolin and Sanalene are also very useful for painting the woodwork of a room. Plain distempered walls can also be very effective. Hall's Sanitary Washable Distemper is one of the best to use. It is easily washed when the walls begin to show signs of dirt, and proves one of the cheapest and most economical wall decorations it is possible to have. A pretty paper frieze can be used with advantage to finish off the decoration of distempered walls.

Dadoes, Panelling and Relief Work.—Dadoes make a very effective finish to wall decoration, being especially suited to rooms with lofty walls. The Japanese leather papers sold at from 3s. 6d. a yard are often used in dado work. Lincrusta is another good material which can be had at prices varying from 1s. a yard and upwards, a very good quality being procurable for 3s. or 4s. per yard. The brown lincrusta is much used for dining-room dadoes. "Anaglypta" is also a very useful material both for dadoes and ceiling relief work. It may be had in all designs and qualities, 4s. a yard representing a good average price for ordinary purposes. A pretty dado of white anaglypta makes a very graceful finish to drawing-room walls.

Dadoes should always be finished with ornamental mouldings called dado rails. These serve not only to set them off to advantage, but also as a protection to the lower part of the walls from the knocks of chairs and other furniture.

Wood panelling makes a very effective decoration for dining-room, library, or study where the rooms are large and lofty. A panelling is carried much higher up the walls than a dado, a deep frieze being as a rule the only other wall decoration required. Oak, mahogany, and cedar panellings give a most handsome effect. The cheapest oak panelling is 1s. 6d. a foot. Good English oak may be had from 2s. 3d. a foot, whilst mahogany panelling may be had from 2s. a foot. Though the initial expense is necessarily very great, yet from the point of view of wear wood panellings are unequalled. They are easy to keep clean, and can be bodily removed and fitted in other rooms if desired. Wood panelling enamelled or painted white is often used in drawing-room decoration. In very elaborately decorated period drawing-rooms the wood is often carried up the walls in very narrow panels, alternating with panels of silk in delicate tints. Such an elaborate scheme of decoration, however, would only be suitable in very large and luxuriously furnished dwellings. Where white wood panelling is used in the drawing-room of the average household it is only carried to the height of a dado. Needless to say, in very small rooms panelling of any kind would look altogether out of place. (For Chimney-piece Decorations, see p. 22.)

COLOUR SCHEMES FOR DIFFERENT ROOMS

The Dining-Room.—For the decoration of a dining-room reds, yellows, buffs, dark greens, and russet browns are the colours most often selected. There is a certain tradition in regard to the decoration of a dining-room which dies hard. Everything about the room must be imposing, hence a rich red is a very favourite colour. It is, however, not so fashionable for this purpose as of yore, its use being to a certain extent superseded by the present vogue for papers of buff and russet tints, which are now being used extensively in the dining-room decoration of the most tastefully furnished houses.

The choice of colour must of course be guided by the aspect of the room—red, yellow, and the warmer shades being the most suitable where it has a north-east aspect, whilst cool dark greens and mauves are ideal colourings for rooms with sunny aspects. Red and green, russet and green, and buff, brown and green, mauve and grey make admirable dining-room colour schemes. For instance, a dining-room papered in red might have dark green curtains, a dark green table-cover, and an Axminster carpet in which dark green is the prevailing tone, or else one of these many-toned oriental carpets, the soft tones of which combine so well with almost any scheme of colouring; russet-coloured walls would look well with green curtains, green table-cloth, and a warm red carpet-square over a dark parquet or polished wood flooring.

A plain patternless buff paper thrown into relief by a rich brown dado would make an exceptionally handsome background for mahogany furniture and pictures in dark brown frames, whilst walls papered in soft mauve with a frieze of silver grey, mauve curtains, a tapestry carpet-square with a subdued pattern on a grey ground, and a tapestry table-cover to tone with the carpet, would set off a dining-room suite of oak in Queen Anne style.

The Drawing-Room.—The drawing-room is the room of all others which lends itself to light and delicate treatment. The general effects of the decorative scheme should be one of brightness and cheerfulness, and, above all, of refinement. Delicate mauves, soft greens, turquoise blues, white, pinks, are all suitable colours for wall decoration. The aspect of the room must of course be considered. Warm soft pinks and yellows are best for rooms facing north-east, whilst soft cool greys, blues and greens form ideal colourings for rooms with sunny aspects. White is particularly suitable in small rooms, as it gives an impression of greater space. As a background for Adam's or Empire furniture it is especially effective. Pretty striped papers in light colours with floral friezes go well with Hepplewhite furniture.

A drawing-room papered or painted in white would look well with a frieze or floral border of a pretty shade of blue green with a carpet and curtains in the same colouring. The entire woodwork of the room, including mantelpiece, overmantel, and dado (if any) would also be white.

A drawing-room with a north-east aspect would look well with a pink satin stripe paper in a soft tone, an art green pile carpet, and curtains of the same shade of green.

Soft grey wall-paper with a rose-coloured floral frieze, rose curtains, and rose and grey in the colour of the carpet would make another effective colour scheme.

Nothing could be calculated to set off drawing-room furniture to better advantage than a light well-polished parquet flooring adorned here and there by one or two choice oriental rugs. The cost is, however, prohibitive to those who are not superabundantly supplied with this world's riches.

Many people who have carpet-squares or rugs as floor coverings in all the other rooms of the house prefer a fitted carpet in the drawing-room. Where square carpets are used " parquet " makes the best surround, but this is necessarily expensive. Failing parquet a good floor stain should be applied to the surround. Many good stains are sold to imitate oak, dark oak, light oak, walnut, rosewood, satinwood, and other woods. Both parquet and stained floorings require to be kept well polished (see p. 66).

The Library.—The library should be painted or papered in sober colours such as brown, red, tan, and dark green, in keeping with the dignity of the room. To paper a library in the pale art shades of blue or green would be to go against every law of what is fitting and proper. A good soft Turkey carpet forms a favourite floor covering for this room. The shades of Turkey and other oriental carpets are so skilfully interwoven that they will tone with almost any colour. Brown walls and a deep red carpet and curtains are very effective. All the wood should be in brown. Oak and other wood panellings are largely used for wall decoration in the libraries of the rich. They have a very handsome and imposing effect. Dadoes in dark shades of anaglypta or lincrusta are very suitable. Red is a favourite colour in library decoration. Walls papered in red with brown woodwork, a carpet in deep tones of green and red, and curtains to match makes a very effective background.

Breakfast-Room.—The colour treatment of a breakfast-room will, of course, depend upon its aspect. In well-planned houses it usually has a sunny position. A paper with an unobtrusive rose floral pattern on a white ground would tone well with an art blue carpet-square. A plain blue paper with white woodwork, pretty chintz or cretonne curtains with a pink floral pattern on a white ground, a pretty cord carpet with a rose pattern on a fawn ground would also be very suitable.

Bedrooms.—The bedroom papers should be bright and cheerful-looking; never heavy, and, above all, intricate designs should be avoided. These are apt to be particularly irritating to an invalid who is forced to spend a number of days in bed, and worrying over the intricacies of a wall-paper can at times have an almost maddening effect upon a person so situated. As illness is a factor which will have to be reckoned with in almost every household, let the bedroom paper be bright yet restful in design; in fact, nothing can be better than an absolutely plain wall-paper. Washable distemper also forms an admirable decoration, and can be had in all the best and most artistic shades. Distempered walls, however, should always be finished off with a pretty frieze. A plain white paper or distemper, with a pretty floral border of roses to form a panelled effect, would go well with a green art square carpet, rose curtains, and ivory-white woodwork: soft blue paper would tone well with a pretty tapestry carpet with a rose design on a fawn ground, whilst pretty white and rose chintz curtains would complete the colour scheme. White papers with pretty floral friezes and borders to tone with the rest of the decorative scheme form the most characteristic feature of present-day bedroom decoration; a plain white paper with a very deep wisteria frieze is especially effective and would look well with a mauve carpet and mauve curtains.

The Hall.—It is a mistake to think that gloomy colouring is essential to the decoration of a hall—so much depends upon whether it is a bright hall or a dark one. Plain papers or distemper are as a rule the best to use unless the hall is a very lofty one. Warm shades of red and terra-cotta are very suitable, or green where the hall is a particularly bright one. White dadoes, friezes, and woodwork will go a long way towards brightening up a dark hall. Very deep friezes can be used with good effect. A rich pile carpet to tone with the stair carpet and laid over linoleum is a very effective floor covering. When the hall is separated from the outer door by a small vestibule, the door of the latter should be draped with curtains to tone with the rest of the colour scheme. Where linoleum is used as floor covering it should be of a simple parquetry pattern. Any valued trophies, such as swords, other armour, fox brushes, &c., &c., form most suitable decorations for the walls of a hall.

FURNISHING THE HOME

The choice of furniture for the home should not be undertaken lightly. It is a matter which calls for the exercise of much discrimination and forethought, careful consideration of ways and means, and, above all, much ingenuity in cutting one's coat according to one's cloth, and at the same time getting the best possible value for money expended.

The requirements of the different rooms in the house should first be carefully studied, and a list made out of every piece of furniture necessary for each separate room, including carpet, fire-irons, window-curtains, curtain rods, blinds, &c.

It may take some time to make out a thoroughly comprehensive list, but it will prove to be time well expended. To go to a furniture shop with only a vague idea of the general wants of the different rooms is to court disaster at the outset. Money which should have been expended upon essentials goes to purchase articles which may be ornamental, it is true, but which are totally unnecessary for use, whilst the important essentials that make for comfort are either overlooked, or else remembered too late.

It is most important, therefore, to set about buying furniture in a business-like way. Lack of method in buying will inevitably result in chaos, and the shopping for the home, instead of being a pleasure, as it should be if undertaken in the proper spirit, will prove a positive ordeal for the unfortunate shoppers.

Many people who have only a very small sum to spend upon furniture make the mistake of taking little interest in their shopping, resigning themselves to the purchase of anything, no matter how ugly, so long as it is cheap. Never was there a greater fallacy. Good taste should be the guiding spirit in the furnishing of the home, and good taste goes a great deal further than mere money in this respect. The most beautiful homes are not necessarily those which have been furnished without any regard to cost; rather are they those upon which care and trouble have been expended in making a judicious and tasteful selection.

A woman of refinement and taste will make a room in which the furniture largely consists of the results of her own handiwork and skill look better and much more desirable than the room of the woman with unlimited wealth at her command, who does not possess the necessary taste to guide her in steering clear of mere vulgar display. Money is a most important factor in the furnishing of a home, it is true, but a very little money can be made to go a long way if only a little trouble and care are exercised in the spending of it. A great deal, of course, will depend upon the resourcefulness of the young couple. Some men, for instance, have a taste for carpentering and carving, then how can this taste be more satisfactorily employed than in the furnishing of the home ? Pretty shelves and book-cases and even tables can be made in this way at a very trifling cost. Ordinary orange or soap boxes can be turned into wall brackets, boot cupboards, and even book-cases. Cosy window-seats and pretty ottomans can be turned out by the home upholsterer and carpenter at a trifling cost. It is wonderful what can be done with a few yards of chintz and a liberal supply of enamel. Dainty hangings for impromptu curtain cupboards, wall draperies to hide ugly corners, cushions and window-curtains can be fashioned from the chintz by deft and skilful fingers, whilst ordinary deal tables and shelves may be converted into very dainty pieces of furniture indeed by means of a good coating of enamel well applied. As a general rule, the homes which require the exercise of so much care, ingenuity, and ability to make a sum of money go a long way in the furnishing are those that give the most real satisfaction to their occupants, and what greater pleasure can there be than in the realisation of the fact that the little pinchings and contrivings have brought their reward. The young wife who hears a friend congratulate her on the appearance of a pretty rug which she has fashioned from a piece of carpet bought as a traveller's sample for a few shillings at a furniture shop, will experience a much more genuine thrill of pleasure than will her richer sister who is complimented upon any article of furniture upon the purchase of which she has not expended a single thought.

It should be every woman's aim, therefore, however small a sum she may have to invest on the purchase of furniture, to see that it is expended to the best advantage, both from the point of view of taste and also from that of suitability and wear. Do not aim at handsome effects which cannot be achieved with the small sum at your command ; cheap imitations should also be shunned. Let what you have be good of its kind. It is better to buy one or two really *good* pieces of simple and unpretentious furniture and add to them by degrees, than to buy a quantity of cheap imitation which will be shabby in a year.

A good deal of furniture is sold upon the hire system nowadays ; that is to say, that, after the payment of a certain stipulated small sum as a deposit by the purchaser the furniture is delivered at his premises, and is paid for in monthly instalments until the purchase is complete. When a hire contract is entered into with a good and reliable firm the transaction often proves satisfactory, and for people who have not the command of a sum of ready money, however small, with which to buy their furniture it is a most convenient method, but in many other respects the hire system is open to objection. To begin with, it will mean a great strain upon the income of the young husband during the years in which he is first beginning to realise his added responsibilities, a strain which is apt to become a veritable burden in the case of those ups and downs of fortune to which every one more or less is liable. Should any reverse of fortune occur owing to which for a time he is obliged to suspend his payments, he is confronted with the probability of having the furniture taken away, even though he should have paid off all but the last few instalments. Again, when a person has a fixed sum to spend, he knows he must keep within its limits, whereas when it is a question of payment by degrees he often ends by buying more than he can afford. As a matter of principle, therefore, from the point of view of the young couple who are just starting upon the management of a home, the hire system has much in its disfavour, and, however small the sum available, it is better to pay outright for the furniture, beginning married life clear of the money responsibilities which would be otherwise involved. One can always begin in a small way, launching out further as the savings accumulate or the income increases.

A small flat with two bedrooms, a sitting-room, bath-room, and a kitchen can be very well furnished for £50, and much less than that if the young couple are adept at contriving in the way already described.

Young engaged couples who have to set about choosing furniture for their new home would do well to get some assistance in drawing up a list of their requirements. Knowledge of the ins and outs of furnishing is best attained by experience, and for this reason the bride's mother will often be able to make many useful suggestions.

Having made out their list it must next be their aim to divide up the sum to be spent upon the various rooms in suitable proportions. For this they will have to acquire some knowledge of the prices of the various articles, and for information in regard to this point they cannot do better than send for the catalogues of one or two of the best furnishing firms. Furniture catalogues in these enlightened days are not only true objects of art in regard to illustrations, but they usually contain all possible information in regard to the question of furniture, which makes it exceptionally easy for the buyer to make a suitable selection. Comprehensive lists are drawn up containing details in regard to each article necessary in furnishing the home from the table in the dining-room to the saucepans in the kitchen, and all the prices are marked in plain figures.

In addition, people are advised as to how to spend certain sums of money on their furniture to the best advantage. Nearly every furniture list contains schemes for furnishing flats and houses for sums varying from £50 to £500 and upwards. These schemes are drawn up especially for the use of people of average means who have a certain sum to spend and must keep within its limits.

Furthermore, all the large firms show model houses on their premises completely furnished in accordance with the details in their catalogues. A visit to any of these model houses is an education in itself, and nothing is calculated to be of greater assistance in giving reliable guidance to the shopper as to how her money may be spent. The model dwellings are completely furnished in every detail, and in each room a list is usually hung up in some prominent position giving full particulars in regard to every piece of furniture necessary with the price of each separate article. The decorative scheme is complete, including fire-place and fire-irons, window drapery, curtains and wall paper, though the estimate in most cases does not include the latter. A careful study of these rooms both in regard to the colour scheme and also to the arrangement of their actual contents cannot fail to be a useful guide to any purchaser as to her requirements.

Not only one but three or four furniture showrooms should be visited. The shopper can have no better opportunity of studying really practical furniture schemes, and even though she cannot afford to purchase furniture of the kind so displayed, she will gain many helpful ideas in planning out her own little furniture scheme according to the limitations of her purse. (See Maples' Ninety Guinea Flat, p. 35.)

FLOORING AND FLOOR COVERINGS

Parquetry. — It should be ascertained that the floors are well levelled, smooth, and free from cracks and holes before laying down carpets. Plasticity and elasticity are very necessary attributes to all good flooring. It should also have a good surface capable of easy polish. Particularly where the floor, or at any rate the borders of the floors, are stained and polished is the last quality necessary. Parquetry is the ideal flooring for hall and reception rooms, but its cost is very great, and for this reason it is a luxury to be enjoyed only by the favoured few. The cost of laying parquetry flooring in a moderately sized square hall of the kind so often seen in modern houses and flats might in many instances be met by economies practised in the general furnishing of the rooms. The first impressions gained of the interior of the house upon entering the hall goes a long way to help the visitor to form an opinion of the whole, and for this reason the question of hall decoration should never be relegated to the background when the decorative scheme is planned.

Where parquetry is used for the entire flooring it should be of the best. The thin makes are, however, quite effective as surrounds for central carpets. They can be purchased at prices ranging from 3d. per foot and upwards.

Carpets.—The choice of carpets for a house must first of all depend upon the sum of money to be allotted to their purchase. This should not amount to more than one-sixth of the sum allowed for furnishing. Where a house or flat has to be furnished for £90 to £100, for instance, not more than £15 should be spent on carpets, whereas out of a sum of £200 for furniture, the outlay on carpets should not be more than £30.

It requires the exercise of no little forethought to make a small sum of money go a long way in the purchase of floor coverings. First and foremost cheap showy carpets should be avoided. One cannot expect good wear out of a very cheap carpet. It will very soon become faded and shabby looking, and nothing tends more to spoil the appearance of a room than a shabby carpet. For those with limited purses there can be no more economical and, at the same time, more durable floor coverings than plain felts and linoleums.

Felts are now largely used as entire fitted floor carpets. They wear much better, and are much more effective in every way than the cheaper varieties of carpets, for whereas the latter are very seldom obtainable in really good colourings, the plain felts are to be had in all the best art shades and are most soft and harmonious in effect. They lend themselves admirably to the soft subdued colour schemes now so greatly in vogue, and act as a very effective background to furniture. When felt is used as a floor covering there should always be in addition one or two pretty rugs scattered here and there about the room. Felt is also largely used as a surround for a square carpet, many people preferring it to linoleum owing to the fact that it gives the room an appearance of greater warmth in winter. Oriental rugs show up especially well upon a plain felt carpet. Brussels, Wilton, and Axminster rugs are also very effective. Many a bargain in rugs may be picked up at the annual sales of any large furniture establishment. In many cases the large furnishing firms and carpet manufacturers sell what are known as "traveller's samples" of carpet. These run at times into lengths of a yard and over. They only require to be finished off with a little gallon, and very pretty and handsome rugs are thus made at the cost of a few shillings. Pieces of the very best Brussels, Axminster, and other well-known makes may be had in this way, and when the buyer is able to make a good selection, she will find that she has a much better rug than it would have been possible for her to procure when buying in the ordinary way.

Carpets wear much longer if an underlay is provided to keep them from direct contact with the floor. Plain grey felt is admirable for the purpose, and serves not only to preserve the carpet, but also to make it softer to the tread. A good underfelt may be had from 1s. to

1s. 4½d. per yard running from 46 to 54 inches in width. Brown paper also makes a very good underlay, and may be purchased for 2d. a yard. What is known as felt paper is also suitable and costs 3d. per yard. A species of coarse canvas is also used for putting under carpet and may be purchased for 4½d. a yard.

Art square carpets as a rule do not require fastening to the floor, as the heavy furniture of a room would keep them in place. Heavy rich pile carpets, however, require to be fastened here and there. The most handy fastening for a square carpet consists of a patent brass nail which fixes into a groove of the same metal. The groove is screwed into the floor, a hole being drilled into the latter to receive it. The carpet can thus be lifted when necessary with very little trouble, the nails coming easily out of the grooves when it is pulled gently upwards (see illustration).

Patent Carpet Nail.

Measuring Rooms for Carpets.—Most carpet manufacturers send representatives to take the measurements of their customers' rooms for carpets, but long distances and various other circumstances sometimes make it impossible

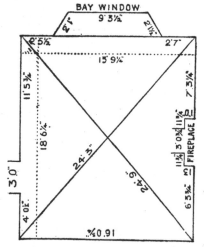

Plan showing Method of Measuring Room for Carpet.

for them to do so. The diagram here given shows how a room should be measured for carpet and surround. When ordering carpets a similar plan should be sent showing position of windows, doors, and fire-place, and giving the measurements in feet and inches. The dimensions should be accurately taken, though the plan need not be drawn to scale; carpets of any kind can be made up from such a drawing.

Different Kinds of Carpets.—For good wear, artistic colouring, and handsome appearance generally the various oriental carpets are unequalled. They are hand-made and the design and colouring are so skilfully interwoven that they will be found to tone well with almost any colour scheme. Skill in designing is almost a tradition with the peasants of the East, for the various designs are handed down from father to son, and are woven from memory, the keen eye for designing and colouring being thus an hereditary gift.

The carpets are sold in the eastern bazaars. Most large carpet-dealers in Europe have agents in the various well-known centres of the carpet industry who are entrusted with the purchase of carpets on behalf of their firm. Turkey carpets are very rich and handsome in appearance. They are favourite carpets for the dining-room, library, or study. The Anatolian Turkey carpets are particularly noted for their delicate colourings, especially in the lighter shades suitable for drawing-room carpets. Persian carpets have a particularly varied range of colouring from the handsome rich tints suitable for dining-room and study, to the soft delicate tints for drawing-room use. They are also durable, being very close in texture. Indian carpets are lower in quality and consequently less expensive than most other oriental carpets. The patterns are worked on various light grounds for drawing-room wear and also darker grounds suitable for dining-room and library. The cheapest varieties should not be chosen as they do not wear well. The better qualities are, however, very satisfactory, as the pile of these is close and deep and the colouring light and harmonious.

Brussels Carpets seem to retain a perennial hold upon the public favour. They make very beautiful and durable floor coverings, but a fair price should always be paid for them. Increase of competition in the carpet trade has induced many manufacturers to place very cheap carpets upon the market, advertising them as " Best Brussels " and quoting very low prices for them. It is impossible to obtain a good " Brussels " at a low price ; 4s. 9d. a yard represents a good average figure for best Brussels carpets, and as a general rule not less than 3s. 9d. a yard should be paid if a really good quality carpet is desired. The pattern of a Brussels carpet always shows through on the wrong side. The carpets are made by weaving thread through a canvas over wires, the latter being withdrawn after the carpet is woven, leaving the loops which form the pile of the carpet. A good quality Brussels carpet can always be judged by the length of the loops or pile. These carpets may be bought by the yard or in seamless woven squares.

Axminster.—The real hand-made Axminster carpets make luxurious and therefore costly floor coverings. They take their name from the town of Axminster in Devonshire where they were first made. They have a rich deep pile and are woven in the most beautiful designs and colourings. More within the reach of the average purse are the machine-made Axminster Pile Carpets. These are to be had in many qualities and in a great variety of colourings— in light tones suitable for drawing-room use, and in the deeper colourings suitable for dining-room and library, and may be purchased for from 4s. 6d. per yard. The patent Axminster and the Crompton Axminster are the best of the machine-made varieties.

Wilton Carpets.—The Wilton carpets are noted for their soft appearance and plush-like surface. They are closer in texture, though shorter in pile than the Axminster carpets. They are made in a very similar manner to Brussels carpets with the exception that the wires are not taken away until the loops are cut. They are made in a variety of designs and colourings, the design in self colours being especially beautiful. Wilton carpets may be purchased by the yard or in seamless woven squares.

Kidderminster Carpets.—These are reversible carpets without pile. They are mostly suitable for bedrooms. It is never advisable, however, to use them as fitted carpets, as the dirt gets very quickly through the carpet to the floor, remaining there in thick layers if the carpet is not frequently lifted. Kidderminster squares, with linoleum surrounds, are the best to use. Seamless Kidderminster squares are now sold under a great many different names, each manufacturer having his own name for his special make of carpet. The carpets known as " Roman Squares " are well-known varieties of the Kidderminsters, as also are the Cheviot and Shetland squares.

Tapestry Carpets are not unlike Brussels in appearance, but the pattern does not show through on the wrong side. They are inexpensive, and may be had in many pretty designs, but are not suitable for hard wear.

Velvet Pile Carpets.—Many varieties of velvet pile carpets are manufactured in imitation of Wilton carpets. They are inexpensive, but unsuitable for hard wear.

Stair Carpets.—Stair carpets require to be very carefully laid over underfelt or stair-pads. A sufficient quantity should be bought to ensure an extra half yard for each flight of stairs. This will allow for a periodical shifting of the carpets at the treads about four times a year so that the wear is evenly distributed, the extra half yard being always kept neatly folded under the last tread of each flight or under the carpet on the landing. The carpets will be found to wear much longer if this simple precaution is taken.

It is always advisable if a saving can be

effected elsewhere to spend a little more money on stair carpets and to have them of as good a quality as possible. They are subjected to an enormous amount of wear and tear, and the very cheap kinds will soon become shabby looking. Good pile carpets are the best for wear, Brussels, Wilton, and Axminster stair carpets being very effective. Tapestry carpets are also suitable and may be had at moderate prices.

Plain felt in one of the art shades makes a very effective and economical stair covering especially suitable for a house furnished in soft subdued tones.

Those to whom an inexpensive carpet is a *sine quâ non* cannot do better than try the cord stair carpets sold by the Abingdon Carpet Co., of Thames Wharf, Abingdon, which are both cheap and durable.

Stair Rods for keeping the carpet in place on each tread are indispensable to the staircase equipment. They are usually of brass and fit

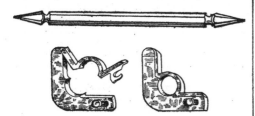

Stair Rod and Eyelets.

into specially made eyelets. The thin round rods are the least expensive; the price varies with the degree of their thickness. The flat sexagonal brass rods are the most handsome, and add not a little to the appearance of a well-carpeted staircase.

LINOLEUMS

The inlaid linoleums are the best, as their colourings and designs are so worked into the materials that they cannot wear off or be obliterated. One of the best of the inlaid linoleums is that known as "Greenwich Linoleum." "Duroleum" is also very good and durable.

The entire hall can be covered to advantage with Greenwich linoleum or duroleum. The pattern should be very judiciously selected. Needless to say, floral patterns are quite out of place, the most suitable being the simple geometrical patterns in imitation of tiles or parquetry. Linoleum requires to be very carefully laid and should be pasted to the floor with the edges of each breadth fastened by a few headless brads.

In many houses linoleum is largely used instead of carpets in all the bedrooms. It is certainly the most hygienic floor covering for a bedroom, as it does not accumulate dust and can be easily swept and washed, and it is at the same time the least expensive. In bedrooms carpeted with linoleum rugs are usually placed at either side of the bed and in front of the toilet table. Twelve square yards will be required to carpet a room 12 feet by 9 feet. The outlay will therefore be most moderate, and to those with inelastic purses this is a very important consideration.

Linoleum is also a suitable floor covering for bath-rooms and nurseries. Cork carpet is also largely used for these rooms. It has the advantage of being noiseless to the tread, and in the opinion of many has a warmer appearance than linoleum. It may be had at 2s. 2d. per yard, the shades in dark green and dark blue being particularly effective.

CURTAINS AND BLINDS

The decorative effect of a room can be made or marred by the selection of its curtains in regard to material, colour, and suitability to the various rooms in which they are placed.

In dining-room and library, for instance,

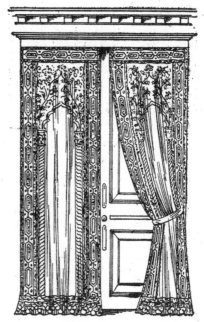

Portière Curtains.

there should always be curtains of tapestry, chenille, velvet, serge, or other similar materials. In the drawing-room curtains of dainty materials such as lace or silk and the various art linens are most appropriate, whilst light chintz, cretonne, lace, muslin, and all other light washable curtains are suitable for the bedrooms.

The cornice poles from which the curtains are to be hung must also be suitably chosen. These will form an item in the general cost of window decoration which should not be overlooked. Ninepence per foot represents an average price for a brass pole one inch in diameter. For brass poles three inches in diameter 3s. 3d. per foot would represent a fair price. White enamelled cornice poles are suitable for drawing-room and other brightly furnished rooms and are cheaper than the brass ones. Mahogany poles three inches in diameter suitable for dining-room and study may be had for 1s. per foot. For bay windows

Casement Curtains.

the prices are higher. Rings to match these poles are sold at prices also varying with their sizes.

Portière curtains are often hung over doors, both for decorative purposes and the exclusion of draughts. They should be of materials such as chenille, velvet, silk, or serge, and should be hung by means of rings to a rod across which they can easily be drawn backwards and forwards. Where there are curtain cupboards in the bedrooms, the hangings should always be of cretonne, linen, or other firm washable material substantial enough to keep out the dust.

Casement Curtains, are now largely used instead of the ordinary roller blind, so casement blinds would be the more correct name to give them. They present a very pretty and decorative appearance and look best with casement windows, but can also be used with sash windows. In the latter case there must always be separate blinds for both upper and lower sash. The casement curtains (or blinds) only reach to the window sills, and the ordinary side curtains are used with them. Cretonne, chintz, casement cloths, silk and Bolton sheeting are the best materials for these blinds. The selection of both material and colour will of course depend upon the decoration and upholstery of the room in which they are used.

Arrangement of Curtains.—Much may be done to improve an ugly-looking window by the manner in which the curtains are arranged. A very narrow straight window may be made to look wider by extending the cornice pole a few inches beyond the window on each side. From this the curtains should hang straight without being looped up in any way. When two or three very narrow little windows come close to each other a top valance can be made to include them as one wide window. From either side should hang curtains of the same material as the valance, whilst lace casement curtains hung over the divisions of the other windows would serve to complete the one window illusion, giving a pretty casement effect to the whole. The casement window lends itself more readily than any other to decorative treatment. Special fabrics are sold by all furniture dealers for this favourite type of window. In this connection it is interesting to note the great revival in old-fashioned fabrics including the actual repetition of the patterns of the quaint chintzes and printed linens which were in vogue during the seventeenth and eighteenth centuries.

The alcoved casement window is always the most effective. Pretty casement curtains in two tiers can adorn the windows, whilst the broad recess may be occupied by a quaint old-world window-seat of the same material as the curtains and valance by which the alcove is enclosed.

Blinds.—Venetian blinds, if of good quality, are always suitable and useful as the laths can be easily cleaned. Their use has to a great extent been superseded however by the more ornamental linen or holland blinds trimmed with lace edging and insertion and working on spring rollers. Very good quality blinds may be had for eight or nine shillings each, the cost of the roller depending upon the particular patent used. Inexpensive linen blinds suitable for bedrooms may be had for about four shillings. With most firms the prices quoted for the blinds include both the measuring and fitting. Blind materials are also sold by the yard for people who prefer to make and fix their blinds themselves. Furniture firms usually send pattern books of these materials when applied for, giving the price per yard and also the price of the whole blinds including making and fixing.

Mantelpiece Decoration.—The decoration of the mantelpiece and its surroundings must conform with the general decorative scheme of the room. Period furnishing requires that the chimney-piece decoration should have a special treatment, and its decoration should therefore be placed in the hands of the firm which is supplying the rest of the furniture.

The ugly gilt-edged mirror which formed the conventional chimney-piece decoration of the time of our grandmothers is now mercifully buried in oblivion. Artistic wooden chimney-pieces and overmantles combined now form part of the decorative equipment of most tastefully furnished houses. These are constructed of mahogany and oak or in other dark woodwork for dining-room and library, and in wood painted white for drawing-room and morning-room. The mantelpieces of bedrooms do not require the elaborate treatment given to those

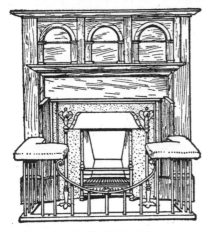

Illustration showing Artistic Chimney-piece and Club Curb.

of the reception rooms. Either a picture or a small overmantle may be placed over the chimney-piece of the latter, and where the woodwork is carried up over the mantelpiece it is only carried up to a very small height.

Where there are no fitted overmantles in connection with the chimney-pieces of the reception rooms the latter must be bought separately. Very pretty overmantles may be purchased in oak, walnut, mahogany, and wood painted white.

Mantelpiece drapery is seldom seen now, but at times it is absolutely necessary to hide an ugly chimney-piece. In these circumstances the material used should be as light and graceful in appearance as possible. Pretty liberty silks and satins in the delicate art shades make most effective draperies.

Tiled hearths and marble fenders are much favoured in present-day house decoration. Brass and steel fenders should always be kept

well polished. A very ornamental type of fender is that known as the "Club Curb." This consists of plain brass or iron rails which reach at times to a height of two feet and which are surmounted by an upholstered seat, usually of morocco. Sometimes the upholstery goes all round the top of the curb, but more usually the seats are only at the sides and corners. A pair of fire-dogs and the necessary fire-irons, i.e. shovel, poker, and tongs, should form part of the equipment of the fire-place. Very useful for morning-room, study, and bedrooms are the little combination set of fire-irons now sold, which fit on to a specially constructed stand. These are inexpensive to buy and look very well. As the stand is of a good

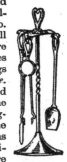

Fire-Irons.

height the fire-irons can easily be taken from it without having to stoop as in the case of the ordinary fire-dogs.

FURNISHING THE VARIOUS ROOMS

The Drawing-Room.—This is essentially the domain of the house mistress, and it is stamped as it were with her own individuality. The woman of refinement and taste makes her personality felt not only in the general furniture scheme of the room, but in the many dainty little finishing touches without which there always seems to be something lacking in even the best furnished drawing-rooms. This something is invariably absent from the drawing-room of the wealthy uncultured woman, who, though she may have had the good sense to give *carte blanche* to a reliable furniture dealer in regard to the choice of furniture, yet fails utterly in imparting that atmosphere of refinement conveyed by the subtle touch in the arrangement of details which is always characteristic of the drawing-room of the gentlewoman, however poorly furnished it may be.

All stiffness and awkwardness of arrangement in drawing-room furniture should be avoided. There should be an air of daintiness and grace and at the same time of cosiness about the room. The drawing-room of to-day is not a room for show but a room for use. It is no longer thrown open on strictly state occasions, nor are children nowadays trained to look upon it as a sort of Bluebeard's chamber only to be entered upon occasions when both Sunday frocks and Sunday manners must be donned and the maxim "Little children may be seen, but not heard," most rigorously observed. There are still some middle-class people who keep their drawing-room as a show-room, only using it on "At Home" days and for other similar functions; but such rooms always wear an air of stiffness and lack of comfort which is often reflected in the manner of the house mistress upon the rare occasions when she is called upon to sit in it in state to do honour to her guests.

Pretty occasional tables and daintily upholstered tapestry settees, one or two cosy tapestry easy-chairs, a tea-table, a drawing-room cabinet, an escritoire, and a piano should be present in every well-furnished drawing-room, to say nothing of such ornamental accessories as tapestry screens, flower-pots on stands, and the innumerable trifles which go to complete the furnishing of a really cosy room. Needless to say, heavy furniture of all kinds should be banished; everything in the room should be as dainty and artistic as possible.

Inlaid mahogany and rosewood are largely used in the construction of present-day drawing-room furniture. There is much that is French in the modern style, which is of graceful and refined design. Furniture manufacturers seem to have taken as their groundwork some of the best characteristics of the old world styles,

Corner Chair.

Occasional Table.

evolving from them a style particularly suitable for present-day needs. Drawing-room chairs are of a dainty spindle-legged design, the pretty little corner chair being especially typical of present-day drawing-room suites. Tables are small, light, and graceful. The needs of the slender purse are particularly well catered for by the modern furniture dealer. People of average means are no longer compelled to furnish their drawing-rooms with all sorts of odds and ends, and chairs which quarrel with each other in both colour and design are now seldom seen in even the most poorly furnished rooms, as complete furniture suites in inlaid mahogany or satinwood can be purchased for quite a moderate sum. The less expensive suites do not contain so many pieces as the more expensive kinds; sometimes only a settee, two small chairs, two corner chairs, and a round table are provided. In these circumstances the furnishing scheme must be completed by purchasing by degrees one or two upholstered arm-chairs, and, if possible, a small sum should be expended upon one or two dainty little occasional tables to match the rest of the suite. A cabinet and an escritoire might also be added as soon as the purse allows. The settees pro-

vided with drawing-room suites are always of the same spindle-legged pattern as the chairs, and an added air of cosiness will therefore be imparted by the addition of a pretty drawing-room Chesterfield or some other similar type of softly upholstered settee or couch. A jardinière to match the furniture will also be effective; and where a brass standard lamp with a soft delicately coloured silk shade, may be had, the effect of the pretty subdued light it gives at night is very pleasing. A little "tea companion," upon which plates of cake and bread and butter may be handed round at afternoon tea, is a piece of furniture the usefulness of which must be by no means overlooked. A tasteful fire-screen, preferably one draped in delicate silk, liberty style, should be placed before the grate. The clock should be in keeping with the general daintiness of the room. Very pretty designs may be had in the refined Sheraton and Chippendale styles for quite a moderate outlay. An art tapestry screen in a framework of mahogany or any other wood of which the furniture may be composed may also be added with effect. The drawing-room is essentially a room to which little extras may be added by degrees, but—and this is very important—the additions must always be in keeping with the general furniture scheme.

The larger the room the more advantageously can the daintiness of drawing-room furniture be displayed. It is a mistake, however, to crowd too much furniture into a small room, not only from the point of view of space, but owing to the fact that its effect will be completely lost and the room made to look smaller than it is.

A small drawing-room should, if possible, be papered in white. A white satin striped paper with a very narrow floral frieze would be effective. (For Drawing-room Decoration, see p. 15.) Water-colour sketches and delicate engravings are the most suitable pictures for drawing-room walls.

A pretty Indian carpet with a light ground makes a very effective floor covering. Wilton, Brussels, and Axminster carpets in the lighter tones are also suitable (see carpets, p. 20). Where a seamless woven square carpet is used in a small room plain Japanese matting will be found to make a very good surround.

Many drawing-rooms are furnished nowadays in reproductions of famous period styles such as Chippendale, Adam, Sheraton, Hepplewhite, Louis XV., or Louis XVI. Needless to say, where such a style is adopted everything must be in keeping. Chairs of one period must not be mixed up with tables of another, and a bureau of still another epoch; wall papers and carpets must also be chosen in accordance with the particular furniture scheme.

Arrangement of Furniture.—A great deal will depend upon the suitable arrangement of the room. The position of a piano, for instance, has spoiled the effect of many otherwise well-arranged drawing-rooms. Very often it is necessary to place an upright piano against the wall through exigencies of space. A more graceful effect, however, is usually obtained by placing it at a convenient angle. Where it is an old and shabby-looking instrument the face of it can be turned towards a corner of the room hidden from all but the pianist, whilst the back can be draped in silk of a delicate art shade. Whenever an upright piano is placed with its back turned away from the wall it should be draped in this manner.

Grand pianos give an air of "finish" to a drawing-room which is achieved by no other means. A pretty silk cover should be kept over the top if photographs or ornaments of any kind are to stand upon it. It is bad taste to have too many ornaments or photographs on a piano, a panel photograph in a very handsome frame and one or two choice ornaments being quite sufficient. It requires a very large room to show off a grand piano to advantage. Demi-grands look very well, and the "Baby Grands" are very suitable both for large and moderately sized rooms. Piano-stools are not now inartistic as of yore. The high round piano-stools are things of the past; more attention is now paid to both comfort and appearance in regard to this piece of furniture. The design pictured in our illustration is much in vogue at present.

Piano-Stool.

Choice of a Piano.—In choosing a piano four important things must be considered, *i.e.* size, volume of sound, tone, and touch. In connection with the first two the size of the room must be taken into consideration so that both size and volume of sound are in proportion. In regard to tone, where singing is an accomplishment in the family it must be seen that the piano has a good singing tone. The pianist of the family should also try it before it is purchased to see that it is in every way to his (or her) satisfaction in regard to touch. There are many makes of pianos noted for their soft beautiful tones, such as those bearing the names of Rud Ibach, Sohn; Bechstein, Erard, and innumerable others.

Hall, Staircase, and Landings.—Within recent years good taste in hall furniture has decidedly increased. There is a leaning towards the artistic in every way. Instead of the one time conventional combined hat-rack and umbrella-stand we find the quaint, old world monk's settle and the separate umbrella-stand and neat wall rack for hats and coats. Oak is a very favourite wood for hall furniture. Imposing looking richly carved oak settles with chairs to match are pieces of furniture upon which very

large sums of money may be spent, but the needs of the shopper with the slender purse have been by no means overlooked in this connection. Plain artistically designed settles may be had in fumed oak for as small a sum as £1, 1s.; a neat fumed oak umbrella-stand can be purchased for six or seven shillings, whilst high-backed oak chairs may also be had for very moderate prices. Where there is an outer hall or vestibule both hat-rack and umbrella-stand should be

Hat-Rack.

placed there. A grandfather's clock is a very effective piece of hall furniture. It should always occupy a prominent position near the staircase. Mats to be placed outside the various room doors should not be overlooked when furnishing the hall. There should also be a good fibre mat in the vestibule.

If the hall is a bright one some pictures can be displayed to advantage upon the walls, also any military or hunting trophies (see Hall Decoration, p. 16). Where there is a high white dado crowned with a projecting rail or

Umbrella-Stand.

shelf, one or two good pieces of china might be displayed upon this.

Where the hall is carpeted staircase and landing carpets should match the hall carpet. In high houses, however, the flight of stairs leading to the servants' room may be covered with oilcloth. If a tenant is fortunate enough to secure a house with a tiled hall, she will be spared the expense of purchasing a floor-covering of any kind, for a few mats will be all that is necessary. One or two pictures may be hung on the walls of the stairway if the light is sufficiently good for them to be properly seen.

Where there are good landings these are capable of tasteful decorative treatment. In houses where there is a large alcoved landing leading from the first flight of stairs to a side wing of the house, the alcove should be prettily draped with curtains. A low-standing book-case enamelled white could be placed upon the side facing the stairs with one or two choice pieces of art pottery displayed upon it. A small table and two chairs could occupy the curtained recess to the left. Those who are the fortunate possessors of some good piece of statuary might display it here to advantage. One or two tall jardinières containing palms

Monk's Settle.

would also be effective. Such a landing, if cosily furnished, can easily be used as a smoking lounge. We do not all possess large square landings, however, but even very tiny landings, if of the proper shape, can be gracefully treated by means of hangings and appropriately placed jardinières.

There are so very many different types of halls and landings that it is rather difficult to lay down hard and fast rules for their treatment. The ordinary passage hall does not lend itself to much decoration. Very often there is only room for settle, hat-rack, and umbrella-stand. Chairs are really unnecessary where there is a good oak settle, but they should always form part of the hall furniture where there is none.

The Lounge Hall.—This description covers two widely different types of hall. The large square hall of the country mansion, with its carved wood panelling, deep wide staircase, and handsome furniture, need not here be dealt with. Such halls are only possessed as a rule by people with whom money is no object and who can afford to pay for the most expert advice upon the question of furnishing. But there is another type of square hall which is often met with nowadays, *i.e.* that which forms a characteristic feature of the modern type of bungalow or flat.

In the smaller flats where there is only one sitting-room a hall of this kind has to do duty as another sitting-room or lounge. In these circumstances it should be furnished as much like a room as possible. Screens should be used to keep off the draught from the front door, whilst curtains should hang from the doors of the rooms which lead out into the hall. A cork carpet in a shade of art green could be used as a floor-covering, with two or three warm cosy-looking mats scattered over it. Umbrella-stand and hat-rack should be banished away in some hidden corner. Near the fire-place might be placed a glass-fronted cupboard, painted white, in which either dinner or tea-set could be displayed. If space permits there might also be a low white enamelled book-case, upon which one or two pretty vases in Wedgwood blue could stand. Two low chairs and a cushioned settee would complete the "sitting-room" illusion. A bright fire burning in the grate in winter will increase the homely and comfortable appearance of the hall sitting-room. In flats with only one sitting-room such an arrangement will be found not only cosy but convenient. Care must be taken, however, to reduce draughts to a minimum. All doors leading on the hall should be kept closed when it is in use and the portières drawn well over them.

Dining-Room.—Large sums of money are very often spent upon dining-room furniture with very poor results. There is a tradition with most people that the dining-room must be sombre and heavy looking, and in the effort of living up to that tradition they often succeed in turning out a room which is so gloomy in appearance that to spend any amount of time in it is to become hopelessly depressed.

This is a great mistake. The dining-room, it is true, must be furnished in a dignified manner, but cheerfulness must not be banished from it. We have gone past the days of the ponderous Victorian sideboard and hideous horse-hair chairs. All should realise the fact that our dining-rooms may be dignified and at the same time pleasing and artistic.

There was a time when the cost of furnishing the simplest type of dining-room was so great that people of slender means could seldom afford to furnish the room outright, but were forced to purchase the various articles by degrees. Nowadays things have changed—furniture manufacturers supply complete suites at reasonable prices, as a visit to any of their show-rooms can prove, and, what is more, the workmanship is good and the design excellent.

In former times the design of cheap furniture was seldom good, hence the public belief in the "cheap and nasty" theory which is still so widely spread. It is true that to obtain really good furniture one must pay a good price, but the fact remains that manufacturers and dealers

Model Dining-Room for small Flat (*Maple*).

A Simple Bedroom (*Heal & Sons*).

are studying more and more the needs of those to whom money is an object, recognising that it is not of people with unlimited wealth at their disposal with which to indulge their most extravagant tastes that the major part of the great army of shoppers is composed, but rather of those who have only a certain sum to spend, and who must necessarily keep within its limits.

Dinner-Waggon.

First of all, the dining-room must be suitably decorated (see p. 15). A few well-chosen oil-paintings and family portraits (if any) may adorn the walls. Failing these some very good engravings in frames of the same wood as the furniture. A good Turkey carpet is the carpet *par excellence* for a dining-room, but we cannot all afford to indulge in luxuries of the kind. Let the carpet at any rate be as soft in appearance as possible, with a good pile. Oak, mahogany, and walnut are the principal woods utilised in the manufacture of dining-room furniture. Especially inexpensive, and at the same time good, furniture may be had in what is known as " fumed oak."

At one time even the cheapest makes of sideboards cost a fair sum, and so very often this article of furniture had to be banished from the list of many a young couple furnishing on very small means. Nowadays a most artistic style of fumed oak sideboard, something akin to a Welsh dresser in appearance, may be obtained for an outlay of only a few pounds. This type of sideboard is very effective in dining-room decoration. It is a type also which is very fashionable at the present time. One or two pieces of china should always be displayed on the shelves, Dutch fashion. Blue and white china looks prettiest with oak. Of the expensive sideboards in the old Dutch styles richness of carving is the chief characteristic. In most of these glass in any shape or form is conspicuous by its absence.

A dining-room can be well furnished at a cost of between £18 and £20, the furniture including an inexpensive fumed oak dresser of

the kind described, some high-backed fumed oak chairs neatly upholstered in green leather, a good oak dining-table, a dinner-waggon, or butler's tray, an easy-chair, a small writing-table, and the necessary equipment in the way of cloth table-cover, curtains, cornice pole, fender, fire-irons, coal-scuttle, carpet and surround hearthrug. Where strict economy has to be practised the easy-chair and the writing-table may be omitted. Very inexpensive black iron coal-scuttles, gipsy pattern, may be purchased for a few shillings, and can be made to do duty where a better kind cannot be afforded. A pretty cloth or art serge table-cover can be made at home for a very small outlay, and casement curtains may also be made for a trifling cost by the clever home worker. (See Furnishing Lists, p. 36.)

Morning and Breakfast-Room.—These two titles are bracketed together because in the generality of houses, where there are but three or four reception rooms at most, the terms " morning-room " and " breakfast-room " are synonymous. The " breakfast " or " morning " room may be taken to indicate the most generally useful room in the house. It is writing-room, sewing-room, and school-room in turn. Many a morning is spent in this room by the busy house mistress in writing letters, going over accounts, and attending to innumerable small household details. It is also often the room where the elder children, emancipated from the nursery, prepare their lessons, and partake of that ever favourite meal of childhood—the five o'clock tea.

The furniture for the morning-room or breakfast-room must therefore be chosen with due

Gate-legged Table.

regard to the uses to which it will be put. As meals are to be served in this room a sideboard will be necessary. This can be much smaller and of lighter design than that of the dining-room. Then there must be a table—a fair-sized round gate-leg table of fumed oak would be useful and at the same time inexpensive, as a good one may be purchased for about £3. Fumed oak chairs with rush seats may be purchased for from 12s. each. In addition, there should be a large lounge easy-chair or two small tapestry arm-chairs, a small writing-table for the special use of the house mistress, and a book-case or some book-shelves for the children's school books.

Where there are no children, the morning-room will be probably utilised as her own special room by the mistress of the house. In these circumstances she will be able to give full scope to her taste for dainty and graceful effects. Chairs may be upholstered in tapestry, pretty engravings can be hung upon the walls, and, apart from the sideboard, which is a necessity in a breakfast-room, the whole scheme of furnishing may be such that it might be aptly termed a "boudoir."

There are many possibilities in the furnishing of a morning-room, possibilities which must always, however, be guided by individual circumstances.

The Library.—There should be an air of restfulness about the library, conducive to reading and study. A flat leather top desk with drawers on either side should be placed in a good light. The writing equipment should be complete in every way—inkstand, pen-rest, blotter and letter weight, a stand for note-paper and envelopes and telegram forms and postcards should all be there and should be kept neat and tidy. To go with this desk there should be a low desk-chair—the round leather upholstered revolving-chair is the most comfortable type. A very large arm-chair in which the master of the house can lounge at ease while reading one of his favourite works is also

Flat Library Desk

a necessity in the well-furnished library. Near this chair should be one of the ever-handy revolving book-cases from which the reader may select a volume at will. A large stationary book-case will also be necessary. This should be with adjustable shelves in order that books of all sizes can be placed upon it. A very good sectional extending book-case may be purchased for a little over £3. One or two high-backed

chairs should also be in the room, and a good hassock footstool should be placed near the easy-chair.

In houses where there is little money to spend upon book-cases and other similar articles of furniture, much may be done by the home worker towards its equipment. With a little knowledge of carpentering inexpensive shelves can be made and fitted round the walls. These should always have some sort of border, not only as a finish but to keep off the dust. It may be often found advantageous to purchase the writing-table from one of the large office-furnishing firms, as very often

Revolving Book-case.

these firms have second-hand goods which they are willing to sell at quite a moderate sum. Desk-chairs may often also be purchased in this way. A little smokers' cabinet should also find a place upon the wall.

There should always be dark curtains in the library—red or green are particularly suitable. Where there is a portière over the door it should be of the same colour as the window curtains. (For Library Decoration, see p. 16.)

Bedroom Furniture.—The stiffness, ugliness, and lack of comfort generally which characterised the furniture of the early Victorian era, was in no way more clearly demonstrated than in regard to furniture for the bedroom. Happily the heavy, cumbersome high chest of drawers, the ungainly wardrobe, and the deal muslin-bedecked table which, surmounted by a looking-glass of the most conventional pattern, did duty as toilet-table in even the best rooms of the average middle-class household, are now things of the past, at any rate with all those who prefer the present-day artistic furniture to the atrocities of the early Victorian tradition. There are still some people, it is true, who, whilst sparing neither trouble nor expense in the suitable furnishing of dining-room, drawing-room, and other reception rooms, barely give a thought to the furnishing of their bedrooms. So long as the reception rooms are nice anything will do for the bedrooms seems to be their guiding principle, and whilst money is spent ungrudgingly upon the decoration of the other rooms a totally inadequate sum is set apart for the furnishing of those rooms in which after all they spend a very considerable portion of the twenty-four hours.

Happily in these enlightened days there are comparatively few people who take so decidedly unenlightened a view of things. With those who do, it must be presumed that tradition dies hard and that they are simply carrying on the tastes of their grandmothers. Sensible people are keenly alive to the fact that, apart from the usual number of hours spent in the bedroom, intervals of illness are apt to occur in the lives of every one of us. In these circumstances should not our bedrooms be as bright, cheery, and as pleasing to the eye as possible ? Neither ungainly inartistic furniture nor hideous wall paper will be conducive to the cheerfulness of an invalid in that period of convalescence, during which a morbid and depressed state of mind will do more than anything else to retard recovery. On the other hand, a prettily decorated room, with a bright pleasing wall paper, tasteful furniture, however simple, and a cheery aspect have more influence in keeping up the spirits of the invalid and assisting her to a speedy recovery than one would generally suppose.

The ideal bedroom has a sunny aspect. There is something especially exhilarating about the morning sun. Care should be taken, however, to see that the rays of the sun do not beat down direct upon the forehead of the sleeper on those summer mornings when sunrise occurs at a time when she has not completed more than three-quarters of her full amount of sleep. Needless to say, suitable blinds should be provided for every bedroom, and these should be kept well lowered, or, if there is a casement window, the curtains should be drawn. When the plan of the room allows of such an arrangement, the bed should be placed so that the window does not face, but comes to one side of it. In this way the discomfort of the early morning glare will be avoided.

It is also essential that the bed should not be placed in a draught. The head of the bed should never be facing the window, for instance, neither should the fire-place be on the same side of the room as the door. If only for purposes of ventilation, there should always be a fire-place in the bedroom—an open gas-fire is especially useful, as it does away with the labour of setting fires and carrying up coals, and can be turned off and on as required without involving any trouble.

When taking a house a woman should be careful in looking over the bedrooms to note if they contain any fitted cupboards. These are a boon in every household, and, painted a pretty white to match the woodwork, they add considerably to the ornamentation of the room. The presence or absence of these cupboards should always form a consideration in the taking of a house. It is also advisable to study the structure of the walls. In many cases where cupboards are lacking there may be convenient alcoves where these may easily be fitted, or, if money is a consideration, they may be utilised for making pretty curtain cupboards. Suitably placed alcoves are capable of treatment, by which they may add considerably to the decoration of a room. An alcove just

over the bed, for instance, lends itself to tasteful curtain drapery. Where one occurs over the window it may be treated in the same way.

In the Queen Anne style of house especially, many of the quaint old-world casement windows are set into deep alcoves. What prettier effect may be obtained than by furnishing the window with a dainty chintz-covered window-seat, and draping the alcove with head valance and curtains of chintz to match that used in the upholstering of the seat ?

The furnishing of the bedroom should be studied first of all from the point of view of hygiene and comfort. Where there is a fitted carpet to the room, or a square carpet which goes under the bed, it should be seen that the mattress of the latter stands at a sufficient height from the floor to enable the dust to be easily taken from underneath it. There are many makes of bedsteads nowadays, more especially those of the various modern French styles, which are so low as to almost touch the floor, leaving little or no space between the floor and the mattress. Such a style of bed may be artistic, but it is certainly far from comfortable, and in no circumstances should comfort be made to give way to art, the ideal furniture being essentially that in which art and comfort are combined.

Medical authorities have laid much stress upon the fact that carpets in bedrooms are merely harbingers of dust and dirt, and therefore unhygienic. They maintain that there should be no carpets under beds, as these cannot always be moved every day for sweeping purposes and dust is apt to accumulate there because unseen. Bedroom manufacturers have, however, found a way out of this difficulty, and Messrs. Heal & Sons, of Tottenham Court Road, London, sell beds which are furnished with patent rails upon which they can be moved with the greatest ease.

There is no doubt that linoleum is the best floor covering for a bedroom from the point of hygiene. It can be easily swept and washed, and one or two nice rugs will serve as a concession to the claims of comfort and warmth.

The next best thing would of course be a square carpet with a linoleum or a stained floor surround. There are people who object, however, to the cold look of the bare boards or of linoleum even if they only appear on the border of the room. In these circumstances a plain felt surround to tone with the carpet is very useful.

The brass bedstead is much in vogue at the present day. It is not the cumbersome-looking object of yore, but a well-designed and useful piece of furniture. When fitted with swinging Italian wings it can be prettily draped with dainty cretonne or other artistic hangings to tone with the colour scheme of the room. Draperies of this kind suspended from wings, and wall draperies hung in artistic fashion from the wall against which the head of the bed stands, are the only form of bed-curtains used nowadays, excepting in the case of the old-time four-poster

Bedstead on Metal Tramway.

which is still to be found in many homes, and revivals of which many bed manufacturers are placing upon the market. Valances are as a rule limited to the latter type of bedstead.

The wooden bedsteads now on the market are artistic in every way and free from that ugliness which characterised those of Victorian days. They are no longer ungainly, cumbersome pieces of furniture, too heavy to move and consequently difficult to clean. Fitted with all the most up to date improvements, including iron frames and wire mattresses, they do not now act as harbingers of dust and dirt. To the many hygienic disadvantages of the old-time wooden bedstead may be ascribed the subsequent craze for *anything* in metal, however ugly in pattern. Some of the most ornamental wooden bedsteads are those of inlaid mahogany in Sheraton style. Iron bedsteads can be had for the most moderate outlay. A white enamelled iron bedstead always looks dainty and clean. It is one of the best and most useful types of inexpensive bedsteads, and looks especially well with brass tops. The ordinary low iron bedsteads are very suitable for servants' rooms.

Bedding.—It is of the utmost importance that the bedding should be of the best. Many people are apt to study show more than comfort when furnishing their bedrooms, with the result that the important question of bedding is very often neglected. It never answers to purchase very cheap bedding, for the latter is apt to prove

only too dear in the long run. A cheap mattress is not only uncomfortable, but it is an actual menace to the health.

Woven wire spring mattresses with good horse-hair or wool over mattresses should be used where possible. Good hair mattresses, however, are apt to be somewhat costly, and therefore are not always within reach of the average purse. Good wool mattresses are infinitely preferable to cheap hair ones. They should in all cases be purchased from a reliable furniture dealer, preferably from a firm who make a speciality of bedroom furniture and bedding, for in this case good value is assured.

In buying mattresses never be misled by an attractive covering, which too often hides much that is deficient in the quality of the material of which it is comprised. For this reason it is seldom advisable to purchase what are described as "bargains" at sales. The common qualities of horse-hair mattresses are filled with various sorts of "short hair" which afford no hold to the "ties," and therefore tend to move and work into those uncomfortable "lumps" which so often turn a bed into a regular instrument of torture. On the other hand, the fine long horse-hair used in good

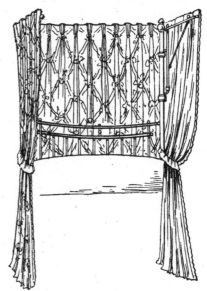

Italian Wing-Drapery.

mattresses gives a proper hold to the "ties" and is kept in place by them. The French mattresses, which contain a special quality of hair mixed with white wool, are exceedingly soft and comfortable. Cheap flock mattresses, which are made up from any sort of rags, should be always avoided.

The wire mattress should be covered with a piece of ticking or Hessian to prevent it from rubbing the hair mattress which is placed over it.

The colour scheme of a bedroom should be as bright and cheery as possible, and always chosen with due regard to the aspect of the room and to the furniture which it will contain (see p. 16). Where the hygienic method of covering the floor with linoleum or cork carpet is adopted, care should be taken to prevent the room from having a bare appearance by putting down a number of warm and cosy-looking rugs of as good a quality as can be procured for the sum available. Everything that tends to harbour dust and dirt should be absent from the bedroom. There should never be an excess of ornamental trifles and knick-knacks about the room. Girls are especially prone to collect these little ornaments, to the despair of many a hard-working housemaid.

Furniture.—The best-designed bedroom furniture of to-day combines much of the artistic effects of the famous epochs in furniture history with a strict attention to convenience of construction as necessitated by modern needs. Modern bedroom furniture manufacturers also make a special feature of reproductions from the antique. Needless to say, when a bedroom is furnished in accordance with a certain period, decoration, carpet, hangings, all must conform with this furniture scheme.

Oak, mahogany, satinwood, rosewood are very favourite materials for bedroom suites. There is also a great vogue at present for white enamelled furniture. This fashion comes as something in the nature of a blessing in disguise for the woman with a slender purse, as the white enamelled suites show a wide range of prices, the cheaper kinds being procurable for a few pounds.

Every furniture suite should comprise a wardrobe, a dressing-table, a wash-stand and two chairs, although in some of the more inexpensive suites only toilet table, chest of drawers, and wash-stand are included. When the latter is not fitted with rails for towels a towel-horse should be provided. It should be ascertained that the locks of drawers and wardrobe cupboards are in order, that the drawers open and shut easily, and that the inside of each piece of furniture is in as good condition as the outside. The wash-stand should have a marble top and be tiled at the back. A sheet of emdeca might also be fixed up at the back of the wash-stand instead of the ordinary " splasher " for the protection of the wall. A cosy easy-chair and a table should also be included in the bedroom furniture where possible. Very daintily upholstered little tapestry arm-chairs may be obtained at quite moderate prices. For an inexpensively furnished room an ordinary basket chair painted to tone with the furniture and with pretty cretonne cushions can be made to answer the purpose. A box ottoman daintily upholstered in cretonne is a most useful piece of furniture, more especially in flats where the cupboard accommodation is necessarily limited. This may be either purchased from a furniture shop or fashioned by the deft fingers of the home upholsterer. Pretty cretonne, chintz, lace, or other washable curtains are the most suitable for the bedroom. Heavy hangings of any kind should be avoided. The walls should not be covered with pictures—one or two engravings in light-coloured frames will be sufficient.

The toilet-table linen should always be fresh and spotless. The pretty duchesse sets consisting of a narrow lace-edged or hem-stitched toilet cover and mats are the most suitable for the present-day type of table. These sets are often used also for the wash-stand. They are apt to get very wet, however, if they are left on during the toilet ablutions, and for this reason most people prefer to do without them. The general equipment of the toilet-table in regard to pin-cushions (well supplied with pins), hat-pin and hair-pin tidies must not be neglected. Any silver displayed on the table should be kept clean and well polished. All these are details, attention to which will go a long way to securing the cosy effect in bedroom decorations which some people find it so hard to achieve.

THE DRESSING-ROOM

The decoration of a dressing-room should conform with that of the bedroom which it adjoins. It should contain a good roomy gentleman's wardrobe, a shaving-stand with mirror, also washstand and suit-case stand. A shaving-stand is to be preferred to the ordinary toilet-table, not only because it takes up much less room, though this is an important consideration as dressing-room space is usually limited, but also because a shaving-glass is much more easily adjusted to the correct angle required by the person shaving, and, being very light, it is easily moved to any convenient position.

Shaving-Mirror

Toilet Ware.—Over-elaboration of design in toilet ware should be avoided in tastefully furnished homes. Artistic yet simple patterns should be chosen. Patterns after the style of Wedgwood and Spode are much favoured by those whose furnishing is on artistic lines. Plain colours and simple shapes go best with the present-day style of bedroom furniture. The self-coloured art wares are largely used, and with these the quaintly shaped ewer with a spout like that of a teapot is often seen. On the whole, the ewers of a more conventional design are preferable to these.

In addition to the regular toilet set there should be a white china slop-pail, a water-bottle, and a glass in every bedroom.

THE BATH-ROOM

In the bath-room the sanitary fittings should be beyond reproach. In a rented house this will of course be the landlord's affair, so when looking over a house particular attention should be paid to the bath-room fittings. A good fitted iron bath of the latest type with taps for hot and cold water and waste and without any wooden casing is the best. Iron baths are preferable to the more luxurious porcelain, as the latter take a great deal of heat from the water, taxing the capacity of the kitchen range to the utmost, whereas with iron baths the heat of the water is retained. There are several methods of covering and finishing the interior surface of iron baths. Of these the porcelain enamel process is perhaps the most effective. Where this process has been applied the interior of the bath presents the same enamelled surface as earthenware—the enamel is also very durable.

A fitted lavatory basin with hot and cold water-supply is very desirable in a bath-room. Beyond the actual fittings very little furniture is required. There should be a towel-rail, a cane-seated chair, a stool, and a rack for sponges and soap to be hung on the wall next to the bath. One of the new bath-racks which fit across the centre of the bath to act as receptacle for the soap and sponge which the bather is actually using is also useful, as it does away with the necessity of reaching up whenever anything is required to the rack on the wall. A cork bath-mat and one or two warm bath-rugs are also necessary. There should also be a mirror on the wall, preferably the regulation bath-room mirror, with a drawer for brushes and combs. Cork carpet or linoleum are the best floor coverings for bath-rooms. (For Bath-room Wall Coverings, see p. 14.)

FURNISHING A BED-SITTING-ROOM

The bed-sitting-room represents the home of many a woman worker, who often takes more pride in the arrangement of the few simple articles she can call her own and the purchase of which in many instances have involved several little acts of self-sacrifice than does the possessor of the most luxurious furniture which money can buy.

It is wonderful what good results may be achieved with comparatively little outlay in the furnishing of a room of the kind, but necessity nearly always proves " the mother of invention," as the many ingenious yet simple contrivances

which can be resorted to in furnishing a bed-sitting-room will go very far to prove.

The great object to be attained in furnishing a bed-sitting-room is to arrange it in such a manner that it gives no idea of a bedroom during the daytime. This result is not so difficult to achieve as one would suppose. Before taking the room, first of all ascertain that the wall-paper is not one of those glaring atrocities so often met with in the present-day lodging-house. If the room is suitable in every way and the wall-paper is the only drawback try and get the landlady to have it re-papered. If she is not disposed to do so offer to share part of the expense, which will not be much. Very simple and effective paper may be bought for an ordinary-sized room at an entire cost of from 15s. to 20s., including the work of hanging, and rather than put up with ugly wall-paper it will be found better in the long run to bear the cost oneself, if the landlady is obdurate on the point.

It is well to observe when taking the room if there are any cupboard fitments. A good

The "Divan" Bed.

roomy cupboard will save the purchase of a wardrobe which, besides being somewhat expensive to buy, would go a long way towards destroying the sitting-room illusion during the day. If a wardrobe is a necessity then one of the plain inexpensive bamboo cupboards without any glass in front would be the best to purchase. If the cost of a carpet cannot be afforded, stain the floor with permanganate of potash and polish it with bees'-wax and turpentine—the cost of this will be very trifling if you do the whole work yourself. Two or three pretty rugs may be purchased for a few shillings each. A fairly good art square carpet for a small room may be purchased for about 25s. ; with this only the surround of the floor need be stained.

The furniture should include a bed which can be made to look as much like a couch in the daytime as possible—a perfectly flat bed of the camp variety without any upstanding head or foot-piece would do. With this there should be a good soft wool mattress. The bed should always be placed against the wall. In the daytime the bed-clothes can be neatly folded up and placed underneath the mattress, and the whole can be covered with a pretty Indian rug. Arrange on this one or two cushions and the result is a very cosy and effective-looking eastern divan. Special couch beds are now largely sold by furniture manufacturers.

A small plain deal table with one or two drawers may be purchased for five or six shillings. This should be stained a shade corresponding

Dwarf Cupboard.

with the rest of the furniture of the room and placed against the wall, and a good-sized looking-glass hung on the wall directly over it. The table will do duty as both toilet-table and writing-table. In the daytime the brushes and hand-mirror, together with the toilet-cover and mats, may be put aside in the drawer, their places being taken by a neat blotting-pad, an ink-stand, and the necessary writing materials. A dwarf cupboard could be made to do duty as a washstand, the toilet ware being placed inside the cupboard during the daytime; or, if the conventional wash-stand is preferred, this could be placed in a corner of the room and completely hidden by a large screen.

Then there must be a table large enough for meals. A round deal gate-leg table would be very useful, as the flaps can be let down and the table put on one side when the meal is not in progress. A large box ottoman in which clothes may be kept should also form part of the furniture; one or two smaller ones made out of sugar-boxes and upholstered in cretonne to match that of the ottoman would also be useful, acting as handy receptacles for millinery.

At one side of the room there should be a low table or cupboard which can do duty as a sideboard. The usefulness of corner brackets and shelves in a room of this kind cannot be too highly estimated. A hanging corner cupboard with a glass door would be especially useful for the display of a dainty afternoon tea service which cannot safely be trusted downstairs. Very many large general stores, such as Whiteley's in London, make a special feature of the sale of white wood articles for carving, poker work, or enamelling. Very well-designed pieces of

furniture may be had in this white wood at a comparatively small cost. Thirty shillings will purchase a pretty china cabinet in white wood, whilst a small book-case with sliding doors may be had for even less, and a hanging book-case 27 inches high would cost from twelve to fifteen shillings. Small book-shelves and wall-brackets may be bought for from 1s. 11d. and upwards. When properly stained or enamelled this furniture looks very well indeed. For an extra change it can be stained at the shop where it is purchased

Three or four small chairs and one or two easy-chairs will complete the furniture of the room. Upholstered tapestry arm-chairs may now be had for as little as fifteen shillings. Wicker chairs when prettily upholstered can be made to look very cosy. When bought ready upholstered they necessarily cost more than when the work is undertaken at home. In the section upon home carpentry and upholstery many useful hints are given in regard to the making of inexpensive little odds and ends for the home which the proud possessor of a bed-sitting-room would do well to study. Pretty curtains and draperies, dainty table-

Ottoman

cloths, all can be made by the deft fingers of the woman who takes a pride in making her surroundings as cosy and dainty as possible, however heavily she may be handicapped in regard to means.

Period Furniture.—Distinctive style in furniture is becoming cultivated to a very great extent nowadays, and people who have the means with which to indulge their taste in this direction like to furnish at least one room in their house in accordance with one of the famous furniture periods. Genuine "antiques" can as a rule be only indulged in by those with well-filled purses. Other people, however, may be fortunate enough to possess one or two pieces of really good antique furniture which has come to them by inheritance. These should be cherished as articles of real value, and placed amongst surroundings in keeping with their character.

A good piece of furniture is apt to prove somewhat costly at times in the expenditure entailed by living up to it. A Louis XVI. cabinet, for instance, will demand that not only the rest of the furniture in the room but also the decoration be in the same style. It seems superfluous to remark that no woman of taste would allow such a piece of furniture to be placed in a room furnished in accordance with the early Victorian tradition.

All women should have at least an elementary knowledge of the characteristics of the various styles of furniture belonging to the famous epochs. Without this knowledge they are apt to make somewhat glaring errors when attempting to furnish their rooms in accordance with any particular period. The study of the evolution of furniture has a fascination peculiarly its own. Through it the manners and customs of our forefathers may be traced step by step from the time when primitive man first began to carve out of wood or stone those crude implements suited to his needs, through the centuries of progression marked by the Gothic, Tudor, Jacobean and Georgian periods to the Victorian era (which last, strangely enough, marked a time of positive decadence in the art of furniture designs), and thence to the present day.

The connoisseur does not need to concern herself with the styles of furniture which prevailed prior to the fourteenth century, however. The needs of our ancestors in those days were too simple for the evolution of any really characteristic style, which could be adapted to present-day needs. The real evolution of artistic furniture in this country began with the Tudor period. Many Italian craftsmen settled in England during Henry VIII.'s reign, and the influence of the Italian Renaissance has left its mark upon the furniture of the period. The furniture of the "Jacobean" period has a dignity all its own. Many people like their dining-rooms furnished in this particular style, which prevailed during the reign of James I., 1603—until the end of the reign of James II., 1685. It was during the eighteenth century, however, that English furniture reached its greatest degree of artistic perfection, and it is with this period, therefore, that collectors are most concerned. It gave birth to such artist-craftsmen as Chippendale, Adam, Hepplewhite, and Sheraton, whose names will ever live in the annals of furniture design. Contemporaneous with these famous English styles were the French styles of Louis XV., Louis XVI., the Directoire, and the First Empire.

As has been already remarked, during the Victorian era art in furniture went through a marked decadence. The furniture of this recent period is marked by its stiffness, ungainliness, and general air of discomfort. It may safely be said that connoisseurs of the future will not readily advocate a revival of the Victorian style.

Those who wish to make a study of the characteristics of the best periods in furniture cannot do better than read some good books upon the subject. Mr. Edwin Foley, in his book entitled "Decorative Furniture," traces the evolution of artistic furniture from the most remote times,

explaining the main characteristics which distinguish the art of each particular period. Much valuable assistance is given to the collector by the many coloured illustrations of the various styles which are to be found throughout the book. She should also make a point of visiting museums and other places where specimens of old furniture may be seen; such as the Victoria and Albert Museum, South Kensington, London; the Royal Scottish Museum, Edinburgh, and the Dublin Museum. For French decorative furniture in particular the Jones Collection, South Kensington Museum and the Wallace Collection, Hertford House, Manchester Square, should be visited.

SOME FURNISHING ESTIMATES

The following lists, giving suggestions in regard to the best way of spending two fairly representative sums of money on the furnishing of a small house or flat, will prove useful to the young couple who are about to furnish a home, and who require guidance not only as to the furniture to be purchased, but also in regard to the cost of the various articles. The first list of this has been compiled by Messrs. Maple in connection with a ninety guinea model flat displayed at their show-rooms. The second scheme for furnishing a house for £300 has also been largely compiled from information obtained from the same firm—

THE NINETY GUINEA FLAT

The sum of ninety guineas is apportioned amongst the various rooms as follows :—

	£	s.	d.
Dining-room	18	5	3
Drawing-room	22	17	6
Bedroom	20	19	1
Servant's room	4	3	3
Bath-room		17	3
Hall	3	4	3
Kitchen	2	1	5½
Linens, blankets, &c.	7	8	4
China and glass	3	6	7½
Electro-plate and cutlery	5	5	2
Ironmongery	6	1	10
	£94	10	0

The following lists give detailed expenditure for the various rooms :—

DINING-ROOM

	£	s.	d.
Seamless tapestry carpet (12 ft. by 9 ft.)		2	6	6
Linoleum surround (say) 8 yds. at 1s. 1¼d.			9	0
2 pairs casement curtains with rod and fittings			17	6
Cloth table-cover			10	0
Black curb fender			7	6

	£	s.	d.
Set of fire-irons		4	6
Coal-scoop		10	0
Fumed oak sideboard	4	8	6
Dining-table (3 ft. 6 in. by 5 ft.)	2	5	0
1 Elbow-chair with rush seat	1	2	6
4 Small chairs with rush seat at 13s. 9d.	2	15	0
Oak side-table		17	6
1 Lounge easy-chair	1	3	6
Hearth-rug		8	3
	£18	5	3

DRAWING-ROOM

	£	s.	d.
Axminster pile carpet (12 ft. by 9 ft.)	4	4	0
Linoleum surround (say) 10 yds. at 1s. 1½d.		11	3
2 pairs of Mapleton damask curtains with rods and fittings	1	6	0
Curb fender		7	6
Set of fire-irons		4	6
Brass coal-scoop		10	0
2 "Neston" easy-chairs upholstered in tapestry at 22s. 6d.	2	5	0
1 "Neston" settee upholstered in tapestry	1	18	6
1 Arm-chair with tapestry seat	1	1	0
2 Small chairs with tapestry seat at 13s. 9d.	1	7	6
Inlaid mahogany cabinet	4	15	0
Inlaid mahogany centre table	1	12	6
Inlaid mahogany occasional table		9	9
Mahogany escritoire	2	5	0
	£22	17	6

BEDROOM

	£	s.	d.
Felt carpet planned to room (say) 12 yds. at 3s. 9d.	2	5	0
2 pairs cretonne casement curtains with rods and fittings		18	4
Curb fender		7	6
Set of fire-irons		4	6
4 ft. 6 ins. Bedstead, white and brass	1	8	9
Wire-woven mattress		10	6
Sanitary pad		5	9
Extra thick wool mattress	1	11	6
Feather bolster		10	0
2 Pillows at 6s. 9d.		13	6
Decorated white bedroom suite, comprising dressing-chest with jewel drawers, double wash-stand, wardrobe, bevel plate glass mirror, pedestal cupboard, towel-horse, and 2 chairs	10	5	0
Double set toilet ware		13	6
Easy-chair		12	9
Bed furniture		12	6
	£20	19	1

SERVANT'S BEDROOM

	£	s.	d.
Linoleum for covering floor		9	9
Bedside rug		3	9
2 ft. 6 in. iron bedstead and wire mattress, wool mattress, pad bolster, and pillow complete	1	7	9
Japanned oak wash-stand		5	3
Simple set of toilet ware		3	6
Japanned oak chest of drawers with dressing-glass fixed	1	5	6
Cane-seated chair		2	6
Japanned oak towel-rail		1	9
Fender		3	6
	£4	3	3

BATH-ROOM

	£	s.	d.
Covering floor with linoleum		4	6
Cane-seated chair		3	6
1 pair casement curtains with rod and fittings		5	6
Bath-mat		3	9
		17	3

HALL

	£	s.	d.
1 pair casement curtains with rod and fittings		6	0
Fumed oak umbrella-stand		15	0
Fumed oak hat-rack		6	6
Linoleum for covering floor (say)		11	3
Black fender		4	6
Fumed oak settee	1	1	0
	£3	4	3

KITCHEN

	£	s.	d.
15½ yds. linoleum at 1s. 1d.		16	3
4 ft. kitchen table		13	6
2 Kitchen chairs at 2s. 10d.		5	8
Kitchen fender		5	6
	£2	0	11

LINENS, BLANKETS, &c.

	£	s.	d.
1 pair blankets (84 by 104 in.)		17	9
1 Under-blanket		4	6
1 White quilt		12	9
1 Down quilt		17	6
2 pairs cotton sheets at 10s. 6d.	1	1	0
2 pairs pillow-cases at 2s. 4d.		4	8
1 pair blankets for servant's bed		8	11
1 Under-blanket		2	11
1 Coloured quilt		3	11
2 pairs cotton sheets at 5s. 11d.		11	10
1 pair pillow-cases		1	11

	£	s.	d.
2 Damask table-cloths (2½ by 2 yds.) at 5s. 11d.	11	10	
6 Napkins for		3	9
6 Huckaback towels for		4	9
3 Bath towels at 1s. 1½d.		3	4½
6 Servants' towels at 6½d.		3	5
6 Tea-cloths for		2	11
6 Glass-cloths for		2	6
6 Dusters for		2	0
2 Kitchen table-cloths at 1s. 11½d.		3	11
2 Roller towels at 1s. 1½d.		2	3
	£7	8	4½

CUTLERY

	£	s.	d.
6 Table knives for		6	3
6 Small knives for		5	3
1 pair meat-carvers		4	9
1 pair game-carvers		4	9
1 Steel		2	0
6 Electro-plated table forks for		11	3
6 Electro-plated dessert forks for		8	3
4 Electro-plated table spoons for		7	6
6 Electro-plated dessert spoons for		8	3
6 Electro-plated tea spoons for		5	3
2 Egg spoons		1	8
1 Butter knife		2	6
1 pair sugar tongs		2	0
2 Electro-plated sauce ladles at 2s. 6d.		5	0
1 Electro-plated cruet with mustard spoon		13	6
2 Electro-plated salt spoons at 9d.		1	6
Electro-plated teapot		15	6
	£5	5	2

CHINA AND GLASS

	£	s.	d.
Dinner service for six persons		16	0
Tea and breakfast service for six persons	1	2	0
Service of glass for 6 persons, viz.: 6 port glasses, 6 tumblers, 6 sherry glasses, 2 decanters complete		9	3
Water-bottles and glass for bedroom	1	5	
Water-bottles and glass for servant			10
China and glass for kitchen use—			
6 Plates, assorted sizes		1	6
1 Vegetable dish		2	3
3 Dishes for		2	9
1 Sauce boat			6
2 Breakfast cups and saucers at 5½d.			11
2 Plates at 3d.			6
1 Sugar basin			4
1 Milk jug			7
1 Salt cellar			3½
2 Tumblers			5
1 Set of 3 jugs		1	3
2 Pie dishes		1	6

	£	s.	d.
2 Pudding bowls		1	2
1 Teapot 6d., 2 store jars for 1s. 5d.		1	11
1 Bread pan		1	3
	£3	6	7½

IRONMONGERY (*Kitchen List*)

	£	s.	d.
1 Bath (galvanised)		2	6
1 Bowl (hand)		1	0
1 Bread grater			7
1 Cake tin			8
1 Chopping board		1	4
1 Clothes horse		5	0
1 Coal scuttle		1	11
1 Coffee canister		1	0
1 Coffee pot		1	9
1 Corkscrew			6
1 Colander		1	0
1 Set of dish mats		1	11
3 Dish covers : 1 each, 3s. 6d., 6s. 3d., 7s.		16	9
1 Dust pan		1	0
1 Egg slice			8
1 Egg whisk			6
1 Fish kettle		3	3
1 Fish slice			8
2 Iron spoons for			6
3 Tea spoons			7
1 Set steps		7	0
1 Slop-pail		3	0
1 Tea canister		1	3
1 Tea tray		2	9
1 Tin-opener			6
1 Toasting fork			6
1 Glass tub (pulp)		2	6
1 Nutmeg grater			2
1 Gravy strainer		1	2
1 Housemaid's box		2	9
1 Tin kettle		1	2
1 Iron kettle		3	0
1 Knife board			7
1 Knife tray		1	8
3 Knives and forks (table)		2	9
1 Galvanised pail			10
2 Flat irons for		1	6
1 Flat iron stand			6
1 Flour dredger			6
1 Flour tub		2	9
1 Frying pan		1	0
1 Funnel			3
1 Paste board		2	3
1 dozen patty pans			4
1 Pepperbox			4
1 Plate basket		3	0
2 Plate leathers		2	0
1 Kitchen poker			9
1 Rolling pin			6
1 Salt box		1	9
3 Iron saucepans, 1 each, 1s. 4d., 1s. 9d., 2s. 9d.		5	10

	£	s.	d.
1 Enamelled saucepan		1	3
1 Set skewers			7
1 Soap-dish			4
1 Towel roller and brackets		1	0
1 Wire sieve			10
3 Wood spoons			7

Brushes—

	£	s.	d.
1 Hair banister brush		1	3
1 Whisk brush		1	1
1 Long hair broom		2	6
1 Carpet broom		2	6
1 Dusting brush		1	0
1 Nail brush			4
1 Scrubbing brush		1	3
1 Bass scrubbing brush			8
2 Plate brushes for		1	9
1 Set shoe brushes		2	9
1 Set stove brushes		2	9
1 Sweep's brush			9
	£6	1	10

£300 HOUSE

Summary

	£	s.	d.
Hall	9	13	3
Dining-room	55	4	0
Drawing-room (with piano)	84	13	3
Morning-room	18	14	11
Best bedroom	32	16	8
Spare bedroom	19	8	5
2nd spare bedroom	14	17	11
Servants' bedroom	9	13	0
Kitchen	4	7	2½
Bath-room	1	14	3
Plate and cutlery	9	0	0
Linen and blankets	17	18	5
China and glass	8	0	0
Ironmongery and extra fittings	10	0	0
	£296	1	3½

This leaves a balance of £3, 18s. 8½d., which will go towards any extra expenditure upon clocks, cushions, portières, and fancy table-covers which have not been included in our lists.

DETAILED LISTS

HALL

	£	s.	d.
18 yds. stair and landing carpet at 4s.	3	12	0
2 doz. rods, eyes and pins		16	0
Covering floor with linoleum (say) 12 yds. at 1s. 6d.		18	0
Hat-rack		8	6
Fumed oak settle	1	1	0

	£	s.	d.
Fumed oak umbrella-stand	1	8	9
Rug		17	6
1 pair casement curtains with rod and fittings		7	0
Fender		4	6
	£9	13	3

DINING-ROOM

	£	s.	d.
Axminster pile carpet 12 ft. by 12 ft.	6	4	0
Linoleum surround (say) 12 yds. at 1s. 1½d.		13	6
2 pairs casement curtains with rod and fittings	1	3	6
Table-cover	1	5	0
Pierced steel fender	1	1	0
Set of fire-irons		9	0
Coal-scoop		11	0
Mahogany sideboard	8	17	6
Mahogany 2-tier serving-table	2	10	0
Dining-table	4	12	6
6 mahogany small chairs upholstered in morocco at 22s. 6d.	6	15	0
Easy-chair upholstered in tapestry	4	4	0
Easy-chair upholstered in tapestry	3	5	0
Mahogany occasional table	1	11	6
Mahogany escritoire	4	11	6
Mahogany book-case	7	10	0
	£55	4	0

MORNING-ROOM

	£	s.	d.
Seamless tapestry square carpet 12 ft. by 9 ft.	2	6	6
Linoleum surround		9	0
2 pairs curtains with rod and fittings		17	6
Curb fender		7	6
Set of fire-irons		10	0
Coal-scoop		5	0
4 small rush-seated fumed oak chairs at 13s. 9d. each	2	15	0
Fumed oak sideboard	4	8	6
Easy-chair	1	5	0
Hearth-rug		8	3
Gate-leg table	2	0	0
Sectional book-case	3	2	8
	£18	14	11

DRAWING-ROOM

	£	s.	d.
Axminster pile carpet 10 ft. 6 ins. by 9 ft.	4	4	0
Felt surround (say) 12 yds. at 3s. 9d.	2	5	0
Pierced fender	1	1	0
Set of fire-irons		12	0
Brass coal-scoop		11	0
2 pairs casement curtains with rod and fittings	1	3	6

	£	s.	d.
Inlaid mahogany Sheraton cabinet .	8	17	6
Inlaid mahogany writing	2	17	6
Piano	40	0	0
Piano-stool with velvet cushion . .	1	2	6
Inlaid mahogany circular table . . .	2	5	0
Settee upholstered in tapestry . . .	5	7	6
Easy-chair	2	12	0
1 Inlaid mahogany elbow-chair . .	1	17	6
4 Inlaid mahogany small chairs at 22s. 6d.	4	10	0
1 Inlaid mahogany occasional table .	1	6	9
Hearth-rug		18	0
Screen	3	2	6
	£84	**13**	**3**

KITCHEN

	£	s.	d.
Covering floor with linoleum . . .	1	5	0
4 ft. kitchen table		17	9
2 Kitchen chairs at 6s. 6d.		13	0
1 Windsor chair		8	0
1 Carpet deck-chair		6	6
Alarm clock		5	6
Coal hod		2	2
Strong shovel		2	3½
Kitchen poker		1	6
Rug		5	6
	£4	**7**	**2½**

BATH-ROOM

	£	s.	d.
Covering floor with linoleum . . .		10	0
Cane-seated chair		3	6
Glass with drawer for brush and comb		11	6
Bath rack		5	6
Bath mat		3	9
	£1	**14**	**3**

BEST BEDROOM

	£	s.	d.
Gobelin carpet 12 ft. by 12 ft. . . .	3	12	0
Linoleum surround (say) 12 yds. at 1s. 1½d.		13	6
Curb fender		7	6
Set of fire-irons		4	6
2 pairs casement curtains with rod and fittings	1	0	0
4 ft. 6 in. brass bedstead	3	5	6
Wire-woven mattress		10	6
Sanitary pad		5	9
Hair mattress	2	3	9
Feather bolster		10	0
2 Pillows		18	0
Inlaid mahogany bedroom suite, comprising : — Wardrobe, dressing-chest with glass, washstand fitted with cupboard, and towel-rail and two chairs	12	15	6

	£	s.	d
Double set of toilet ware		15	0
Easy-chair		12	9
Hearth-rug		8	9
Occasional table		14	9
1 set of bed draperies to match curtains		18	6
Oval Sheraton mirror	1	5	0
Screen	1	9	6
Linen basket		5	11
	£32	**16**	**8**

SPARE BEDROOM

	£	s.	d.
Caledon carpet 12 ft. by 9 ft. . . .	2	14	0
Linoleum surround (say) 10 yds. at 1s. 1d.		10	10
2 pairs Mapleton damask curtains with rod and fittings	1	0	0
1 set of bed draperies to match . . .		17	6
Fender		7	6
Set of fire-irons		4	6
3 ft. White and brass bedstead . . .	1	5	0
Wire-woven mattress		7	9
Sanitary pad		3	9
Hair mattress	1	7	6
Bolster		6	0
Feather pillow		9	0
White bedroom suite, comprising :— Wardrobe, dressing-chest, with glass, washstand fitted with towel-rail and 2 chairs	7	10	0
Single set toilet ware		7	11
Hearth-rug		8	9
Easy-chair		12	9
Occasional table		9	9
Linen basket		5	11
	£19	**8**	**5**

SECOND SPARE BEDROOM

	£	s.	d.
Fumed oak bedstead with wire spring mattress	2	4	9
Sanitary pad		3	9
Hair mattress	1	7	6
Bolster		6	0
Feather pillow		9	0
Fumed oak suite comprising :—2 ft. 6 ins. wardrobe, 2ft. 6 ins. dressing-table, washstand, and one chair .	4	10	0
Oak shaving-stand	1	9	6
Easy-chair		12	9
Set of toilet ware		6	9
2 pairs casement curtains with rod and fittings	1	0	0
Clothes-basket		2	11
Linoleum to cover floor (12 by 9) . .	1	10	0
2 Rugs at 7s. 6d. each		15	0
	£14	**17**	**11**

SERVANTS' BEDROOM (2 *maids*)

	£	s.	d.
Covering floor with linoleum . . .		9	9
2 Bedside rugs		6	0
Two 2 ft. 6 ins. iron bedsteads and wire mattresses, wool mattresses, pads, bolsters, and pillows complete at £1, 7s. 9d. each . . .	2	15	6
2 Painted chests of drawers at £1, 9s. 6d. each	2	19	0
2 Painted washstands at 12s. 6d. . .	1	5	0
2 Painted dressing-glasses at 4s. 6d. each		8	9
2 Painted chairs at 4s. 3d. each . .		8	6
Double set of toilet ware		7	0
Fender		3	6
1 pair casement curtains with rod and fittings		10	0
	£9	**13**	**0**

(For Ironmongery, see p. 37.)
(For China and Glass, see p. 37.)
(For Electro-plate and Cutlery, see p. 37.)

LETTING A FURNISHED HOUSE

Speaking generally, it is unadvisable to let a well-furnished house. To do so is to place your precious household goods at the mercy of strangers, who will not appreciate them or care for them as you do. Dilapidations and breakages of various kinds are bound to occur, and even if their money value is received, there are some things that cannot be replaced in the owner's estimation.

Very often, however, a woman finds it absolutely necessary to let her house. She may be called abroad, and might not care to leave the house shut up or in charge of a caretaker. Again, the finances for the annual holiday might depend to a great extent upon her ability to let it. In these circumstances, therefore, she must take the utmost precautions to ensure that it is let to careful tenants. The house should be put in the hands of a good agent, who will see that all the formalities in regard to suitable references from the prospective tenant are proceeded with, and who can make judicious inquiries apart from these references.

The agent will charge a commission upon the amount received for rental, together with fees for drawing up agreement and taking inventory. An inventory has always to be taken of every piece of furniture, plate, and linen left in the house. Where the house is large it may sometimes take a whole day to go over this carefully. The mistress of the house should see that this important piece of work is properly done, drawing the agent's attention particularly to articles she wishes to be carefully noted.

It is usual to leave a certain small supply of plate and linen; but the bulk of this with other cherished articles should be locked carefully away. A very large cupboard or a room, sometimes both, should be reserved for locking-up purposes, and the agent should see that the doors of these are carefully sealed.

If the furniture is very good, never let the house to people with young children, as these are often responsible for a great deal of damage. Dogs, if not under proper control, also often cause a large amount of wear and tear. It is as well to have a clause inserted in the agreement that no dogs must be kept without the landlord's consent. This consent should not, however, be unreasonably withheld. Many people would not dream of taking a house without taking their pets with them. Let it be impressed upon the tenants, therefore, that they will be held responsible for any additional wear and tear which the keeping of these pets might entail.

Before letting the house it should be thoroughly cleaned from cellar to attic, and the chimneys should be swept. The tenant should also leave it as clean in every way as when he (or she) took up the tenancy.

QUARTER DAYS

English			Scotch		
Lady Day	.	Mar. 25	Candlemas	.	Feb. 2
Midsummer	.	June 24	Whitsuntide	.	May 15
Michaelmas	1	Sep. 29	Lammas	.	Aug. 1
Christmas	.	Dec. 25	Martinmas	.	Nov. 11

Half-Quarter Days

Feb. 8, May 9, Aug. 11, and Nov. 11.

MISTRESS AND SERVANTS

THERE is an old and very true saying that "knowledge is power." Nowhere does this maxim more fittingly apply than in the case of the woman who is thoroughly acquainted with every detail of the work of the home, and knows how the various domestic duties can be most efficiently and, at the same time, most expeditiously performed.

Even to the woman who is so comfortably endowed with this world's goods that she can afford to maintain a staff of highly trained servants at liberal wages, a knowledge of housewifery is an invaluable asset. Then hers must be the brain to supervise and direct the smooth running of the household machinery, to see that each servant performs conscientiously and efficiently the work allotted to her, that the whole establishment is maintained in that perfect working order which is a typical feature of the good housewife's régime.

In this section each phase of the servant question is carefully considered. The duties of the mistress in regard to the treatment and management of servants and the proper organisation and supervision of their work are clearly outlined, as are also the duties of each servant in accordance with the number kept. Useful information is also included in regard to the engagement of servants, prevailing scale of wages, allowances and holidays.

DUTIES OF THE MISTRESS

Knowledge of Housewifery Advisable.—Like every other profession the profession of home-making requires a certain amount of training and apprenticeship. It is quite a mistaken notion to think that housewifery comes instinctively and naturally to every woman, and that the woman who is unfitted for any other career in life can stay at home and "keep house." Domestic skill can only be acquired by training.

Whatever other calling a girl or woman may choose to select, be it nursing, teaching, medicine, art, or any other of the professions open to women, both time and money are expended in order to qualify her for her career. Why should housekeeping be left out when training in this is just as essential, seeing that the happiness and comfort of so many will depend upon her fulfilling her duties in an intelligent manner ? A woman who has no knowledge of the right way to manage a house has no more right to marry and be responsible for her husband's worldly goods than a man would have to accept a post the duties of which he was quite ignorant.

A servant is quick to grasp the fact when her mistress is not versed in the arts of domestic science, and quicker still to take advantage of the ignorance thus displayed. She knows that there is no trained eye to detect flaws in her work ; that a room half dusted will seldom evoke a protest—a table carelessly or slovenly laid will as often as not pass unheeded. The mistress will be made to suffer in many little

ways for her ignorance in respect to household duties until by bitter experience she will awaken to the realisation of the fact that knowledge is indeed power, and strive to learn what she should have known when she first began to reign as mistress of her own home.

To the girl who is destined to begin married life in such humble circumstances that she will not be able to afford to keep even a general servant, ignorance of the rules of household work is apt to become something in the nature of a calamity. An untidy, ill-kept home, to say nothing of ill-cooked meals, is not conducive to the good temper or cheerfulness of a husband, more especially when he comes home after a hard day's work to find chaos reigning supreme, and that atmosphere of discomfort which few can analyse, and only those who have experienced it can understand. Indeed, it may be said that many a little " rift within the lute " has been occasioned by nothing less prosaic than the lamentable ignorance of her household duties displayed by the young wife.

Training in housekeeping may be acquired in different ways. Firstly, a young girl may be trained in her own home under a good mother or guardian, and this is the best training of all. The training may be given gradually throughout early life by allotting her little home duties to perform and teaching her the importance of the small things on which the comfort of the home depends. Or, if the greater part of the girl's life has been spent away from home in a boarding-school, then the training may be given in a more concentrated form when the school life is over. The practical nature of a real home training is of much greater value than any isolated courses of lessons, which may be taken later on in life. Training can also be acquired at one of the numerous schools of Domestic Science now established in various parts of the country, and if only sufficient time is allowed this is another excellent way of learning various branches of household routine. Finally, knowledge can be gained by experience, but this unfortunately may be at the expense of needless worry and anxiety not only to oneself, but to the other members of the household as well.

Modern housekeeping requires an expert and not an ignoramus, and there should be nothing degrading about having to look to the ways of one's household. In fact, it will generally be found that the better educated and the more intelligent a woman is, the higher will be her housekeeping capacities. A sound knowledge of household details does not tie one more to one's own four walls, but it enables one to get the best results with the least expenditure of time and energy.

Oversight and Inspection.—It is the duty of the mistress to see that her house is kept as spotlessly clean as it is possible to make it. Each part must receive her attention, not only the principal rooms of the house, such as the sitting-rooms and bedrooms, but the kitchen, scullery and servants' bedrooms as well.

She must also see that food is neither wasted nor thrown away. This will necessitate a daily visit to the larder (see p. 101), and even the scrap-pail and dust-bin must not escape her notice. Constant watchfulness in this respect is all-important, and if a mistress thoroughly understands what ought to be, she will detect waste from the beginning and be able to put it right.

Sinks and lavatories must also be included in the tour of inspection, and if there is any unpleasant smell it must be seen to at once.

It will also be the duty of the mistress to see that the locking up of the house at night is attended to—that all low windows and doors of unused rooms are locked and back and front doors bolted. She must see that silver is carefully put away, and that all fires are in a safe condition to leave.

Order and Arrangement.—The wheels of domestic machinery will not run smoothly unless the mistress is orderly and methodical in all her arrangements.

She must first of all have a clear idea of what she wishes to have done, and then make her plan accordingly, so apportioning the work among the different workers that for each detail some one person is responsible. There must be a fair division of labour, so that too much does not fall to one person and not sufficient to another.

There must also be a proper time for everything and everything should be done in its time. Punctuality and method will contribute essentially to the comfort of the home, and if household work is systematised there will be little fear of friction or neglect.

It is impossible to draw out a model plan which will suit the requirements of all households, so much depends upon the size of the house, the number of the family, the style of living, and the means at disposal; it therefore rests with each mistress to devise her own particular working scheme. She may not always succeed in attaining her ideal, but she can at least have a certain standard at which she aims and which she does her best to attain. This amount of method must not prevent departure from routine should circumstances require it. It must always be remembered that rules are made for people not people for rules, and the mistake must not be made of subordinating everything to the keeping of the ménage.

If there is one thing worse than an uncomfortable and disorderly home, it is the household where order and system are carried to such a pitch that all those pleasantly diverting pursuits, which tend at times to upset the general arrangement of things, are reduced to a minimum in order to avoid unnecessary work, to save the carpets, keep the furniture in good condition, or something else of a like nature. This is to make a desert of a home.

Order and system should be silent factors which do not obtrude themselves, necessities which are best kept out of sight, but which act none the less as drops of oil on the machinery of domestic routine.

Daily Duties.—The duties of the mistress of a household are very numerous and very varied, and it will be well for her to try to draw out a plan and time-table of her own daily routine.

The extent of her duties will naturally depend upon her income, the staff of servants at her disposal, and the size of her household.

To house the members of her household in comfort and health, to feed them properly and nurse them in sickness, to keep household accounts, to engage servants and allot to each their proper share of work, and to do the work herself when occasion requires, are among a few of the duties which will rest upon her shoulders.

Details of the various branches of work for which she will be responsible will be found under their respective headings, such as The House, The Table, Nursing, &c., and it is hoped that the instructions there given will prove helpful to the woman who desires to be a real home-maker.

The Duty of Cheerfulness.—Cheerfulness is one of the most valuable of possessions; it is really the sunshine of life, the promoter of health and happiness. To be able to keep up the spirits of those around us not only adds to the brightness of the home, but helps to make all duties comparatively light and easy. It is a woman's duty to make the life of the home as happy and gay as possible, and however depressed she may sometimes feel she ought to struggle against the feeling and not damp the spirits of those around her.

No one can be more trying than the person who continually gives way to low spirits, going about with a martyr-like expression, and making a habit of airing her grievances at every meal or family gathering. Such a person is a constant source of irritation to the other members of the household.

Unfortunately, it is often upon the home-loving woman that the little worries, the small contretemps of daily life weigh most heavily. She takes it too much to heart if her house is not so spotlessly clean as she would like, or if her well-planned arrangements have been upset, and she finds it difficult to look at things from a right perspective.

It requires some strength of will to grapple against this spirit of worrying and getting depressed, but the home-maker ought to think of others before herself and do her utmost to keep these little troubles in the background.

Health and happiness are a thousand times more important than all the spotless homes in the world, and to worry over every speck of dust, over every broken dish, or such-like trifles will only result in greater miseries, broken-down nerves, and premature wrinkles and old age.

Home Touches.—The duties of the mistress are not finished when the routine of household work is set agoing and cleanliness and order have been established. The little finishing touches, the small elegances, the tasteful arrangement, the special provision made for individual comfort must come from her or be wanting altogether. She must endeavour to make the rooms as pretty as possible and give to them an air of repose and restfulness. Who does not know the difference between a room that is merely kept in order by a servant and one in which the lady of the house takes an interest as well. It is perhaps attention to the small things of the house that has the most to do with the comfort of it, and it is just these minor details that require the most thought, as they are outside the ordinary routine. If they are neglected or forgotten all the cosiness, all the home feeling and soothing influence will be gone and bare utility alone will remain.

The true home-maker is also one who has the intuitive power of divining the tastes and feelings of others and who is ever ready to minister to their needs. With a ready tact she will put herself in the place of those around her, will be able to perceive their unspoken worries and disappointments, and sympathise with them without remark. She will even be able when occasion arises to shield them from unkindly notice or an ungenerous remark. Tact of this kind is perhaps innate, and yet much of it may be acquired by observation and kindly feeling.

Women are the real home-makers, and it rests with them to make the four walls in which they live something more than a mere dwelling.

Happy is the woman who can so surround her own fireside with the true spirit of home, as to make it the spot where the brightest and most desirable of everything is to be found, a harbour from all outside cares and worries ; she will find that not alone to herself, but to those around her as well, it has become the best place in the world.

Duty towards Herself.—Last but not least, it is the duty of the mistress to take care of herself and attend to her health. However busy she may be, she ought to contrive to have a period of leisure and to be out of doors for some time every day. Self-sacrifice in the cause of duty may become almost a fetich with many women. No woman, however, is justified in making herself a domestic drudge. She confers no benefit upon any one by being a slave to her family and to her home. The best house-mistress is undoubtedly the one who allows herself time for both relaxation and diversion, realising that without it not only her health, but also her nerves and her temper would suffer in the long run.

The head of the house must also find time for her own toilet and make the best of her personal appearance. There is no occasion for her to wear costly apparel unless she can afford it, but she must always be neat and wear what suits her and looks attractive. A lady cannot expect servants to look up to her and pay attention to their dress if she herself goes about in slovenly attire ; in this, as in everything else, she must be the example to be copied.

Beyond the Home.—We often hear it said that if a woman does her duty in her own home this is all that can be expected of her. But this is a very narrow view to take of life, and such a limited existence is bad not only for the woman herself, but for the other members of her household as well. In fact, the reason that so many heads of families break down in health is because they wrap themselves up too much in the cares of their own household and worry so much over every trifle that it ends in their requiring a rest cure or something of the kind.

A woman ought, as a responsible member of society, to use her powers to help and encourage those beyond the borders of her own home. If she did this, even to a small extent, she would find that the strain of constantly thinking of household affairs was very much relieved, and that she gained strength for renewed effort.

Then there are social duties to perform—the paying of calls, the giving of entertainments, the cultivation of friends, &c., and these are claims which cannot be neglected. If we shut ourselves up from our friends and live entirely within our own small circle we very soon become narrow-minded and end in being forgotten.

ENGAGING SERVANTS

There are several different ways of obtaining servants. If one can be heard of by recommendation, either through friends or through a servant in one's employment, this is certainly the most satisfactory and easiest way, but it is only occasionally that one is favoured by such a chance.

Then there is the registry office, which may or may not be good. While there are offices of high standing, where business is done in an honest and upright manner, there are many others whose dealings can by no means be relied upon. As a rule, city registry offices are of little use for supplying servants for the ordinary middle-class household, as they cater more for hotels and other large establishments; and while they may have on their books a long list of butlers, cooks, lady's-maids, parlourmaids, and other specialists in domestic service, the cook-general, house-parlourmaid, or general rarely seeks for a situation through that channel. A good suburban registry office may, on the other hand, render valuable assistance, especially if a girl belonging to a special district is required.

A well-drawn-up advertisement inserted either in a local paper or in a good general newspaper with a wide circulation is one of the best means, and this method often enables one to have a better choice. The wording of the advertisement must be concise, and at the same time it must neither be vague nor misleading. A few particulars as to requirements should be given, and it should be stated whether the applicant is to write or to apply in person and at what hour. The following specimen advertisements may serve as a guide to those who are inexperienced in this work :—

General Servant.—For small flat, three in family, must understand plain cooking, no washing. Wages £16–£18. Good health and references essential. Apply after 4 P.M.

Cook General.—Wanted immediately, small house, four in family. Wages £18–£20. Late dinner. Age 25–30. Apply after 7 P.M.

Parlour-maid.—Wanted 1st July, good at silver and needlework, a little housework. Age 22–28. Wages £20–£25. Three servants. Apply ——

Young girls trained in domestic work can also be obtained from charitable institutions, but this plan should not be resorted to unless one is prepared to devote a considerable amount of time and trouble to their training. Although the girls have had training of a kind in their institution, they are as a rule quite unaccustomed to the niceties of a private house, and are apt to be very uncouth in their manners. There is difficulty, too, in getting other servants to take

kindly to a girl of this class, and not infrequently it proves an unhappy arrangement on both sides.

It is always wise to have a personal interview with a servant before engaging her. This not only helps the mistress to judge of her character by her appearance, but it also enables the girl to see the house to which she may be asked to come, and gives her a better idea of the work that will be expected of her.

The mistress should begin the interview by asking the maid some questions as to what experience she has had, how long she remained in her last place, and what reason she had for leaving it—what wage she had been having, and what she would now expect. Some inquiries should be made regarding the girl's family and also whether she has good health or not. Attention should also be paid to her personal appearance, whether she is clean and tidy in her person, neatly and suitably dressed, and of a prepossessing manner. If the information thus obtained is in the main satisfactory, the mistress should next give an outline of the duties she would expect her to perform, and if after a little mutual conversation the arrangement seems likely to suit both parties, details may be entered into a little more fully.

A servant must never be engaged under false pretences, and it is never a wise plan to make things appear better than they really are. It is better policy to make it quite clear what will be expected in the way of work, so that there may be no chance of future misunderstanding.

Some information should be given as regards the habits and customs of the family, the number of servants kept, and the amount of entertaining likely to be done. The mistress should also state her wishes as regards dress, caps, aprons, &c., and whether she will allow visitors or not. The question of wages must also be discussed and a clear statement must be given as to what time will be allowed off and what holiday will be given, also what notice must be given should either party wish to terminate the engagement. If a cook is being engaged, there should be a clear understanding about perquisites.

The first conversation in a matter of this kind counts for a great deal, and there is nothing like making everything clear at the outset.

If a maid has been asked to come some distance in order to have this interview, it is usual to pay her expenses.

With regard to references, a personal interview with the maid's last employer should be obtained if possible. There are a few occasions on which a written character may be safely accepted, but these should be the exception and not the rule, and written particulars should be accepted with a certain amount of caution. Besides, ladies will always give more information verbally than they will by writing, and there is always something to be gained by seeing the house in which the girl has been previously employed, as this also serves as an index as to what has been expected of her in the way of service. In fact, it is never a very wise plan to take a servant who has been employed in a house out of one's own rank in life. For instance, a servant who has been employed by a lodging-house keeper, by small trades-people, or even in an hotel is not suitable for private service with gentlefolk, as she would be unaccustomed to the ways of refined people. Each branch of service has its own standard, and what may be ideal in one line of life, falls very far below the ideal in another.

During the above interview the mistress should ascertain the reasons for the maid leaving her place and also her capacity for work. She must also make inquiries as to her moral character, whether she is clean, neat, good-tempered, also whether she has good health and is an early riser.

If the answers to such inquiries prove to be satisfactory and the mistress considers the girl likely to suit her requirements, the next step is to write to the maid or to ask for another interview in order to fix the date of arrival, and to make the final terms of engagement. In Scotland and the North there is an old-fashioned custom of giving arles or earnest money as a token of engagement. The sum of 2s. or 2s. 6d. is given to the maid as sealing the contract. But this is merely an old custom and not a necessity.

The usual custom of hiring a servant is from month to month; this means that they are paid once a month and the engagement can be terminated on a month's notice. (See Law of Master and Servant, p. 377.)

Character-giving.—Although a mistress cannot be compelled to give her servant a character, it is customary to do so when a girl is leaving her employment. The fact of refusing to grant a reference would almost imply inability to testify to any good qualities in the girl's character, and this would be most prejudicial to her future career.

A character must not, however, be given lightly; it is essential to state only what is true. There must be no exaggeration either of the good or of the bad points, and the mistress in search of a maid must be considered as much as the maid herself.

A mistress has no right to hide some serious fault from a desire to give the girl a better chance, but she must be absolutely frank and impartial in every way. (See Law of Master and Servant, p. 377.)

WAGES, ALLOWANCES, AND HOLIDAYS

Wages.—The wages of an indoor servant should be paid monthly, dating from the day the maid enters your service. Or, for convenience sake, where there are several servants, a fixed date may be chosen, say the 1st of the month as general pay-day. In this case, the odd days when a girl arrives would have to be paid for separately. Wages must always be paid regularly, and under no circumstances should a servant be obliged to wait for her money.

The amount payable as wages varies very much in different localities, and one has to conform very much to custom in a thing of this kind. The wages in town are usually higher than those paid in the country.

The following table may serve as an approximate guide as to what is usually paid :—

Butler	£45—£90
Housekeeper	30— 80
Cook	20— 40
Cook-general	18— 25
Parlour-maid	16— 25
Housemaid	16— 20
House-Parlour-maid	15— 25
Kitchen-maid	12— 20
Scullery-maid	8— 14
General Servant	10— 25
Lady's-maid	25— 50
Footman	20— 30
Valet	30— 50
Tweeney	10— 16
Hall Boy	9— 12

Licences.—An annual licence is required for each man-servant in addition to wages (see p. 384).

Board Wages.—When servants are left in charge of a house during the absence of the family, or if they are sent away temporarily for the same reason, it is usual to put them on board wages. This means that in addition to their regular wage they are paid a sum ranging from 7s. 6d. to 12s. 6d. for a woman-servant, and from 12s. to 15s. for a man-servant per week as food money. The amount varies according to the style of living, and the district in which they are living. When several servants are left it is very usual for them to club together and for one, generally the cook, to do the catering ; but this is a matter of arrangement amongst themselves. If they are obliged to find their own accommodation as well as board, an extra allowance should be paid for lodging or the fare paid to their own homes.

Food Allowances.—In a small household where only one or two servants are kept it is not usual to have food allowances. In fact, the less difference there is made between the meals of the family and those of the servants the better.

When there are several servants it is very customary to make an allowance of such articles as tea, butter, and sugar, but here, again, unless there is a large establishment it is seldom wise to make a difference in the quality of these commodities, unless it be tea, where a special brand such as China tea is frequently used for the dining-room and another, better liked by the domestics, is given for kitchen use. Otherwise to give an inferior quality of anything to the servants only leads to discontent, and the saving of expense is scarcely noticeable.

The usual allowances for tea, butter, and sugar are the following :—¼ lb. tea, ½ lb. butter, and 1 lb. sugar per week for each servant.

As regards the different meals, the following is a very usual rate of allowances :—

Breakfast.—Tea, bread and butter and porridge (if wished) with some little addition, such as dried fish, egg, or boiled bacon. There are some houses where this addition is not granted, but this is poor fare when we consider that a girl is expected to do a morning's work on the strength of this early meal.

Lunch.—This is not a recognised meal, but when breakfast is taken very early, a little bread and butter, with a cup of milk or a cup of cocoa, should not be denied, especially as some girls are unable to take much breakfast.

Dinner.—This meal is usually the same as the dining-room lunch or early dinner, and consists of meat with at least one vegetable, and pudding, or soup and cold meat with a little cheese or stewed fruit.

Tea.—Bread and butter with a little jam or dripping cake in addition to tea.

Supper.—Cocoa or coffee with bread and butter and cheese, or the remains of any salad, savoury, or simple pudding left from dinner. Meat is never given unless there are men-servants, but a basin of soup may sometimes take the place of the cocoa or coffee.

Laundry Allowance.—If the washing is not done at home, servants are usually allowed from 1s. to 1s. 6d. for their laundry bill ; if the lesser sum, some of the smaller articles would require to be washed by themselves.

Holidays and Time Off Duty.—There is no hard-and-fast rule as regards this, and it is best for each mistress to arrange the matter with her maids. The usual allowance is an evening or afternoon once a week with an afternoon and evening on alternate Sundays; while a fortnight's holiday in the year is very general.

TREATMENT OF SERVANTS

It is most important that when a new servant arrives, the house, or her department of it at least, should be in good order. It is very disheartening to have to commence by cleaning out cupboards and clearing away some one else's disorder before any good work can be started.

In small houses the mistress should take the maid round and show her where her work will be, and where she will find the necessary implements to perform it. A list of her duties should be written on a card and hung in some convenient place, such as the kitchen or pantry, and it will be just as well to have the time off duty stated on the same card. The details of the maid's work should be given her by degrees. There is no use confusing the girl's mind by telling her too much at once; the necessary instructions for the first day's work will be quite sufficient to begin with. For the first few days a little patience and forbearance will be necessary until the girl learns the ways of the household and the wishes of her employer, and allowance must be made if everything is not done exactly as one would wish.

Then, later on, though a mistress cannot expect perfection, it is her duty to see that the work is properly and regularly done, and if anything is wrong, to speak about it at once and not allow it to slip. This should always be done in a kindly spirit and without any show of temper. In fact, if she is very much annoyed about anything, it is much better to wait until the first feeling of vexation has passed over and she is able to speak calmly and firmly without showing unnecessary vexation.

A servant should never be corrected before a third person, neither should a message of reprimand be sent through a child or a fellow-servant.

Then, again, it is a bad plan to be constantly going after a servant and doing oneself any work that may have been slurred over or omitted. This is frequently done to save oneself the trouble of speaking, but it will not make a capable nor a reliable maid. A girl ought to be given a reasonable amount of work to do and then held responsible for its fulfilment ; if it is found to be more than she can properly do it is much wiser to relieve her of some of it than to have the constant feeling of dissatisfaction.

Above all things, a mistress must make an effort to be absolutely fair and consistent, and there should be nothing underhand in her dealings. By these means she will have a better chance of obtaining faithful service. A good servant likes to feel that there is a firm hand over her, and that the mistress notices whether her work is well or badly done.

While reproof should be given when necessary, praise must not be withheld when work is well done. A word of commendation is very welcome to all of us. To those who clean our rooms, cook our food, brush our boots, &c., we cannot be too grateful, as, at the best, it is monotonous work, and one's maids are certainly due more consideration than is frequently given. They are not all demons trying to "do us" at every turn, but human, often very human, and they should certainly be treated reasonably and their rights respected.

As we exact and expect civility and courtesy from our maids it is only fair that we should render them the same. A fear of familiarity should never be an excuse for a curt answer, nor justify the omission of "please" from our requests, nor a word of thanks for any service rendered. Neither should we be reluctant to wish them the common salutations of "good morning" and "good night."

Servants who are treated with this courtesy of manner will, as a rule, like their place and try to render faithful service.

It is also fitting that well-performed duties which tend to make the home happy and comfortable should be rewarded by little kindnesses—a gift now and then in acknowledgment of some special service or at a special season, such as Christmas or on return from a holiday, or an occasional holiday or treat. A little encouragement of this kind goes a long way towards making the drudgery of housework pleasant and easy.

One should not be backward either in raising the wages of a girl who has worked well. If she has been in our service for a year or eighteen months, she is worth more than when she first came, and the rise will be appreciated so much more if it is given unsought. Then when a gift is given, let it be something that shows a little kindly thought—a length of print, a muslin apron, or a pair of stockings are very useful and sensible, but they are not pretty, and every girl who is earning a fair wage ought to be able to afford these necessaries. How much nicer would be a little handbag and purse, a pretty work-basket, a set of toilet brushes in a case, or something which she would not likely buy herself, which would show the friendly thought and serve as a little keepsake.

There is much said nowadays about the dislike of the lower classes for domestic service. One reason to account for this is the increased education which they receive in the elementary schools. This naturally creates a spirit of independence and a wish to rise in the social scale, which is not altogether unworthy. An employer, to be successful, must therefore take this new spirit into consideration and make allowances for it by respecting the rights of those who serve. Many mistresses fail to move with the times, and cannot see that the requirements of the working-classes are altering, and that more liberty and more wages is demanded.

Fortunately, much is being done to raise domestic service to a higher level, and it depends very much upon the employers whether these efforts succeed or not. If the mistress herself despises household work, and allows it to be seen that she looks down upon those who do it, it will not be surprising if her domestics cultivate the same ideas. On the contrary, she ought to be able when necessary to take part in the household work without in any way losing her dignity.

A lack of leisure and want of privacy are other reasons for making domestic service unpopular. It frequently happens that a maid has no time she can call her own, and that she is continually under the eye of her employer. Now although there is no limit regarding the working hours of a servant, beyond the fact that she must be allowed a sufficient time to sleep, this does not entitle us to demand service without relaxation. A certain amount of leisure must be granted and then strictly adhered to. An effort, too, should be made to make this leisure time happy by letting servants have a comfortable place to sit in. Often the only means of freedom from work is to go out of the house, no matter what the weather is like. A few books or magazines or even the daily paper sometimes might be passed on to the kitchen with advantage.

Then a certain amount of privacy is due, especially at meal times. Servants have a right to take their meals free from interruption, and they should not be called away if it can possibly be avoided. Although a mistress should feel free to enter her kitchen at any time, she ought to choose her times for doing so and not be continually passing in and out.

Allowing a servant her independence does not prevent a mistress from taking a kindly interest in her affairs, and she must remember, too, that from the time the girl enters her house until the hour she leaves it, she is morally, although not legally, her guardian. It is an exception when a girl resents being spoken to as a fellow-woman, and yet some mistresses hesitate to do this and thus fail to win respect and affection. Servants should be encouraged to tell their little ailments, and to say at once when they are not feeling well. It should be seen that they go to bed in good time and that they take proper and sufficient food.

It is especially necessary in the case of a young servant to exercise this supervision, and particularly so if she has been brought a long way from her own home and her own people. Then it will be the duty of the mistress to ascertain where she is going to spend her time off. In fact an " evening out " should scarcely be granted unless she has friends to go to or can go out with a fellow-servant. An effort should rather be made to let her go out during the day until she has made the acquaintance of some respectable girls with whom she can be trusted.

A word might be said here about servants' bedrooms. The places in which some maids are asked to sleep are a disgrace to civilisation, and not infrequently it is in the houses of the wealthy that the worst accommodation is found—underground bedrooms which, besides being dark and airless, are sometimes damp and insanitary as well. For her own sake as well as theirs a mistress should see that her maids are provided with proper sleeping quarters, and each servant must have her own bed, a good mattress, and sufficient covering. The room itself should be light and airy, and it must be cleaned and attended to in the same way as the other rooms of the house. A servant herself is not always fastidious and particular about her room, and will sometimes be lax as regards the cleaning of it, but none the less we must see that sufficient time is given to clean it and that our wishes in this respect are carried out. There is no reason either why the servants' bedroom should be the only ugly room in the house— a place to hang useless pictures and store unsightly pieces of furniture. A pretty wall-paper or, better still, a washable distemper of a nice colour, a nice clean coverlet on the beds, tidy furniture, &c., is a training in itself and helps to increase the girl's self-respect.

And, finally, let us treat our servants with a spirit of trust and confidence, and we shall seldom have reason to regret it. For instance, a too strict locking up of daily necessaries is not always a good plan, as it shows a lack of confidence which a good servant will often resent, while a dishonest one will find a way of being dishonest whatever precautions we may take, and she is better out of the house. Besides, for one's own sake, it is bad to live in an atmosphere of suspicion and watchfulness. Human nature is the same all round; the best in us responds to trust, and the worst rises to the surface if we are constantly being rubbed the wrong way. Servants, like other people, would often do better if they were trusted more.

DUTIES OF SERVANTS

In drawing up a scheme of servants' duties it is not possible to make a plan which will suit all requirements, as every household has its own individual arrangements and no two are exactly alike. All that can be done is to furnish a broad outline of the work which requires to be done, and the following paragraphs must be looked upon as suggestive only. It is to be hoped that they will serve as a guide to the inexperienced and help them with their ménage until they have gained sufficient knowledge to make their own plan.

The amount of work to be done before breakfast by the different maids must depend upon the hour of that meal, and if before 8.30 or 9 o'clock some of the duties put down in the following lists must be delayed until later in the morning.

There has been little or no provision made for home washing, but where this is undertaken it must be looked upon as the special work of the day and time given for it in accordance with the amount to be done.

The exact time for doing the various pieces of work has not been stated, because, as a rule, it is a bad plan to tie a worker down in this way and to say that a certain piece of work has to take a certain time, and so on; it makes her grow into a sort of working machine, and takes away from her all responsibility.

If the servant is active she has no inducement to work quickly if she finds that her spare moments are just filled up with more work, and, on the other hand, if she is slow it is very discouraging to find that her work is never finished at the time expected.

The Cook.—The cook, as her name implies, is the one who prepares and cooks the food of the household. She is the chief servant in the kitchen, where she reigns supreme.

There are different grades of cooks. First we have the *Professed Cook*, who is only found in large establishments. In former years a chef or man cook frequently filled this post, but women cooks have now come more to the fore, and a chef is rarely employed in a private ménage. The professed cook has always one or two maids under her—(kitchen-maid and scullery-maid)—to whom she assigns the cleaning of the kitchen premises, the preparation, and possibly the cooking of vegetables, the cooking and serving of servants' meals and also nursery meals if there are such, while she devotes herself to the higher branches of cookery only, assists the mistress in drawing up the necessary menus, and orders the stores required for her department. She does no cleaning nor housework, but is waited on by her underlings.

Then we have the *Good Plain Cook*, who in large households, where there are a number of meals to be served, will undertake all the cooking that is required and the cleaning of the kitchen and kitchen premises. Sometimes she will have the help of a charwoman once a week to do the heavy cleaning or scrubbing, or that of a "tweeney," a young girl who divides her time between the house and the kitchen, working generally under the housemaid in the morning and under the cook from lunch time onwards. She may or may not undertake the cleaning of her own bedroom, but beyond that will do no work in other parts of the house.

And finally we have the *Cook-General*, who is usually found in middle-class households, where only two or three servants are kept. Her duties extend somewhat beyond the kitchen. She is expected to take some share in housework proper, such as the cleaning of the dining-room or library, the cleaning of the front hall, door-step, and brasses, and to give some assistance to the housemaid.

Qualifications Necessary.—There are certain qualities necessary to the making of a good cook, whatever her grade may be. She must first of all have some knowledge of cookery more or less extensive according to what is required of her. She should at least know thoroughly what she professes, and if it be only the simplest cookery, it must be good of its kind, palatable, and nicely served. She must also be punctual in all her duties, and especially so in the serving of meals. There is nothing which upsets the ways of a household so much as having meals served at uncertain hours, and for this the cook is usually responsible.

It is also important that a cook be clean and tidy in her work. All the kitchen premises and utensils should be kept spotlessly clean, and while cooking is going on there should be tidying up and clearing away at the same time. An untidy and littered kitchen is very dispiriting for other servants, even if the cook herself does not mind the disorder. No good work can be done in a muddle; in fact, the best cooks make the least mess and use the fewest utensils. The kitchen should be tidied up after every meal and made to look as bright and comfortable as possible, especially in the afternoon when the heavy part of the day's work is usually over.

A cook should also be an early riser. With her rests the lighting of the kitchen fire, upon which the hot-water supply for early morning baths, &c., depends, not to speak of the cooking of the breakfast. The amount of actual work done before breakfast will naturally depend upon the hour at which the meal is served, but unless an early start is made the cooking of the breakfast will be hurried and unsatisfactory, the water will only be tepid, and the rest of the work will be behindhand all day. The other servants, too, look to the cook as an example of what is required in this respect, and if she rises late the others will doubtless follow her lead.

Method and forethought are also valuable qualities for a cook to possess, as by their practice the labours of the day can often be considerably lightened. In cooking so many little things can be prepared in advance, and if the bill of fare is known a day beforehand one day's work can often be fitted in with another's. Then, when it comes to the actual cooking of the meal, the cook must consider carefully what dish requires the longest time, and so arrange that everything is ready at the hour appointed. Forethought, too, in the ordering of stores and provisions may save many a worry and bustle at the last minute. Then, again, in the matter of breakfast it is often possible to prepare what has to be cooked the night before, so that if anything should happen in the morning to make her a little late, the first meal may still be prepared with a calm mind.

And last, but not least, a cook ought to have consideration for her fellow-servants, and although the kitchen is her domain, there is no reason why it should ever be a place where others are afraid to enter, and where she acts as tyrant. On the contrary, she should do her best to make the place cosy and comfortable for them, as it is often their only resting-place when they have a little leisure to sit down. It is the cook's duty, too, to see that the kitchen meals are served properly, and while it is right that she should have no interference with the larder, she must provide a sufficient supply of well-cooked food and that which has been ordered by the mistress herself. A word of warning, too, is sometimes required to cooks who have young servants working under them, as they are often tempted to put an undue amount upon them, especially of the heavy work, while she herself does only what requires little output of strength.

Personal Appearance.—A cook should pay special attention to her personal appearance, and specially from the point of view of cleanliness and neatness. Her hair must at all times be neat and not allowed to come beyond bounds. There is nothing more revolting than to see a woman preparing food with her hair hanging round her head in an untidy fashion, or, what is worse still, brushing or combing her hair in a kitchen.

A cook should always try to keep her hands in good condition, and they must always be washed before any cooking is commenced. Gloves should be worn when doing any dirty work, such as the flues, the grates, and the cleaning of tins. In winter-time, if the skin is inclined to become very rough, a little glycerine should be rubbed in occasionally.

A dress of washing material, such as print, drill, or galatea should be worn in the early part of the day; in fact, there is a large amount of cooking to be done in the evening, and as the cook is not expected to leave her kitchen, it is very usual for her to remain in her cotton dress. Or she may if she chooses wear a light print dress in the morning, changing to a darker cotton one in the afternoon. Cotton, being easily washed, is a much more suitable material for kitchen use than any woollen stuff. The dress must be short enough to clear the ground by two inches. White linen aprons with bibs should be worn while cooking, and these should be furnished with a good-sized pocket. White linen sleeves, too, are sometimes slipped on, but a shorter dress sleeve or one that can be well rolled up is in many ways preferable, as the white sleeves to the wrist become very soon soiled, and in warm weather are very heating. A strong coarse apron should be donned while doing the rougher work or standing at the sink. A neat and simple cap should also be worn. If the cook has very little cooking to do in the evening, it is usual for her to dress in a dark navy blue or black dress, and to wear a muslin apron like the other house-servants. Tidy and comfortable shoes should be worn at all times.

Duties of the Cook.—It is the duty of the cook to do all the cooking that is required either single-handed or with the help of a kitchen-maid or scullery-maid. Then beyond this her duties will vary according to the number of servants kept and the style of living of the household.

Although it is impossible to draw out a plan which will suit all cases, the following table of duties may serve as a guide where the cook takes a share in the work of the house. In larger establishments where the cook's services are entirely confined to the kitchen it is very easy to delete the other duties, and the order of the remaining work would continue in very much the same way.

Duties of the Cook-General.—Rise at six, strip bed, and leave bedroom airing. Downstairs at 6.30. Open up kitchen premises and air where necessary. Light kitchen fire and clean range. (If the boiler is not a self-filling one, it should be filled the night before.) Fill kettles with water, and if there is anything for breakfast which requires long cooking, such as porridge, put this on to cook before leaving the kitchen and leave other things ready for breakfast as far as possible.

Then go to dining-room, draw up blinds and open windows, clean fire-place and light fire if necessary. Sweep room with carpet-sweeper, dust it carefully and fill coal-box. Sweep and dust hall, clean doorstep and brasses and shake mats.

Then serve kitchen breakfast and prepare what is required for the dining-room. Clean gentlemen's boots and sweep any backstairs or passages.

Clear away dining-room breakfast things, and take up crumbs. Wash all or some of the dishes.

Tidy kitchen and larder, and be ready to receive mistress. In the forenoon prepare and cook early dinner or luncheon and prepare late dinner as far as possible. Dust and tidy cook's bedroom and commence any special work of the day.

Answer the front-door bell until 1 o'clock, while the housemaid is engaged upstairs, and attend to any messages which come to the back-door.

Serve lunch, then kitchen dinner and wash up, leaving kitchen tidy. It is usual for the cook to wash the dinner service used in the dining-room, although glass and silver are done by the housemaid. Finish special work of the day, and dress if there is no late dinner or a very simple one. Kitchen tea.

Prepare and cook late dinner or supper and coffee if ordered. Wash up (this can often be done while the meal is going on, and need not be a troublesome matter). Kitchen supper.

Leave everything tidy for the night and fuel ready for lighting fire in the morning. The back-door should be locked as soon as it is dark and windows the last thing before going to bed. Bed at 10 o'clock.

Special Weekly Duties.—Besides the daily routine some special cleaning should be undertaken each day so as to keep all in order.

This might be arranged in somewhat the following manner :—

Monday—Downstairs windows.
Tuesday—Backstairs and passages.
Wednesday—Clean dining-room and hall alternate weeks.
Thursday—Clean tins, brasses.
Friday—Larder and cupboards.
Saturday—Kitchen (flues before breakfast).

Notes.—The above plan presupposes that the dining-room breakfast is at 8.30; if earlier some of the housework must be left until that meal is over.

It is sometimes customary for the cook-general to help the housemaid with the beds except when there are young ladies in the house, when they generally undertake this piece of work.

The clearing of the breakfast-table and washing of some of the dishes is also frequently done by the ladies of the house, especially if the family is large and only two maids are kept.

The cook-general is often expected to do some washing, such as all the kitchen towels and dusters, her own washing, and sometimes the flannel washing as well. When this is the case, this should be done on Monday or Tuesday and be regarded as the special work of the day. It should be started as early in the forenoon as possible, the cooking being made as simple as possible that day, and a little extra help might be given by members of the household.

The cook-general is also expected to take the housemaid's duties when the latter has her evening out or her free time.

The Nurse.—See under Section " The Child."

The Housemaid.—A housemaid is employed to do work about the house and more especially in the bedrooms and sitting-rooms. This work will vary according to the number of servants kept and the style of living. In larger establishments where there are many bedrooms and a constant coming and going of visitors, there may be several housemaids—an upper housemaid and two or three under-housemaids. In this case the upper housemaid would be responsible for and supervise all the work done in the bedrooms and sitting-rooms, although most of the actual cleaning and all the rough work would be undertaken by the junior maids.

The upper housemaid would do the lighter and more difficult work in the principal rooms, would see that the bedrooms were properly prepared for guests, answer the bedroom bells, and attend to the wants of the ladies of the house. Sometimes she is required to act as lady's-maid to her mistress if there is no special maid for this purpose. She would take charge of the bed-linen, giving out the necessary supplies, and keeping an accurate account of the stock. She would also take charge of all curtains and hangings, cushion-covers and table-covers, see that the suitable articles were in use and all kept in good order. She might also have time for some of the mending.

It would be her duty to take early tea and water into the principal rooms in the morning, and again give the necessary attendance in these rooms throughout the day and in the evening.

Some of the locking up at night might also fall to her share.

The under housemaids would do all the cleaning proper, such as the sweeping, dusting, and scrubbing. The cleaning of the bath-rooms, lavatories, and housemaids' pantry, the cleaning of all grates and the lighting of fires. If there is a school-room or nursery it would be the duty of one of them to do all the cleaning and waiting required in that department. The junior maid would also have charge of the servants' bedrooms and back staircase. The boot cleaning, too, would be shared by the under-housemaid unless there was a boy or man employed for the purpose.

In smaller households where only two or three servants are kept, the housemaid will have to do the work of the bedrooms single-handed, and the sitting-rooms are generally divided between the different maids. She may or may not have some mending to do ; this will depend upon the extent of her other duties.

A single housemaid is also expected to give the parlour-maid some assistance in waiting at table and answering of bells, and to take her duties during off-duty times.

She will also have the cleaning of ladies' and any children's boots.

The House-parlourmaid combines the duties of housemaid and tablemaid, and, in addition to her house duties, she will have charge of the table, *i.e.* the setting and clearing of the table for all meals, all the waiting required, and the washing of the silver, glass, and china. She should answer all front-door bells after one o'clock and might have to undertake a little washing. The cook may or may not give some assistance with the housework.

Qualifications Necessary.—A housemaid must be clean, orderly, and an early riser. Much of the comfort of the household depends upon getting a fair amount of cleaning done before breakfast. She must be quiet and unobtrusive in her work and make as little disturbance as possible with her cleaning. She must be polite and courteous in her manner and always respectful. She must also be methodical, arranging her work so that too much does not fall to one day and not sufficient to others.

Dress and Appearance.—A housemaid should at all times be neat and tidy in appearance, and pay particular attention to her hair and the cleanliness and freshness of her person.

In the morning she should be dressed in a neat print dress with a plain white apron with bib, a linen collar, and a simple cap with cambric frill. A coarser apron may be put on when doing any rough work, and a pair of gloves while cleaning the grates. In the afternoon the cotton dress should be changed for the orthodox dress of some black woollen material, plainly made, but neat fitting with tight sleeves and of a smart walking length. A muslin apron should then be worn with a becoming cap and turn-down collar and cuffs usually fastened with bows of black ribbons. Quiet shoes should be worn at all times,

Duties of the Housemaid.—(Three maids—cook, housemaid, and parlour-maid.) Rise at 6 or 6.30, dress, turn down bed and leave room airing.

Open up drawing-room or any other sitting-room under her care, clean fire-place, sweep and dust room, and light fire if necessary. Sweep and dust stairs. Take hot water to the bedrooms and early cups of tea if required. Prepare baths. Kitchen breakfast. Clean front hall and doorsteps unless done by cook, clean any boots, make her own bed, and tidy bed-room.

While family are at breakfast go into bed-rooms, and see that windows are open and beds left to air. Then empty slops and attend to the wash-stands. Make beds with the parlour-maid's help. Dust bedrooms and put them in order and then do special work of the day. Kitchen dinner. Dress. In the afternoon finish off any lighter pieces of work which are not dirty, and do mending if required.

Kitchen tea. In the evening take hot water to the bedrooms half-an-hour before dinner is served. Draw down blinds, and light up at dark, closing windows if required.

During dinner it is usual for the housemaid to do the carrying of the dishes from the kitchen to the dining-room and *vice versâ*, so that the parlour-maid may never require to leave the room, and also to give what assistance she can with the waiting. When dinner is over, return to the bedrooms, empty slops, and give fresh supply of water, turn down beds and lay out clothes for the night ; remove any dirty boots and see that all is in order.

Kitchen supper. Bed at ten o'clock.

SPECIAL WEEKLY WORK

Monday—Clean drawing-room and spare bedroom alternately.
Collect and count washing.
Tuesday—Clean two bedrooms.
Wednesday—Clean servants' bedrooms and housemaid's pantry.
Thursday—Clean bath-room, lavatory, and staircase.
Friday—Clean library or morning-room and front hall, unless done by the cook.
Saturday—Put away linen from washing and make things generally tidy for Sunday.

Duties of the House-parlourmaid.—(Two maids, cook general, and house-parlourmaid.) Rise at 6 or 6.30, dress, turn down bed and leave room to air.

Sweep and dust drawing-room or library, and light fire if required. (The dining-room is done by the cook.)

Sweep and dust stairs. Take hot water to the bedrooms and call the family.

Kitchen breakfast. Lay sitting-room breakfast and clean boots, serve breakfast. Empty slops and see that beds are left airing. Dust and tidy own bedroom. Clear breakfast-table and wash up, unless this is done by the cook. Make beds with the assistance of the cook or some member of the family.

Dust and tidy bedrooms and proceed to special work of the day. Dress by one o'clock. Set the table and serve lunch or early dinner.

Kitchen dinner. Clear the dining-room table, take up crumbs and leave room tidy. Wash up silver and glass and finish any light work. Answer front-door bell in the afternoon and evening and indoor bells all day.

Prepare and take in afternoon tea. Kitchen tea. Wash up afternoon tea things.

Draw down blinds, close windows (if required), and light up at dusk.

Lay dinner-table and serve dinner. Wait at table, clear and wash up. Serve coffee if required.

Attend to bedrooms, emptying slops, laying down beds, and removing any dirty boots.

Kitchen supper. Bed at ten o'clock.

SPECIAL WEEKLY DUTIES

Monday—Clean drawing-room or spare bedroom alternately.
Collect and count washing.
Tuesday—Clean one or two bedrooms.
Wednesday—Clean bath-room, lavatory, and staircase.
Thursday—Clean servants' bedroom and pantries
Friday—Clean silver and brasses.
Saturday—Put away washing and tidy up generally.

The Parlour-maid.—A parlour-maid or table-maid's chief duty is to look after the table and see to the serving of all meals. It is a very important position, and one which would be filled by a butler in houses where men-servants were employed.

The parlour-maid takes the sole charge of the silver, glass, china, and other valuables in daily use, and is mistress of the pantry. She also has charge of the sideboard, the wine, cake, fruit, &c., and sees that fresh supplies are ordered as required.

The care of the table-linen will be another of her duties. She must see that the table is sufficiently supplied, and that an accurate account is kept of the stock. The mending, too, might be done by her if time permitted.

A parlour-maid usually undertakes the cleaning of one or two sitting-rooms, usually the drawing-room and one other smaller room as well. She attends to the sitting-room fires, and lamps and candles if used.

She answers the front-door bell throughout the day, unless relieved for part of the time by the housemaid, and announces all visitors.

She may also be responsible for the floral decorations of the table and for the arrangement of flowers and plants throughout the house, unless the mistress herself undertakes this piece of work.

If there is no man-servant the parlour-maid valets her master, attending to the brushing of his clothes and the cleaning of his boots. If there is no lady's-maid she may be called upon to wash up and do lace and other fine articles belonging to her mistress and also any fancy articles, such as d'oyleys and tray-cloths for table use.

She might also be called upon to assist the housemaid with bed-making, and would do housemaid's duties in the latter's off-duty times. She is usually responsible for the shutting of the sitting-room windows at night and the front door, unless done by some member of the family.

Personal Appearance and Requirements.—A parlour-maid should be tall and elegant in appearance and rather slight, so that she can move about easily and be graceful in her movements. The dress, which is similar to that worn by the housemaid, must be neatly made and fit well, and the apron, collar, cuffs, and cap must always be spotlessly clean, and especially so when the maid is waiting at table.

A parlour-maid should pay particular attention to her hands, in order to have them nice for giving attendance to the members of the family, and her hair should be neatly done without being too elaborate or fussy in style. She must be orderly and punctual in all her doings, and have a thorough knowledge of waiting at table and other table requirements.

As a parlour-maid comes into such close contact with the family, the post can only be filled by a woman who is capable and conscientious, and who has the interests of her master and mistress at heart. Her manner must be pleasant and respectful at all times, she must know how to receive and address people of refinement, and be able to give in an intelligent way any information that may be required.

Daily Duties of Parlour-maid.—Rise at 6 or 6.30, according to time of breakfast. Dress, turn down bed and leave room to air.

Open up sitting-rooms under her charge, light fires if necessary, and do the sweeping and dusting. Give any attendance required by the master of the house and clean his boots.

Kitchen breakfast. Then set sitting-room breakfast-table and make toast, tea and coffee unless done by the cook. Serve breakfast and wait if required. Finish any work in the sitting-rooms. Clear breakfast-table, take up crumbs, and leave room in order. Help housemaid with beds. (This might be done before the clearing of the table if breakfast is a very prolonged meal, but at the same time the beds should be left sufficient time to air.)

Dust and put in order her own bedroom, unless done by the housemaid. Wash up dishes, including silver. See that all cruets are filled ready for the next meal, also jam and sugar dishes attended to, and butter rolled or made into pats. Attend to the sideboard and see that the necessary wine is decanted, and that fruit and cake dishes are clean and tidy. Make a note of any stores required. Attend to any floral decorations and water-plants. Attend to lamps and candles if used in the sitting-rooms.

Dress by one o'clock, in time to lay luncheon table. Make up sitting-room fire, and put room in order before setting the table. Serve luncheon and wait as required.

Kitchen dinner. After dinner clear luncheon from sitting-room table, leave room in order, and wash up. If time permits, do mending in the afternoon or a little ironing. Take in afternoon tea and attend to all visitors. Light up sitting-rooms at dusk and draw down blinds.

Kitchen tea. Prepare for dinner, lay table, and at the appointed time announce the meal in the drawing-room or sound a bell or gong. Wait at table either alone or assisted by the housemaid. Carve if required. Then clear and wash up. Serve coffee or any other refreshment that may be required.

Kitchen supper. Bed at ten P.M.

SPECIAL WEEKLY DUTIES

Monday—Collect and count table linen, wash out towels, dusters, wash-leathers, &c., and give special attention to plants.

Tuesday—Clean drawing-room or other sitting-room.

Wednesday—Clean second sitting-room (morning-room or library) or assist housemaid with special cleaning.

Thursday—Clean silver.

Friday—Clean pantry and her own bedroom, or any brasses and other ornaments.

Saturday—Count and put away washing, general tidying up and preparations for Sunday.

The General Servant.—The general servant is employed to do the entire work of the house, except that which is undertaken by the mistress herself or some other member of the family.

If the household consist of more than two or three persons it will be necessary for the mistress to give a considerable amount of help, if the work is to be done properly. She may either do the cooking or the lighter parts of the housework, such as dusting, laying the table, washing of silver and glass, &c.; this depends entirely upon her own tastes and inclinations.

Although a general servant cannot be expected to be an expert in all branches of household work, she ought to have a good all-round knowledge and be able to cook simple dishes in a wholesome and appetising manner.

Her work need not necessarily be harder than that of another servant who only performs special duties, but it must be systematically arranged, and she must be quick and active if the day's proceedings are to be carried through in a satisfactory manner. A general servant is not infrequently looked down upon as holding an inferior position, a sort of "jack of all trades and master of none"; but this entirely depends upon the maid herself and upon the house in which she serves. If she does her work well, she is a most valuable person, and her position, if conscientiously filled, may become one of trust. If she has the good fortune to be employed by a kind and considerate mistress, her life should be a very happy one. She will enter into much closer relationship with the family than it is possible to do where there are several servants, and she will get full credit for all her work. A good general is always particular about her personal appearance; the fact of being busy should never be an excuse for having a dirty and dishevelled appearance; in fact, this state only denotes a slovenly worker. It ought also to be a source of pleasure to be dressed in good time in the afternoon. The dress should be that worn by any other house servant, *i.e.* a nice print dress in the morning, with a white linen apron, linen collar, and cap, and a black or dark blue dress in the afternoon with a muslin apron and more dressy cap. A coarse apron or overall should always be kept at hand to slip on when doing any dirty work.

Daily Duties.—Rise at 6 or 6.30, dress, turn down bed and leave room to air. Unbolt door, draw up blinds and open kitchen and sitting-room windows. Light kitchen fire and sitting grate. Fill kettle and put on porridge if required. Clean boots, sweep and dust sitting-room, lighting fire if necessary. Sweep and dust hall and clean doorstep and brasses. (If breakfast is at an early hour this may be left until later.) Prepare sitting-room breakfast and have kitchen breakfast.

Empty slops and air bedrooms. Tidy and dust her own bedroom. Clear breakfast-table, wash up and tidy kitchen. Take orders for the day.

Make beds with assistance, dust and tidy bedrooms, and sweep and dust stairs. Prepare early dinner or lunch and do special work for the day. (If late dinner is the rule, the mid-day meal should be as simple as possible, and most of the cooking should be prepared in the morning.)

Serve lunch and have early dinner. Clear and wash up. When kitchen has been tidied, change dress, attend to any light duties in the afternoon, and serve tea. Attend to all bells promptly. Serve supper or dinner at the hour appointed, and do what waiting is required. Clear and wash up and have kitchen supper. Light up at dusk, draw down blinds, and close windows as required. After dinner turn down beds and attend to the bedrooms. Collect sticks and coals for the morning. Bed at ten P.M.

SPECIAL WEEKLY DUTIES

Monday—Wash towels and dusters, &c. (Heavy washing can scarcely be undertaken unless the maid is relieved of most of her other work for the forenoon.)

Tuesday—Clean drawing-room and dining-room alternate weeks.

Wednesday—Clean bath-room, staircase, and hall.

Thursday—Clean bedrooms.

Friday—Clean pantry, larder, and any back premises, also silver and tins alternate weeks.

Saturday—Clean kitchen.

The Housekeeper.—The housekeeper is the representative of her mistress, and in large households she fulfils the duties which naturally fall to the mistress herself in a smaller ménage. This leaves the lady of the house free to attend to social and other claims.

The housekeeper is second in command, and answerable only to the head of the house. She engages and dismisses servants and pays their wages—with the exception of the nurse and lady's-maid—arranges their work, and is responsible in every way for their appearance and behaviour and the fulfilment of their duties.

The housekeeper is responsible for the proper keeping of the house in every part, and she sees to the needs and comfort of the whole family and domestic staff.

She orders and gives out all stores, keeps accounts, and pays the bills. If there is a butler he relieves her of some of those duties, and he is always responsible for the men-servants.

The housekeeper should see her employer at stated times in order to give in a report of the various departments, and also to receive her instructions and learn her wishes.

The housekeeper has always her own sitting-room in which her meals are served by one of the under-maids, except dinner, which she usually takes with the other servants.

Her sitting-room may be shared by some of the upper servants, such as the lady's-maid, the butler, and the valet.

The Butler.—The position of butler is usually one of great trust. He is head of the men-servants, is responsible for the work of those under him, arranges their off-duty time, and often engages them as well.

He has sole charge of the wine cellar, and gives out the wine required, keeping a note of the stock, and frequently seeing to the buying in of supplies.

To his care is confided the silver and other articles of value in daily use.

He is responsible for the arrangement of all meals and the table appointments. He announces when meals are ready, puts the dishes on the table or does the carving, pours out the wine, and waits assisted by a footman or parlour-maid.

He is responsible for the care of the billiard-room and smoking-room or library, and the fires and lighting arrangements of the other rooms.

If single-handed, his duties would be very much the same as those already detailed for the house-parlourmaid. If there is no valet he waits upon his master. He also looks after any carriage or motor rugs and lamps, and in the country would be responsible for shooting and picnic lunches.

When there is no housekeeper the butler frequently pays the bills and does the marketing. He usually goes out every day.

The butler is also responsible for the shutting up of the house.

In the early part of the day his dress should be dark trousers and waistcoat and black tail coat, with a white front and collar and black tie —in the evening the regulation dress suit with a white tie.

The Footman.—The footman is generally an all-round useful man and his duties may be very varied. If there is a butler, he would work under him, but in houses where he is the only man-servant his duties might be somewhat after the following :—

He would clean boots and shoes, knives and windows, fetch coal and see to the filling of coal-scuttles and the keeping up of fires.

He would lay the table and wait, assisted by a parlour-maid or housemaid, and wash up the silver, glass, and china after each meal.

He would valet his master and go out with the carriage if required, attending to any rugs.

The charge of lamps and window-plants would also fall to his share. He would answer bells, announce visitors, and take in afternoon tea.

He would also be responsible for the locking up of the house at night.

A footman may or may not wear livery. If this is not supplied it is usual to give two suits in the year, either new or from his master's wardrobe.

The Lady's-maid.—The lady's-maid devotes herself to the personal requirements of her mistress and looks after her needs in every way.

She undertakes the charge of her wardrobe and sees that all her belongings are kept in good order and proper repair.

She assists her mistress with her toilet, helps her to dress and undress, brushes and dresses her hair, selects and lays out the clothes she is going to wear.

She does any packing and unpacking and travels with her mistress when required.

She requires a bedroom for herself, which is sometimes fitted as a bed-sitting-room, where she can do her sewing and other work.

She will keep her own and her mistress's room in order, do the dusting, and make the beds with some assistance ; but she will not be expected to clean grates nor do any hard cleaning, and she will take no part in general housework.

If well filled the post of lady's-maid is no sinecure, as a varied knowledge is necessary to do all that is required. A woman who undertakes this work must be able to sew well in order that she may both make and mend neatly. She must also have some knowledge of dressmaking and millinery so as to be able to alter and renovate, to change the style of an evening dress, to make a tasteful bow, retrim a hat or bonnet, or give the necessary finishing touches to a lady's toilet. She must be a woman of taste, and be able to give advice as to the choice of dresses, &c.

She ought to know enough laundry work to enable her to wash and do up laces and silks and muslin, wash shawls and feather boas, and other fancy articles.

She must be a good hair-dresser, and if a fashionable coiffure is required, it is a good plan to take a lesson occasionally from a first-class hairdresser in order to learn the newest modes.

If she travels with her mistress a knowledge of languages, especially French, is invaluable, and she should know how to make travelling arrangements, see to tickets and luggage, and be responsible for the exchange of money.

A lady's-maid wears no uniform, but ought to be quietly and neatly dressed when in attendance on her mistress.

Her manner must be pleasant and respectful, and she must know how to exercise self-control. As she comes into such close contact with the private life of her mistress, it is her duty to give her faithful and loyal service as long as she remains in her employment.

The Valet.—The valet attends to the personal wants of his master just as the lady's-maid waits upon her mistress. He helps him with his dressing, and takes full charge of his wardrobe, brushes his clothes, cleans his boots, and attends to any repairs.

He sees that his master's wash-stand and toilet-table are supplied with the necessary requisites, and is responsible for all his belongings being kept in order and in the proper place.

He must know how to pack and unpack, and if he travels with his master he must know how to make all arrangements, take tickets, and see to luggage, &c.

The valet is sometimes expected to give assistance in waiting at table.

The Laundry-maid.—The laundry-maid is responsible for the washing and dressing of the household linen.

She will have full charge of the laundry, seeing that it is kept clean and in perfect order. She will also be responsible for all the linen confided to her care.

If the family is not large, she may be expected to take part in some of the housework as well.

(For fuller details of her duties see Guide to Laundry Work, p. 271.)

The Scullery-maid.—The scullery-maid ranks lowest amongst the kitchen servants, and if there is a kitchen-maid she works under her.

A scullery-maid is employed primarily for cleaning all the dishes and utensils used in the kitchen; she washes the kitchen floors and does the scrubbing. She will assist with the preparation of vegetables and be responsible for the keeping up of the kitchen fire.

If there is no kitchen-maid, the scullery-maid will assist the cook and work under her direction.

Although the work may be somewhat laborious, it is a good beginning for a young girl who aspires to be cook, and if she is quick and willing she may learn a great deal, and gradually rise to a better position.

The Kitchen-maid.—A kitchen-maid is employed to work under a cook, to be her apprentice as it were. She is responsible for many of the plainer dishes, thus leaving the cook free for more important duties. She prepares and serves the kitchen meals, and also cooks for the nursery and school-room if required.

If there is no scullery-maid, the kitchen-maid will also undertake the cleaning of the kitchen utensils, the kitchen stove, and some of the kitchen premises.

Provided a kitchen-maid serves under a good cook, this is the best way for her to learn the art of cooking.

The Tweeny.—This is a title given to a young girl who divides her time between the house and the kitchen. In the forenoon she may work under the housemaid or the nurse and do the housework, and from lunch time onwards assist the cook. She does all the odd jobs and must be ready to make herself generally useful.

The Hall Boy.—The hall boy or boy in buttons is sometimes kept in place of a single manservant, and if clever and willing he may be an extremely useful member of the household.

He will be found of special value in the house of a professional man, such as a doctor or dentist, where there is much answering of bells required, and perhaps running of messages as well.

A capable boy will soon learn to clean knives, boots, and windows, to fill coal-scuttles and look after fires. He will also be able to set the table, do some waiting and most of the washing up.

The boy in buttons must be provided with clothes; a livery suit of some dark cloth, navy serge, dark green, or dark crimson with the coat buttoning to the neck, and for doing cleaning or rough work he should have a cotton jacket of dark blue or striped drill or strong holland and some good stout aprons.

HOUSEKEEPING WITHOUT A SERVANT

In these days of flat life, when accommodation for housing a servant is very limited, it is often found more convenient to do without one altogether, or to manage with either daily help or the services of a thoroughly competent worker once or twice a week.

It ought to be quite possible for a newly married lady to undertake the work of a small flat with perhaps the occasional help of a char-woman, and to have time for other interests as well. Or if, as is often the case, two sisters or two friends live together, the work should be all the more easy to manage, as each can take her share of the household duties.

Some knowledge of housekeeping is, however, necessary for the successful management of a " no servant " ménage, and if one is entirely ignorant of the ways of doing things, it should scarcely be attempted unless absolutely necessary, as the results are not likely to be satisfactory.

Good health is also a *sine qua non*, although no great physical strength is required ; so much is done nowadays to make the work of a house simple, and especially the work in a flat. There are no stairs nor front door-step to keep in order, the cooking and water heating can be done by gas, and all provisions, &c., can be brought to the very door without the trouble of going up and down stairs. Yet with all the conveniences possible, success in the undertaking will depend to a large extent upon the order and method displayed in its organisation. The work must be planned carefully, or one will either be in a constant muddle, or be continually at it, and have time for nothing beyond the daily round of house duties.

To begin with, the woman who does her own work must dress suitably when performing her household duties—a short skirt, a cotton or other washing blouse, and a big apron or overall is the most suitable attire ; or a complete wash-ing dress might be worn if the weather is warm. A large overall to slip on over a good afternoon dress will also be found useful.

It will be well also to secure as many labour-saving apparatus as possible, such as gas-cooker, carpet-sweeper, knife-cleaner, mop for washing dishes, &c.

Care, too, must be taken of the hands. Because a woman is her own maid-of-all-work this is no excuse for her being careless in this respect. Gloves should be worn as much as possible, and after doing washing up the hands should be well dried and a few drops of glycerine and rose-water should be rubbed into the skin.

Do not commence by doing too much before breakfast. Unless one has been accustomed to early rising it is apt to knock one up for the rest of the day without any reason. Do not attempt to light fires and clean out a sitting-room before a meal has been taken. Sometimes it may be possible to prepare a certain amount the night before, and in any case there should be a small gas or even an oil-stove upon which the morning meal can be prepared. If the sitting-room has not a stove which can be lit without much trouble, there is no reason why the kitchen should not be pretty enough and tidy enough for the first meal to be taken there.

On rising in the morning put on a large kettle of water. If there is porridge for breakfast this should have been soaked over-night in a double cooker. Put a light under this also. Then dress, and when ready let breakfast have the first attention, taking time to have this meal leisurely and in comfort. Next collect the dishes and clear the table, and either put the dishes to one side while the bedrooms and sitting-room are being done, or wash them up straight away.

The sitting-room should be done next, as it will be as well to let the bedrooms air as long as possible. If a fire has to be laid, do this with order and method. Go over the floor with a carpet-sweeper, then dust every part and leave the window open. Next turn your attention to the bedrooms, put these in order, and then sweep and dust the passage. Now return to the kitchen, wash up all the dishes, and sweep and dust. If breakfast has not been very late, all the cleaning should be finished by eleven o'clock, unless some special work has to be done, such as the thorough cleaning of a room, silver, brasses, &c., but if any help is given with the work this could also be fitted in.

The cooking for the day should now be thought of, and although it is always possible to have meals at a restaurant, or to order various dishes from a caterer's, it must be remembered that this is an expensive way of living, and with the necessary knowledge of cookery it should be quite possible to have dainty little meals at home, and so feed well with very little trouble. The woman who does her own work will not require to spend much time considering what is in her larder ; she will no doubt have arranged in her own mind what the different meals have to be whilst doing her other work. All the cookery required should either be done in the morning or at least prepared as far as possible, so that what must be left for the evening will take very little time to get ready when required. Light utensils should be used, such as aluminium, enamelled tin, or earthenware saucepans, as they are easier to handle and keep in order. One or two steamers would also be invaluable, as so much cooking can be done in these without trouble and attention.

After the mid-day meal it is a good plan to rest, even if, only for half-an-hour, and then, after dressing, one ought to feel quite fresh to go out and turn one's thoughts in a different channel. The afternoon should be free from household cares.

If the evening meal has been prepared in the morning it will not take long to get it ready, and half-an-hour as an ordinary rule should be sufficient. Then if washing up in the evening is found awkward, there is no occasion to do more than the silver, which it is never wise to leave, and the other dishes, if they are not required in the morning, could be packed up and washed with the breakfast dishes.

Marketing.—The time for doing this will depend upon circumstances, and need not be rigidly fixed. If it is inconvenient to go out in the morning in the midst of the other work it may be possible to order in the afternoon for the following day, or another way is to arrange for the tradesmen to call, and for everything to be brought to the door at a certain time.

Outside Help.—This may be obtained either daily or once or twice a week, according to circumstances and individual needs. If a young girl is engaged to come in for an hour or two every morning, she might do the washing up, prepare the vegetables, and attend to the other kitchen work, also clean the boots and stoves and assist with the rooms as well. Many prefer, however, to have more competent help even if it is not so often. A good worker for half a day could do all the hard cleaning, including the stoves, scrubbing of the kitchen, and thoroughly clean one or two rooms each visit. If the rooms can be prepared for her, and any ornaments and other trifles dusted and afterwards arranged, it will be a great saving of time, and in this way half the rooms could be cleaned one week, and the other half the next.

Advantages.—Besides the actual saving of board and wages of an indoor servant there will be a feeling of independence. It will be possible to leave home for a day or a week without any need for worrying about the house. There will also be freedom from that feeling of close proximity to a servant which is impossible to avoid in a flat, and which destroys the sense of liberty which is essential to the happiness of both parties.

Warning.—It must be remembered that housework must not crowd out everything else; one must have time to read a little, rest a little, and keep in touch with the outside world as well. The economy that saves money at the expense of health and the capability of enjoyment is in reality one of the worst extravagances.

Another point is that the housekeeper must remember to feed herself. If the mid-day meal is taken alone, she is only too apt to make it as meagre as possible to save trouble, and also to take it too quickly, whereas time would be well spent in eating something really nutritious, and if the quantity is small the quality should be all the more carefully considered.

One must also learn to do without many things, and not expect to live in the same style as those who have plenty of servants at their command, but this can quite well be done without falling into a slovenly way of living and losing any of the refinement of life.

WAGES TABLE

Giving the rates per Month, Week, and Day of Yearly Incomes from £10 to £50

Year.			Month.			Week.			Day.			Year.			Month.			Week.			Day.		
£	s.	d.	£	s.	d.	£	s.	d.	£	s.	d.	£	s.	d.	£	s.	d.	£	s.	d.	£	s.	d.
10	0	0	0	16	8	0	3	10¼	0	0	6½	17	0	0	1	8	4	0	6	6½	0	0	11¼
10	10	0	0	17	6	0	4	0½	0	0	7	17	10	0	1	9	2	0	6	8¾	0	0	11½
11	0	0	0	18	4	0	4	2¾	0	0	7¼	17	17	0	1	9	9	0	6	10½	0	0	11¾
11	10	0	0	19	2	0	4	5	0	0	7½	18	0	0	1	10	0	0	6	11	0	0	11¾
11	11	0	0	19	3	0	4	5¼	0	0	7½	18	10	0	1	10	10	0	7	1½	0	1	0¼
12	0	0	1	0	0	0	4	7½	0	0	8	18	18	0	1	11	6	0	7	3¼	0	1	0½
12	10	0	1	0	10	0	4	9¾	0	0	8¼	19	0	0	1	11	8	0	7	3¾	0	1	0½
12	12	0	1	1	0	0	4	10¼	0	0	8½	19	10	0	1	12	6	0	7	6	0	1	0¾
13	0	0	1	1	8	0	5	0	0	0	8½	19	19	0	1	13	3	0	7	8	0	1	1
13	10	0	1	2	6	0	5	2¼	0	0	9	20	0	0	1	13	4	0	7	8¼	0	1	1¼
13	13	0	1	2	9	0	5	3	0	0	9	21	0	0	1	15	0	0	8	1	0	1	1¾
14	0	0	1	3	4	0	5	4½	0	0	9¼	22	0	0	1	16	8	0	8	5½	0	1	2½
14	10	0	1	4	2	0	5	7	0	0	9½	23	0	0	1	18	4	0	8	10¼	0	1	3
14	14	0	1	4	6	0	5	7¾	0	0	9¾	24	0	0	2	0	0	0	9	2¾	0	1	3¾
15	0	0	1	5	0	0	5	9¼	0	0	9¾	25	0	0	2	1	8	0	9	7½	0	1	4½
15	10	0	1	5	10	0	5	11¼	0	0	10¼	30	0	0	2	10	0	0	11	6½	0	1	7¾
15	15	0	1	6	3	0	6	0¾	0	0	10¼	35	0	0	2	18	4	0	13	5½	0	1	11
16	0	0	1	6	8	0	6	1¾	0	0	10½	40	0	0	3	6	8	0	15	4½	0	2	2¼
16	10	0	1	7	6	0	6	4¼	0	0	10¾	45	0	0	3	15	0	0	17	3¾	0	2	5½
16	16	0	1	8	0	0	6	5½	0	0	11	50	0	0	4	3	4	0	19	2¾	0	2	9

GUIDE TO HOUSEHOLD WORK

THE object of the following pages is to furnish the housewife with directions for the performance of such details of household work as are not dealt with under special headings.

The directions are the result of many years practical experience of everything pertaining to household management.

The various details of household work are dealt with separately under their own headings, and the many useful hints with regard to cleaning, &c., are the result of actual test.

It is hoped that the information given will afford valuable help to the harassed housewife in the little difficulties which are continually cropping up in the course of daily duties. If it does this the mission of this section of the book will be abundantly fulfilled.

THE CLEANING OF ROOMS

Before beginning to clean a room of any kind it is very important that everything required for the work should be collected together, so that there need be no unnecessary running about to seek for this or that duster or brush. So first consider what has to be cleaned, and then take with you the necessary implements, seeing that everything is in order for the work to be carried out satisfactorily and systematically, with the least possible waste of time.

TO CLEAN AND TIDY A BEDROOM

Daily Work.—First draw up the blinds as far as they will go, being careful to keep them straight, and open the windows top and bottom. Then turn down the bed and spread out any night garments on a chair. Allow the room to air for an hour at least before the bed is made. During this time the slops may be emptied, towels hung up evenly, and any clothing or other articles left lying about the room put away in their places. It is always better if two people can make the bed. When this is neatly finished, fold up the night-dress or sleeping-suit, put it in a neat case, and lay it on the bed just beneath the pillow.

If there has been a fire in the room attend to the grate next, being careful to make as little dust as possible.

It will not be necessary to sweep the room every day, but the floor must be gone over with a short brush and shovel or with a carpet-sweeper, so as to take up any pieces or surface dust. Be careful too that all fluff is removed from underneath the bed. Some people prefer to have the carpet wiped over with a slightly damp cloth or leather.

Then dust the room. Commence at one corner and go steadily round, dusting each article until every part has been done. Pay particular attention to the toilet table. Lift each article and dust underneath it, arranging everything with order and taste.

If the edges of the floor are polished or covered with linoleum, rub them round with a slightly damp duster, or, better still, with the flannel or cloth which has been used to rub up a polished floor. The latter will have the remains of a little wax upon it, and will keep the floor in good condition.

If a candlestick has been used, see that this is in order, putting in a fresh candle if required, and removing any old matches.

Finally fill up the ewer and water-jug with fresh cold water, and lower the blinds and windows a little if desired. Look round the room to see that everything is in order and that no duster or brush is being left behind, and close the door quietly on leaving.

Weekly or Thorough Cleaning.—Once a week, or at least once a fortnight, a bedroom will require a more thorough cleaning if it is in constant use.

After the slops have been emptied, the bed-room ware and any gas globes should be carried away to a bathroom or housemaid's pantry, where they can be washed. If this is not convenient, they must be covered over and washed afterwards in the room.

Before making the bed, brush the mattress on both sides and well round the edges, as this is one of the best means of keeping away moths. Dust also the bedstead under the mattress and then make the bed, but do not put on the top cover; this is better kept off until the cleaning is finished. Tuck up the valance all round, if there is one, and brush and pin back any curtains out of the way.

Next lay some sheets of clean paper or a large towel on the top of the bed. Dust all ornaments (keeping aside any that may require washing) and other small articles, and lay them on the top of the bed over the paper, or towel. Shake and fold up the toilet cover, and all table-cloths and towels; shake and remove any short window-blinds, and lay these also on the bed. Cover all with a large dust-sheet, which will hang well over the sides.

Dust and remove from the room as many as possible of the small articles of furniture, and cover over what is left with dust-sheets or old newspapers. If any of the chairs are upholstered, these should be brushed with a furniture brush before being covered. All clothing must be taken down from the back of doors and kept out of the room or under cover.

Roll up all rugs or mats, and take them outside to be beaten later on. If this cannot be done they must be brushed with a short brush in the room and then removed.

If there has been a fire in the room, remove all the cinders and dust, but do not polish the grate until the room has been swept. Next close all windows and doors, and see that drawers too are shut.

Sprinkle the carpet with tea-leaves or bran, and sweep it thoroughly. When the dust has all been collected in a shovel, the window should be thrown open and the room left for a little while to allow the dust to settle.

Meanwhile the dust in the dust-pan should be taken away and burnt at once. If left lying about it is very apt to be knocked over and the contents perhaps scattered around. The articles that have been outside can also have attention. The rugs should be brushed or beaten outside and carried back in readiness to be laid down, the ware in the bathroom washed, and the small furniture rubbed up.

Then return to the room and finish off the fireplace, using a hearth-cloth.

Roll up the dust-sheets, which should afterwards be shaken in the open air. One word about dust-sheets—too often these are used until they reach such a dirty state as to be rendered almost useless. They should be washed whenever necessary.

The dusting may now be commenced. First mount a pair of steps, dusting all out-of-reach places, such as blinds, curtain poles, inside of windows, pictures, top of wardrobe and door, &c. Then dust and polish, if necessary, the furniture that remains in the room; also dust round the skirting board, panels of doors and floor where it is uncarpeted.

When the dust has as far as possible been removed from the room, it is time to do any necessary washing. Wash the top of the washstand if it is marble, the tiles round the fireplace, the window ledges if they require it, and any finger-marks off doors. The windows and mirrors too if they require special cleaning should now have attention. Also finish off the edges of the floor in a suitable manner, according to whether they are linoleum, varnish, or matting.

Now put back in their places the articles which were laid on the bed, let down the bed valance, and put the bed in order.

Then bring back the things from outside and arrange everything in order. Supply the wash-stand with fresh water and new soap if required.

Spare Bedrooms.—These will not require to be cleaned so often as the rooms that are in constant use. If they are aired and dusted regularly they ought to keep in good order without being turned out more than perhaps once a month. Of course, this depends a good deal upon the locality in which a house is situated. A room in a smoky city will require much more cleaning than one in a fresh country district.

Note.—For details of the various operations, see under special headings.

TO CLEAN A SITTING-ROOM

The order and method for this is very much the same as for a bedroom, except of course there is not the bed and wash-stand to attend to.

Daily Work.—Draw up the blinds and open the window. Remove any table-covers, shake them and fold them up, and roll up the rugs (sometimes this is done over-night).

If there has been a fire in the room, attend to that first. Lay down the hearth-cloth before commencing, and finish off the grate completely.

Then with a dust-pan and short brush—or, better still, with a carpet-sweeper—go over the floor, taking up any crumbs and pieces and all surface dust. Be careful to make as little dust as possible. Lay down the rugs and brush them over also.

Then take away the dust and burn it at once, also the contents of the waste-paper basket.

Next dust the room carefully, commencing at one corner and going steadily round.

If there is a polished or linoleum surround to the carpet, wipe this round with a *slightly* damp duster and then with a dry one. Dust at the same time the skirting-boards. Replace the table-covers, and see that cushions, books, &c., are all in order.

To "Thorough-Clean" a Sitting-room.—A room that is in constant use will require to be cleaned more thoroughly once a week. A drawing-room or room that is only used occasionally will not require it so often. The mistress of the house must decide for herself how often it is necessary to turn it out.

To Prepare the Room.—First remove all plants and flowers, and these should be attended to and arranged outside before they are brought back into the room.

Pull up the blinds as far as they will go. Shake or brush the curtains, and pin them high up out of the way. Remove any short window-curtains, shake them and fold them up.

Then dust thoroughly all ornaments, odd books, music, &c., and either remove them from the room or cover them over on a table or side-board inside.

Dust also and remove, if possible, all small articles of furniture.

Roll up all rugs, and have them taken out of doors to be shaken or beaten later on.

Take off all table-cloths and antimacassars, shake them and fold them up. Beat all cushions, but not too roughly, and then cover all these small things with a dust-sheet.

Upholstered furniture and footstools should be brushed, and all furniture which cannot be removed should be covered over with large clean dust-sheets.

To Clean the Room.—Follow the same order for sweeping, dusting, and doing the grate as for a bedroom. (See 59.)

After sweeping, and while the dust is settling, the things outside should be seen to. Rugs should be shaken, dirty ornaments and glass globes washed or cleaned, and any necessary polishing done.

After the inside dusting is done, put back the furniture in its place, and put on table-cloths and antimacassars. Bring back all ornaments, &c., take down the curtains and see that all is in order.

Finally replace any plants and flower decorations.

CLEANING OF HALL AND STAIRCASE

Before commencing to clean these, close all doors leading into them. Take up all mats and have them shaken outside the house. In houses where there is much going up and down stairs the latter will require to be swept down daily, but with a quiet household it may be sufficient to sweep them two or three times a week, and to simply dust them on the other days.

Begin at the top landing and work downwards. If there is a long stretch of landing on any of the floors, this should be swept with a long broom or carpet-sweeper instead of the short brush, as it will save unnecessary kneeling.

To sweep the stairs, take a banister or stair-brush and a dust-pan. A double brush, with bristles on one side and hair on the other, is the most convenient for the purpose. Sweep the top and front of each step, catching the dust in the dust-pan. Use the bristle side of the brush for the carpet and the soft hair side for the paint or varnish.

When the bottom of the stair is reached take the dust away at once and have it burnt; if left lying in the dust-pan it is very liable to be knocked over and spilt. And here a word of warning may be given about the danger of leaving cleaning materials on a stair; most serious accidents have happened owing to carelessness in this respect.

Allow the dust to settle before doing the dusting. Stairs and banisters will require to be dusted thoroughly every day, and each banister rail should be done separately.

The varnished or painted sides of stair and landing should be wiped first with a *slightly* damp rubber, as this will prevent the dust flying about, and then polished with a dry one.

Doors, door-handles, and window ledges must also have attention. Lay down the mats last of all.

Weekly Cleaning.—Once a week the stairs will require a more thorough cleaning.

When sweeping the steps, pull out the ends of the rods and sweep away the dust from underneath. The banisters too, if they are of wood, should be carefully brushed. If made of painted iron, they may be washed after the sweeping is finished with a wash leather wrung out of warm water and a very little soap. Care must be taken to wring the leather rather firmly, so as to prevent drops of water falling on the steps.

After the stairs have been thoroughly swept, and while the dust is settling, the rods may be cleaned. While doing this an old newspaper or large duster should be laid on the steps to protect the carpet, and not more than one or two rods must be taken out at one time.

Then after the steps and banisters have been carefully dusted, polish the hand-rail with a little furniture polish and the sides of the stairs and landing with floor polish, or bees'-wax and turpentine. If of varnished wood, or if of enamelled white paint, wash them carefully with a little plain soap and water, and rub up with a dry cloth.

A stair carpet will require lifting more frequently than other carpets; twice a year at least, and oftener, if there is much going up and down. When the carpet is up, the steps should be well scrubbed with a little carbolic soap before it is relaid.

If there is a linen drugget over the stair carpet, this should be lifted frequently. Roll it up as gently as possible so as not to disturb the dust. Then have it taken out of doors, well brushed and rubbed over with a damp cloth. The carpet underneath should be well brushed before laying it down again. Change the position of the drugget a little each time it is relaid, so as to ensure equal wear.

To Clean the Hall.—The rugs having been removed, sweep the floor carefully, keeping the dust down as much as possible. Take the dust up in a dust-pan and have it burnt. Then allow the dust that has risen to settle, and dust all the furniture, skirting-boards and doors. If the hall is tiled or covered with linoleum, it ought to be washed once or twice a week, or as often as necessary.

The hall mats should be shaken or beaten outside the back-door if possible, and they must not be relaid until the floor is dry. The door-steps must be washed every day (see p. 73), and as early in the morning as possible. If there is not time for much work before breakfast, then the steps can be done first and the hall left until later in the day. Empty the scraper, and black-lead it brightly. Polish all brass door-handles and plates; those inside once a week and those outside every day.

Once a week the furniture in the hall should be well rubbed up, all brass or other ornaments cleaned, gas globes washed, gas bracket dusted, and any windows and mirrors cleaned.

Note.—For details of the various operations, see under special headings.

THE BATHROOM AND LAVATORY

To Clean Baths.—All baths should be thoroughly well rinsed and wiped out after having been used. If the soapy scum which rises on the top of the water is allowed to lie on them, they will be found much more difficult to clean.

Enamelled Baths.—Empty or run out all the soapy water, and then let in some clean warm water. Take a flannel or soft brush and wash the sides and all over with this, using a little soft soap, or Sunlight soap if necessary; but if the bath is in constant use this will not likely be required every day. If the enamel becomes stained or discoloured, dip the flannel in a little dry salt before applying it. Rinse with clean warm water if soap has been used, and then dry with a cloth. This treatment should be sufficient to keep the bath in order, but if the enamel becomes very dirty use a little Sapolio along with the ordinary soap. Care must always be taken not to roughen the surface of the enamel, because if once the polish is spoilt it is much more difficult to keep it in order.

A Porcelain Bath can be treated in the same way as above, but Brooke's soap may be used instead of Sapolio if the ordinary soap and water is not sufficient to make it clean.

A Zinc Bath is a little more difficult to keep in order. It should be washed out as above, and, if much soiled, rubbed with a mixture of soft soap and Brooke's soap. Shred down some Brooke's soap and mix it in a saucer with some soft soap. Apply this to the bath with a flannel, rubbing it well in, rinse and dry thoroughly. Fine bath-brick dust mixed with a little paraffin is also an excellent thing for cleaning zinc, but it requires a lot of rinsing to get rid of the smell.

The Water-closet Pan.—This should be well flushed out with water every day and brushed round with a special brush, which is kept for this purpose only. Then once a week at least a good pailful of hot soda-water should be poured in and the brush used again.

If the pan has become discoloured or a coating of fur collected on the sides, empty out as much of the cold water as possible and scrub it well with sand and soft soap, or use a little coarse salt. If this is not sufficient to bring it into good condition, dissolve a penny-worth of spirits of salt in one quart of boiling water; pour this into the pan and allow it to remain there for a short time. Then brush round vigorously and rinse. Care must be taken that the mixture does not touch the hands, as it is very poisonous and liable to burn.

The lavatory brush should, if possible, be hung on a nail outside the window. Each lavatory should also be provided with a towel hung on to a nail by a loop.

It is very important that no rubbish be put down the lavatory, such as burnt matches, hair combings, faded flowers, pieces of orange peel, &c. It must be remembered that the pipes are usually made with a bend, and

Lavatory Brush.

such articles would be likely to obstruct them. Young servants should always be warned against throwing any scraps they find in the bedrooms into the slop-pail.

The window of the lavatory should always be kept open and the door shut.

The Lavatory Basin.—If this is emptied immediately after use and rinsed with a little cold water, it will be easily kept in order. It is when dirty soapy water is allowed to remain in the basin that it becomes more difficult to clean. When necessary wash with hot water, soap, and a brush, using a little Brooke's soap or Sapolio if required for any stains; rinse with cold water and dry with a cloth. Every day the taps ought to be dried and rubbed with a duster, and twice a week at least they should be polished with a little metal polish to keep them bright and shining.

CARE OF CARPETS AND RUGS

To Sweep a Carpet.—In these days of carpet-sweepers and suction dust-lifters much of the old-fashioned hand-switching has been done away with. A carpet-sweeper is now to be seen in almost every house, and it is certainly an immense saving of labour. The price varies from 10s. 6d. upwards. It is quick and simple, and takes up the dust where it lies instead of raising it to float about the room in an unhygienic way. It must be rolled across the carpet with even strokes, and there is no occasion to press too heavily. Care must be taken not to use it near heavy furniture, so as to avoid knocking it, and a brush will always be required as well to brush all corners and places where

Carpet-Sweeper.

the sweeper cannot reach. The sweeper must be emptied each day after use, and any fluff, hairs, or thread ends removed from the brushes. If attention is not paid to this the sweeper will very soon become clogged and out of order.

When cleaning a carpet which has a thick pile, such as an Axminster, it is better to use a brush in preference to a sweeper, as the rollers on the latter are liable to leave marks on the soft surface.

Patent suction dust-lifters or vacuum cleaners are also coming into use, but the really practical ones are still much too expensive for the ordinary private house.

When none of these patent cleaners are available, then a carpet must be swept. It will not be necessary to sweep it with a hard broom every day; it will be sufficient just to go over it with a short-handled brush and dust-pan, taking up any pieces or surface dust. Then once a week, or once a fortnight, according to how much the room is used, the carpet must be brushed more thoroughly.

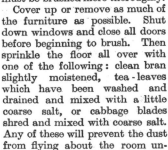

Cover up or remove as much of the furniture as possible. Shut down windows and close all doors before beginning to brush. Then sprinkle the floor all over with one of the following: clean bran slightly moistened, tea-leaves which have been washed and drained and mixed with a little coarse salt, or cabbage blades shred and mixed with coarse salt.

Short-handled Brush.

Any of these will prevent the dust from flying about the room unnecessarily and also help to freshen the carpet.

Then take a carpet broom or switch and brush all over the floor with short sharp strokes. Commence at one of the corners and work methodically, sweeping all the dust towards the fireplace or door. Sweep in such a direction as to flatten the pile, or the carpet will have a rough appearance and be apt to collect dust. The brush ought to be turned occasionally so as to wear it equally. The dust must be kept together as much as possible and not sent flying over the room. When brushing a thick pile carpet, such as an Axminster or Turkey, be particular to brush the way of the pile, or the dust will only be swept into it. Collect all the dust together in a heap, brush into a shovel and take it away to be burnt. Then open the window, and leave the room for a short time before doing any dusting.

To Revive the Colour.—If the carpet is old and somewhat faded, the colour may be somewhat revived by washing it over with a flannel wrung out of ammonia and water; or if the carpet is soiled as well, wash over first with carbolic or Sunlight soap and water, and rinse with ammonia and water.

To Remove Stains.—*Ink.*—As much as possible should at once be absorbed with a piece of blotting-paper. Then pour on some fresh milk, rub it in, and off, then take some more milk and repeat the process, finally washing with a little clean warm water. If this fails, which may be the case if the ink has been on the carpet for some time, try Sanitas, or a tea-spoonful of oxalic acid mixed in half a teacupful of water.

Grease.—If it is candle grease, remove as much as possible with a spoon or bone paper-knife; then place a piece of thick brown or blotting-paper over the stain and apply the point of a hot iron, allowing the grease to sink into the paper. Move the paper and repeat the process. Other grease stains may be removed by covering them with a paste made of Fuller's earth and water. Allow this to remain for twenty-four hours and then brush off. *Black-lead* stains can also be removed with Fuller's earth.

Chiver's carpet soap is also very good for removing stains.

To Beat Carpets.—If a carpet has to be beaten at home it should be taken into the garden and carried as far from the house as possible. If the distance cannot be very great, all windows and outside doors should be closed while the beating is going on to prevent the dust entering the house. Hang the carpet over a clothes-line with the wrong side out, and beat it well with strong canes or carpet-beaters. Care must be taken that there are no sharp points in the sticks which would be likely to injure the carpet. When the wrong side seems clean and no more dust rises, turn the carpet and repeat the same process on the right side. Then if there is some nice clean grass, spread the carpet over it and sweep off the surface-dust with a strong broom. The carpet may even be drawn over the grass to freshen it.

Rugs should if possible be taken out of doors to be beaten or brushed. If they are too heavy to be shaken by hand, they should be hung over a rope and beaten with a stick, or laid on the grass and brushed thoroughly. When there is no garden or yard they must be swept in the room to which they belong. If much soiled, wash them over in the same way as carpets.

White Skin Rugs.—If these are large it is wise to send them to a professional cleaner to be cleaned, as it is too much of an undertaking to attempt them at home, and the result is not likely to be satisfactory. A small skin rug can, however, be washed without much trouble. Prepare a tub of warm water and make a strong lather with melted soap or soap powder, adding enough ammonia to make the water smell rather strongly. Put the rug into this and knead it well with the hands, or put it on to a washing-board and brush with a brush. Repeat the process in a second soapy water if the first is not sufficient to clean the rug. Rinse thoroughly in warm soapy water; put it two or three times through the wringing-machine. It is always better to leave a little soap in the skin, as this helps to keep it soft. Shake the rug well, in the open air if possible, and dry in a good wind or indoors in a warm atmosphere, but not too near a fire. Whilst drying the rug should be shaken and rubbed occasionally to keep the skin soft.

Cocoanut-Fibre Door-Mats.—These should be beaten right side downwards, and on a green if possible. When very dirty, wash them with hot water and soda and a very strong brush. Then dip the brush in salt and water and wash over again. The salt will help to keep the fibre stiff.

GENERAL DIRECTIONS FOR DUSTING

It is very important that all dust should be removed from our rooms, not only because dusty rooms are uncomfortable and unpleasant to look upon, but also because dust is one of the sources of disease when we inhale it into our lungs.

The first point in dusting is to be provided with the proper sort of duster. This should be made of some soft material that will gather up the dust, and something smooth that leaves no fluff. In large families there is generally some old material that can be used for the purpose, such as remains of old curtains, or print dresses, old window-blinds, or even thin bed-covers, which have become too shabby to serve their original purpose. Cotton is as a rule better than linen. A duster must always be hemmed. A ragged duster should never be used for fine work, as it is very likely to catch on to some ornament or pointed furniture and cause an accident. Old dusters can always be used up in the cleaning of grates, brasses, and the like.

It is a good plan when dusting a room to work with two dusters, one slightly damp to gather up the dust, and the other dry to follow after and polish up. The aim in dusting must be to remove the dust and not merely to flick it from one part of the room to another. The duster ought to be rolled up into a sort of pad, the dust collected in it and then shaken out of the window from time to time. The work must be done on some distinct plan to ensure every part of the room having attention. Commence at one corner of the room and work steadily round it until every article has been dusted. High and out-of-reach places should be dusted first, as then any dust falling from the upper part will be removed when the lower part is being done. It is not only the tops of furniture and the places that are seen that require dusting, the backs of chairs, chair and table legs, the ledges of wainscoting, and other out-of-the-way places all require attention. When dusting a chimney-piece or table where small ornaments, &c., are placed, lift each article separately, dust it and also the surface underneath it before laying it down again. A furniture brush should be used for the dusting of ornamental furniture.

THE CLEANING OF FURNITURE

All furniture requires regular dusting to keep it in good order. A soft duster is necessary; in fact, it is best when dusting and polishing to work with two dusters, one with which to hold the article of furniture, and the other to do the dusting and rubbing up. A soft brush will be a help for any twisted or ornamental parts.

Upholstered furniture will also require a brush, and especial attention must be given to the crevices, and folds and buttons on chairs. Furniture brushes can be bought in many

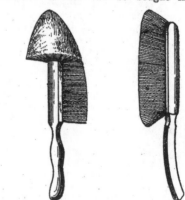

Furniture Brushes.

different patterns, and it is as well to choose the one that is best suited to the work to be done.

It must be remembered when dusting and rubbing up furniture that more can be done by plenty of " elbow grease " than by any amount of furniture polish; in fact, this latter is often used in far too lavish a manner.

In addition to the regular dusting a more thorough cleaning and rubbing up will be required at periodic intervals, and then some furniture polish may be applied. This may be prepared at home in one of the following ways :—

(1) Put into a bottle equal quantities of boiled linseed oil and brown vinegar—shake together and use as required. This is very simple and very good.

(2) Take equal quantities of linseed oil, turpentine, brown vinegar and methylated spirits and mix all together in a bottle.

Many other formulæ might be given, and melted bees'-wax is a very favourite ingredient, but although a good thing it requires an amount of very hard rubbing to remove the effect of its sticky properties. Furniture polishes may be bought ready prepared, and many of these are so good and so inexpensive that it is just a question whether it is worth one's while to go to the trouble of making one's own.

Furniture polish must never be used until the furniture has been well dusted, or it will smear and clog. Shake the bottle before beginning, and apply a little with a flannel or soft cotton pad. Rub it well into the wood, and evenly according to the grain. It should never be used in excess. Afterwards rub off with a soft duster and polish with a second duster or chamois leather.

When working with furniture polish be careful to place the bottle where it is not likely to be knocked over.

At spring-cleaning time, or at least once a year, most furniture will be improved by being washed before polishing.

Mahogany Furniture should be washed either with cold tea or with vinegar and water. Use a soft flannel or sponge for the plain pieces and a soft brush for any carved or ornamental parts. Dry and then polish as above.

Oak Furniture.—A little warm beer is the best thing for washing this, as it improves the colour. This is better than soap and water, and especially for old oak, as soap would spoil the appearance of the wood. When dry, polish with furniture cream.

Highly Polished Furniture should be washed with methylated spirits and water. Put two table-spoonfuls of methylated spirits into three breakfast-cupfuls of warm water, wring a small sponge out of this and wash the furniture all over. Dry and polish with a chamois leather. No further polishing will be necessary.

Pitch-Pine Furniture may be washed with warm water and a little soap, but care must be taken not to make it too wet.

Stains on Furniture.—*White Stains*, which are due to hot dishes having been placed upon the wood, can be removed with spirits of camphor. Rub well in with a soft rag and then polish the wood in the usual way. *Ink Stains* can be removed by rubbing them with a little oxalic acid. Do not spread the acid over the wood more than is necessary. A cork is a good thing to use for the application. Wash off with warm water and then polish.

Upholstered Furniture.—To clean this thoroughly it should be well beaten and brushed in the open air. If the material with which it is covered becomes soiled and dirty, it may be considerably restored by rubbing it over with warm bran or fig-dust, which can be bought from any corn-dealers. Benzine will probably remove any obstinate stains.

Leather Chairs.—These can be washed when dirty simply with soap and tepid water. Rub very lightly with a sponge, and then wipe off the soap and dry with a soft cloth. Very little water must be used. When dry, polish with the linseed oil and vinegar polish, or with an application of white of egg slightly beaten.

White Wicker Chairs.—Wash with soap and warm water and a soft brush. Rinse off the soap, and rub the cane over with equal quantities of lemon juice and water, or with a pennyworth of oxalic acid mixed in two cupfuls of water ; this will help to whiten the cane. Put the chairs in the open air to dry.

Grease stains may be removed from wicker by rubbing them with a little methylated spirits.

FIRES AND FIREPLACES

Before beginning to lay a fire or clean a grate, the hearth-rug, if there is one, should be rolled up and put on one side and a hearth-cloth laid down over the carpet. Any coarse close material will do for this, such as sacking, tick, or an old cretonne curtain ; but care must be taken to spread always the clean side next the carpet.

Have at hand everything that will be required for the cleaning of the grate and the laying of the fire. Some old newspaper, dry sticks, and a supply of small coal ; a sweep's brush or grate brush, a small shovel, black-lead or other stove polish, with brushes for putting it on and polishing ; one or two dusters, the necessary materials for cleaning steel or brass, and a pair of gloves. The best plan is to keep all these in readiness in a housemaid's box, which is usually fitted with small divisions for keeping the different requisites, and is sometimes provided with a cinder-sifter as well. A pair of gloves should always be worn, as there is nothing worse than black-lead for the hands, and there is no occasion to have them unnecessarily spoilt.

First remove the fire-irons and place them on the hearth-cloth. Then clean out the fireplace, using a piece of stick for the purpose, as this will make less noise than the poker. Be careful to make as little dust as possible. Next brush the back of the grate and inside the fireplace with the sweep's brush, and remove all ashes and cinders. The latter must be reserved for laying the fire, or if there are too many, burnt in the kitchen or boiler stove. The grate must now be thoroughly dusted before any black-leading or polishing takes place.

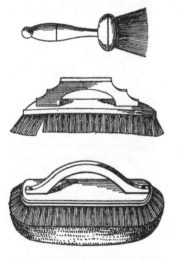

Sweep's Brush.

If the stove requires black-leading, apply a very little black-lead that has been moistened with water and a few drops of turpentine, by means of the black-lead brush. Or instead of black-lead a specially prepared stove polish may be used, such as Nixelene or Enameline; and this is almost simpler and cleaner, as there is no danger of it being splashed over any surrounding tiles, or even on the carpet. Brush off with a polishing brush, and then finish off with a firm polisher. There is no occasion to use much black-lead or polish; in fact, if a stove is in constant use, it will not likely be required every day; a rub up with the polishing brushes will be sufficient, except

Black-lead Brushes.

perhaps once a week when the room is having a more thorough cleaning.

The bars of the grate will always require a little extra attention, and may require to be blackened more often.

Next lay the fire. Many people never succeed in laying a fire that will burn well, because they pack it too tightly and do not leave enough space for the air to get through between the paper and sticks. Commence by laying a few cinders at the foot of the grate with some lightly crumpled paper on the top. Next place in some sticks crossways, allowing some of the ends to rest on the bars of the grate, and then some more large cinders or small pieces of coal on the top. The fire should be made to slope backwards, so that when it is first lighted the smoke will not blow into the room. Fire-lighters may be used instead of ordinary sticks; they are resined and burn up very quickly.

If the front and sides of the grate are tiled, rub these over daily with a duster, and occasionally wash them with a flannel wrung out of warm water and a little sunlight soap; rinse, dry with cloth, and polish with a chamois leather. If the tiles are stained, a little Sapolio rubbed on the flannel and applied rather dry will generally remove the marks; then wash over and finish as before. Do not use too much water when doing the cleaning, as it will be liable to sink into the cement and ultimately loosen the tiles.

Then finally clean the fender curb and fire-irons. If these are of brass, copper or steel, it will be sufficient to rub them well with a dry duster or chamois leather each day, and to give them a more thorough cleaning, say once a week. (See cleaning of brass, steel or copper, p. 72.) If they are made partly of iron and partly of steel, &c., the iron part may be brushed over with the polishing brushes, or a little Brunswick black may be used to the fender if it becomes very shabby. Black-lead must on no account be put on the handles of fire-irons.

If an iron grate is not to be used for some time, it is a good plan to rub it up with a little Ronuk; this will not only keep it looking bright, but will prevent rust. Directions for use are given with each tin.

If by any chance the grate has become rusty, rub well with a mixture of bath-brick dust and paraffin, then wash off and dry before polishing. Grates that are seldom used are sometimes painted with Brunswick black to keep them in good condition.

CARE OF CHIMNEYS

Chimney on Fire.—This can to a large extent be prevented by keeping the chimneys clean. Every chimney should be swept once or twice a year at least, and oftener if the fireplace is in constant use. Kitchen chimneys should be swept oftener; three or four times a year will not be too much if large fires are kept burning daily.

In addition to the thorough cleaning given by the sweep, any soot which accumulates near the fireplace should be swept away with the sweep's brush when the different grates are cleaned.

If the chimney should catch fire the first thing to do is to close the door and window to prevent a strong current of air from increasing the flames. Then throw over the fire a few handfuls of salt, when it will as a rule burn itself out in a very short time.

HOW TO SCRUB A ROOM

The room must first be cleared of as much furniture as convenient, and all rugs and pieces of carpet rolled up and put on one side. Then sweep the room with a soft broom, and remove all the dust in a shovel.

Have ready a kneeling-mat, a pail of warm water, a scrubbing brush, a piece of house flannel or a swab, and a little soft soap.

Commence at the corner of the room farthest from the door. Wring the flannel out of the

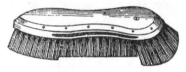

Scrubbing-Brush.

water, and wet as much of the boards as the arm can conveniently reach. Put a little soap on the brush and scrub each piece thoroughly backwards and forwards, and with the grain of the wood. This loosens the dirt, and it is now important to have it removed. Wring the flannel again out of the water and wipe the portion of board that was scrubbed until all the soap is gathered up; then dry with a coarse cloth. Do not make the boards wetter than is necessary to make them clean, especially if it is a floor that has a ceiling underneath, and change the water as soon as it becomes dirty. Work methodically over every part of the floor until all is finished.

If the wood is greasy, a little soda may be added to the water, and when washing boards that are much soiled a little sand used along with the soap will be a help. A bad stain can be usually removed from a floor by spreading it with a paste made of Fuller's earth and hot water, allowing it to remain overnight and then washing off.

When finished, allow a good current of air to pass through the room to dry it; or on a damp day it is better to have a fire burning, more especially if it is a bedroom or a room that will be used immediately.

CARE OF POLISHED FLOORS

These should be swept and dusted every day. First remove as much as possible of the surface dust with a soft short-handled broom and dust-pan, or, if there is a large surface of flooring under treatment, a long broom can be used. Then rub the floor with a dry duster, or what is

better still, with a floor-duster. If there is much polished flooring to be kept in order, it is very important that the worker should not do it on

Floor-Duster.

her knees. Then once a week the floor should be polished.

To Prepare Floor Polish.—Shred down $\frac{1}{4}$ lb. bees'-wax, and put it into a jar with $\frac{1}{2}$ pint turpentine; allow this to melt slowly in the oven or on the side of the stove, stirring occasionally with a wooden stick.

Rub a little of this on to the floor with a piece of flannel and then polish with a pad, which can be bought for the purpose, or with a floor-polisher.

Special floor polishes can also be bought prepared, such as Ronuk, Jackson's Camphorated

Floor-Polisher.

Polish, &c., and the use of one of these would of course save the trouble of making, but it would come a little more expensive than the simple bees'-wax and turpentine.

TO CLEAN LINOLEUM OR FLOOR-CLOTH

Much washing and scrubbing is bad for the ordinary linoleum. It should be well swept every day, and only washed when necessary. Take a pail of warm water, some plain yellow soap, and a piece of house flannel, and wash the linoleum with this. Wring out the flannel and take up as much of the moisture as possible. Then dry with a clean dry towel. If the linoleum is very dirty and requires a brush, then a soft one only must be used. The use of soda, ammonia, or washing powders must be avoided.

Greenwich Linoleum, which has the pattern all the way through, can be washed with warm water, a flannel, and a little Brook's soap. This revives the colour and makes it look like new. To give the linoleum a more finished appearance, it may be rubbed over with a little skimmed milk after washing and finished with a dry cloth ; or with a little glue water made thus :—Take one ounce of glue powder or shredded glue, dissolve it in one pint of boiling water and allow it to melt, stirring occasionally with a stick. The linoleum may of course be polished if a brighter gloss is desired. (See Polished Floors, p. 66.)

Indian Matting.—This should be washed on the floor with a strong solution of salt and water and then dried quickly with a soft cloth. Or, if it becomes very much soiled, take it up and scrub with soap and water and a moderately hard brush. Rinse on both sides and dry with a cloth or in the open air. If there are stains on the matting a little ammonia might be added to the water or some benzine applied to the spot.

Care of Tiled Floors.—Sweep every day with a soft broom ; and once or twice a week, or oftener if necessary, wash them over with soap and water. Take some water in a pail and add to it a little soap powder or melted soap. Use either a house flannel or brush to wash with. If the tiles are very dirty a brush will be required. Rinse off the soap, and then make as dry as possible with the flannel. A little Brook's soap or Sapolio will be useful for removing any stains. If it is desired to have a polish on the tiles, they may be rubbed over with a little milk after washing, or with linseed oil and turpentine mixed in equal quantities.

THE MAKING AND CARE OF BEDS

However well chosen and hygienic a bed may be, if it is not well made, the comfort of it will be greatly reduced, if not altogether spoilt.

A bed must be thoroughly well aired every day for an hour at least before making. The windows of the bedroom should first be thrown open top and bottom, the bed-curtains drawn back, if there are any, then the clothes stripped off the bed one at a time and placed over the back of a chair or chairs. The pillows and bolster must be well shaken and beaten, and placed near the open window if possible, and then the mattress raised on its two ends so as to form an arch for the air to pass through. If there is a feather mattress, this should be laid over the end of the bed.

In making a bed individual taste should always be considered. Some like all the surplus length of blanket doubled over at the top, while others like the covering only to reach to the shoulders ; and in the case of a feather-bed some like the bed made so as to slope towards the foot, and others prefer it perfectly flat, and so on. These may appear fads, but it entails no extra trouble to give in to them—only a little thought ; and

attention to these small details may add very much to the comfort and real repose of the sleeper.

It is always better and more expeditious if two people can be engaged in the making of the beds ; and needless to say their hands should be spotlessly clean, and they should each wear a clean apron or overall.

The mattress must be turned each morning —one day from top to bottom, and the next from side to side—so as to ensure equal wear.

If there is a feather-bed, it must be thoroughly shaken to prevent lumps. Take the two opposite corners and shake the feathers towards the centre, then the other two corners and do the same, and next the sides. When the feathers seem perfectly light and free from lumps, smooth the mattress over, being particular to fill the corners with feathers. If any feathers should come out during the process, it will generally be from a hole in the seam, and this should at once be attended to and sewn together with a needle and cotton.

In laying the clothes on the bed each article must be put on separately, and not thrown on in a mass to save time. They must be put on evenly, allowing the same amount to come over each side of the bed and be tucked in all round. It is also most important to have them free from wrinkles or folds of any kind.

When the mattress is arranged, next put on the binder or under-blanket. This should be wide enough to tuck in well at the sides of the bed, when it will hold the mattress together and make the bed smoother and more comfortable. The under-sheet is now put on and tucked in all round, and the bolster laid on the top at the head of the bed, unless no bolster-slip is used, when the under-sheet must be left long enough to fold over the bolster and completely cover it, but this is not such a comfortable arrangement. Next, place on the top sheet with the wrong side uppermost, and the widest hem at the top to turn over the blankets. On the top of the sheets lay the blankets with the open end at the top (as it is easy then to throw off one fold if the occupant of the bed should find it too hot). Then a coverlet or sheet should cover all, and must be light in weight, as it is meant for night use. This should be turned in over the blankets at the top, and the end of the sheet turned over it ; the blankets are thus preserved from dust, and the bed has a more inviting appearance when it is turned down for the night. Then slip in the pillow or pillows on the top of the bolster without flattening them down, and on a double bed place the opening of the slip to the inside of the bed. Lastly may be put on a pretty counterpane, which is removed at night. This should not be tucked in, but allowed to hang over the sides in graceful folds. If there is a centre pattern, be sure that this comes to the centre of the bed, and any surplus length may be laid in folds at the foot. If carefully folded up at night and always in the same folds, the counterpane will keep clean for quite a long time, and it adds very much to the dainty appearance of the bedroom during the day.

If an eider-down is used it should be rolled up or folded double at the foot of the bed. Those who like warmth without weight will find it a great advantage to make the bed with the eider-down between the upper sheet and the blankets. The warmth is thereby sensibly increased, and if the eider-down is well ventilated it is not unhealthy.

If pillow shams and sheet shams are used, the pillows should be placed on the outside of the counterpane during the day, and the sheet sham slipped under the bed-clothes and arranged so that the embroidered edge rests on the counterpane.

If there are curtains, draw these back and arrange the ends neatly on the pillows.

Turning down a Bed.—First remove the eider-down; then take off the counterpane and sheet and pillow shams, if there are such, and fold all these up very carefully, and place them where they will not be crushed nor sat upon. Then turn down the clothes about a foot or a foot and a half at the top of the bed, and one corner, or two corners if it is a double bed, may be turned back again towards the centre, but this is a matter of taste. It is also a question of taste whether the clothes be left tucked in at the sides or loosened. Let down and draw any curtains. See that pillows are nice and smooth and all straight and even, and then replace the eider-down, spreading it out over the bed this time.

Care of Beds.—The strictest cleanliness must be observed as regards beds, not merely in the changing of the linen, but in the bed itself and everything about it.

One hears of beds the spars of which are never dusted except at the annual period of spring cleaning, and sometimes not even then. We ought to remember that the dust in our houses, and especially in our bedrooms, is not only earth dust, soot, fraying of carpets and curtains, &c., but that there is a large admixture of animal matter, for our outer skin or cuticle is constantly peeling off and being removed; and added to that, this dust if not removed becomes impregnated with noxious gases exhaled from our lungs and from the pores of our bodies, and poisons the air we breathe, thereby greatly lessening the beneficial effects of sleep. Every part of the bedstead should be carefully dusted once a week, a small brush being used if necessary. The best time for this will be before the bed is made on the day the room is thoroughly cleaned.

The bedstead itself, and especially the under-part, should be washed with warm water and carbolic soap at least once a year. If at any time insects should appear, the bedstead should be rubbed over with paraffin or very strong ammonia.

Japanned bedsteads may be revived by rubbing them over with a little paraffin, and then polishing with a leather or soft duster.

Brass bedsteads should be dusted daily, and occasionally rubbed over with a little sweet oil and polished with a leather. Metal polish should not be used, as the brass is lacquered. If this wears off it will require special treatment.

If the mattresses and pillows have been covered with cotton slips (see p. 258), it is very easy to have these taken off and washed as soon as they become soiled. The bedding can then be thoroughly brushed and beaten, special attention being paid to the edges and to the little corners where the mattress is tacked down. If this can be done out of doors, so much the better.

The mattresses ought to be taken to pieces and re-made every few years—not merely because they will, even with the most careful treatment, eventually form into hard lumps and hollows, but because they will really require to be purified from animal matter. Although it is possible to do this at home, this course is scarcely to be recommended. It is much wiser and simpler to send them to a good upholsterer.

Blankets, too, must be washed or cleaned whenever they require it. Once or twice a year will be sufficient under ordinary circumstances, provided they have proper care in the way of airing, shaking, and being kept covered from dust; but if they have been used in the case of illness they must of course be washed specially, and if the illness is an infectious one, disinfected as well.

EMPTYING OF SLOPS AND CARE OF THE WASH-STAND

The appliances necessary for this portion of household work are: a slop-pail, a can of boiling water in which a little soda has been dissolved, a small mop, two slop-cloths, and a glass-towel. The slop-pail used for carrying about is best made of enamelled tin, as it is easily kept in order and there is no danger of its breaking. It should always be fitted with a lid.

The slop-cloths should be of some thin open material, which can be washed and dried easily.

Slop-Pail.

One must be used for the basin and wash-stand and the second for the chamber and bedroom slop-pail. It is important to keep each cloth for its special purpose.

Commence by emptying everything into the slop-pail. Pour a little of the hot soda-water into the chamber, and allow it to remain there while the wash-stand is being put in order.

Rinse out the basin with clean water, using a little of the soda-water if necessary to remove any stain or soap-suds. Then pour a little clean water into the basin and rinse the tumbler and water-bottle, and dry them with the glass-towel.

Next rinse any sponges or loofahs, &c., and either hang them up to dry or place them in a sponge basket. Then pour out the water, and wipe the basin thoroughly with its special cloth. Empty the ewer and wash it out if necessary. If rain water is used there is frequently a considerable amount of sediment which settles at the foot of the jug.

Wipe also the wash-stand, lifting each article and wiping it clean. Pay particular attention to the soap-dish.

Wash the chamber with the mop, using the water that has been standing in it; rinse and dry with the special cloth. If there is a slop-pail belonging to the room, empty this also, wash with hot water, using the mop. Then rinse with cold, and dry with the chamber cloth.

Finally fill up the ewer and water-bottle with fresh water. The former with soft water if available, and the latter with drinking water. It is very important that the ewer should be quite emptied every day; if old water is allowed to remain and just a little fresh added, the water will very soon begin to smell. So let it all be *fresh*.

Cover the slop-pail before taking it from the room, and have the contents emptied at once. Care too must be taken to keep this pail very clean and fresh. It should be rinsed out every day with hot soda-water; rinsed, dried, and then left with the lid off to air. The lid should have the same treatment, and then be hung up until required again.

The two slop-cloths should be washed every day and hung up to dry. The glass-towel if properly used ought to last a week.

Once a week, usually on the day the bedroom is being turned out, the wash-stand, &c., will require a more thorough cleaning.

The ware should be taken out of the room if possible and well washed in the housemaid's pantry or bath-room. Use hot water and a little paraffin soap or soap-powder. Pay particular attention to the handles of ewer and chamber, and use small brush for the corners, if necessary. The inside of the ewer too must be washed as well as the outside, and a little soda-water may be required to remove discoloration.

If the water-bottle has become stained and dim, it ought to have special treatment. (See p. 75.)

Wash the wash-stand with a little soap and water, using a washing flannel or soft brush; wipe off the soap and rub up with a towel. Then replace the ware, and supply with water and soap too if required.

TO CLEAN WALLS AND CEILINGS

Papered Walls, when they become dirty, should be thoroughly dusted. To do this, tie a clean soft duster over the head of a long-handled broom. Any soft broom will do, provided the wall is not very high, in which case it is almost necessary to have a special wall-broom, or Turk's-head broom, which has a jointed bamboo handle, and can be shortened or lengthened as required. Sweep every part of the wall, moving the brush up and down in long straight lines, and be particular to remove all dust from any cornice or mouldings. The duster must be changed when it becomes dirty.

Turk's-head Broom.

If the paper has still a soiled appearance after dusting, it may be further improved by rubbing it all over with stale bread. Cut a plain dry loaf in four pieces, and rub the paper all over with it. It will be necessary to mount on a pair of steps to do this. Commence at one of the top corners and rub with light even strokes, undertaking about a yard at a time. There is no need to rub very hard; too much vigour would only destroy the surface of the paper. Go over each piece in a careful methodical way, and in the order most convenient to yourself. This manner of cleaning will make a considerable difference to dirty wall-paper.

The *ceiling* of a room can be cleaned in the same way, and special attention must be given to the corners, where cobwebs so frequently lodge.

Varnished Paper and Painted Walls may be washed *after* dusting. Take a pail of tepid water, and add to it enough melted soap to make a light lather. Use a sponge, and wash the wall all over with this. Then carefully remove the soap with a second sponge or chamois leather wrung out of clear cold water. Leave the wall to dry without any further wiping.

TO CLEAN WINDOWS

Windows must never be cleaned in frosty weather, as the glass is then very brittle and would be liable to break as soon as moisture were applied. Choose a dull dry day when the sun is not shining upon them.

First dust the windows inside and out, and also the woodwork surrounding them. A painter's brush or any other soft brush is the best thing for the purpose. Then take some tepid water and add enough liquid ammonia to it to make it smell slightly, or a small quantity of paraffin. Wring a sponge or chamois leather out of this and wash over the window with it, paying particular attention to the sides and corners. Finish off with a linen duster or a dry chamois leather. No material of a fluffy nature must be used. Clean soft newspaper makes a very good polishing-pad. Commence always at the top and work downwards.

Paint or other stains can be removed from the glass with a little vinegar or oxalic acid.

Various powders are now sold for cleaning windows without water, and these in many cases are found quite satisfactory. Directions for use are given with each special make.

It must be remembered that no woman is allowed to sit or stand outside an upstairs window in order to clean it; so that for large windows which cannot be cleaned from the inside, it will be necessary to employ a man. These men usually bring their own apparatus. The usual charge for cleaning is about 2d. a window.

Painter's Brush.

TO CLEAN BLINDS

Venetian Blinds.—These ought to be thoroughly dusted once a week. Let the blinds down, and by means of a pair of steps, dust all the webbing and the cords. Then with a soft duster dust each lath separately. Commence at the top and work downwards. Do one side first, all the way down, then turn the blind and dust the other side. Put the duster over the finger and rub well round the cords where they pass through the laths.

Once a year, or even oftener, Venetian blinds should be washed. Take a basin or small pail of warm water in which a little soap and borax have been dissolved, wring a sponge out of this, and wash each lath separately. Then dip the sponge into clean warm water and rub the soap off the wood. Dry with a soft towel. Or, if found easier, the laths may be removed. To do this, undo the knot at the foot of the cord which runs through the blind. Then pull out the cord and remove the laths. Wash them as above, and when thoroughly dry, put them back in their place and lace the cord through them.

Linen or Holland Blinds.—These should be dusted weekly. Let the blind down as far as it will go and with a soft duster wipe it well on both sides. Dust also the cord and roller.

To clean them more thoroughly they should be taken down, laid flat on a table and well dusted on both sides. Then take some stale bread or bran, and rub this lightly and quickly all over the material. Dust off with a clean duster. If this is not sufficient to clean them, they will require to be washed. Unless the blinds are small in size, it is not wise to attempt this at home, as they really require special washing to give them a good gloss and keep them in shape.

TO WASH PAINT

Dust the paint first, using a soft brush for the purpose, as this is less likely to drive the dirt into the wood than a cloth. Then have ready at hand a pail of warm soft water, to which a little dissolved soap has been added, and a soft flannel; a second pail of cold or tepid water with a sponge, and a soft cloth or chamois leather for drying. Wring the flannel out of the soapy water, and wash the paint gently with it. Do not use the flannel too wet, and be careful to avoid splashing the surrounding wall. Then rinse off the dirty soap with the sponge and tepid water, and this will prevent the wood having a smeary appearance. Finish off with the dry cloth or leather.

Do not wet too much of the paint at one time; if there is a large quantity of woodwork to be done it will be a great advantage if two can be engaged at the work; one to wash, and the second to follow and do the rinsing and drying. The water must be changed as soon as it becomes dirty.

For *varnished paint* use tepid water only; in fact for any paint care must be taken not to have the water too hot.

Soda must never be used, but a little borax may be added with safety to water that is hard. Care must be taken, too, that the soap used is of a pure and simple kind. Good yellow soap, mottled soap, or carbolic soap are to be recommended. Then as regards the flannel, the ordinary house flannel is too rough, and housekeepers would do well to save up any pieces of old flannel, woven under-garments, old blankets, &c., for this purpose. The towels, too, that are used must not be of a fluffy nature; old huckaback bedroom towels are excellent for the purpose.

The woodwork in a house should be washed at least twice a year. Flies and other insects lay their eggs along the crevices of doors and windows, and by keeping these clean we can do much to avoid the arrival of these unwelcome visitors. Finger-marks and other marks should, of course, be removed as need arises; a little benzine applied on a flannel, or simply a gentle rub with a soapy sponge, will be sufficient. All hard rubbing must be avoided.

White Enamel Paint.—The following is a very good preparation for cleaning this special kind of paint :—

Take one gill of vinegar, one gill paraffin, and half-gill linseed oil, and shake them together in a bottle. Apply this to the paint with a clean sponge or soft flannel and the result will be excellent. No washing is required.

TO CLEAN MARBLE

When marble is in good condition, it can be kept in order by simply washing it with soap and water, rinsed off and then dried. This would apply to marble wash-stands and slabs which are in frequent use.

A chimney-piece which is not cleaned so often may require a little stronger treatment. Dust it first, and in this case a little shredded Brook's soap or Sapolia used along with ordinary yellow soap or soft soap will be efficacious, and a brush should be used for any ornamental parts. Always rinse off the soap, and take a second water if necessary. Dry with a cloth and polish with a chamois leather. Black or grey marble may be rubbed over with a little linseed oil after washing to give it a gloss.

If the marble is stained, the appearance of it may be improved by the following treatment :— Take 1 oz. powdered chalk, 1 oz. powdered pumice-stone and 2 ozs. soda—pound these together and pass them through a sieve. Then make them into a paste with boiling water, and spread this over the marble, especially over the stained parts. Allow it to remain overnight, and wash off as before.

Another way of cleaning marble is to coat it all over with a layer of thick hot-water starch (see p. 280). This starch penetrates into all the crevices and absorbs the surface dirt. When dry it will scale off in large pieces, bringing the dirt away with it. Then wash with soap and water and dry as before.

Oxalic acid, too, will sometimes remove a stain, but it must be rubbed on and washed off again very quickly, as it will discolour the marble if allowed to remain. If a stain is very deep-seated the only sure way of eradicating it is to have the marble repolished.

Marble Statuary should be washed with soap and water only. Sunlight or paraffin soap is good, but nothing of a gritty nature must be used. The washing should be done with soft brushes, small ones being used for any corners or intricate parts. The water must be changed whenever it becomes dirty, and care must be taken to rinse off all soap. Allow the marble to dry, and then polish with a leather or soft dry brush.

Marble statuary may also be cleaned with a paste of starch as above.

TO CLEAN PICTURES

The Glass.—To clean the glass of pictures, dust it first with a soft silk or muslin duster. Then put one tablespoonful of methylated spirits into a small basin of warm water (about two breakfast-cupfuls), wring a sponge out of this and wash the picture glass all over. Be careful not to wet the frame when cleaning the corners and edges. Pay particular attention to any fly-marks or other stains. Then dry with a fine towel and polish with a chamois leather.

Oil-Paintings.—These require very careful treatment. They should be dusted frequently with an old silk handkerchief or feather brush, but if the latter is used one must make sure there are no sharp pieces of quill or wire fastenings which might scratch the canvas. The picture must be taken down to be cleaned thoroughly. First of all it should be dusted, back and front. Then sponge the oil-painting very carefully with a fine sponge or piece of cotton-wool wrung out of lukewarm water. Soap must on no account be used. Rub the surface over lightly and quickly, and do not allow it to remain wet longer than is needful. Dry with a fine cloth or chamois leather. This can of course only be done to oil-paintings that have a coating of varnish over them, as it is the varnish only that will bear the washing. If this gets rubbed or worn off, the picture must be dusted only. If an oil-painting becomes very much discoloured and dirty through age, it is better to send it to an expert to have scientific treatment, as trying different things at home might easily end in injuring the picture.

Brass Picture-Chains.—These become very dirty after they have been exposed to the atmosphere for some time, but they can be made to look quite fresh again by the following treatment :—Brush them first with a soft brush, so as to remove as much of the dust as possible. Then plunge them into a pail of boiling water to which a good handful of soda has been added, and allow them to remain until that is cold. Next wash them in clean hot water with soap and a brush, rinse and hang them up to dry. Finally they may have a rub with the chamois leather.

Gilt Picture-Frames.—If the frames are made of inferior gilt they will not endure much cleaning. Dust them carefully with a soft brush, and if the gilt has chipped off in places it may be touched up with a little gold paint, which can be bought at any oil-shop.

To clean good English gilt frames, dust them first with a soft brush or silk handkerchief, then wash gently with a small fine sponge wrung out of equal quantities of methylated spirits and water. Or a camel's-hair brush may be used instead of the sponge. Dry with a chamois leather.

A little onion water applied with a sponge

sometimes helps to restore the colour of the gilding, and also keeps off flies.

Prepare it thus :—Remove the skin from two or three onions and boil them in two breakfast-cupfuls of water until all the goodness is extracted. Strain through a very fine strainer or piece of muslin and use warm.

JAPANESE TRAYS OR PAPIER-MACHÉ ARTICLES

Clean these by washing them gently with a sponge wrung out of tepid water. Then dry with a cloth and polish with a little dry flour rubbed on with a soft duster or chamois leather.

TO CLEAN MIRRORS

First remove all dust. Then take a basin of tepid water and add enough ammonia to make it smell slightly. Wring a sponge or chamois leather out of this, and wash the glass all over, going carefully round the edges and into the corners to avoid wetting the frame, and especially if it is a gilded one.

Dry with a soft towel, and polish with a chamois leather or old silk handkerchief.

If the mirror has not been cleaned for some time, and is smeared and stained, instead of washing it, make a paste with fine whitening and methylated spirits, and rub this well over the glass with a piece of flannel. When dry, rub off with a duster and polish as before.

For gilt frames see p. 71.

TO CLEAN STEEL

If steel is rubbed daily with a dry duster or leather, and so kept free from dust and moisture, it ought to retain its brightness for a considerable time. When it requires extra cleaning, use very fine emery paper ; No. 0 is best. Rub the steel backwards and forwards with this, and always in the one direction. Cross-rubbing will not polish properly. Emery powder, fine bath-brick dust or crocus powder made into a paste with paraffin or methylated spirits are all good things for the cleaning of steel. These should be applied with a piece of flannel and well rubbed on to the metal. Then a little of the dry powder used for polishing and the chamois leather for the final rub up.

The emery paper is, however, cleaner and simpler to use, and unless the steel is allowed to get into bad condition, it ought to be sufficient to keep it in excellent order.

TO CLEAN BRASS

There are many different materials used for the cleaning of brass, but perhaps nothing is better than fine bath-brick dust or powdered rotten-stone made into a paste with a little paraffin or oil of turpentine. Apply this with a flannel, rubbing the brass well ; then rub off with a second flannel, using a little dry powder, and polish with a duster or chamois leather. There are also many modern polishes that can be used, but with some of them the result, although good to begin with, is not lasting ; the brass tarnishes and becomes dim very rapidly.

The " Blue-bell " polish is one to be recommended, and it has the advantage of being very clean to use. Directions for its use are given with each tin. If a paste of any kind is used, care must be taken that none of it is left sticking to the brass.

Outside brasses may be kept from tarnishing by rubbing them over with a little vaseline after cleaning.

Benares Brass should be washed in very hot soapy water, and well rubbed with a flannel or soft brush. If the brass is greasy, add a little borax to the water, then rinse in hot water and dry with a towel. If the brass still remains stained or discoloured, rub it over with the squeezed half of a lemon and wash again. Finally polish with a chamois leather. It is better not to use any polishing paste for chased work, as it is almost impossible to remove it entirely ; but a little dry whitening may be used to polish with, if it is very carefully brushed off.

Lacquered Brass requires very careful treatment, and especially so if it is not of a very good quality, as the application of paste and a great deal of rubbing would then be liable to remove the lacquer, which is only a sort of varnish which can quickly be worn off.

Lacquered articles should be rubbed up frequently with a leather, and if this is not sufficient to keep them in order, wash them in warm water with soap and a flannel. Then dry and polish. Soda must never be used when washing lacquered goods, but a little borax may be added if the water is hard.

THE CLEANING OF BOOKS

Books should be kept as free from dust as possible. If the book-case is covered with glass this is comparatively easy, but when the books are placed on open shelves they will require more attention. Care should be taken to always cover them with a dust-sheet before any sweeping is done in the room. Then from time to time, or as often as necessary, the books should be removed from the shelves and thoroughly dusted. Take them two at a time, and clap them together to disperse the dust, then dust them gently with a very light duster or soft clothes'-brush. The dust must not be rubbed into the leaves. The shelves, too, should be dusted before the books are returned to them.

THE CARE OF A PIANO

The most important point is to protect it from all damp. It should never be in a temperature under 60 degs. Fahrenheit, therefore it is unwise to have it standing in a room where there is no fire in winter. Great heat is also injurious.

A piano should never be placed against an outside wall, unless it can be protected in some way, neither should it stand in a direct draught.

A strip of felt or a pad of silk is sometimes placed over the keyboard to protect it from damp and dust.

It is a bad plan to pile books and ornaments on the top of a piano, as any weight is apt to spoil the tone of the instrument. A flower vase with water should be especially avoided, as there is always the danger of the water being spilt and soaking between the keys.

Pianos should be carefully dusted with a soft cloth or silk duster, and polished when necessary with a chamois leather. Any marks on the keyboard may be removed with a damp chamois leather, but soap and water should never be used.

A piano, whether it is in use or not, should be tuned regularly by a competent tuner. An arrangement can be made for this to be done periodically, generally four times a year, for a very moderate charge. This will preserve the instrument and keep it at the necessary pitch.

BRASS CHANDELIERS OR GAS BRACKETS

Keep these free from dust with a soft brush or duster. When they become soiled, wash with a sponge wrung out of vinegar and water. Dry with a soft cloth, and polish with a chamois leather.

TO CLEAN BRONZE ORNAMENTS

These must never be *washed*. Dust with a muslin or silk duster, and use a soft brush for any ornamental part. If this is not sufficient to make them clean, sponge the ornaments with stale beer, using a small sponge, and when dry, polish with a chamois leather.

TO CLEAN IVORY

Wash in lukewarm water with plain yellow soap, using a soft brush if necessary to remove dirt from any carved parts. Rinse and dry. Then polish with a chamois leather. If the ivory is stained, rub with a little salt and vinegar, or salt and lemon juice, after washing; rinse and dry as before.

Or, if the ivory is discoloured, lift it out of the soapy water and stand it in the sun. Before it becomes dry, repeat the process if necessary. It must not be allowed to remain dry in a hot sun, or it will warp. Rinse and dry as before.

TO CLEAN DOOR-STEPS

First sweep away all the dust with an old broom kept for the purpose. Then take a pail of cold or tepid water, a piece of strong floor-cloth or swab, and some rough hearth-stone, which can be bought at the rate of two or three pieces for a penny. A kneeling-mat must always be used. Wring the cloth out of the water, and wet over as much as is convenient of the steps at one time. Then rub over with the stone evenly backwards and forwards, and not in curves.

Kneeling-Mat.

Next wring the cloth again out of the water, and wipe the stone again to prevent it having a patchy appearance when dry. Then go on to the next piece of step and do it in the same way, and so on until all is finished. The sides and front of the steps must also have attention.

In frosty weather a handful of salt should be put in the water, and this will prevent its freezing.

GENERAL DIRECTIONS FOR " WASHING UP "

Before commencing the actual washing of dishes, &c., a certain amount of preliminary arrangement is necessary. First of all, one must see that a plentiful supply of hot water is available. If there is a hot-water supply in the house, this is a simple matter if the fire is first attended to, but if only a side boiler or kettles are to be relied on, some looking ahead will be necessary to see that these are filled in time, and then refilled, when once they have been emptied, in order to cause no delay in having to wait for the water to boil.

Then everything that requires washing must be collected together and put within easy reach. The contents of dishes on which food has been served must be put away on clean plates or basins. All scraps of food, crumbs, remains of mustard or jam, &c., must be removed from plates; slops must be poured out of teacups or coffee-cups; remains of tea and tea leaves from the teapot, and so on.

If this were not done before starting the washing, the water would not only become unnecessarily dirty and require more frequent changing, but the work itself would be disagreeable.

Arrange all articles of one kind together, plates of different sizes in neat piles, saucers by themselves in another pile, cups by themselves, and so on.

Silver and glass ought to be kept apart on a tray, or in the case of the former in a plate-basket, until they can be washed. They must not be mixed up with other dishes.

Knives should be placed blades downwards in a washer or jug of hot water. (See p. 76.)

If attention is paid to these small points, " washing up " will be a much simpler affair than if it were just started in a muddle. Much time too will be saved, as all unnecessary turning round and walking about with wet and soapy hands will be avoided.

Two basins or small tubs will be necessary for the washing, one for hot water and the second for a cold or tepid rinsing water. For silver, glass and fine china, a small wooden or pulp-ware tub is best, as this is less liable to scratch or break fine articles ; but for ordinary dishes, and especially greasy dishes, zinc or tin is preferable, as it can be kept clean more easily.

If the water is hard, it must be softened with a little soda or borax, and a little soap or soap-powder must be used if required. Care must, however, be taken to avoid unnecessary extravagance in the employment of these materials; there is frequently considerable waste caused by their needless use, and this must be guarded against.

With regard to dish-cloths, these are best made of some open material which will not retain the grease, such as thin old towelling, or a cheap canvas-like material sold for the purpose.

Some people prefer a mop or dish-brush instead of the dish-cloth, and both are useful.

When all is arranged, commence with the glass and silver, and when these are out of the way start on the cleanest and least greasy of the dishes. If there are two people to do the work, then one can wash while the other does the drying.

The water must be changed whenever it becomes dirty ; continuing to wash in the dirty water would only result in smeary dishes, with probably an unpleasant smell. This is one of the most important points to pay attention to.

Another very important point is the use of dry and clean towels. The thickness of the towel must be regulated according to the kind of article being dried. Glass, silver, and china will require fine smooth towels without a fluffy surface, while coarser dishes will require a coarse and stronger material. In all cases the towels must be clean and free from grease, and as they become wet should be hung near the fire to dry.

Finally, when the " washing up " is finished and everything put away in its place, the dish-cloths or flannels that have been used must be washed out and hung up to dry, and also any towels that require it. The tub or basin must be well washed and rinsed and set on end to air. All then will be clean and ready when wanted again, and a good worker is recognised by attention to these small details.

See also detailed directions under special articles.

For the washing of kitchen utensils, see pp. 92–94.

CARE OF SILVER

The daily care of silver is much more important than the thorough cleaning which is given to it at stated intervals. In fact, if a little extra time were spent over the regular washing and drying, the " thorough cleaning," as it is called, need not be oftener than once in three weeks or a month.

The keeping of silver requires a good deal of care, but it is not difficult if the work is done with method, and attention paid to a few special points.

Table silver should be washed as soon as possible after it has been used. A papier mâché or wooden tub is the best for the purpose, as then there will be little danger of it scratching the silver. Take water as hot as the hand can bear, add a few drops of ammonia and enough melted soap, " lux " or soap-powder to make a nice lather. Wash the silver in this, using a piece of flannel or soft towelling to rub it with. Rinse in clean hot water, and dry with a fine towel while the silver is still warm. If allowed to lie wet, it will be difficult to remove the water-marks. For this reason, if a large quantity of silver is being done, it is better not to start it all at one time, but one lot can be finished as far as the rinsing, and the second lot put to soak in the soapy water while the first lot is being dried. When dry give each article a good rub up with a chamois leather, and then arrange the silver neatly and in order in the plate-basket, or on a tray ready to put away.

Throughout the process the greatest care must be taken not to scratch the silver, and with this in view it is really better if forks can be kept by themselves. In the case of real silver, a careful worker will first lay a towel or piece of flannel on the tray on which the silver is drained, and, in fact, never allow it to touch a hard surface, which might be liable to injure it.

Another important point to remember is, that both towel and lather must be perfectly clean and free from grease, and in the case of the former it must be changed when it becomes too damp. A wet towel is practically useless.

From time to time the silver will be improved by having a more special cleaning. One of the best things to use for this is fine Spanish whitening or some good plate powder and liquid ammonia.[1] Put a little whitening (not more than one dessert-spoonful at a time) into a saucer and mix into a perfectly smooth paste with the ammonia. It should be of the consistency of thin cream. Apply this to the silver with a piece of soft flannel, rubbing each article well, and especially the parts which are most likely to be

[1] Elkington & Co. Ltd., Birmingham, sell a plate powder which is thoroughly to be recommended. It is free from mercury, and does not contain chalk in any form. Chalk is very injurious to silver and electro-plated articles from its cutting nature, and unfortunately forms the basis of many of the plate powders in existence.

stained. Allow this to dry on the silver, then rub off with a second piece of flannel, using a soft silver brush wherever necessary to remove the whitening. Forks require special attention, as the powder is apt to lodge between the prongs. The " Selvyt " fork polisher is useful for this purpose. Then polish well with the chamois leather. When finished, it must not be handled more than necessary.

There are many other plate powders which can be used in place of the whitening, but care must be taken to use one that is thoroughly reliable, as so many of them are mixed with mercury, which is injurious to the plate. Rouge and hartshorn powder are both very good, but unless the former is carefully removed it looks bad. Methylated spirits may be used instead of ammonia, and will be found very satisfactory, but when once a good method is adopted it should be adhered to, as it is easier for the worker and better for the silver.

Silver Brush.

Silver forks and knives with ivory handles should not be allowed to soak in water, or at least the handles must be kept out of the water, or the heat will melt the cement which fixes them together. The best plan is to hold them in the hand while washing and to place them in a jug for rinsing with enough boiling water to reach just up to the handles.

Egg spoons that have become very much stained with the sulphur from the egg should be rubbed with a little fine dry salt and then washed.

A silver teapot may be washed in the same way, only if it has a wooden handle or wooden or ivory rings on the handle, it must not be allowed to soak in hot water. A teapot must on no account be left standing with the remains of tea and tea-leaves in it, but should be emptied and rinsed out with boiling water as soon as possible after use. When it begins to have a discoloured appearance inside or to smell musty, fill it to the brim with boiling water, and add a piece of washing-soda. Close down the lid and let it remain thus all night. Next day pour out the soda-water, wash with soap and water, using a small brush, and rinse thoroughly. A teapot must be dried inside as well as outside, and left with the lid open until quite free from moisture.

Silver should be exposed as little as possible to the action of the atmosphere, more especially in damp foggy weather, when it will very readily tarnish. That which is in daily use should be kept either in a baize-lined plate-basket and covered with a piece of felt or flannel, or in a baize-lined drawer covered in a similar way.

Articles that are not in constant use should be kept in the lined cases, or in bags made of flannel or chamois leather.

A lump of camphor stored with silver will help to preserve its brilliancy.

Britannia Metal Goods.—Messrs. Dixon and Sons, manufacturers, Sheffield, have kindly supplied the following directions for cleaning :— Rub the article all over with a piece of woollen cloth, moistened with sweet oil, and then apply a little pounded rotten-stone, or polishing paste, with the finger till the polish is produced ; after which, wash it well with soap and hot water, and when dry wipe off smartly with soft wash-leather and a little fine whiting. This simple method will effectually preserve the colour.

By attending to the above, Britannia metal goods are warranted to stand their colour any duration of time.

THE WASHING OF GLASS, WATER-BOTTLES, DECANTERS, &c.

Glass requires very special care if we want it to look nice. Tumblers should be washed first in warm water, with a very little soap or a few drops of ammonia, using the fingers or a fine cloth to rub them with. Then rinse them in clear cold water and place them upside down on a tray to drain. Use a very fine towel for drying, as one that is fluffy would leave small particles on the glass. Care must be taken, too, that the towel is dry and free from grease, or it would give the glass a smeared appearance. A final polish with a chamois leather is sometimes given ; but this is objected to by some people, because they think it gives the glass a taste. When a tumbler has been used for milk or any other liquid of a greasy nature, it should be filled with cold water as soon as possible to prevent the grease sinking into the glass and making it troublesome to wash.

Wine-glasses should be treated in the same way as tumblers, only the greatest care must be taken in the drying, because of the slender stems.

If a little vinegar is added occasionally to the water in which table glass is rinsed, it will give it an extra brightness.

Moulded or Cut-glass Dishes.—When washing these use a light lather of soap and warm water, and a few drops of ammonia as well, if the articles are very dirty. A soft brush, too, will be found useful for removing any dust or dirt from the crevices. Always rinse well in clear cold water to remove all trace of soap, and dry and polish as before.

Water-bottles and Decanters.—When these become stained or discoloured, they may be treated in one of the following ways :—Fill the bottle half-full of warm soapy water, and put in some pieces of brown paper, some tea-leaves or small pieces of raw potato ; let it soak for some time, shaking it occasionally, then pour out, rinse and drain. Crushed egg-shells or fine ashes used along with a little soap are also very good. If none of these are enough to remove the discoloration, try vinegar and coarse salt— one part salt to two parts vinegar, undiluted with water (this can be used more than once);

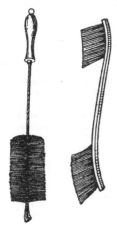

allow them to remain some hours in the bottle, then pour out and rinse and dry as before. Sometimes a brush is an assistance in the washing of decanters.

If the *stoppers* become fixed in wine decanters, it is a good plan to pour a few drops of oil round the neck and place the decanter near the fire, and in a short time try to loosen it gently; if it still sticks, wash it in warm water and repeat the process.

Sometimes a few gentle taps with another stopper will help to loosen the fixed one. Glycerine, too, is a good thing to use instead of oil.

Bottle-Brushes.

Flower Vases should be washed inside with a small brush, and if stained, treated in the same way as decanters.

TO WASH CHINA AND OTHER DISHES

Tea Dishes.—If these are in daily use, it will be sufficient to wash them in hot water with a soft dish-cloth; rinse in cold or tepid water and dry with a fine towel. If the water is very hard, a little borax or soap-powder may be added to it, but soda must never be used for fine-coloured china, and especially if there is any gilt on it. Excessive rubbing, too, must be avoided when finely painted china is under treatment. The water must not be used too hot, and the china should not be put in until the heat has been tested with the hand. If the water is too hot for the hand to rest in, it is too hot for the china. Commence with the cups, then the saucers, and lastly the plates and any jugs or basins. Particular attention must be given to the handles of cups and jugs to see that they are clean.

Care, too, must be taken in the drying of fine china; it will require very gentle handling.

Tea stains may be removed from cups and teapots by rubbing them with a little common salt, or by rubbing a little Brook's soap on a flannel, and then applying it to the mark. This will also remove burnt stains from meat-dishes or pie-dishes.

China Ornaments which are washed only occasionally will require a little more rubbing, and the addition of soap to the water will be a necessity. A soft brush will also be found useful when washing any intricate parts. After washing, rinse well; drain, dry, and polish with a chamois leather.

Dinner Dishes.—As these are stronger and generally more greasy than other china, the addition of a little soda to the water in which they are washed will be advisable, except in the case of gilded ware, when borax or soap-powder must be used instead.

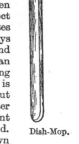

When using soda in the water, it is a good plan to use a small mop instead of a cloth to wash with; the hands will not then require to come into such direct contact with the water. Plates and other dishes must always be washed on both sides, and must always be rinsed in clean cold or tepid water before being put aside to drain. If there is a rack, the plates may be put straight out of the rinsing water into that, and a certain amount of drying will thus be saved. They should be taken down

Dish-Mop.

when dry, and rubbed over lightly with a clean dry cloth to give them a polish.

THE CARE OF KNIVES AND STEEL FORKS

Soiled knives must never be put into a basin or tub of hot water and allowed to soak, as this would melt the cement or glue in the handles, and cause the blades to come apart.

Stand them blade downwards in a knife-washer or jug with sufficient hot water to reach just up to the handles, and add a small piece of soda. Allow them to soak for some little time, then wipe them well, handle and blade, with a dish-cloth, and dry them carefully with a towel or coarse cloth kept for the purpose. If an ordinary towel is used, the greatest care must be taken that the knives do not cut it, as this accounts for many holes which appear far too soon in kitchen and pantry towels.

With regard to polishing the knives, this can be done either on a board or in a knife-cleaning machine. These latter can now be bought for a few shillings, and they are certainly a great saving of labour, but care must be taken in their use. The knives must in all cases be put in clean and free from grease, and the machine must be turned gently and not more than is necessary. If the knife-board is used it is a good plan to remove the worst stains from the knives, and especially from the points, before beginning to rub them on the board. This may be done either with a piece of raw potato dipped in bath-brick dust or knife-powder and rubbed on the knife, or with a piece of cork used in the same way. This will lessen the rubbing considerably and lessen the wear and tear of the knife. Then sprinkle the knife-board with a little of the powder, and rub the knife quickly and lightly backwards and forwards on this. Any pressure must be brought to bear on the back of the knife rather than on the sharp edge, and the point must never be rubbed down. The knives must finally be well dusted to free them from all powder, and must be kept in a dry place.

Should the ivory or bone handles of knives become stained or discoloured, they may be improved by rubbing them with a cut lemon and a little dry salt, or vinegar and salt, then wipe off with a damp flannel and dry. Fine emery powder moistened with a little water and applied with a flannel is also a good thing to use for stains.

When knives are not to be used for some time, it is a good plan to rub the blades with sweet oil and then to roll them, one by one, in a piece of flannel or felt, and in such a way that they do not touch each other. This is especially necessary in damp districts, because if once rust is allowed to attack the steel the appearance of the knife is spoilt.

Steel Forks must be treated in the same way as knives, only instead of rubbing them on the board apply the knife-powder or bath-brick with a piece of flannel. Particular care must be taken to dust well between the prongs.

THE CARE OF LAMPS AND OIL-HEATING STOVES

If lamps are used in a household, the care of them should be in the hands of one person, and unless there is a capable maid who has time to devote herself to the work, it is really better for the mistress to undertake this duty herself. The value of a lamp depends upon its being properly attended to, and if it is allowed to smoke and smell, it is not only worse than useless, as far as light is concerned, but there is nothing more disagreeable.

To begin with, lamps must be cleaned and filled by daylight, as there is always a certain amount of danger in working with oil by artificial light. Needless to say, this must not be done on the kitchen table, nor where any fine work is in progress, as lamp-oil stains are very difficult to eradicate. If a small table cannot be reserved for the purpose, then the best plan is to use an old tray or a piece of thick mill-board.

A lamp in daily use should be filled three parts full every morning, as it is dangerous to use when the oil is very low in the reservoir or container. The oil should be poured in by means of a feeder, and not from the can itself, for in the latter case it would be apt to come

out by jerks and be spilt over, or the lamp would be made too full. It is very important also to use oil of a good quality. In fact, it is no economy to buy cheap oil, as it not only gives an inferior light and burns more quickly, but it is also more dangerous to use. Good oil should give a white light, have no smell, and be as clear as water.

Then with regard to the wick; it is of the utmost importance that this fits the burner well, and it should be just long enough to reach the bottom of the reservoir. A wick should last for three months, after that time it is best to renew it, when the end to be lighted should be dipped in the oil first. As a rule the wick should not require cutting, but should be turned low and the uneven charred part gently rubbed off with a piece of card-board and the surface made smooth with the top of the tubes. If it still remains uneven, it may then be trimmed carefully with a pair of lamp scissors. After this any black pieces of wick must be removed from the burner, and the outside of the lamp rubbed first with a piece of newspaper and then a soft rag, until free from oil.

From time to time, both the reservoir and the burner will require to be thoroughly cleaned. The reservoir should be emptied of all oil and washed out with warm suds to which a few drops of ammonia have been added. Rinse thoroughly, and then turn upside down in a warm place to dry. When the burner becomes clogged and dirty, it should be taken to pieces (care being taken to notice how it is fixed together), and put into an old saucepan with a lump of soda and enough cold water to cover it. Bring to the boil, and boil for half-an-hour. Then rinse in warm water, and use a brush if necessary to remove any charred wick. When quite clean place in a warm place, or a cool oven to dry. The lamp must not be refilled until both reservoir and burner are quite dry, or the oil will splutter.

Pains must be taken to keep both the chimney glass and the globe very clean and bright. The chimney should never be washed, but may be cleaned with lamp-brushes, or a pad of chamois leather or felt fastened to a stick. The Selvyt lamp-cleaner is a most useful article for this purpose. If the glass becomes marked or very much soiled, a little methylated spirits may be used to remove the stains. The outer globe should be dusted every day and occasionally washed in warm water with a little soap, then rinsed and dried with a glass-cloth.

If a lamp burns badly or smells, it is generally due to one of the following causes :—

(1) It has been filled too full, and the oil when heated expands and runs over the sides.

(2) The receiver and burner have not been wiped after filling.

(3) The wick does not fit properly, or it has been badly trimmed.

(4) Inferior oil has been used.

(5) The lamp-glasses are not clean.

When lighting the lamp, turn up the wick only slightly and keep it burning low until the chimney is thoroughly heated; then turn it up as far as it will go without smoking.

When not in use the wick must be kept low, otherwise the oil oozes up through it and over the sides.

To extinguish a lamp (if there in no patent extinguisher attached), turn down the wick until it is level with the tube, and blow quickly across the top of the chimney.

The best lamps are fitted with a patent burner which permits of the lamp being blown out with safety, or, if overturned, will extinguish itself at once. Should an accident, however, happen and the oil be spilt and catch fire, it must be remembered that water poured over it would only spread the flame. The best thing to do is to throw sand or earth on the burning oil, or to smother the flame with a thick rug. Door and window should immediately be shut.

The same remarks apply to the keeping of oil-stoves. It is almost impossible to prevent their smelling a little, but with proper care this smell should be so reduced as to be almost imperceptible.

TO CLEAN BOOTS

Boots should never be cleaned when damp. If they have been brought in very muddy, they should be wiped with a damp flannel or a small wet brush. Then put on to boot-trees, or if these are not available, stuff the inside with some crumpled newspaper, and this will help to keep the boots in good shape. Never put boots close to the fire to dry, as too rapid drying will harden, and perhaps crack the leather. It is much better if they can be allowed to dry slowly in a warm atmosphere. If the leather should become hard, a little vaseline or sweet oil may be applied. This should be rubbed well in and then off again with a piece of flannel.

It is very important that the inside of boots should be kept clean during the process of cleaning. For this reason it is a good plan to cover the hand that is placed inside the boot with a clean duster. Gloves, too, should be worn to protect the hands. Thanks to the many good boot polishes which can now be obtained, the old-fashioned liquid blacking, which was liable to be splashed or spilt where it was not wanted, is now a thing of the past, and boot-cleaning may be quite a clean and tidy occupation. So much so that many ladies who do not keep a lady's-maid prefer to clean their own shoes, and especially those of a fine quality. In fact all the necessary requisites can be kept in a very small tin box, and cause no inconvenience anywhere.

First remove all dust or mud with a brush—then with a piece of flannel or an old stocking-leg, apply a little boot-polish, rubbing it well in and all over the boot, not forgetting the heels and the back part. Then polish with a polishing-pad; one covered with velvet or selvyt cloth is best.

When boots are new and they are found difficult to polish, a few drops of paraffin added to the paste will be found a help.

Brown Boots should be cleaned in the same way, using brown boot-polish instead of black, or the ordinary bees'-wax and turpentine (see p. 66) does very well. Stains may be removed with lemon-juice or methylated spirits, or with the inside of a banana skin.

Patent Leather Boots require rather different treatment. Wipe them first with a damp sponge and dry them. Then rub over with a flannel dipped in a little milk. When the leather becomes shabby it is better to use one of the special polishes sold for the purpose at any bootmakers; or a small quantity of vaseline well rubbed in will keep them soft and bright. The edges of the soles should be blackened.

White Shoes.—Those made of canvas or drill should be cleaned with pipeclay or whitening mixed to a creamy consistency with cold water, then applied evenly with a sponge or piece of soft rag. Place the shoes in the sun to dry, and then lightly brush off any superfluous powder. White kid shoes should be cleaned with a special dressing sold for the purpose.

CARE OF BRUSHES

House Brushes should all be soaked in cold water for some hours, and then well dried before they are used. This prevents the hairs or bristles from coming out, and increases the durability of the brush.

When house-brooms and such-like become dirty, they should be washed. Put a little boiling water in a pail, and add a handful of soda to it. Then pour in cold or tepid water until the pail is three parts full. Take the brushes one at a time, carefully remove from them all fluff, thread ends, hairs, &c., and work them up and down in the soda-water. Rinse thoroughly in cold water and shake well to get rid of as much moisture as possible. Dry in the open air or hang up in a warm atmosphere.

Brushes should never be left lying or standing on their bristles. Small brushes can be hung up, and the longer brooms should be kept in a rack. No pieces of wool nor fluffy matter should be left sticking to the bristles.

It is also very important that brushes be kept for the special purpose for which they are intended, and not used for all and sundry purposes.

EXTERMINATION OF PESTS

Beetles.—These objectionable insects infest usually the ground floor and kitchen premises of houses. They disappear in the daytime and come out at night through the cracks in the flooring, and they multiply so rapidly that

Brush-Rack.

sometimes they can be counted by the thousand. They will attack food of all kinds, and the leather of boots and shoes; in fact, everything that comes in their way.

Many different kinds of traps have been invented, and they all serve their purpose for the time being, but one of the safest and surest methods of extermination is the use of " Blatol." Spread this paste upon pieces of thick paper about three or four inches square. Lay these at night in the places most frequented by the beetles. Remove the papers in the morning and burn them. Lay fresh papers with the paste every night for a week, or more, then every second or third night until all the beetles have disappeared. The " Blatol " so effectively destroys them, and at the same time so completely dries them up, that their dead bodies do not emit the slightest smell.

Fleas.—Strict cleanliness, good ventilation and plenty of light and sunshine are the greatest enemies of this kind of pest. Fleas flourish in warmth, dirt and darkness; these are just the conditions which favour their development.

If a bed becomes infested, the best thing is to have the mattress brought out into the sunshine and thoroughly brushed. The blankets, too, should have the same treatment. Then the bedstead itself should be well washed with carbolic soap and water, and also the flooring under the

bed. Throw the windows of the room well open and let it be thoroughly aired. Various powders are also used for the destruction of fleas, and most of these contain the plant substance " Pyrethrum," which has accordingly been popularly known as " Fleabane." This can be bought in powder form from any chemist, and other ready-made insect powders can also be obtained. Lumps of camphor laid between the bedclothes, or carried in a small muslin bag on the person, is also a preventive, but the chief destroyer of all is cleanliness.

Moths.—It is very important that all moths on the wing should be destroyed as soon as they are seen. They lay their eggs in all kinds of woollen materials, carpets, blankets and bedding, upholstered furniture, &c.

Any article that is likely to be attacked should be brushed frequently, and special attention should be paid to them in the month of September, which is about the time when the eggs are laid, and then again in the month of March, when the insect is still in a dormant state.

Care, too, must be taken of woollen things that are laid away for any length of time. They should be well brushed, and then folded up in a newspaper or sewn into cotton with something aromatic, such as cloves, caraway seeds, camphor, naphtha balls, or sprigs of the common bog myrtle put between the folds of the material as preventive. The moths seem to dislike the printer's ink on the newspaper, and they won't eat through cotton. When a mattress or piece of upholstered furniture is once really attacked by moths it will require to be sent away to be professionally stoved and cleaned.

Bugs.—These are rarely found in clean and well-kept houses, although occasionally through accident they may be introduced. They must be attacked at once, as they breed very rapidly. Whenever their presence is noticed in a bedroom, the bedding must have the most careful attention. The mattress should be well brushed, and especially in the corners and crevices, where eggs may possibly be laid. Then the bedstead itself should be taken to pieces, thoroughly washed with hot water and carbolic or paraffin soap. When dry, paint it over with turpentine and allow it to air. Any woodwork too that seems to be infested should be painted over with turpentine.

A formaline lamp left burning in the room is very good for fumigating.

Mice.—The best plan is to starve them out. All eatables should be enclosed, and nothing left uncovered that would supply them with food. A cat or small dog which is a good mouser are also preventives. A trap, too, is often very effectual in catching a stray mouse here and there, and in frightening away others. There are many different kinds, but perhaps the old-fashioned make, which catches the animal alive, are the most humane; others, which are supposed to kill instantaneously, often succeed in only half doing it, and so causing unnecessary suffering.

There are different poisons too which can be bought for the destruction of mice, of which phosphorus paste is perhaps the best; but care must be taken in using them, and especially if there are domestic animals in the house.

Rats.—When rats enter a house, it is often a sign of insanitary drainage, and if that is the case the wrong must be seen to at once, and the necessary repairs carried out. Or it may be that the house is in the close proximity to a stable, and the rats have made their way into the house through some holes. A trap is sometimes of good service for catching the rats, and directions for baiting them are usually given with each special kind. Poisoning is another method; but this must be done with caution, and especially if there are any domestic animals in the house. Another danger of poisoning is that the dead bodies of the rats sometimes decompose under the flooring, and cause a very bad smell. A small dog, a terrier, sometimes keeps them away most effectively.

If the rats become numerous, a rat-catcher should be employed, who will hunt the rats out with trained ferrets. When once the vermin have been got rid of, all holes by which they have entered should be carefully filled up with cement or plaster.

Flies.—When flies are numerous, it is a good plan to wash the windows and window ledges with a strong solution of carbolic, or if the smell is an objection, sprinkle with Persian powder at night, and then sweep up in the morning. Fly-papers will also catch a number, but they are rather disgusting things to use. They should if possible be put in out-of-the-way places, such as the tops of cupboards. A very simple fly-paper can be made by spreading treacle or honey on brown paper, and sprinkling it with Persian powder or other insect poison. Fly-papers prepared with some sticky substance to which the flies adhere and endure a slow torturing death should be avoided. Another good way of getting rid of flies when they become numerous is to disinfect the room with sulphur.

The blow-fly, which is larger than the common house-fly, is the kind most to be dreaded, as it is a great enemy in the larder. It frequently lays its larvæ in meat, which causes it to decompose very quickly. In hot weather all meat should be examined when it is received, and if anything is suspected, it should be carefully washed with a solution of Condy's fluid and water. The proportions to use will be found printed on the bottle. The meat should then be well sprinkled with pepper or other spice, which will help to keep the flies away. It is a good plan to fasten a piece of muslin or fine gauze over the larder window to prevent the flies entering.

Ants.—These are very troublesome creatures to get rid of when once they infest a house, and sometimes different remedies have to be tried before one succeeds. One of the best is to find the opening through which the ants come, drop in some quicklime, and wash it over with boiling water. A strong solution of carbolic acid or spirits of camphor might also be tried, as ants are very averse to strong smells. Or, again, some petroleum or tobacco juice poured over their nests is sometimes effectual.

SPRING CLEANING

Every year, as soon as the cold days of winter are over, and the promise of fine weather bids fair to be realised, the thoughts of the busy housewife turn towards preparations for the inevitable "Spring Clean." There are still some people who look upon this yearly cleaning as a perfectly unnecessary fetish before which the housewife bows down in deference to a mere time-honoured tradition. This point of view is erroneous, and those who share it show but little knowledge of the art of housewifery. However clean a house is kept, and however regularly the various rooms go through their daily and weekly cleaning, it is always necessary to have a special cleaning from cellar to garret once a year at least. This is not intended to take the place of the daily or weekly cleaning, but rather to supplement it, and to give an opportunity of attending to such matters as can most conveniently be seen to at this season, when all necessary renovation, papering and whitewashing can also be undertaken.

This annual cleaning need not necessarily take place in the *spring*—the time may be arranged according to the convenience of the household; but spring is the season which appeals to most people as being the most natural time for having a good "turn out." After a long winter, things have put on a dark and dingy appearance, and seem very much out of keeping with the fine weather and the bright sunshine. There is a desire to get rid of all dark curtains and other hangings that have been in use all through the wintry months of the year, and to replace them with something light and pretty, and to give things generally a fresher appearance.

The best time for this cleaning is the beginning of May, when fires are required less regularly, and the weather is likely to remain fine. If, however, the autumn or summer suits the arrangements of the household better, it is by no means necessary to adhere to any rigid rule.

A spring cleaning may be hard work while it lasts—a few days of undesirable toil; but there is another side to the picture. What a feeling of satisfaction and air of content there is when all is accomplished, and how fresh and bright the rooms look after they have had their yearly overhauling, and put on their spring dress.

The spring is also the time to see to any repairs and renovations, as, for instance, the re-covering of any furniture which has grown shabby, the re-gilding of any picture-frames which require it, the mending of all locks and door-handles, and so on. Then a new shelf or cupboard might be put up here and there, and any little additions made which might add to the comfort of the home. Deficiencies in stock, too, should be replenished, broken and cracked dishes discarded or given away, and numbers and sets of things made up as completely as possible, so that the work of the house may start anew with a sufficiency of materials and implements.

Importance of Method. — In former times the advent of the annual spring cleaning was looked upon with positive terror by the unfortunate householder. To him it represented a period when he would return home from his hard daily work in the city to find a tired, untidy-looking, cross-tempered wife, furniture heaped pell-mell in all the passages, pails of water and scrubbing brushes at every turn, and curl-papers bristling in the hair, and a liberal display of smuts upon the face of " Mary Jane." His evening meal, more often than not, would have to be taken haphazard in the kitchen, where pots and pans and other culinary paraphernalia in the various stages of the cleaning process would not add to the comfort of his surroundings. Small blame to the man who under these circumstances would seek refuge in the comfort and cheerful society to be found at his club !

In these days of up-to-date cleaning contrivances such a state of affairs should be inexcusable, yet in many houses to-day the words " Spring Cleaning " and " Discomfort " are still synonymous. The extent to which cleaning becomes a nuisance depends very much upon the way in which the work is performed. Some system should be decided on beforehand, and a haphazard way of doing things must be avoided. By the exercise of a little foresight much time and worry may be saved, and method, organisation and thoroughness will bring the work to a speedy conclusion. For instance, if painters, joiners, plumbers, or any other workmen are likely to be required, they ought to be engaged in good time ; the services of the sweep too must be retained, and if extra help is required, a charwoman must be engaged.

Before the work is started in real earnest, the housewife should make sure that she has in stock a good supply of all the necessary cleaning materials, such as carbolic soap, soft soap, soda, soap-powder, borax, ammonia, methylated spirits, bees'-wax, &c., and also a sufficiency of towels, cloths, dusters and brushes to carry on the work. Of course the ideal way to do a spring cleaning is to have the house emptied of all its occupants, except only those who are taking part in the work. Then the correct order in which to do it would be to commence at the top of the house, and to work downwards, beginning with the lumber-room, if there is one, then the bedrooms, next the sitting-rooms, bath-room and lavatory, finishing with the kitchen, cellars, and any outhouses. In the case of a flat a different order may perhaps be taken. If this ideal plan cannot be followed, then it is best to do the cleaning by degrees, and not to plunge the whole house into discomfort by undertaking the whole performance at once. In fact, some mistresses find it more convenient to clean half the house in the spring and the other half in the autumn, or even to clean only a single room now and again. In this way it does not seem such a formidable undertaking for servants.

Each day's work should be carefully planned. Too much must not be undertaken at a time, but only what can be done without undue effort. There is never anything to be gained by over-taxing one's strength. A point should be made of having comfortable meals served all the time, as without this the end of each day would simply mean exhaustion.

There will be a great saving of time when the actual cleaning begins if all cupboards and drawers can be turned out beforehand. When they have been emptied of their contents, the insides should be scrubbed out with carbolic soap and warm water, and then left some time to air. Meanwhile the contents should be looked over, and all rubbish disposed of. The remainder should then be dusted, brushed or washed, according to the nature of the various articles, and put in good order. Then the shelves and drawers should be neatly lined with clean paper, and the contents put back in an orderly fashion. Any winter coats or dresses which are not likely to be required for some time should be well brushed, and if possible hung in the open air for some hours ; then carefully stored with some preparation which will keep the moth away. (See p. 314.) Winter curtains should undergo the same treatment.

Books, and book-cases too, and stands with music, should all be cleaned and sorted out beforehand, and any magazines or pamphlets that are of no further service destroyed, or sent to some hospital for the use of the patients.

Spring Cleaning a Bedroom.—The first thing to do before having a room spring cleaned is to make it as empty as possible. If it is a bedroom, the bedding should first be seen to. All the coverings, including the covers of mattress and pillows, should be sent either to be cleaned or washed. Then if there is a garden to which things can be taken easily, everything which requires shaking and brushing should be taken outside, such as mattress, pillows, cushions, rugs, upholstered chairs (unless too heavy to be moved), &c.; and after they have been cleaned either left in the open air or in an adjoining passage until the room is ready to receive them.

All pictures, ornaments, and small articles of furniture should be dusted before they are removed from the room, to avoid having dust carried to another part of the house; and that which must be left because of its size or weight must be dusted first, and then carefully covered. If there is a nailed-down carpet, this must be lifted, and folded up carefully to prevent the dust flying about, and then taken away to be cleaned or beaten. The floor should then be sprinkled with a little wet saw-dust or bran, swept with a soft brush, and the dust burnt at once.

Should the chimney require sweeping, this should now be done, the sweep having been engaged beforehand. It is well also to see that the work is properly carried out, and that the brushes have been carried up the whole length of the chimney.

When this is finished, the room is now ready for any papering and painting that may be required, and must perforce be left in the painters' hands until their work is completed. If nothing of this kind is necessary, the cleaning must be done in the following order :—First, get rid of all dust by dusting all walls, curtain poles, blinds, and woodwork; secondly, black-lead and polish the grate; and thirdly, do all the washing that is required, such as woodwork, marble, furniture, including windows, bedsteads, floors, &c. Then the room ought to be left to air and dry with door and window wide open.

Meanwhile the articles of furniture, &c., outside can have attention, and as far as possible everything should be cleaned before it is brought back into the room. When everything is dry, all necessary polishing should be done. Pictures can then be re-hung, and everything as far as possible returned to its proper place. The carpet should of course be re-laid as soon as it is ready; only if this has been sent to the cleaners, it may be necessary to wait for two or three days.

Fresh curtains should then be put up, clean chair-covers, and cushion-covers where they are needed, and dainty touches given to make everything look pretty.

A Sitting-room.—The order in which a sitting-room is " spring cleaned " would be very much the same as that followed for a bedroom (with the exception of the bed), but there will probably be more furniture and odds and ends to attend to.

Hall, Staircase and Bath-room.—It is always well to leave the staircase and bath-room until all the other rooms are finished, as there will of necessity be more tramping up and down the former while the cleaning is going on, and the latter has frequently to be used for the washing of ornaments, bedroom ware, &c. The walls of the bath-room should always be of a washable nature, and then the cleaning is a very easy matter, as it simply means that every part must be washed from the top downwards, finishing with the floor. If the bath itself has become very shabby

it should be re-enamelled. This can be done at home, although as a rule home enamelling is not very satisfactory, and if the extra expense can be afforded, it is much better to have it done by a skilled workman. When the washing is finished, the door and window should be left open to dry and air the room, and then the polishing of brasses, woodwork and floor should be undertaken.

The hall and staircase is a more difficult undertaking. The rugs and stair-carpets having been removed, and all pictures, &c., taken from the walls and moved out of the way, the first thing to see to will be the cleaning of the walls. If they are very high, it is scarcely work that can be undertaken by maid-servants, especially if the walls require washing; if it is simply a matter of dusting them down with a long broom, it may be possible. The stairs, railings, and banisters must next be well brushed and washed, and also the floor of the hall and any passages. Wash also any pieces of furniture that require it, including gas globes, flower-pots and ornaments. Next polish all woodwork, stair-rods, brasses and furniture, and lay the carpet and rugs last of all.

The Housemaid's Pantry.—In a well-appointed house where there are several servants there is generally a small room set aside for the housemaid's requirements. It is usually upstairs in close proximity to the bedrooms. This little

Housemaid's Box.

room should contain all that the housemaid will require for cleaning purposes. (See list on page 83.)

It should be fitted up with a sink and be supplied with hot and cold water. There should also be a shelf at a convenient height for holding hot-water cans, hot-water bottles, dust-sheets, &c., and, if room, a rack for hanging brushes and a small pulley or towel-rail for drying the various cloths. It will also be convenient to have a small cupboard in which cleaning materials could be kept in jars, also paper and sticks for lighting fires. A small solid table would also be most useful if space permits, as on this the housemaid could do any special cleaning of silver or brass required for the bedrooms and also the brushing of clothes that come under her care. A few hooks should be put up along the edge of the shelf and at the sink, as they will be found handy for hanging up small articles, such as taper-holder, bottle brushes, sink brush, tin jug, &c.

The following is a list of the articles which the housemaid's pantry might contain :—

A housemaid's box, a slop-pail, a pail for housework, a pair of steps, a kneeling-mat, a dust-pan, hot-water cans, hot-water bottles, a large can for carrying water, a tin jug, a soap-dish.

Brushes.—A carpet switch, a long broom, a small short-handled broom, a banister brush, a wall-broom, a carpet-sweeper, a furniture brush, boot brushes, black-lead brushes, two scrubbing brushes, a bottle brush, hearth brush, clothes' brush.

Cleaning Materials, &c.—Washing soda, Brook's soap or Sapolio, yellow soap, polishing paste, furniture polish, boot polish, turpentine, ammonia, bees'-wax, coarse salt, emery paper, black-lead, paper and sticks, or fire-lighters, matches, taper in holder.

Towels, &c. — Dusters, glass towels, slop-cloths, washing cloth, swabs, coarse towels for drying floors, &c., old soft towels for drying paint, two chamois leathers, pieces of flannel for cleaning purposes, dust sheets, hearth cloth, grate cloths, a pair of gloves.

A REMOVAL

Introductory.—Thanks to modern enterprise on the part of removal contractors, this does not require to be the dreaded affair it was in days gone by. Although a removal is undeniably somewhat of an undertaking, it can be robbed of many of its terrors if it is put into the hands of a reliable firm, and the preliminaries are arranged with some thought and care.

Of course, if money is no object, it is quite possible to step out of the old house in the morning and spend the day enjoyably in town, or with friends, and to walk into the new home in the evening to find there that one's belongings have been bodily transported and placed in position, leaving very little to be done except the arrangement of personal belongings to one's own liking, and other small details.

But this expeditious and easy way of managing the business means money, and we are not all lavishly endowed with this world's riches. People of modest means must be prepared to buckle to when such an important affair as a removal is on hand, and undertake some of the work and arranging themselves.

Thought, advice and experience can, however, do much to lessen discomfort, and prevent chaos, and the more carefully the order of the removal is planned the easier the change of house will be.

Making the Contract.—The first point to decide is how the furniture has to be removed, and by whom. It is always best to choose ex-perienced removers, for although the initial expense may appear more, the ultimate saving in the avoidance of breakages and kindred annoyances is unquestionable. It is better, if possible, to choose a firm near at hand, who will send a representative to look at the things and furnish an estimate free of charge. He will also tell you what arrangements it is necessary to make, and what preliminaries must be attended to. Removals can now be conducted to all parts of the United Kingdom in vans of the most improved construction (pantechnicons), and all risks and responsibilities are undertaken. The charge will depend on the quantity and quality of the furniture, and upon the distance it has to be moved.

Preliminaries in the Old House.—Before the actual removal takes place there are certain preliminaries which must be attended to, both in the old house and in the new.

One very important point to attend to before leaving the old house is to turn out all the rubbish. Clothes that are of no further use, broken and hoarded crockery, damaged and soiled knick-knacks, old saucepans and kettles, empty bottles and jam-pots, all should be disposed of ; in fact everything should be done to avoid the carriage of dirt and worthless stuff. Old papers should, however, be kept, as these will be found useful when packing.

Then all the furniture should be sorted out and considered with a view to its place in the new abode, and that which is unsuitable should be sold or otherwise disposed of. It sometimes happens that an incoming tenant will only be too pleased to buy odds and ends of furniture, and even a carpet or two.

Furniture which requires repairing, cleaning or re-covering, and pictures requiring new frames or re-gilding, should be sent away to have the necessary attention, and not returned until the new house is ready to receive them. The decoration and colouring of the new house must of course be borne in mind when choosing any new upholstery, and shades must be chosen which will tone well with the new surroundings.

All carpets should be lifted and sent away to be beaten or cleaned, according to what is necessary. Curtains, too, which require cleaning or dyeing, and any heavy extra washing, such as bed-covers, spare blankets, &c., should be sent from the old house, and returned to the new, as in this way some of the removal expenses will be saved.

Of course this means a certain amount of dismantling beforehand, but upon the whole it is better to have the discomfort before the removal rather than after it has taken place. Once in the new quarters one is naturally anxious to get settled as quickly as possible, and it is annoying to have to wait for this or that to arrive upon the scene.

Preliminaries in the New House.—The business

of a removal can be very much simplified if one can obtain possession of the new house some time before it is necessary to move into it. The house can then be made ready, and entered with comfort.

First of all, every chimney should be swept. Then whatever whitewashing, papering or painting that is necessary should be done. It is fortunate for a new tenant when the landlord undertakes to do up the house throughout, and will give the choice of papers and colouring.

When the workmen have finished, it will next be necessary to have all the floors scrubbed with carbolic soap, soda and a brush, and under no circumstances should one be satisfied with the superficial cleaning given by the painters, or even by the late tenants. Grates and windows can then be cleaned, and if it is winter time, coal should be ordered in and fires put on so as to thoroughly dry and air the rooms. The lighting and heating arrangements should be carefully tested and necessary alterations made, as it is most annoying later on to have to disturb carpets or linoleum for the sake of laying a new gas-pipe or an electric wire. The water-pipes and taps should also be seen to, and the cistern thoroughly cleaned out.

Then the question of floor covering should be considered. It is an immense help if all linoleum and any nailed-down carpets can be laid before the furniture is brought in. This is really the secret of being quickly settled. When once the carpets and linoleum are satisfactorily laid, then the furniture can be brought in with the happy feeling that it will not require to be moved again. Besides, it is much easier to fit and lay down a large carpet in an empty room than it is when heavy furniture has to be lifted and moved from one place to another. Of course, if the carpets consist merely of small squares or large rugs, it would be wiser to defer laying them until later on in the proceedings. Linoleum in any case, and especially that which surrounds a room, should be put in position previous to the moving in of the furniture.

Then with regard to curtains and blinds, if any of these can be put up beforehand, it will greatly add to the comfort of the first few days, even although the old house has to be robbed of them a trifle sooner in consequence.

Packing.—While years ago it was deemed necessary to pack all furniture, to tie wisps of straw round the legs of tables and chairs, and even sew each article into a sheet of sacking in order to preserve it from ill-treatment, now one can confidently leave the tables, chairs, and such-like to the removal men, who are in most cases trained specialists to the work. The large vans, or pantechnicons, take most things, and especially the heavier articles of furniture, just as they are. It is also better to leave the packing of glass, china, and other breakables to the men, who will

bring the necessary crates and straw for the purpose. They will be much more likely to avoid breakages than any amateur packer, however careful he (or she) may be. It must be remembered too, that a removal contractor can only be held responsible for things he has packed himself, and not for those packed by the owner.

Of course there are always a few things which can be packed beforehand, and if all small things can be stowed away in portable cases, the actual removal is done in a very short time. Books, for instance, can be safely packed; they should be dusted first, and then put in cases lined with paper. Any precious volumes with fine or delicate bindings should be wrapped separately in paper, in order to prevent them from being scratched or rubbed. In the case of large heavy books, it is better to make them up in bundles, and put a piece of cord round them. If they have a valuable binding, they can be wrapped in paper as well. The packages must not be made too heavy. Music too may be tied up in the same way.

Clothing and personal belongings should also be packed. These will go very well in boxes and drawers. The latter can quite well be utilised, as the men simply carry out the different pieces of the chest, and put them in position again in the van, and nothing can come to harm. A towel or large cover should be laid over the contents and well tucked in. Household linen should be packed away in the same manner. If there is no room for blankets and eider-downs, they can be made into a bale which can easily be lifted. Silver and other valuables should be put in a chest, and securely fastened.

The Removing.—This should always be commenced early in the morning, at six o'clock in the summer, and at eight o'clock in the winter at the very latest. Although everything may be left to the workmen, as a rule, it is better for the members of the household to take a share in order to expedite matters. In fact, if the removal is to be got over rapidly, the only way is for each one to give assistance where he or she can.

Beds and bedding should always be sent in the first van, and placed where they will come to hand easily at the other end. Things should, as far as possible, leave the old house and arrive at the new in the sequence in which it is most convenient to handle them.

As soon as the packing into the van is well on its way, a responsible person should, if possible, act as pioneer and start for the new house, so as to be on the spot when the first van arrives to direct the carrying in of the furniture. If this cannot be done, then each piece of furniture should be marked, or labelled, so as to indicate the room for which it is destined. As far as possible, each article should be carried to its own room and nowhere else; and in fact it may, in many cases, be actually put down in its proper place.

A strip of coarse matting should be laid over each carpet, to prevent the men's feet making marks.

It is a good plan to get every bed that is to be slept in put up and made early in the evening, and then, even if it is ten o'clock before the last vanful of furniture is unloaded, one can shut the door and feel that at least a place of repose is secure. Otherwise, one is inclined to go on working at other things until a late hour, when there is little strength left to make a bed far less put one together.

The question of refreshment on the day of removal is also an important one. It is often a saving of time if the men can be provided with a lunch of bread and cheese, and beer or coffee ; and if it is intimated to them beforehand that this will be ready at a certain hour, it will save their time going off to some public-house in order to get refreshments.

A good tea at the other end should also be provided, if at all possible.

For the members of the family, cold refreshments, supplemented by hot drink, must suffice, and those who are not strong enough to support this frugal régime should be out of the way, if possible, on the removal day. Of course it sometimes happens that kind friends come forward and invite the party to a comfortable meal, and this of course is an untold blessing, not only from the point of view of the mere food question, but in regard to the respite afforded from the bustle and hurry of the day's work. Then at the other end, if a maid can be sent over in good time to light a fire and take a picnic basket with her with necessaries for tea, this little meal will prove a comfortable welcome to the new home.

Settling Down.—As soon as the bedrooms have been put fairly straight, it is perhaps best to give one's first attention to the sitting-rooms and kitchen, as when once these are in order and meals can be served with comfort, the worst of the removal is practically over.

The stair carpet and hall rugs should be put down last of all, when all the carrying and extra walking backwards and forwards is at an end.

Then there will no doubt be extra furniture required, and additions of various kinds to make, but it is just as well not to hurry the buying of new things, as it is much more easy to judge what is needed when everything is in its place, and one has been in the house for a few days.

It will of course be weeks before all the odds and ends are put finally in their places, but these trifles do not matter, and once the real work of removal is over and the new house begins to look ship-shape, it should only be a pleasure to arrange the various trifles and knick-knacks to one's liking.

SHUTTING UP A HOUSE

If a house has to be shut up for three months or longer, it is better to lift all carpets, and to take this opportunity of having them sent away to be cleaned or beaten. Take down all curtains and other hangings, shake them well and fold them up neatly. Remove all chair-covers, table-covers, antimacassars, &c., brush or shake them, and fold them up likewise. Keep the furniture as much as possible to the centre of the room, where it will be safe from damp or soot, and cover everything with dust-sheets or large sheets of paper. Any valuable pictures should either be taken down from the walls or covered with fine gauze or muslin, to preserve them from dust. Light and fragile articles, such as ornaments and clocks, should also be covered in this way.

All soiled linen should be collected and sent to the wash if possible.

Close and fasten all windows, and leave nothing open where rain can enter.

Grease any metal fenders or fire-irons with mutton fat, draw them away from the fire-place, and cover them over.

Turn off the gas from the main, and leave all waste-pipes connected with the water open.

No food must be left behind, which would be likely to smell or encourage mice and other vermin. Kitchen premises especially should be left well swept and as clean as possible.

All valuables, such as silver and jewels, should be packed in a strong box and sent to the bank.

Pull down all blinds, or if there is danger of their being spoilt with the sun, cover the windows with brown paper, fastening it up with strong drawing-pins. Close and bolt the shutters, and shut and lock all doors.

Notice should also be given to the police that the house is closed, and they will give it special attention.

WHAT TO DO IF FIRE OCCURS

Fire accidents, large or small, are liable to occur in every house, and one ought to be prepared to take the necessary precautions to prevent the spreading of the flames.

In the case of a partial fire, speedy action may be the means of putting it out at once. For instance, if a curtain catches fire, which frequently happens owing to its too close proximity to a gas-bracket, it should be pulled down quickly (provided the person who does so is clothed in a woollen dress), and the flames crushed out with a piece of carpet or a rug, or, if the damage has not gone very far, they might be beaten out with a rug or wet cloth.

A wet blanket or cloth is valuable for beating out flames wherever they are, or if the fire is on the ground water may be poured over it. A syphon of soda-water is also a good fire-extinguisher, and in the case of sudden fire, *fire grenades* are excellent, and no large household should be without them. All that is necessary is to break the glass globe and sprinkle the contents over the burning place.

Burning oil, as in the case of a lamp being overturned, should be extinguished by throwing sand, earth, or ashes over it. Water would only help to spread the flames.

If a person's clothing should catch fire the wearer ought to at once throw herself down on the floor and roll over and over, first wrapping herself in a rug or any other heavy woollen article if anything of the kind is handy. If, when the accident occurs, another person is present, the latter should endeavour to extinguish the flames by covering the victim with any heavy woollen articles in reach, pressing them well over her and forcing her to maintain a recumbent position. Heavy table-cloths are amongst the best things to smother the flames. It is a fatal thing for the burning person to rush out and call for help: as long as the upright position is retained the flames will spread, and it is always the face and upper parts which will be the most severely attacked.

In all cases of fire the doors and windows should be kept closed as much as possible, as any draught only helps to fan the flames; smoke follows the current of air, and flames follow the smoke.

If the fire is of a more serious nature, the alarm should be given at once and the fire-engines sent for. Every effort must be made to escape and to help others to escape by the first means of egress. If aroused at night to find the house on fire, wrap yourself in a blanket or rug and get out of the room at once. If the room is full of smoke tie a wet towel or handkerchief or even a wet stocking over the nose and mouth, and this will exclude the smoke and still permit of breathing. If the smoke is so dense that you are unable to stand upright, crawl along on the hands and knees, as the clearest air is always next the floor.

Should the ascent and descent of the stairs be impossible, try to make your way to the window of a front room and if there are others in the house try to get them to do likewise. Unless some one is in the burning room the door should not be opened, and no attempt must be made to extinguish the fire until life has been saved.

On no account should you throw yourself from the window, and if in extremity and no assistance is at hand tear up the sheets and tie the pieces together to form a rope, allowing good ends so that the knots will not slip. Fasten one end to a bedstead or other heavy piece of furniture near the window. Then slip the improvised rope out of the window and let yourself down hand under hand, taking advantage of the knots to keep yourself from slipping too quickly.

Those who are helpless to let themselves down should have the end of the sheet tied round their waist and be lowered through the window. A mattress should if possible be thrown out of the window, as this might be the means of softening a fall if the sheet should happen to be too short.

The most important thing in all cases of fire is not to lose one's presence of mind and not to waste a moment in taking action.

FOOD AND THE KITCHEN

THIS article deals with all that a housewife should know in regard to the management of the culinary department of her household. Useful hints are given as to the suitable furnishing and efficient cleaning of the kitchen premises, care of the kitchen range, and cooking by gas, electricity, and on oil-stoves. Each aspect of the commissariat department has also been considered, including such important questions as the marketing and storing of provisions. The article concludes with a complete calendar of meat, fish, poultry, game, fruit and vegetables in season, which has been compiled for the purposes of easy reference.

HOW TO FURNISH A KITCHEN AND SCULLERY

The furnishings and fittings of the kitchen premises are very important—so much of the comfort of the household depends upon this department and the way in which it is managed that it is well worth while to fit it up comfortably and suitably. When we consider that servants not only have to live in a kitchen as we live in our dining-room and drawing-room, but that their weekly " afternoons " or " evenings out " constitute the only change they have from their surroundings, we ought to try to give the room in which they spend so much of their time as homelike an appearance as possible.

It often happens, however, that people who are most particular about having the other rooms of their house dainty and comfortable grudge the bare necessaries when anything in connection with the kitchen is concerned.

The kitchen itself should be bright, airy, and roomy. Unfortunately, it is not always possible to have all these conditions fulfilled, especially where there are underground premises and an area, and the kitchen-window looks out on to a stone wall, but in such cases the best must be made of a bad job and a few additional inside comforts must make up for the want of outside view. Sometimes the light in premises of this kind may be increased by having the outside wall painted white or a light cream colour.

The ventilation must be good, and in addition to the doors and windows it is well to have a ventilator placed in the wall above the height of the window to allow the fumes of cooking to escape.

The sanitary arrangements should also be carefully attended to, and there must be a good supply of water.

The kitchen ought to be within easy reach of the dining-room, and yet so placed that the odours of cooking do not reach other parts of the house. The larder and storeroom should also be close at hand to avoid any unnecessary going backwards and forwards from one place to the other.

Walls and Ceilings.—The ceiling of the kitchen ought to be smoothly plastered and then whitewashed. This whitewash must be renewed every year, not only for cleanliness, but also to give more light. For the walls glazed tiles are the ideal covering, as they can so easily be washed, or a high-tiled dado with distemper or other suitable finish above. But both these methods of wall-covering prove somewhat expensive, and people of moderate means have to content themselves with something a little cheaper. The walls may be washed all over with a simple distemper, and as this process costs very little the distemper may be renewed whenever it becomes dirty. Pretty light colours, such as buff, pink, pale blue, or pale green are the most effective. Varnished paper makes another appropriate covering; it lasts well, looks bright, and can very easily be cleaned; or, again, the Sanitary or so-called Washable paper might be used—this is less expensive than varnished paper, but it will not last so well nor stand so much cleaning. Specially prepared paints, such as Ripolin, Sanalene, and Muraline are also to be recommended; they are to be had in a variety of shades, and make a kitchen look very pretty. The woodwork in the kitchen should either be painted the same colour as the walls in a darker shade, or with white paint or a light oak stain.

The Floor.—The flooring of a kitchen varies very much according to locality. In some parts of the country we find red flags, in others glazed tiles, in others red or yellow bricks, concrete, or wooden boards, &c. When the floor consists of flags, tiles, or bricks it does not, as a rule, require further covering, as it can be easily washed, and one or two rugs or mats for standing on are all that is necessary. But when there is a wooden floor it is important to cover it with some material that is easily washed, as boards soon become soiled and are very difficult to keep in order. Good linoleum is the best kitchen floor-covering, and one with a pattern is to be preferred to a perfectly plain one, as it does not show marks so quickly. Inlaid linoleum is the best, as its pattern is ingrained in the material, and although the initial outlay is greater it comes cheaper in the end, as it is so much more durable than the other makes. (See also p. 21.)

Fixtures.—The number of immovable fixtures in a kitchen varies considerably with the style of the house—they usually comprise a dresser, shelves, cupboards, a pulley for hanging up towels, &c., a roller for towel, gas or electric fittings, bells, sink and kitchen range or stove.

The dresser is really the kitchen sideboard, and as a rule it is fitted against one of the walls and belongs to the house. If it has to be made

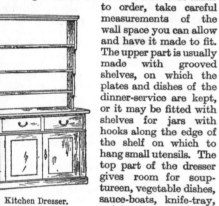

Kitchen Dresser.

to order, take careful measurements of the wall space you can allow and have it made to fit. The upper part is usually made with grooved shelves, on which the plates and dishes of the dinner-service are kept, or it may be fitted with shelves for jars with hooks along the edge of the shelf on which to hang small utensils. The top part of the dresser gives room for soup-tureen, vegetable dishes, sauce-boats, knife-tray, weights and scales, &c.

—beneath there should be two or three drawers for holding spoons, knives, &c., and kitchen towels, while the lower part is fitted up with cupboards for holding dishes and the larger cookery utensils. If the kitchen is small, make the most of it by using the walls. It is a good plan to have a shelf carried round all the available wall space, and just as high as a servant can reach. When a number of hooks are required a strip of wood might be fixed below the shelf, and nails or hooks put into that. It is a bad practice to drive nails into the wall itself, as they are sure to come out and bring some of the plaster with them.

Then there should be a well-constructed sink. Stone-ware or tiled sinks are the best, as they are the easiest to clean and keep in good order. The back of the sink should be made of some material which will not spoil with the splashing of the water; if not already fitted with tiles,

a sheet of zinc might be fitted up or a sheet of "Emdeca," which is an imitation of tiles and very practical. (See p. 14.) Above the sink should be a plate-rack in which plates can be drained, and the necessity of drying thus avoided. Underneath might be one or two shelves or a

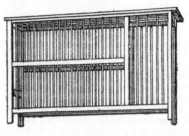

Plate-Rack.

small cupboard for keeping cleaning requisites—and at the right-hand side of the sink a sloping grooved board on which to lay dishes, &c., to drain. A flap table might also be arranged at the side on which to place dishes when they are dried if table space is scanty.

If there is a separate scullery this would naturally contain the sink, &c., and here all the washing up would be done. The walls of the scullery should be lined with shelves, and as much as possible made of the available space. The shelves on which saucepans are placed should be sparred, as this allows the air to get inside to dry them. If there is not much room for shelving, a saucepan-stand which can be placed either in kitchen or scullery is often found most valuable. A small cupboard or shelves underneath the sink will be found useful for keeping cleaning materials. The scullery, like the kitchen, should be light and well ventilated, and unless the floor is tiled or flagged it should be covered in the same way.

Cupboard accommodation is also most valuable in a kitchen. If this is inadequate, it is sometimes possible to have a cupboard fitted up on the wall for holding a small store of provisions. A recess or a corner can also be utilised for this purpose, and a joiner

Saucepan-Stand.

will be able to fit up a few shelves with a simple door at a very small cost.

Every kitchen should be supplied with a pulley on which to dry kitchen towels (unless these can be hung elsewhere) and also a roller with brackets on which to hang a roller-towel.

The lighting of the kitchen is another important point, and the light, whether it be gas or electricity, should be so arranged as to make it possible to see clearly both at the table and at the stove.

The Kitchen Range.—The most important fixture of all is the kitchen range. It is impossible to do good cooking without a good stove. The open grate limits one's sphere of work considerably, and there is always the risk of getting food smoky and saucepans dirty. It is certainly best for roasting (a roast never tastes so well as when cooked in front of an open fire), also for broiling and grilling, but with these its merits end. An open range is scarcely to be seen now in modern houses, the kitchener or close range has taken its place.

There is an endless variety of kitcheners, all more or less similar but going under different names. A tenant has not usually a choice in this matter, but before taking a house it should always be seen that a proper stove has been provided and that it is in good working order.

In choosing or buying a stove, do not look out for the cheapest kind procurable, but buy one of a thoroughly good make, and have it well fitted up. The material must be good. Cheap stoves are usually made of some light metal which wears out very quickly, causing great waste of fuel and much annoyance as well, while a well-constructed one will be made of malleable iron, wrought iron or steel.

A good stove should be provided with an adjustable bottom, which can be raised or lowered according to the size of fire required. Thus, when the stove is not being used for cooking purposes the fire may still be kept in and the water warmed, but with a very small consumption of fuel. There should also be a well-ventilated oven, a good boiler and water-supply, and a plate-rack on which to warm dishes.

The best type of stove is usually convertible into an open range, and a cheerful fire can be arranged in the evening by simply sliding back the top plate.

It is a good plan to have a light screen made which can be hooked on to the front of the fire, as this serves as a great protection when any one has to stand near the stove to stir a sauce or do other cooking.

Very often the reason why a kitchen range does not burn well is that it is not understood. It is important, therefore, that both mistress and servant should thoroughly understand the working of it, and also the method of cleaning before the stove is condemned as being inefficient. For cleaning, see p. 91.

Furniture.—For the ordinary kitchen there is very little movable furniture required. The table is the chief article, and this ought to be as large as is convenient. If there is not much floor space available it is better to have it made with flaps, which can easily be put down when not in use. It ought to be made of plain unpainted deal, and should be of a convenient height to work at and very steady on its legs. Kitchen tables are generally made oblong with one or two drawers at the ends, which are always an advantage. Sometimes too a narrow shelf is put underneath on which articles can be placed when cooking is being done, thus keeping the table itself more clear.

In larger kitchens a second table will always be found useful—a smaller and lighter one which can be moved about, or even a collapsible one which can be put aside when necessary.

A fender may also be required and a simple curb is all that is necessary, although one made of steel will of course be more ornamental. In very small kitchens the fender might be dispensed with altogether, and a light screen hooked on to the front of the fire to prevent the cinders falling out will take up much less space. A strong poker, coal shovel and scuttle should also be provided. The best shape of scuttle is that known as a coal-hod; it takes up little room,  and is not easily knocked over like the scoop shape. The flue-rake and flue-brush are generally supplied as part of the stove.

Coal-Hod.

The chairs should be of plain varnished wood, and the number will depend upon how many maids there are—there should be one for each and one over. Then if the kitchen is used as the maid's sitting-room, there ought to be one or two comfortable chairs for resting in the evening. Strong wicker ones or the light-coloured Windsor arm-chairs are both suitable—or even camp-chairs with a strong carpet cover might be used, as they can be folded up during the day and put out of the way. In any case it should be remembered that our maids require something a little better than a straight-backed wooden seat when their day's work is over.

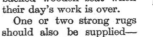

Windsor Chair.

One or two strong rugs should also be supplied— something of a nice bright colour. Pieces of stout carpet neatly bound at the edges will serve the purpose very well. A rule should be made that these rugs are rolled up at night and not put down again until the principal work in the kitchen is finished the following day.

A dark serge cloth might also be supplied to cover one of the tables and give it a less forbidding appearance.

The arrangement of the window depends very much upon the style of the house. As a rule, a short muslin curtain across the window is all that is necessary and all there is room for. Madras or strong washing muslin is the best to use for the purpose, or, if preferred, a light casement cloth ; but it must be of a material that will wash well and not lose its colour in the tub. The curtain should be simply made with a hem top and bottom. If the window is wide it may be better made in two parts with a division in the middle, but, if narrow, it will look better in one piece. The curtain should be half as wide again as the width of the window to allow for fulness. A light brass rod should be fitted across the window at a convenient height and the curtain fixed to that either by means of small rings or by slipping the rod through the upper hem of the curtain. If the kitchen is large and the window wide, short side-curtains, of some pretty cretonne, linen, or casement cloth might add very much to the comfortable appearance of the room. These are easily washed, and, provided they are not made too long, they will not be found an inconvenience. A simple brass or bamboo rod should be fixed across the window and the curtains attached to that by means of rings sewn on to the upper hem or heading. By this means the curtains can easily be slipped off when they require washing.

A good clock must not be forgotten when furnishing the kitchen—either one to hang on the wall above the kitchen mantelpiece or a small alarm clock, which can easily be carried about or taken to the maid's bedroom at night.

Utensils.—The number and kind of utensils must be determined somewhat by the size and circumstances of the household.

Unless there is a kitchen-maid it is a mistake to buy a large quantity of utensils which require polishing and keeping bright. In fact, it is never wise to buy too many to begin with ; the more you have the more there will be to keep in order, and when means are limited and service difficult to procure it is much wiser to start with what is strictly necessary and add by degrees to the supply.

In small houses and flats the kitchen utensils must be reduced to a minimum. Shelf accommodation is scarce and there are few if any cupboards ; large and heavy saucepans would then be quite out of place and a multifarious collection of moulds and dishes only in the way. At the same time it is unreasonable to expect dainty cooking to be done without implements, and every facility should be given to those who undertake the work.

It will generally be found that the better the cook the fewer utensils she will require, but still maids have different ways of working, and it is always wise to give them what they ask for within reasonable limits.

And, again, when service is short an effort should be made to give as many labour-saving appliances as possible, such as a knife-cleaner, a mincing machine, a gas stove or gas ring, &c.

Whatever is bought should be good of its kind. Buy plain and well-made articles and they will last a lifetime.

Saucepans.—Except for a large establishment where cooking has to be done in big quantities it is a mistake to invest in a number of heavy iron saucepans. One or two will be quite sufficient. The others might be made of steel, copper, aluminium, enamelled tin, or fire-proof ware.

Both steel and copper saucepans are excellent and very durable, but they are expensive to buy, and those made of copper are liable to verdigris unless well looked after.

The enamelled tin saucepans will be found most useful, but they should be bought in a good quality. The hard grey enamel lasts better than the white, and will stand any amount of hard wear. The cheap make of this kind of saucepan should be avoided, as the lining soon begins to crack and peal off and then they become dangerous to use.

Aluminium saucepans are also to be recommended, and they are rapidly supplanting all others made of metal, as they are absolutely safe from all fear of verdigris and they do not rust. They are easily cleaned (see p. 93), and nothing could be lighter to handle.

Then there are the clay terrines and brown stoneware saucepans, so dear to the heart of the French housewife, and which are coming more and more into favour in this country (see p. 148).

When once a trial has been made of the lighter style of saucepan, there will seldom be a return to the heavy iron make which are such a labour to clean, not to speak of the lifting.

The following list of utensils with approximate prices may prove useful to those who are starting housekeeping for the first time. It is suitable for a small house with one or two servants.

	s.	d.
1 Galvanised bath	2	2
1 Galvanised pail		10
1 Tin enamelled basin	1	0
1 Fish-kettle	3	3
1 Frying-pan	1	0
1 Iron stewpan	2	0
1 Iron saucepan	1	9
2 Enamelled saucepans, 1s. 3d., 1s. 9d.	3	0
or 2 Earthenware saucepans	2	0
or 2 Aluminium saucepans	3	6
1 Iron kettle	3	6
1 Tin kettle	1	6
1 Wire sieve	1	2
1 Cooking board	2	3
1 Pot-rest		3
1 Rolling-pin		6
1 Flour dredger		6
1 Sugar dredger		6

	s.	d.
1 Funnel		3
1 Cork-screw		6
1 pair of scissors		10
1 Tin-opener		4
2 Oven tins	1	4
1 Cake tin		8
1 Tray	2	0
1 Sink tidy	from	6½
1 Gridiron or hanging grill	1	4½
1 Steamer	6	0
1 Set of skewers		6
1 Grater		7
1 Poker		9
1 Egg whisk		6
1 Soap dish		4
1 Jelly mould	1	0
1 dozen patty pans		4
1 Palette knife	1	0
1 Cook's knife	1	3
2 Table knives and forks	1	10
1 Potato knife		4½
2 Iron spoons		6
2 Wooden spoons		5
2 Dessert spoons		8
2 Tea spoons		4
1 Toasting fork		4½
1 Gravy strainer	1	0
1 Knife-board		10
1 Pepper and salt box		9
1 Shovel		6
1 Coal-scuttle	1	11
1 Roasting tin and stand	1	6
1 Long broom	1	6
1 Yard broom	1	4
1 Set shoe brushes	2	9
1 Set stove brushes	2	9
1 Sweep's brush		9
2 Scrubbing brushes	1	6
1 Nail brush		2
2 Egg-brushes		3
1 Sink brush		6
1 Dish mop		4½
3 Jugs	1	0
2 Pie dishes	1	6
2 Pudding bowls	1	2
1 Large mixing bowl		10
2 Breakfast cups and saucers		11
6 Plates assorted	1	6
3 Dishes	2	9
1 Sugar-basin		4
1 Salt-cellar		3
1 Lemon squeezer		4½

Jars and tins will also be required for kitchen use, but it is seldom necessary to buy these.

The following might be added if means allow—

	s.	d.
1 Mincing machine	4	8
1 Spring balance	5	0
1 Meat-saw	2	6
1 Knife-sharpener		10
1 Box-cutter	1	0

	s.	d.
6 Small moulds	1	0
1 Frying basket	1	6
1 Set of steps	5	0
1 Omelet pan	1	6
2 Sandwich cake tins	1	0
1 Preserving pan	4	0
2 Fancy moulds	3	0
1 Pestle and mortar	3	0
1 Fish slice		8
1 Vegetable presser	1	6
1 Flour tub or crock	2	6

The above does not include utensils for laundry work. See under special heading.

If the housemaids' utensils are not separate, the following brushes, &c., will be required in addition for household use :—

	s.	d.
1 Plate brush		9
1 Carpet whisk	2	6
1 Double banister brush	2	9
1 Dust pan	1	0

Note.—If there are several servants they should be allowed inexpensive crockery and glass for their own table use apart from the dishes used for cooking.

The Cleaning of the Kitchen and Kitchen Utensils.—The kitchen may be cleaned either all in one day or by degrees. The latter method is generally found the most convenient, as it is less obtrusive and does not upset the comfort of the house so much. The saucepans and tins may be cleaned one day, cupboards and windows another, larder, passages, and outside premises another, flues and range another, with the scrubbing of the floors and tables, &c., to follow.

This is entirely a matter of arrangement and must be planned to suit the ways and circumstances of each individual household.

An effort should be made to have the cleaning done early in the day or at a time when there is no special cooking to attend to.

Instructions for the various cleaning operations will be found below. (See also Duties of the Cook, p. 49.)

How to Clean a Kitchen Range—Weekly Cleaning.—A large strong apron, or overall, a pair of gloves, and a cap which covers the hair should be worn when doing this piece of work. The kitchen, too, should be prepared by removing or covering with a dust-sheet or sheets of paper anything that is likely to be soiled with dust. Remove any kettles and saucepans from the top of the range and put the fender, plate-rack, and fire-irons to one side. Put down a hearth cloth and have sweep's brush, flue rake and brush, shovel and black-lead brushes in readiness. Commence by raking out the fire, and be particular to pass the rake well to the back so as to get all the cinders out of the boiler flue. Brush out all cinders and ashes and save the former for making the fire later on.

To clean the flues commence at the top. Open the dampers and the little doors or slides at the entrance to the flue or flues. Pass the flue brush up as far as it will go, then to the sides and then downwards, working it well against the side of the flue. The loose soot will all fall downwards to the back of the stove and will be removed later on. In a large stove there may be two or even three flues and each one must be done in the same way. Brush the top of the dampers and brush the flue doors or slides and put them back in place.

Now remove all rings and tops from the top of the stove and brush all the soot off the top of the oven with the sweep's brush, letting it fall either down the side of the oven or into the fire-place—the former is the simpler. Also pass the flue brush down the sides and back of the oven if there is an opening. Brush the under-side of all the top pieces and put them back in place. If there is a boiler or second oven at the other side of the range the top and sides of this must be cleaned in the same way. Every part must be freed from soot, and always work from the top downwards.

When the top part is finished remove the little door or slide which will be found underneath the oven, put a good-sized shovel below it, pass the flue rake in at the hole and draw out all the soot. Repeat the same at the other side if necessary. The soot must be taken outside at once, and if there is a garden it should be kept for manuring purposes.

Next dust the stove all over, and if the top is greasy wash it with hot water and soda. Thoroughly dust or brush out the oven. If the shelves are greasy wash them out with hot water and soda, then whiten them with a paste of whitening and water, which will give them a nice clean appearance.

To Black-lead the Stove.—Apply the black-lead very lightly with the black-lead brush, commencing with the highest part of the stove and doing a small piece at a time. Brush off with the hard brush and polish with the polisher (see p. 65).

If there are tiles at the back of the stove these must be washed over with a soft cloth, soap, and water, or, if stained, with Brook's soap or sapolio.

Clean all steel parts with fine emery paper or with fine bath-brick dust made into a paste with paraffin (see p. 72).

Lay the fire, using the cinders along with some small coal, sticks, and paper.

Sweep the hearth, wash it over with warm water, and whiten with soft sandstone. Put back the fender, fire-irons, &c., and put a light to the fire if required.

Daily Cleaning.—The fire should be well raked out every day, the top of the stove brushed with the sweep's brush and polished with the stove brushes. Black-leading should not be required

more than once a week, except perhaps on the special parts which are much used.

Rub up the steel parts with emery paper, or wipe them with a soft duster or selvyt cloth, and clean the hearth.

If properly done, the flues should not require cleaning more than once a week, but if a large fire is kept constantly burning it may be necessary to brush over the top of the oven more frequently—sometimes, too, in the case of small stoves the flues require cleaning more than once a week. This must be regulated according to how the stove burns.

Cleaning Saucepans.—Clean saucepans form one of the first essentials of good cooking. "You can judge a workman by his tools" cannot be better applied than to a cook, as no woman who has any pride in her profession would put up with such a thing as a dirty saucepan. They ought to be her special pride and care.

Now that saucepans are used almost entirely on gas-stoves and close ranges where there is no smoking from an open fire, there is no excuse for having the outside coated with soot or black grease which comes off on everything that touches it. The handle and outside of the saucepan should receive the same attention as the inside.

As soon as a saucepan is finished with, it should be filled with warm water and left soaking until it can be cleaned.

Care must be taken not to pour cold water into a hot enamelled saucepan or there will be danger of cracking the lining; in fact it is always a risky thing to do if the pan is very hot. Saucepans should be cleaned as soon as possible after they are taken from the fire and never allowed to remain dirty overnight except under very special circumstances.

The method of cleaning will depend somewhat upon the kind of saucepan, but the rule that they must be properly clean and free from taint of any kind applies to all.

If the contents of a saucepan have become burnt boil some hot water and soda in it before attempting to do the cleaning.

No saucepan must be laid away before it is perfectly dry unless it is placed where the air can reach the inside, as on a sparred shelf.

Iron Saucepans.—Wash them well in hot water and soda, scrubbing inside and out with a pot brush. Use a little sand, if necessary, to make them clean. The sand must be used almost dry or it will not have so much power. When clean, rinse thoroughly so as to get rid of any grit and dry with a coarse cloth.

Enamelled Saucepans.—Wash well in hot water and soda, and then apply a little Brook's soap or sapolio to take off any marks or discoloration. Salt or fine silver sand may also be used, or even crushed egg-shells are very good for whitening the enamel. Rinse thoroughly and dry with a cloth.

Tin and Steel Saucepans.—Clean in the same way as enamelled saucepans.

Earthenware Saucepans.—Wash first in hot soapy water, then apply a little fine sand or sapolio, if necessary, to remove any marks. Rinse thoroughly and dry with a stout cloth.

Copper Saucepans.—These require very special care, as, if once neglected, they are apt to harbour verdigris, which is very poisonous. For this reason the tinned linings should always be kept intact, and directly there are signs of wear and the copper begins to show through the saucepans should be sent away to be re-tinned.

Clean the inside of copper saucepans with a mixture of soft soap and Brook's soap or soft soap and fine silver sand applied with a piece of flannel or soft cloth wrung out of warm water. For the outside use the skin of a lemon dipped in bath-brick dust, or salt and vinegar applied with a flannel. Well rinse the saucepan with hot water and dry quickly and thoroughly. The outside may be further polished by rubbing it up with a little dry whitening.

Aluminium Saucepans.—Wash well with hot soapy water, using a little silver sand if necessary to remove any discoloration or burnt matter. Rinse thoroughly first in hot and then in cold water and then dry with a soft cloth. Soda must on no account be used with aluminium ware, and patent cleaning mixtures should also be avoided. The outside may be polished occasionally with metal polish.

The vessels should not be scraped, nor should the light brown enamel which will form inside be disturbed, as it is not only quite harmless, but adds considerably to the life of the articles.

Wooden Articles.—An effort should be made to make kitchen tables, boards, and wooden utensils as white as possible. The following will be required for cleaning them : a pail or basin of warm water, a piece of house flannel, scrubbing brush, sand, soap, and a stout cloth for drying. Wash the wood over with the flannel wrung out of warm water. Rub a little soap on the brush, dip in sand and scrub with the grain of the wood. Rinse well in order to remove all grit and dry quickly with a clean cloth. Soda should not be used, as it tends to discolour the wood. Sand helps to whiten it.

When cleaning a kitchen-table the legs should not be forgotten. If plain wood they may be scrubbed in the same way as the top, but if painted they must only be wiped over with a damp flannel and dried.

Wooden utensils must not be put too near a fire to dry or they will warp ; they ought to be placed upright where the air will get round them.

Sieves.—A sieve should be cleaned as soon as possible after it has been used. If any substance is allowed to harden on it the cleaning will be much more difficult. Wash thoroughly with a little hot water and soda and scrub well with a brush. If it is a wire sieve hold it up to the light and see that none of the little holes are blocked up. Be particular also to scrub well round the sides where the rim joins the surface part. Rinse well and dry with a strong cloth. The sieve should then be put in a warm place to dry. If this is not attended to a wire sieve will become rusty and a hair one coated with mildew.

Sieves must always be kept in a dry and clean place.

Tin Lids, Moulds, and Dish Covers.—Hot water with a little soap powder or plain soap should be used for washing these. They must be well rinsed and then dried at once.

Saucepan lids should be washed or at least well wiped with a cloth each time after use. The rim must have special attention, as any grease from a stew or such-like will lodge there. It is a good plan to give all saucepan lids a good washing once a week.

A brush may be used when washing fancy moulds of any kind. When the insides become difficult to clean the moulds should be put into a saucepan with hot water and a little soda, and boiled for half-an-hour. This will loosen any matter or burnt pieces which may adhere to them. They may also be secured with a little silver sand, or Brook's soap may be used to remove any discoloration. Thorough rinsing will be necessary.

All tinned goods must be well dried before being put away, as they are liable to rust.

Polishing.—Tins that are put up for show may be polished to make them look bright, but this should never be attempted before making sure that they are quite free from grease. Make a smooth paste with a little whitening and water—rub this on the tins with a piece of flannel, and, when dry, rub off with a duster. A soft brush may be used to remove the whitening from any corners. The inside of moulds should never be polished.

A few drops of ammonia may be added to the whitening, but as the tinning of some moulds and lids is very thin, strong cleansers should as a rule be avoided.

Zinc.—Sometimes the surround of a sink is covered with zinc, and this may be cleaned in the following way : Scrub first with hot soapy water to which a little soda has been added. Rinse and dry. The zinc may then be polished with a little whitening mixed to a paste with turpentine. Apply with a piece of flannel, and when dry rub off with a duster.

To Clean Floors, Linoleum, &c.—See "Work of the House," p. 66.

Baking Tins.—Wash well in very hot water with a little soda in it, using a strong brush and a little sand if necessary. Rinse well and dry with a coarse cloth. If a roasting-tin has become very brown and is hard to clean, let it soak in hot water and soda for an hour or two to soften the burnt substance.

Kitchen Knives and Forks.—Wipe these with a cloth wrung out of hot water to remove any grease, but do not allow them to lie in hot water, which would tend to loosen the handles. Then rub off any stains with a little Brook's soap or sapolio applied rather dry on a piece of flannel. Rinse off and dry with a knife-cloth. It is not necessary to polish kitchen knives on a knife-board; it only wears them unnecessarily.

Kitchen Cloths.—At the end of the day all cloths which have been used and are soiled should be washed in soapy water with a little soda; then thoroughly rinsed, wrung out, and hung up to dry. At the end of the week they ought to be laid aside in order to have a more thorough washing with the rest of the household linen (see p. 276), and a fresh supply put into use.

Pudding Cloths.—After a pudding cloth has been used it should be thrown into hot water with a little soda and allowed to soak for half-an-hour or so. Then wash out and rinse with care until no trace of the soda water remains. Dry in the open air if possible. Fold up carefully and keep in a clean place. A pudding cloth must only be used for its own special purpose. If the above process is not sufficient to make the cloth clean it ought to be boiled in a saucepan for half-an-hour with hot water and a small piece of soda and then rinsed in the same way. The use of soap and soap powder should be avoided as far as possible.

Jelly Cloths.—Wash in the same way as pudding cloths.

Care of the Sink.—This is a very important matter in the management of the kitchen and scullery, and a sink left in a dirty and greasy state, especially the last thing at night, will at once denote a careless and untidy worker.

Every sink should be provided with a sink basket or tidy and a sink brush. The former is

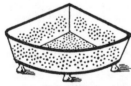

Sink Basket.

used to place over the opening to keep back any tea-leaves, vegetable parings, or other refuse which might block the pipe. An old colander will serve the purpose very well.

Do not throw anything but water down a sink, and if the water is greasy flush it well afterwards with hot soapy water. It is a good plan also to pour down some very hot soda and water when the washing up is finished.

If water in which vegetables have been cooked

is not kept for making soup, it should never be poured down a sink, as it would cause an unpleasant smell, but should be emptied straight into a drain or outside in the garden.

An effort should be made to keep the pipe and trap (an elbow-like bend in the pipe just below

Sink Brush.

the sink) in good order by preventing grease and refuse collecting in them. If these become choked and clogged an unnecessary expense must be incurred to have them cleared out, not to speak of the annoyance. Do not be afraid of plenty of hot water when washing up; it is greasy luke-warm water which clogs the pipe sooner than anything.

When the washing up is finished the sink should be well scrubbed out with some hot water and soda and a little soap, rinsed with hot water, and then finally the cold pipe should be allowed to run. If the sink is discoloured, use a little sand or Brook's soap. The sink brush and any dish clothes must also be washed out and hung up to dry. Also any tub or basin that has been used for washing up.

Refuse.—In every household there must necessarily be a certain amount of rubbish to dispose of consisting of ashes, sweepings from floors, broken crockery, old tins, food remains, &c.

Part of this refuse should be put into a dust-bin or ash-pit, with either of which every house should be provided, while the remainder should be burnt.

The ash-pit is more frequently found in country districts where the removal of rubbish cannot be so frequent as in towns. It is usually built of brick or stone and should be well cemented and placed at some distance from the house.

The best kind of dust-bin is one made of galvanised iron and round in shape. The size will depend upon the needs of the household, but it is better to have two, if necessary, of a medium size than one that is too heavy to be lifted. These dust-bins are very often provided by the landlord and belong to the house.

There should always be a lid to fit the dust-bin to prevent damp from entering or dust from flying about. It should be placed at least a few feet from the house and never near a window, and it must be removed and thoroughly emptied by the dustman twice or at least once a week.

Nothing but dry refuse should be put into a dust-bin unless it can be emptied very frequently, as damp favours decomposition and very soon causes an unpleasant and very unhealthy smell. Animal and vegetable refuse in this case is better burnt, and if there is a kitchen range in use it should not be a difficult matter to dispose of all vegetable parings, tea-leaves, and such-like by this means.

There are two ways of burning food remains. They may either be dried slowly at the back of the fire or underneath the grate, after which they will burn quite readily, or they may be put into the stove in small quantities when the fire is very bright and hot enough to consume them quickly. If refuse is put on to a low fire in a damp condition it will cause a most unpleasant smell.

Needless to say, it is the duty of the mistress to see that nothing is thrown out or burnt except that which is absolutely of no value. In some houses the dust-bin is one of the most fruitful sources of waste. (See Law in regard to Removal of Refuse, p. 382.)

COOKING BY GAS

Gas Stoves.—There is much to be said in favour of a gas stove, and if properly managed it can be a great saving of time, labour, and expense. It can either be used to supplement a kitchen range where there is a large amount of cooking to be done, or in small houses it can be made to take the place of a coal stove altogether.

It is especially useful in flats where ladies very often have to do all their own work or the

Breakfast Cooker.

greater part of it themselves, and where actual labour must be reduced to a minimum.

If the whole stove is not required and the oven part would be of little or no use, a small griller or even a gas ring is often a great comfort and saving. It can be placed on the top

Gas Boiling Ring.

of the range or on a small table in the scullery, and will often save the keeping up of a fire for the sake of boiling a kettle or doing some light cooking in the evening. A little griller would also be found a great boon in the morning when an early breakfast has to be prepared, as it will

not only boil a kettle but make toast or grill fish or bacon at the same time. A very nice griller and boiler can be bought for 7s. 6d. or 8s. 6d., while a small boiling ring will only cost two or three shillings plus the india-rubber tubing (6d. to 9d. per foot) required for attaching it to a gas bracket.

Gas stoves can be had in different sizes and various makes. Improvements are constantly being made, and there is great competition among the different makers as to who will produce the most perfect article. Before buying one it is a good plan to go to one of the Gas Company's offices or exhibitions where all the different kinds of stoves are displayed, and where they can often be seen in actual use. The newest make of gas cookers is well raised above the floor, which saves a great deal of unnecessary stooping, and also does away with the necessity of having a slab on which to place the stove for the sake of protection. Those with enamelled linings are the most easily kept in order. The size chosen must depend upon the amount of cooking to be done and the oven space required, and also upon the size of the kitchen. It is a mistake to have one larger than necessary, as it always means a greater consumption of gas to heat the oven, &c.

The price of gas stoves runs from about £4 to £12 according to size, while they can also be hired at a rental of about 2s. 3d. per quarter and upwards. In fact, in many cases it is better to hire than to purchase, as the Gas Company not only supply the stove but keep it in repair, and will change it when desired for one of another description.

It is very important to have a gas stove properly fitted up and to see that there is the necessary ventilation. The work should be put into the hands of a capable workman, because unless the pipe to which the stove is connected is of the right size and there is sufficient pressure of gas, the stove will not work properly. It is sometimes a good plan to have a separate meter for the gas stove in order to regulate the consumption of gas.

How to Use a Gas Stove.—It is also very important to know how to use a gas stove, otherwise there may be great waste of gas and many spoilt dishes.

The Gas Companies give special demonstrations all over the country where the working of the various stoves is fully explained and a cookery lesson given at the same time. They are also beginning to send out lady demonstrators to private houses to show how each part of the stove should be used in order to secure the best possible results for the smallest consumption of gas; but the hints given below may be of use to those who cannot avail themselves of these special lessons.

Every gas stove is provided with several burners on the top and each burner has a special tap in connection with it. There will also be a special tap for the oven.

A taper is preferable to matches for lighting the gas.

Do not turn on more taps than are actually required at one time, and be careful to turn off the gas directly you have finished using it. When about to use the oven open the door first, turn on the gas, and then apply the light. Be sure that all the little burners inside are lighted and on both sides. If they should become clogged with grease or other matter the little holes must be cleared with a needle or fine wire. Never keep the gas burning longer than is necessary—for instance, when once the contents of a kettle or saucepan have come to the boil the merest flicker of light will keep them simmering.

The large round burner should not be used when the smaller one is sufficient. Then, again, when the griller is being used a saucepan or kettle of water should always be placed on the top to utilise the top heat as well as that of underneath.

Gas may also be economised by using a steamer or patent cooker (see p. 148) in which several different articles can be cooked one above the other with only one jet of gas underneath. It is also a waste of gas to use heavy saucepans, as they require an unnecessary consumption of gas to bring them to the boil. Steel, aluminium, and enamelled saucepans are all suitable, also the fireproof china and the glazed earthenware ones. The saucepans must also be clean at the foot; if there is a coating of soot or black grease it acts as a non-conductor of heat, and this again will cause a waste of gas. It is always better, if possible, to keep a separate set of saucepans for a gas stove and not to use them indiscriminately for a gas cooker and a coal stove.

The flame of gas must not be allowed to blaze up the sides of a saucepan, but only underneath.

When once the oven has been properly heated the light should for most purposes be turned down half way, and in some cases even lower. Then the cooking should be so arranged that when the oven is lighted it should be made use of to the fullest extent, two or three dishes being cooked in it at the same time. For instance, if there is a small roast it may be cooked on a roasting-tin on the bottom shelf, while such things as a milk pudding, potato or macaroni pie, baked potatoes, or stewed fruit might be cooking above. Or, when pastry is being cooked, cakes or scones might be cooked at the same time. It would not, however, do to cook pastry with a roast, as the air of the oven would be too moist. It is a waste of gas to light the oven to cook one dish.

To Grill.—A special grill pan is supplied with every gas stove, and this can be used for many purposes, such as for cooking a chop, steak, kidneys, bacon, fish, or in fact anything that could be cooked on the ordinary grill. Very good toast can also be made under the grill.

Place the grill pan under the griller, light the gas and wait until the griller is red hot before putting the meat or whatever is being cooked underneath. Then proceed as for ordinary grilling (see p. 167), turning the meat and reducing the heat as required.

To Make Toast.—The gas should be turned down after the griller is once hot. The bread must be watched very carefully and turned when necessary. The toast must not be made too quickly or it will be soft and heavy.

To Use the Oven.—A gas oven generally contains two or three grid shelves and always one solid shelf. The latter is used to throw down the heat, and is placed above anything that requires browning. Nothing should be placed on the solid shelf or it will burn, with the exception of liquid things or anything that can be placed in a tin of water. The top of the oven is always the coolest part. When dishes in course of baking are becoming too brown before being sufficiently cooked, the solid shelf should be removed altogether.

It used to be thought necessary to place a tin of water at the foot of the oven, but this is not the case.

When roasting meat the joint should either be hung on a hook attached to a bar which runs across the top of the oven or put on a roasting-tin placed on one of the grid shelves at the lower part of the oven. If the former method is adopted the shelves of the oven will require to be removed and nothing else can be cooked at the same time. The thickest part of the joint must always be hung downwards. Heat the oven well before putting the meat in, and after the first ten minutes reduce the gas one-half or even more according to the amount of pressure; follow in fact the general rules for roasting (see p. 165).

When baking cakes the oven should first be thoroughly heated and then the gas turned down more or less according to the special kind of cake, and whether it requires a moderate or hot oven. Place the cake or cakes on the grid shelf and below the browning shelf, and gradually reduce the heat until the cakes are ready. If the cake is large it may be better to keep out the solid shelf altogether and even to cover it over with a double piece of kitchen paper to prevent its taking too much colour. With large cakes, too, it is a good plan to leave them in the oven for about half-an-hour after the gas has been turned off, and to let them dry slowly in the gradually reducing heat. The same rules will apply to the baking of pastry.

If a little care is taken and attention given to details a gas oven is really very easy to manage, and after a little practice one becomes quite expert at regulating the heat to a nicety.

How to Clean a Gas Stove—Weekly Cleaning.—

Put down a hearth-cloth and have in readiness a pail of hot water and soda, one or two strong cloths or swabs, and black-lead brushes, &c., for cleaning purposes. Remove the bars from the top of the stove and wash these in the pail of hot water, using a brush if necessary. Wash the top of the stove, being very careful to make the burners clean; sometimes it may be necessary to clean out the little holes with a piece of wire or a fine skewer if they have become clogged. Wash also the tray under the burners, the oven shelves, the sides of the oven, which are sometimes fitted with movable linings, and the tin which stands at the foot. If there are enamelled linings, as in some of the stoves, a little salt or Brook's soap may be used for cleaning purposes and also for the oven tin to remove any brown marks or other discoloration.

Then black-lead the bars, the top and body of the stove, and put back the different parts in their proper places. Polish the brass taps with metal polish, rub up the steel with fine emery paper, and the stove is finished.

Daily Cleaning.—If the stove is thoroughly cleaned once a week it will not require black-leading the other days; it will be sufficient to give it a good brush over with the harder polishing brush, to wash the tray underneath the burners, and the oven tin if the oven has been used.

Neither grease nor any kind of food which may have been spilled during cooking should ever be allowed to remain on a gas stove, but must be washed off at once with a cloth wrung out of hot water and soda, otherwise an unpleasant smell will be caused the next time the gas is used.

COOKING BY ELECTRICITY

Although we have long been accustomed to electricity as a lighting agent and even for heating purposes, electric cooking stoves have not yet become common. There are, however, several different makes to be had, and the price of some of them is by no means prohibitive.

One of the simplest and most economical stoves on the market is the "Tricity" cooker; it is so simple, so easily regulated, so perfectly controlled and so safe that it cannot fail to appeal to those who try it. There are different types of this stove—The Single Cooker, The Duplex Cooker, and the Extension Cooker, while the ovens are sold separately.

The Single Cooker can be used for grilling, toasting, boiling, steaming, stewing, heating irons, airing clothes, or as a radiator to warm a room. The round plate on the top of the stove is raised to a dull red or lesser heat controlled by means of two switches, and any degree of heat from " very hot " to " low simmering " can be obtained.

Electric current is brought to the stove through a flexible steel-covered cable which ensures absolute safety. The cable is ten feet in length and is attached to a wall-plug. The

"Tricity" Stove.

1. Single Boiler. 2. Oven. 3. Extension Boiler.
4. Grill Pan. 5. Toaster.

cooker can easily be moved when desired within the range of the length of the cable, and, when in use, should be placed upon a table or on a wooden pedestal as shown in engraving. It should be a convenient height for working at.

Special sets of cooking utensils are sold for use with this cooker. They are quite simple, in both metal and earthenware and without wires of any kind, but one important point about them is that each article is absolutely flat at the base so as to obtain good contact with the hot-plate and thus make the cooking more rapid and economical.

The Duplex Cooker has two hot-plates, and its uses are the same as those of the Single Cooker.

The Extension Cooker has also one hot-plate, and is generally used in conjunction with one of the other cookers or to give top heat to the oven. It is also useful alone for boiling, stewing, and similar simple operations.

Ovens too can be bought in two sizes, and are heated by being placed on the top of a Single or Duplex Cooker. The larger size is quite sufficient for the needs of the average household.

The following is the *working cost* of the " Tricity Cooker " with electricity at a 1d. a unit.

1 Penny runs a " Tricity " hot-plate for 5 hours at lowest heat.

1 Penny runs a " Tricity " hot-plate for 1¼ hours at greatest heat.

Full particulars regarding price, use, &c., can be obtained by writing to the makers, the Berry Construction Co., Ltd., Charing Cross House, London.

COOKING ON OIL STOVES

A small oil stove may sometimes be a convenience when neither gas nor electricity is within reach. In summer, when a big kitchen fire is not required, a stove of this description will often perform all the cooking operations necessary. Being independent of any fittings, it can be moved about at will, and placed wherever it is most convenient. Sometimes, too, in country quarters where the kitchen range is inadequate for the cooking required, an oil stove will be found of valuable assistance, and it can even be used in an out-house if the kitchen is small and inconvenient.

They are to be had in various sizes, ranging from a small stove on which only one saucepan or kettle can be placed, to a large family stove with oven, boiler and accommodation for several saucepans as well. It is important to buy a stove of a thoroughly good make, and of late years there have been so many improvements made in their construction that they are more easily regulated and there is less danger of their smoking than formerly.

It is always well to see the stove at work before buying it, and to obtain full instructions as to its use, as with each special make there are certain points which require explanation. One of the greatest objections to oil stoves is their smell, but this can be to a large extent, if not altogether, avoided by proper management and care.

To secure the best results, care must be taken to keep the stove very clean and to use good oil. The wicks, too, must fit properly and be kept free from all charring. The oil-receivers should be well filled before using the stove, and the oil must not be allowed to burn too low.

It is also important to stand the stove out of a draught, and for this reason, as well as for the sake of convenience, it is better to raise it above the ground. It may be placed either on a simple four-legged stand or if it is a portable stove it is a good plan to have a box made which will serve at the same time as packing-case and a stand upon which to place it when in use. (For Cleaning and Trimming, see p. 77.)

COAL AND OTHER FUEL

Arrangement of the Coal Cellar.—A good-sized coal cellar is always an advantage in a house, as there will then be room to store not only a quantity but also at least two different kinds of coal. The contents of the cellar should be so arranged that each kind can easily be found, and a supply of slack or coal dust should also be kept in one corner.

When a fresh supply of coal is ordered it must not be thrown in on the top of the old dust, but this should first be scraped to one side and used along with the larger pieces. If this is once buried there becomes an accumulation of dust in the cellar which is never used up.

A strong coal shovel should be kept in the cellar, also a hatchet for breaking the coal when necessary. A large lump of coal should always

be broken on the ground and not on the top of other coal, which would in all probability produce an unnecessary amount of small coal and dust.

The Buying of Coal.—Coal is always cheaper if it can be bought in large quantities—by the sack or bag is one of the most expensive ways in which it can be procured. Naturally the amount ordered must depend upon the accommodation there is for storing. The prices are generally much cheaper in summer than in winter, and, if convenient, there is a distinct advantage in laying up a store at this time of year. During the months of June, July, and August is the most advantageous time to buy. Sometimes it is possible to make an arrangement with the coal company that if the purchase is made in the summer the coal will only be delivered a ton or half a ton at a time as required.

It is important to buy the right kind of coal for the different ranges or fire-places. Range nuts or cobbles are excellent for kitchen use, and it would be most extravagant to use finer coal for this purpose. Coke, which is cheaper than coal, is often burnt along with the range nuts. A larger and better kind of coal will be required for use in the sitting-rooms. The housekeeper should see that the coal with which she is supplied does not contain too much dust. A careful watch should always be kept on this.

Coal should always be ordered from a good reliable merchant, and, if possible, from a depôt in one's own neighbourhood so as to avoid any extra charge for carriage. The price of coal fluctuates very much according to the supply. It is also affected by labour disputes involving strikes, lock-outs, &c., and is, as a rule, cheaper in localities which are in close proximity to a coal-field.

Householders who live in flats should ask for their coal to be delivered in half-sacks, as these are easier to carry up a number of stairs.

Economy in the Use of Coal.—An extravagant use of coal is one of the greatest sources of waste in a house, but, with careful management, much can be done to economise in this direction without in any way reducing the amount of comfort to be gained from the fires.

Fortunately the construction of stoves and grates has been very much improved of late years, and what are known as slow combustion stoves are fitted up in all the modern houses. Small coal should always be burnt along with the large. A ton of coal always produces a certain amount of dust, but if this is not sufficient an extra amount can always be ordered by the sack.

When a room is not in actual use or when the weather is mild and it is yet advisable that the fire be kept in, a lump of coal should be put on when the fire is rather low and then a good shovelful of damp slack placed on the top.

This is called "backing the fire," and by this means it can be kept in for several hours, and when a blaze is wanted a little breaking up with the poker is all that is necessary. Continual poking is also a cause of waste; the less a fire is touched the better, and if it is desired to keep the room at an equal temperature the fire should never be allowed to burn too low, but a few pieces of coal put on gently from time to time with a sprinkling of dust.

Sometimes the fire-place in a room is unnecessarily large, and this can be remedied by the use of fire-bricks, which will reduce the space and at the same time throw out heat. Clay balls are sometimes used for the same purpose. Briquettes are also used to economise coal. They are made of coal dust moistened and formed into blocks. Used along with a little moistened slack they will keep a fire in for hours, even all night, and they are a great convenience in this way. The only disadvantage to their use is that they cause a lot of dust when broken up.

Cinders should also be utilised. The larger cinders in the room-fires should be used when laying the next fire, while the smaller ones which have been sifted from the ashes can always be used in the kitchen-fire or in a boiler-fire if one is used.

Wood.—Logs of wood are frequently used as fuel, and in country districts a supply of logs can often be had quite cheaply, and they make a nice cheery fire in the winter. In town, however, they are not as a rule any cheaper than coal. Firewood can be bought quite cheaply in bundles, but even with this extravagance should be avoided. One bundle should be made to light two fires; in fact, with care it can be made to serve for three. There are also different kinds of firelighters to be had, and sometimes these are cheaper than the bundles of wood as they light the fire more easily, especially if the coal is of a hard make.

THE LARDER

A house of any considerable size usually contains a larder in which perishable food can be kept, and the importance of this room cannot be over-estimated. The ideal arrangement is to have it in two parts, so that dairy produce may be kept separate from butcher-meat, &c.

Position.—Whenever possible the larder should have a northerly or easterly aspect and comparative absence of bright sunshine. It is important, too, that it should be conveniently near the kitchen, although not near enough to be influenced by the heat of the range. It should never be placed near a lavatory; neither should the window overlook that part of the premises where the gulleys to receive the contents of the waste-pipes are placed.

Arrangement and Fittings.—The ceiling should be lime- or white-washed. The walls too, if they are not tiled, should be lime- or white-washed or painted with some sanitary paint which can easily be washed.

The shelves are best made of stone, marble, or slate, although wooden ones are sometimes fixed. In any case it is well to have a slab of slate or marble on which special things, such as butter and milk, can be placed to keep them cool.

Window-sills should be lined if possible with glazed tiles, and the floor should be of stone or tiles (red flags) or concrete.

Ventilation.—There should be one or more windows with which to ventilate the larder. If there are two one should be glazed to let in light and the other should be fitted with wire gauze or perforated zinc, fine enough to exclude all flies. If there is only one window it should be kept open constantly, and a piece of muslin should be stretched tightly across it to keep out flies and dust. There must be a through ventilation, and sometimes it is advisable to have one of the panels of the door fitted with perforated zinc in order to secure the necessary draught. Or sometimes perforated bricks are let into the walls, which help considerably to ventilate the larder.

The door of the larder should fit securely.

Requisites for the Larder.—Strong hooks securely fixed in the ceiling or hung from rods of iron running from side to side of the larder, from which to hang meat, game, &c.; a few smaller hooks fixed to the shelves or walls; a wire rack, baskets or wooden boxes for vegetables; bags of netting for lemons; a bread-pan, a large earthenware pan for milk with a piece of muslin as a covering; wire covers for cold meat, odd cups, basins, plates and dishes, also a few muslin bags for holding meat, hams, &c.,

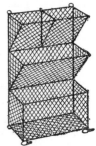

Vegetable-Rack.

and some improvised meat-safes made of muslin bags stretched out by wooden hoops.

A refrigerator is an advantage in a larder but by no means a necessity, except in large establishments or in houses where ices are largely used (see Ices).

Temperature.—This should not exceed 50° Fahr. in summer, nor fall below 38° Fahr. in winter.

Cleaning the Larder.—Absolute cleanliness must be maintained in the larder by daily and weekly cleaning.

Daily Cleaning.—(1) Wipe over the shelves with a damp cloth and put food not being used immediately for cooking on clean plates and dishes.

(2) Wipe over the floor also with a damp cloth or with a brush with a damp cloth or swab

tied over it (sweeping and dusting must never be done while food is in the larder, as it simply raises the dust to let it fall afterwards on the food).

(3) Wipe out the bread-pan.

(4) Burn any scraps not quite fresh of fish, bones, vegetables, &c.

Weekly Cleaning.—A special day should be chosen for this :—

(1) Remove all food from the larder.

(2) Sweep and dust walls and floor ; gather up dust and burn.

(3) When dust has settled, dust and scrub shelves, using carbolic soap, or if the weather is hot some disinfectant may be added to the water, such as carbolic, Jeyes' Fluid, Sanitas, or Izol.

(4) Scrub floor with soft soap or carbolic soap and water.

(5) Leave door open to dry floor, &c. When dry replace the food on clean dishes.

(6) Thoroughly wash out bread-pan and leave it to dry and air before returning the bread.

(7) In hot weather place bowls of charcoal or disinfectant and water on the shelves.

Occasionally—

(1) Whitewash or limewash the ceiling about every six months.

(2) Scrub wire gauze or perforated zinc of windows and doors with disinfectant or carbolic soap and water.

(3) Scald and scrub meat-hooks and wire meat-covers.

(4) Wash muslin covers when necessary.

(5) Fill up any cracks or mouse-holes with cement and place traps when necessary.

Treatment of Various Kinds of Food—Meat, Game, and Poultry.—All uncooked meat should be hung. If there is a cut side keep this uppermost to prevent the juice running out. Examine the meat carefully each day and wipe it with a cloth to keep it dry. It may also be dusted over with a little flour. The marrow should be removed from the bone of such joints as a sirloin, ribs of beef or loin of mutton, before the meat is hung up.

If there is any sign of taint cut off the infected part and burn it, then wash the meat with a weak solution of Condy's fluid and water, vinegar and water, or borax and water. If there is a danger of flies attacking the meat, pepper it well and hang it up in muslin ; or if there is a danger of the meat not keeping, it may be partially cooked.

Frozen meat should be well thawed before cooking ; it should be taken from the larder and kept in a warm kitchen for an hour or two.

Cooked meat should be lifted out of the gravy with which it has been served and put on a dry plate covered over with a meat-screen.

If game or poultry has to be kept some time it should not be plucked, as the feathers are a protection from flies. Tie a piece of string

tightly round the neck to exclude the air and hang it up. A little charcoal may also be put inside the vent to help to preserve it. This may be made by putting a piece of wood in the oven and letting it remain until it is quite black. I should be hung in a current of air and well sprinkled with pepper if there is any danger o flies. If there is any sign of taint the feather should be removed and the bird washed in sal and water or vinegar and water. Repeat i necessary and then rinse in fresh water.

The length of time game should be kep depends partly on the weather and partly on individual taste, some people not caring to ea it until it smells distinctly high, while other prefer to use it comparatively fresh.

To Keep Suet.—If there are any glands o kernels to be seen these should be removed, als any parts which show discoloration, as thes very soon become tainted and spoil the rest. I the suet has to be kept for several days it is good plan to bury it in flour. If it is put int the flour-bin it will not impart any flavour to th contents.

Ham and Sides of Bacon.—Hang in musli bags dusted with pepper or ginger to keep o the flies. If they are to be kept a long time th bags should be made of calico, or strong brow paper may be used for wrapping them in.

Lard.—Keep in a closely covered crock o basin.

Bones (for stock).—If unable to use at onc bake sharply in the oven for a few minutes.

Stock and Soup.—See p. 118.

Fish.—Fish should always be placed in th coolest part of the larder—on a marble or slat slab if possible. It is always better if it can h used fresh, but when necessary to keep it fo a day or two sprinkle liberally with salt, or i hot weather it may be wrapped in a piece o muslin wrung out of vinegar and water. Drie fish should be hung on a rod or hook.

Farm Produce—Butter.—Keep in an earthen ware crock, cover with a piece of muslin wrur out of salted water and then with a tight-fittir lid. If there is a large quantity of butter to l stored it should be packed very tightly in th crock so as to leave no room for air to get down the sides. Place the crock in a cool, dark, and airy place.

To keep fresh butter in hot weather a butter-cooler should be used ; this is made with a cover into which is poured a little water. Failing a butter-cooler

Butter-Cooler.

place the butter in a bowl standing in a larg bowl of cold water. Cover it with a piece muslin, allowing the ends of the muslin to d into the water. The water, which should l changed daily, is soaked up by the muslin and thus kept constantly wet.

Butter must not be put near any strong-smelling substance as it quickly absorbs any flavour.

Cheese.—A cut piece of cheese should be wrapped in grease-proof paper or in damp muslin and kept in a cheese dish or jar or tin in which there is a little ventilation. A large piece of cheese ought to be turned frequently and the rind rubbed occasionally with a cloth to prevent moisture collecting. A ripe cheese must be watched carefully to see that it is not attacked by the cheese fly.

Milk and Cream.—Strict cleanliness is the first necessity. The jug or basin in which the milk is kept must be thoroughly scalded and rinsed with cold water. Milk should always be kept covered, and, like butter, it should not be put near anything with a strong smell, as it readily absorbs odours. It is a bad plan to mix milk—a fresh lot should never be added to some that has been in the house several hours. In hot weather the milk should be scalded if it has to be kept for several hours. Stand the jug containing it in a large saucepan of water and heat to almost boiling-point, or this may be done in a double saucepan. A pinch of carbonate of soda or powdered borax may be added to the milk to preserve it, but this spoils the flavour. The same care must be taken with cream. If it is scalded as above it will keep sweet for several hours. A lump of sugar will also help to preserve it.

Eggs should be kept in a basket or on an egg-stand where they do not touch each other. If there is room for storing, the thrifty house-keeper will buy a quantity of eggs in the spring and store them for winter use. They can be preserved in one of the following methods :—

(1) Place them in an air-tight box between layers of coarse salt. The small end of the egg should be placed downwards and they must never touch each other. Put a layer of salt two inches deep on the top, cover with a thick piece of calico or strong paper, and then a tight-fitting lid. This must be kept in a cool place.

(2) Grease the eggs (they must be very fresh) over with lard, oil, or any pure fat and place them on a tray with a layer of bran above and below.

(3) Pack in lime, in the same manner as for salt, only this renders them so brittle that they are unfit for boiling.

(4) Lay them in a bath of water glass. Water glass can be bought for about 4d. per pound, and full directions for its use are printed on each tin.

Bread.—Bread should be kept closely covered in an earthenware bread-pan with a lid, or in an enamelled iron bin. It must never be put away while hot, but should be allowed to cool where the air can circulate freely round it.

The pan or crock must be wiped out regularly in order to free it from all musty crumbs, and once a week or once a fortnight thoroughly scalded, and then allowed to become cool and dry before the bread is returned to it.

Bread can also be kept well if it is placed in a clean cloth and placed on a shelf.

What to do when there is no Larder.—In many small houses and flats there is no proper larder, and one cupboard has to serve the purpose of larder and storeroom and sometimes as a place for keeping dishes as well.

When this is the case the quantities ordered must be as small as possible and cleanliness and order are all the more necessary. If the shelves are made of wood it is a good plan to have them covered with white oil-cloth, as this can so easily be wiped over or washed. In addition to this cupboard, a meat-safe should be provided and placed either outside or in a cool place. Needless to say, it should not be placed anywhere near a lavatory. A small meat-safe can occasionally be fixed to the outside ledge of the kitchen window. If it is out of doors the top must be protected from rain by a covering of wood or galvanised iron, and it must be scrubbed out every week and just as carefully as an inside cupboard.

Failing a meat-safe, small cane and muslin cages should be bought in which meat can be hung up in any cool and well-ventilated place. They are very inexpensive to buy, or they can even be simply constructed at home by making a bag of muslin drawn in at top and bottom. Place a plate at the foot and keep out the sides with hoops of cane lightly tacked in position.

Economy in the Larder.—No housekeeper should dispense with a daily visit to the larder. A survey of this department will help her in ordering the meals of the day besides acting as a stimulus to the cook to avoid waste and keep things in good order.

The chief points to notice when inspecting the larder are :—

(1) What food there is left from the previous day's meals, and how best it can be made to re-appear at table.

(2) What scraps there are for the stock-pot and odds and ends of fat that can be rendered down.

(3) The condition of any meat or game that is being hung.

(4) The condition of the bread-pan—if there are any scraps that will require to be used up.

(5) What new provisions will be required.

(6) That the larder itself is as tidy and fresh as it ought to be, and that plates on which food rests, as well as any basins and jugs, are all clean.

STORING FRUIT AND VEGETABLES

Vegetables.—When vegetables are only bought in small quantities as required they should be kept in baskets or a vegetable rack and stored in a cool place—the floor of the larder or cellar is the best. Potatoes alone, carrots and turnips together, and green and other special vegetables by themselves. Onions, shalots, chives, and garlic are best hung up by strings or in a net bag and kept away from other food.

Parsley and mint should be kept with the stalks in water, and the water changed every day.

Tomatoes should be kept on a plate or spread out on a shelf without touching each other.

To Store Vegetables.—Although vegetables are at their best when freshly gathered, they can when necessary be kept for a limited period. When potatoes are bought in large quantities and stored through the winter, they should be kept in a dry dark cellar and covered with straw to keep off the frost. If kept in a bright or damp place they will spoil and become milled and withered. Rub off all sprouts and shoots as they appear. Examine frequently and remove any that show signs of decay. In the country potatoes are sometimes stored in a deep hole in the ground lined with straw and banked up with sand.

Artichokes can be treated in the same way.

Carrots, Beetroots, and Parsnips may be preserved in dry sand or earth in a dark cellar.

Turnips should be allowed to lie on the floor of a dark cellar.

Vegetable Marrows and Cucumbers will keep for some time if they are hung up by the stalk in a cool situation.

Small **Cabbages** too, if they are sound and firm and cut before the frost touches them, can be preserved for a few weeks if they are spread on a stone floor in the dark.

Herbs.—If these can be bought fresh in the summer time it is best to dry them quickly beside the kitchen fire. Then strip off the leaves and rub them through a fine sieve. The different kinds should be kept separate and stored in air-tight boxes or bottles.

Fruit.—If only bought in small quantities, such fruit as apples, pears, plums, apricots, and oranges should be wiped and spread out on a tray, on the shelves of the store-room or larder, or on a special fruit-stand.

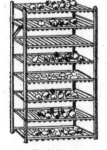

Fruit-Stand.

Bananas and grapes should be hung. Softer fruits, such as currants and berries, should only be bought as required and then used at once.

Lemons should be wiped dry and hung up in nets, or if laid on a shelf they should be turned every day.

All fruit should be kept in a cool place and out of the sun, unless it is a kind which requires further ripening.

When **Apples** have to be stored in large quantities for winter use, they should be dry, sound, and not too ripe. They should be spread out on shelves in a fruit-room or an attic that does not admit too much sunshine. They should not be allowed to touch each other and any decaying ones should be instantly removed. Rough-skinned apples, such as russets, keep best.

Pears, if not ripe, may be kept in the same way or hung up by the stalks.

THE STORE-ROOM OR STORE-CLOSET

If a small room can be set aside for the storage of groceries and other household commodities it will be a great convenience to the careful housewife, and if she has some knowledge as to the stocking and general management of that store-room she will feel a sense of pride in keeping it well plenished and in good order.

A store-room should be dry and airy, tidy and well arranged. A room with a northern or eastern aspect is the best. It should be as near the kitchen as possible in order to avoid unnecessary carrying, and not in the vicinity of a sink or closet.

If a small room is not available a good-sized cupboard can serve the purpose, and goods, &c., must be bought according to the accommodation for keeping them and individual requirements.

Fittings and Arrangements.—The store-room should have its walls and ceiling white-washed or coated with sanitary paint, which can be easily washed. The walls and floor should be examined for any cracks, and if there are such they should be carefully filled up with cement to prevent the entrance of mice, beetles, and other vermin. The floor should be well boarded and either left uncovered or covered with linoleum.

If there is an outside window it should be covered with wire gauze or fine perforated zinc through which no flies can enter.

The walls should be fitted with plenty of shelves, and if these can be graduated in size it will be found an advantage; broader shelves below to hold the bulkier and heavier articles, and narrower ones above for those that are lighter. It is a bad plan to have the shelves so wide that the jars and other receptacles have to be placed one behind the other; it will be a case of "out of sight out of mind," and it will be impossible to see at a glance what the store-room contains. The shelves should be covered with white or brown oilcloth, which is easily wiped down or washed. This can be fastened in position with drawing-pins if there is difficulty in making it lie flat.

If space permits it will be found a great convenience to have a small inner cupboard with one or two drawers, also a strong steady table with a pair of scales or balance.

A few hooks along the edges of the shelves will also be useful for hanging such articles as can be suspended, and they sometimes help to eke out an otherwise limited space.

Requisites.—Besides the stores and provisions it will be found useful to have the following articles in the store-room :—

(1) A dust-pan and brush and one or two dusters for keeping the shelves, floor, &c., in order.

(2) A supply of paper, brown and white, string, pen and ink, and some labels or adhesive papers. A drawer in the table or cupboard might be utilised for these or a special corner of the shelves.

(3) Jars, canisters, boxes, and bottles for keeping the various stores. Any odd jars and

boxes, &c., can be used for the purpose as long as they are sound and have tight-fitting lids or saucers to cover the tops very closely. Empty biscuit-boxes, jam or pickle jars, can be utilised for the purpose. For those who can afford something daintier there are many kinds of store jars to be bought both in earthenware and enamelled tin with the names of the various groceries, &c., printed on the outside, from about 1s. each according to size. Glass jars with lids are also nice for groceries that are bought in small quantities, such as almonds, preserved fruits, cocoanut, chocolate, &c., and neat tin boxes or a small chest for keeping the various spices. Receptacles that have no printed name must be neatly labelled to show the nature of the contents.

Store Jar.

(4) A slate and pencil for noting down what stores require replenishing should be hung in a convenient place in the store-room, or a store

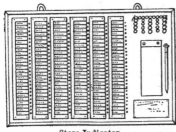

Store Indicator.

indicator may be purchased for about 3s. This useful little remembrancer gives a printed list of the different stores on a neat frame, and a system of pegs and holes indicates what is required.

(5) A few implements will also be required— a pair of scissors, a cork-screw, a knife, a tin-opener, two or three spoons of different sizes, a few scoops, and a cheese and soap-cutter.

(6) It will also be found useful to keep a small tool-box in the store-room containing a hammer, saw, gimlet, screw-driver, a pair of pincers, chisel, and a useful supply of nails, hooks, and tacks.

Grouping the Stores.—In arranging the store-room the various articles must be grouped methodically according to their kind and in such a way that they can be easily found. Keep a special shelf or corner for cereals, another for the different kinds of sugar, another for jams and preserves, another for bottled goods, and so on.

If there is a small cupboard this might be reserved for a medicine cupboard, or for special articles or poisons, which are better kept under lock and key. There should also be a special corner for wine if there is no separate wine cellar, and a special corner for cleaning requisites. Then if there are drawers these might be used for kitchen paper, dish papers, cutlet frills, &c., and another one for an extra supply of dusters, dish cloths, floor cloths, &c., while the nails and hooks can be utilised for such articles as can be hung.

Articles such as tea and coffee, cheese and soap, must not be placed near each other, as the smell and flavour may be imparted from one to the other. Nothing must be kept in paper parcels, and every jar, canister, box, &c., must be clearly labelled on the outside. The heavier jars should be placed on the bottom shelf or on the floor, if dry, and those in constant use readiest to hand.

Cleaning the Store-room.—The store-room must be kept very tidy. The jars ought to be taken down periodically and thoroughly dusted, and the shelves dusted and washed over before they are returned. When necessary, the jars should be washed out and well dried before being refilled. The table and floor should also be scrubbed when they require it, and everything kept in good order. If the stores are dropped about in an untidy manner it will only encourage mice and insects. It is important also that the store-room should be well aired.

Giving out Stores.—Stores should be given out regularly, either daily or weekly and at a fixed date. They should be checked when they come in, and the consumption should be strictly regulated, or the method of buying in quantities will be found an extravagant one.

There are two ways of checking consumption : one method is to keep all stores and provisions under lock and key and to give them out by weight and measure. This method is exact, but it does not always answer ; it is more suitable for a public institution or for a large establishment than for a small private house. It is often a cause of worry and annoyance, and is apt to cause friction between mistress and servants. As a rule, good servants will work most willingly in houses where they are trusted, and if we begin by calculating measure for measure with them they will doubtless do the same with us. Servants who are inclined to be wasteful will waste by ounces just as easily as they can by pounds.

Still, it is not wise to have large quantities out at one time for general use. Smaller jars can be filled with the different stores for daily consumption without actually doling them out by the ounce and half ounce and so much for each person. Some things, such as butter, tea, and sugar, it is very usual to measure out for kitchen use, and where there are several servants this is a wise plan and is thought nothing of (see p. 45).

Another way of checking consumption is by means of the weekly bills. Each housekeeper must draw up her own estimate as to how much should be spent upon certain things and then make an effort to keep within its limit (see p. 365).

GENERAL NOTES ON STORING

Tea and Coffee should be kept in air-tight canisters or in a lead-lined chest.

Dry Groceries.—Keep in covered earthenware jars.

Starch.—Keep in a cool place and well covered, as air turns it powdery.

Soda and Salt.—Keep in a wooden or tin box with a lid. Damp is bad for them; it forms them into blocks.

Spices.—Keep in air-tight tins or in a spice chest.

Flour.—Keep in a wooden or enamelled bin. Sometimes the bin is divided, and one portion can be used for household flour and the other for Vienna flour. If the floor is of stone or damp the bin must be raised.

Jams, Pickles, Bottled Fruits, &c. must be kept in a cool place as they are liable to ferment. If the store-room is hot they should be placed near the floor.

Soap.—Cut in blocks with an old knife or soap-cutter and stack up with a space between each block.

Enamelled Bin.

Candles.—If store-room is warm rub with methylated spirits to harden them.

Biscuits and Cakes.—Keep in tin boxes with tight-fitting lid.

CARE OF WINES

Wines require a great deal of attention, and their preservation in a state fit to drink largely depends upon the treatment they receive. Any carelessness or neglect is sure to be followed by deterioration in quality, and the loss of those properties which can only arrive at perfection if the maturing process is allowed to proceed under conditions which are favourable to their growth and development.

The Wine Cellar.—The cellar should be under-ground if possible, as it will then be less affected by variations in temperature. It should be cool, dry, and well ventilated without any strong draughts. The walls are generally made of brick or stone and white-washed, and the shelves or bins of wood or iron.

Care should be taken to see that the drainage is good and that no foul air enters. The windows or holes to admit light should be small, as any sunshine would raise the temperature which ought to be kept uniform. The thermometer should stand about 55° Fahr. and there should be no variations. If at any time it is necessary to raise the temperature artificially, gas must on no account be employed, as the vitiation of the air which results is injurious to the wine— an oil lamp or small oil stove is better.

Apart from any artificial heating there will always be a slight difference in the degree of warmth between the top bins and the lower ones, owing to the tendency of warm air to rise, and in consequence of this care must be taken to arrange the different varieties of wines in separate parts of the cellar according to their individual requirements as regards heat.

Binning Wines.—Bins are the open divisions in the cellar in which the wine is placed. They may either be fixtures in the cellar or may be bought separately and placed on the floor; if the latter is done, care must be taken that the bin stands steadily or the wine will be disturbed.

In arranging the wines it must be remembered that all wines cannot be treated alike.

As a rule, it is best to bin the light varieties such as Hock, Moselle, and all sparkling varieties at the bottom, Clarets and Burgundies in the middle, and Sherry and Port and other fortified wines at the top.

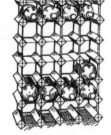

Wine Bin.

The bottles must be placed in the bins horizontally, as the wine would soon deteriorate were they allowed to stand upright. When binning port the bottles should be so placed that the chalk or white paint-mark is uppermost on account of the sediment.

The corks of wine bottles should be examined for signs of decay, because if once they become faulty and the air can penetrate the wine will be spoilt.

Wine should be consumed as soon as possible after the bottle has been opened. The lighter wines are hardly fit to drink if they are kept for even two or three days after being decanted, although the fortified wines, such as sherry and port, will last rather longer. (See also Service of Wines, p. 248.)

Ale, Stout, and Cider.—These beverages require

a temperature of about 50° Fahr. The bottles should be allowed to stand upright a few days before use. Stout should not be kept in the house too long, as it is liable to generate too much gas. If beer is kept in a cask, a stand should be provided in order to raise it about a foot from the ground. A cask should be so placed that there is a space all round it to enable of its being examined from time to time. It must also be perfectly steady and wedges of wood used, if necessary, to keep it from shaking.

Spirits (Whisky, brandy, rum, and gin).—Spirits are best stood upright, and when in bottles require very little attention.

Australian Wines.—These wines are easily handled, being sold in flagons with screw stoppers. Care should be taken to keep the stoppers screwed up very tightly, because if the air is allowed to get to the wine it is liable to turn it acid.

When no Wine Cellar is Available.—If there is no wine cellar in which to keep a supply, wine must be bought in smaller quantities and just enough for immediate requirements. A corner of the store cupboard or some downstairs cellar can sometimes be utilised for

Wine Cabinet.

keeping a moderate supply of bottles, and for convenience sake a small bin might be fitted up. Or a wine cabinet is sometimes found useful, especially in flats and small houses. They are fitted with a strong lock and key, and one to hold four dozen bottles can be bought for about 30s.

MARKETING

General Hints.—It requires a considerable amount of forethought and common-sense to do really good marketing, to buy just what is necessary for the needs of the household, to secure the best value for one's money, and to be economical in the true sense of the word without being parsimonious.

Whether we have much money or little at our disposal it always requires some care to lay it out to the best advantage, and the less there is the more necessity there will be to make the most of it.

Money is often wasted and time lost by the housekeeper not knowing how to choose and order food. It requires some experience to do it well, but with common-sense and good will the art of marketing is easily acquired.

Each purchase should be thoughtfully considered, and when means are scarce money must not be frittered away on any trifle which may strike the fancy and has no real value.

It is always best to deal with good reliable shops and not to be continually hunting after the cheapest market. Try, if possible, to patronise the shops in your immediate neighbourhood, and preferably those in which there is a big turnover, where articles are being constantly sold out and renewed. Avoid shops where the goods are not kept in an orderly and cleanly condition, or where they are exposed to the dust and dirt of the street, or to be touched and handled by every passer-by.

However small the income may be, it will never be found economical to buy goods of inferior quality in order to save a few pence. Aim rather at securing good material of its kind and at avoiding luxuries, except as an occasional treat when they can be afforded.

In order to ascertain whether or not you are being charged a fair price for your provisions, try to obtain a price list from two or three good shops and then compare them.

It is the duty of every mistress to see that her merchandise is good; there is no virtue in allowing short weight and inferior quality nor in permitting oneself to be imposed upon in any way. One only gets the best attention by expecting and demanding it.

Previous to making out her order the mistress should go through the larder and store-room and make a note of what is required, always bearing in mind the bill of fare for the day. Sometimes it is possible to order for two days at a time or to order always one day ahead to ensure having the provisions in the house in good time in the morning. This is often necessary in houses where a very early dinner has to be provided for, and it enables the cook, or whoever undertakes the cooking, time to start her preparations directly the breakfast things are cleared away.

Whenever possible, the mistress of the house or housekeeper should do her own shopping, not necessarily every day, but certainly occasionally. In this way the tradesmen get a better idea of her likes and dislikes and can generally serve her better. Variety will be suggested by what she sees in the shops, and a knowledge of what things are in season is more quickly obtained. With meat especially she will get a better joint or more suitable piece of meat for her purpose if she sees it cut and weighed than if she simply left it to the butcher's discretion. At the fishmonger's, too, a personal visit is a wise plan, as the price of fish varies so much, and even from day to day according to the weather and other circumstances. The more plentiful kind will always be the cheapest for the time being, and it will generally be found that it is the best as well.

Shopping should be done as early as possible, as there is generally a better selection in the forenoon and provisions are fresher.

If this personal shopping cannot be managed by the mistress of the household and there is no responsible person to whom the business may be deputed, a duplicate order book should be used. A separate list for each tradesman should be written out in duplicate form, giving exact quantities required and price if possible. The tradesmen can then send for their orders, one list being given to them and the other retained for reference and for the purpose of checking the house books. This is a safer method than that of giving haphazard verbal orders to message boys.

Small vouchers or weight bills should accompany all goods sent from the shops, and these should be used for checking the various items. (For Payment of Bills, House Books, &c., see pp. 365–66.)

GENERAL NOTES ON ORDERING GROCERIES AND PROVISIONS

When ordering stores there are several points to be considered besides the ordering of what is actually required. We must consider in addition what will keep well, what space there is for storing it, what we can afford, and whether or not it is the best season for a large purchase.

The slate or indicator will help us as regards what is wanted, as when each article is finished or nearly so the fact ought to be noted and then that article included in the next order.

It must be remembered that articles bought in small quantities are often dearer in proportion than when purchased in large quantities; not only is the price per pound less, but the weight of paper and paper-bags is saved.

Good-keeping things should always be bought in large quantities where the purse is not very straitened and where space is not a consideration.

As there is generally a cheap and a dear season an attempt should be made to benefit by the former by buying in as large a store as possible of any special commodity that will keep well and for which there is likely to be use.

All things having a strong taste or smell, such as spices, essences, coffee (when ground), &c., should be bought in small quantities, as they are apt to deteriorate.

All **Grains** and **Cereals, Soda** and **Salt,** may be bought in moderate supplies according to the needs of the household.

Sugar may also be bought in considerable quantities, although moist sugar must be watched, as it sometimes becomes infected with sugar mite. Cane sugar is the best for all preserving purposes; jams made with it will keep longer and have a better colour than if beetroot sugar were used. Beetroot sugar is, however, quite good for other sweetening purposes.

Tea should be bought in moderate quantities. It should be well twisted and the leaves not too small. The special blend to use is entirely a matter of taste.

Dried Fruits will also keep well and should be bought in the autumn when the new fruit comes in. Figs, however, must be carefully looked over, as they often become infected with small maggots.

Soap improves with keeping and may safely be ordered in large quantities. The drier it is the less it will waste when used. There are many different kinds—plain yellow soap, mottled soap, paraffin soap, Sunlight soap, and carbolic soap are all useful for household purposes; also the soft soap, which should be bought in large tins and given out as required.

Candles will also improve with keeping.

Tinned Foods.—Choose tins that are in perfect condition and free from rust. There should be no bulges, which are a sign of fermentation; the tops and bottoms should be rather concave. Foods preserved in earthenware or glass jars are better and safer than tinned ones, but they generally cost more money.

Cheese and Butter must always be chosen by the taste. Cheap butter should be avoided—it is better to use good dripping or lard for cooking purposes than inferior butter.

The choice of cheese is entirely a question of taste. For a moderately priced cheese some of the American cheeses similar to our Cheddar cheeses are to be recommended, also the round Dutch cheeses. In choosing such cheeses as Stilton, Gorgonzola, and Roquefort, select one that combines moisture with green mould. Cream cheeses must always be bought very fresh and used at once.

Eggs if fresh are clear when held up to the light; if stale there is a dark spot or cloudy-looking part. They may be tested by putting them in salt and water—1 ounce salt to 1 pint water; eggs that float in this are not good. They should not be too light, and when shaken the inside should not float about. When eggs are cheap it is sometimes a good plan to buy in large quantity and store them for the winter. (See p. 101.)

Ham.—Choose a short thick leg with a moderate amount of fat. The rind should be rather thin and the bone fine. The quality may be tested by running a pointed knife or skewer in close to the bone; when withdrawn it should not be greasy nor have an unpleasant smell, but, on the contrary, be clean and have a good flavour. Hams vary in price according to the manner of curing and special reputation. In England the Yorkshire and Cumberland hams are generally considered the finest and still command a good price, although some of the southern counties produce hams by no means inferior. In Scotland, the Dumfries and Galloway hams rank among the best, and Irish hams from Belfast are much prized. Canadian and Danish hams are also in the market in large quantities, and although the flavour is not considered so delicate as that of the home-cured variety, their moderate price recommends them to those who have to study economy.

Bacon must be fresh and free from rustiness. The fat should be very white; the lean should adhere closely to the bone and be of a nice red colour, and there should be as little gristle as possible.

The following diagram will give a general idea of the way in which a side of bacon is usually cut in England; there will of course be sub-divisions to make smaller pieces. What is known as " streaky " bacon and the flank are considered the finest, but, being much in demand, they fetch a high price. The back and loin are also prime pieces, while the fore-end and gammon, although not so fine in texture, do excellently for boiled bacon.

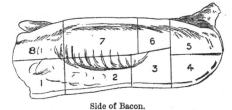

Side of Bacon.

1. Collar.	5. Gammon.
2. Back.	6. Flank.
3. Loin.	7. Streaky.
4. Corner.	8. Fore-end.

HOW TO CHOOSE MEAT

General Hints.—It is very important to buy meat from a good butcher, and one who can be thoroughly trusted.

There are certain signs by which the quality of the meat can generally be judged. The texture should be firm and moderately elastic, and, when pressed, should not leave the imprint of the finger. If the flesh is flabby and moist and has an unpleasant odour it is not good.

The lean part should be finely grained, and the fat, which should not be in any undue proportion, should be free from kernels, brown spots, and streaks of blood.

The meat of most animals that have died a natural death or by accident should be avoided.

Good meat does not waste much in cooking, and when left on a dish the juice should not exude from it in any quantity.

Besides these general points to be remembered each special kind of meat has its individual character by which it can be judged.

Beef.—The best kind of beef is of a nice red colour, almost a cherry red, and the lean has a marble appearance, being slightly intergrained with fat. The fat is a pale yellow colour, not mottled, and the suet hard and dry. It is fine and smooth in texture, with rather an open grain. There should be little or no gristle between the fat and the lean, as this generally indicates that it is the flesh of an old animal. Beef of a dark colour with very yellow fat should be avoided.

Beef is more nourishing and strengthening than mutton, but not so easy of digestion. Ox beef is better than cow beef and generally fetches a higher price. Bull beef is very coarse, and is never sold by a good butcher.

Beef should be well hung before it is used to make it tender; the time it should hang will depend upon the weather, and it must never be allowed to become high.

Mutton.—The best mutton is plump and small-boned. The quality depends very much upon how the animal has been reared, and also upon the age at which it is killed; the mountain-fed sheep are considered the best, and from four to six years old is the best age for killing, only a farmer can rarely afford to keep his sheep so long, and they are generally killed between two and three years of age.

The lean of mutton is not so red in colour as beef, but has a darker and browner hue. It should be firm, close in texture, and not inter-grained with fat. The fat should be hard and very white and waxy. Mutton, like beef, should be well hung.

Lamb is paler in colour than mutton, and the fat is pearly white. When fresh, the veins in the neck end of the fore-quarter have a bluish tinge, and when stale these develop a greenish hue. In the hind-quarter the kidneys should be examined; if they are flabby with an unpleasant smell the meat is stale.

A piece of the caul, a thin transparent-looking membrane, should be sent with each joint of lamb to wrap round it and protect it when cooking.

The New Zealand or Canterbury lamb is much cheaper than the home grown, but as far as taste is concerned it is more like mutton, as it seems to lose its characteristic flavour during the process of freezing.

The flesh of lamb is tenderer than that of mutton, but it is more watery and not so nutritious. Lamb cannot be hung for very long.

Pork.—Pork requires very careful choosing as it is more subject to disease than perhaps any other animal food, and unless one is sure of its source it is safer to leave it alone. The flesh should be of a pinky white colour, smooth, finely grained, and firm to the touch. The skin must not be too thick. The fat should be pearly white with no black specks nor kernels. Small pork is the best. It is much more difficult to digest than either beef or mutton, as it contains such a large proportion of fat.

Veal is the flesh of the calf. It should be very pale in colour, firm, and closely grained. The fat should be white, and if that which surrounds the kidney is hard and without smell the meat is in good condition. Veal is not so nutritious as beef and it is more difficult of digestion. Like all other young meats, it should not be hung very long.

Venison is the flesh of deer. The lean should be finely grained and dark in colour. The fat should be plentiful and of a creamy white appearance.

The age can be judged by the hoof; in the young animal the cleft is small and smooth, while in the older one it has become much deeper and more rugged.

Venison should be hung as long as possible, but it must be frequently examined. Its freshness can be tested by running a knife or skewer into the bone at the haunch; if when withdrawn it smells well and is not sticky this is a sure sign of good condition.

The flesh of the buck is considered superior to that of the doe.

Suet.—This must be very fresh and of good quality. The solid fat, which surrounds the kidney, either beef or mutton, is considered the best. Beef suet should be cream coloured or pale yellow and mutton suet very white and waxy. Both should be very firm and dry.

Internal Meats.—All inside meats such as tripe, liver, kidneys, sweetbreads, &c., must be bought very fresh and used at once.

CALENDAR OF MEAT IN SEASON

Beef, Mutton, and **Veal** are in season all the year round.

Lamb.—House lamb from January to May, grass lamb from May to September, and New Zealand lamb all the year round.

Pork.—All the year round, but best from September to May.

Venison.—Buck venison from May to October, doe venison from October to end of January.

DIFFERENT JOINTS OF MEAT AND THEIR USES

The cutting up of meat varies somewhat according to locality and also according to the special demands of the people with whom the butchers have to deal.

The following diagrams will give an idea of how the different animals are cut up by English butchers, and may also be of assistance to the housewife in knowing what piece to order for the special purpose she has in view.

BEEF

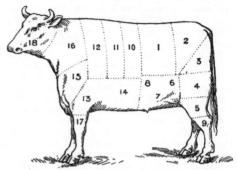

Diagram showing mode of cutting up Beef in England.

1. Sirloin.	10. Fore Ribs.
2. Rump.	11. Middle Ribs.
3. Aitchbone.	12. Chuck Ribs.
4. Buttock.	13. Leg of Mutton Piece.
5. Mouse Buttock.	14. Brisket.
6. Veiny parts.	15. Clod.
7. Thick Flank.	16. Neck.
8. Thin Flank.	17. Shin.
9. Shin.	18. Cheek.

The Sirloin.—This is the best part for roasting, but it is somewhat expensive. It is usually divided into three pieces varying in weight according to the size of the animal. The middle cut is considered the best, as it has the largest amount of undercut. The piece next the ribs has very little undercut, and the one next the rump is a joint difficult to carve, as it has a piece of bone on one side.

The sirloins from both sides of the animal not cut asunder form what is called the baron of beef, corresponding to the saddle in mutton. This is a joint rarely seen nowadays, but was famous at banquets in the days of our ancestors.

The fillet or undercut of the sirloin is the most tender part for entrées or fillets of beef.

Ribs.—The cuts from the ribs are also good for roasting, those nearest the sirloin being the best. Various sizes of joints can be cut according to special requirements. It is more economical to have the bone removed and used for soup and the meat itself rolled. One or two ribs treated in this way make a neat little roast for a small family. When a large cut of the ribs is ordered and roasted whole, it is better to have the thin end cut off and used for a separate dish, otherwise it becomes overcooked before the thicker part is ready. The piece of ribs next the shoulder is better stewed or braised than roasted.

The Rump.—This is divided into three parts—the middle, the silver-side, and the chump end. The middle is an excellent piece of fleshy meat for any purpose. Some of the best steaks are cut from this part; it is also a first-rate cut for pies, for rolled beef, or for a tender stew. The chump end is also good for stewing. The silver-side is very often salted and is good for boiling.

Buttock or Round.—This is another very fleshy piece of meat with little bone. It is one of the best pieces for braising or boiling, and is often salted. It can also be roasted, but, although economical, it is not so fine in flavour as the ribs or sirloin.

Aitch Bone, or Edge Bone.—This is a cheap piece of meat, but as it contains a large propor-tion of bone and wastes very much in cooking it is not really economical. It is an awkwardly shaped joint and very difficult to carve. It is generally boiled and sometimes salted.

Brisket.—This is also sold at a low price, and is used principally for boiling or stewing. It is rather fat, but is excellent when salted and boiled and then served cold.

Flank.—The thick flank is one of the most economical parts to buy, as it contains no bone and very little fat. Suitable for braising, stew-ing, and boiling. The thin flank contains much more fat, and is best salted, boiled, and eaten cold.

The Clod and Sticking Piece are both some-what coarse and only suitable for soup or cheap stews.

Shin.—This is also coarse grained and very gelatinous. It is excellent for stock and soup. The top part will also make an economical stew if slowly and carefully cooked.

Cheek.—Only suitable for stews and for making soup. As it contains so much bone it is not really economical.

Cow Heel is very gelatinous, and is used principally for making jelly, or, along with meat, as a foundation for soups. It can also be carefully boiled or stewed and then eaten with a good and piquant sauce.

Tail.—This is somewhat expensive. It is used for making soups, and can also be stewed or braised.

Heart.—This is rather coarse and very in-digestible, but it can be made palatable by being stuffed and very carefully roasted or braised.

Tongue is usually salted and then boiled and served cold, or served hot with a good sauce, or cut in slices for an entrée.

Tripe.—This is the inner lining of the stomach. It is usually sold partially prepared, although in Scotland it requires many hours' boiling. It is very tender and easily digested, and for this reason is frequently ordered for invalids.

There are several different kinds of tripe popularly known as "honeycomb," "blanket," "double" or "book" (because it is like the leaves of a book), and "reed" the dark-coloured portion.

Liver.—This is a cheap piece, and is nutritious for those who can digest it. It requires careful cooking.

Kidneys.—Used for making soup. Can also be stewed, although rather indigestible.

Midriff.—A thin fleshy piece which runs across the middle of the animal. It is rich in flavour and is very good for stews or beef-steak pudding.

Sweetbread.—In the ox this part is coarse, and can only be made palatable by careful cooking.

VEAL

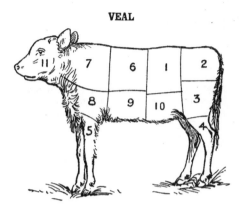

Mode of cutting up a Calf.

1. Loin.	7. Shoulder.
2. Chump end of Loin.	8. Blade-bone.
3. Fillet.	9. Breast.
4. Hind-knuckle.	10. Flank.
5. Fore-knuckle.	11. Head.
6. Neck (best end).	

Veal, which is the flesh of the calf, is cut up into the following different joints :—

The Fillet.—One of the finest pieces, very fleshy with little or no bone. Can be used for any purpose. The best cutlets are cut from this part. It is high priced, but not over expensive, as there is practically no waste.

The Breast.—If boned, stuffed and rolled, this part makes a nice little joint for roasting. It can also be braised or stewed. Entrées are also prepared from this piece.

The Loin.—One of the best pieces for roasting, also for chops.

The Neck.—A good joint for braising or stewing. Can also be roasted. The best end may be cut into chops. The scrag-end is more suitable for broth.

Knuckle.—This is a favourite part for soup or broth and is much used in the making of white stock. The fore-knuckle is more tender than the hind-knuckle and is often stewed or boiled and served with a good sauce.

Head and Feet are sometimes served to-gether as a hash, but, being rather insipid in flavour, they require a good sauce. They can also be used for pies, when some ham should be added, and for different entrées. The head is used for soup—Mock Turtle Soup—and the feet for making jelly—Calf's Foot Jelly.

Sweetbread.—This is considered a great delicacy, and is generally expensive. It is much used for entrées, and is a favourite dish for invalids. The throat sweetbread, which is the thymus gland of the calf, is considered inferior in quality to the heart sweetbread.

Kidney.—Generally sold along with a piece of the loin and roasted. Can also be used separately in the same way as sheep's kidneys.

Brains.—A very delicate morsel for entrées.

Liver and Heart.—Can be used in the same way as sheep's liver and heart.

MUTTON

The following diagram will give an idea of the different joints into which mutton is cut:—

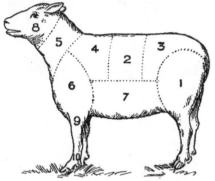

Diagram showing mode of cutting up a Sheep.

1. Leg.	6. Shoulder.
2. Loin.	7. Breast.
3. Chump end of the Loin.	8. Head.
4. Neck (best end).	9. Shank.
5. Scrag.	10. Trotter.

The Leg.—This is one of the most economical cuts for boiling or roasting, as it is lean with a small amount of bone in proportion to its size. It is too large a joint for a small family. It is sometimes a good plan to have it cut in two pieces and to roast one piece and boil or stew the other. When a piece of the loin is cut along with the leg it is called the haunch.

The Loin.—This is generally divided into two parts, the best end and the chump end, or even subdivided into separate cutlets or chops. The loin makes one of the finest and most delicate roasts, but it is not economical owing to the large proportion of fat and bone. If ordering for a roast it must be well jointed by the butcher or it will be found difficult to carve, or sometimes the chine bone, the bone which runs down the centre of the back, is sawn nearly off and then removed altogether after cooking. The double loin from both sides of the animal is called the saddle. It is considered a very fine joint, but too large for an ordinary household.

The Neck.—The best end of the neck is also used for cutlets. It is an excellent piece for broiling and braising, as it is tender and delicate in flavour. The scrag-end, which lies nearer the head, is a cheap piece of an awkward shape and contains a good deal of bone. It is only suitable for broth or plain stews as it is impossible to cut it in neat pieces.

The Shoulder.—This is another good joint for roasting, and some people prefer it to the leg. It is perhaps more delicate in flavour, but is inclined to be fat. It can also be braised or boiled.

The Breast.—Is a cheap piece of mutton with much fat and skin. If boned, stuffed, and rolled it makes quite a nice little roast. It is also very suitable for Irish stew where the potatoes absorb some of the fat.

The Head and Trotters are generally sold at a low price, but they make excellent broth, and can also be served as a dish by themselves with a good sauce or made into a pie and served cold.

The Pluck.—This consists of the heart, liver and lungs, which are often sold together. In Scotland they form the foundation of haggis. The lungs, or lights, are very inferior, and by themselves are seldom used, except perhaps as cats' meat. The heart is sometimes sold by itself, and is very good stuffed and roasted. The liver can also be bought separately, and is generally fried or sautéed along with a little bacon.

Kidneys.—These are very dainty morsels and are a favourite breakfast delicacy. They are generally broiled or stewed, and are also used along with beef in pies and stews. The loin roast often contains one of the kidneys.

LAMB

When lamb is large it is usually cut up and used in the same way as mutton, but when small it is cut in quarters. The fore-quarter consists of the neck, shoulder, and breast, and the hind-quarter of the leg and the loin.

If the hind-quarter makes too large a joint the upper part may be cut into chops and served as one dish, while the lower portion will make a nice little roast or may be steamed and served with a good sauce. Or a larger-sized piece may be cut off the top and made into a stew or braised.

The fore-quarter may be divided in the same way, the breast piece being stewed or braised and the shoulder roasted. The chops from the neck may also be cut off separately and either broiled or fried or used for hotch-potch.

Lamb's Head can be used in the same way as sheep's head and is more delicate in flavour.

Lamb's Fry, consisting of the liver, sweetbread, and heart, is generally cut in slices and fried. The sweetbreads alone are considered a great delicacy and are much used for entrées.

PORK

Diagram showing different cuts of Pork.

1. Spare Rib.	4. Fore-loin.
2. Hand.	5. Loin.
3. Spring or Belly.	6. Leg.

The usual joints of fresh pork are the following :—

The Loin is generally scored and roasted. Pork chops are also cut from this part.

Leg.—Another piece for roasting. The skin must always be scored by the butcher, or it would be impossible to carve the joint. It is sometimes salted and then boiled.

The Hand and Spring or Belly.—These parts are rather fat, and are usually salted. They are best boiled and served cold.

Head.—Usually salted. Can be made into brawn or boiled and served cold.

Feet (Pettitoes) can be cooked in various ways. Usually boiled or stewed.

The Tongue should be pickled and then served in the same way as sheep's tongue.

VENISON

The finest joint for roasting is the **Haunch.** The **Loin** and **Neck** are also good roasting pieces.

The **Shoulder** and **Breast** are better stewed or made into a ragoût. Chops are usually cut from the loin or neck and steaks from the leg.

FROZEN MEAT

Large quantities of meat are now imported from abroad in a frozen condition and sold in this country at a considerably lower price than that of home production. New Zealand, Australia, the United States, S. America, and Canada all send us in supplies.

The prejudice against this kind of meat has to a large extent disappeared, and it is certainly an immense boon to those who cannot afford the high prices asked for our home-fed meat.

Needless to say, this foreign meat does not equal British meat as far as quality and flavour are concerned; the process of freezing apparently takes away from its goodness, but with careful thawing and good cooking it compares very favourably with the more expensive joints, and

in many cases it requires an experienced palate to detect the difference.

Mutton and lamb seem to suffer less than beef from the process of freezing. That known as Canterbury lamb is the best. When ordering frozen meat it must be remembered that it will not keep in warm weather without a refrigerator.

HOW TO CHOOSE FISH

General Hints.—Fish to be good ought to be in season.

Moderately-sized fish are better than very large ones, especially those which are thick and plump in proportion to their size. A short thick fish is always better than one that is long and thin.

There are several signs by which its freshness can be judged; the fish should be firm and stiff, and when held up the tail should not droop; but this alone is not sufficient sign, as fish kept on ice will retain its rigidity although several days old, so we must look for other signs as well.

The gills in fresh fish are a bright red, the eyes are bright and not sunken, and the scales also are bright and can be easily removed when rubbed.

A flat fish should never be bought without looking at both sides, and especially the grey side, as this betrays any want of freshness more quickly than the white.

A plaice, for instance, can always be judged by its spots; when fresh they are a bright red, and after it has been kept some time they take a brownish hue.

In choosing cut fish, such as cod, halibut, or salmon, &c., the flesh should have a firm appearance with a close grain; if it looks fibrous and watery it is not good.

Never choose fish that is bruised or has the skin broken, as it will not keep well.

CALENDAR OF FISH IN SEASON

January.—Barbel, bream, brill, carp, cod, dory, eels, flounders, gurnet, haddock, halibut, hake, herring, ling, mackerel, perch, pike, plaice, skate, smelts, soles, sprats, sturgeon, tench, thornback, turbot, whitebait, whiting.

Crabs, crayfish, lobsters, mussels, oysters, scallops, shrimps.

February.—Bream, brill, carp, cod, dory, eels, flounders, gurnets, haddock, halibut, herring, ling, mackerel, mullet, plaice, perch, pike, salmon, skate, smelts, soles, sprats, sturgeon, tench, thornback, trout, turbot, whitebait, whiting.

Crab, crayfish, lobsters, mussels, oysters, prawns, scallops, shrimps.

March.—Bream, brill, carp, cod, eels, flounders, gurnets, haddock, halibut, herring, ling, mackerel, mullet, pike, salmon, skate, smelts, soles, sprats (tench until 15th), thornback, trout, turbot, whiting, whitebait.

Crabs, crayfish, lobsters, mussels, oysters, prawns, scallops, shrimps.

April.—Bream, brill, chub, conger eel, cod, dory, flounders, gurnet, haddock, halibut, herring, ling, mackerel, mullet, plaice, salmon, shad, skate, smelts, soles, sturgeon, turbot, trout, whitebait, whiting.

Crabs, crayfish, lobsters, mussels, oysters, prawns, scallops, shrimps.

May.—Bass, brill, cod, dace, dory, eels, gurnet, hake, halibut, herring, ling, mackerel, mullet, salmon, shad, skate, smelts, soles, sturgeon, trout, turbot, whitebait, whiting.

Crabs, crayfish, lobsters, prawns, scallops, shrimps.

June.—Bass, bream, brill, carp, chub, cod, dace, dory, eels, flounders, gurnets, halibut, hake, haddock, herring, lampreys, mackerel, mullet, perch (after 15th), pike, plaice, salmon, shad, soles, tench, trout, turbot, whitebait, whiting.

Crabs, crayfish, lobsters, prawns, shrimps.

July.—Bass, bream, brill, carp, chub, dace, dory, eels, flounders, gurnets, haddock, hake, halibut, herring, mackerel, mullet, perch, pike, plaice, salmon, sea-bream, shad, smelts, soles, tench, thornback, trout, turbot, whitebait, whiting.

Crabs, crayfish, lobsters, prawns, shrimps.

August.—Bass, bream, brill, carp, chub, dace, dory, eels, flounders, gurnets, haddock, hake, halibut, herring, lamprey, mackerel, mullet, plaice, perch, pike, salmon, sea-bream, shad, soles, tench, trout, turbot, whitebait, whiting.

Crabs, crayfish, lobsters, prawns, shrimps.

September.—Bass, bream, brill, carp, cod, chub, dace, dory, eels, flounders, gurnet, haddock, hake, halibut, herring, lampreys, mackerel, mullet, perch, pike, plaice, salmon, sea-bream, shad, smelts, soles, tench, trout, turbot, whitebait, whiting.

Crabs, crayfish, lobsters, oysters, shrimps.

October.—Bream, brill, carp, cod, dory, eels, flounders, gurnet, haddock, halibut, herring, mackerel, mullet, perch, pike, plaice, salmon, sea-bream, skate, soles, smelts, tench, turbot, whiting.

Crabs, crayfish, lobsters, mussels, oysters, scallops, shrimps.

November.—Bream, brill, carp, cod, dory, flounders, eels, gurnet, haddock, halibut, herring, mackerel, mullet, perch, pike, plaice, salmon (Dutch), skate, smelts, sprats, soles, tench, turbot, whiting.

Crabs, crayfish, lobsters, mussels, oysters, scallops, shrimps.

December.—Brill, carp, cod, eels, flounders, gurnets, haddock, halibut, herring, mackerel, mullet, perch, pike, plaice, salmon (Dutch), sea-bream, skate, smelt, sprats, soles, tench, whiting.

Crabs, crayfish, lobsters, mussels, oysters, scallops, shrimps.

ON CHOOSING GAME AND POULTRY

General Rules for Choosing Poultry.—All poultry when young should have smooth and pliable legs, with the scales overlapping very slightly. The spur on the leg must be short and not prominent, and the feet should be soft and rather moist. If the spur is large and the legs hard and dry the bird is no longer young. The flesh should be smooth and without long hairs. When choosing a bird that has not been plucked it should be seen that the plumage is smooth and downy with soft young feathers under the wing and on the breast. If freshly killed the eyes will be clear and not sunken; there will be no discoloration of the flesh and the vent will be hard and close.

When poultry is bought quite fresh it may be hung for a few days, but should not be drawn until about to be used. It must never be over-hung, and when it shows the least sign of turning green it is unfit for food.

Fowls.—The comb should be smooth and of a bright red colour. For roasting choose a fowl with black or yellow legs, as they are supposed to be more juicy and to possess a better flavour. For boiling, choose one with white legs, as the flesh will likely be whiter.

A fowl for roasting, frying, or grilling should be young and tender, but for boiling, braising, or stewing an older one may be taken, as old birds are generally cheaper, and long slow cooking makes them tender.

Geese and Ducks.—Young birds have yellow feet and bills with few bristles; as they get older they become darker and redder, although the wild duck has small reddish feet even when young. The feet should be white and smooth and without wrinkles. A goose must always be eaten young; when over twelve months old it is not good for table use.

Pigeons.—A dark-coloured one is thought to have the highest flavour, and a light-coloured one the most delicate. The legs should be of a pinkish colour; when they are large and deeply coloured the bird is old. The tame pigeon is smaller than the wild species and is better for cooking. Tame pigeons should be cooked at once as they soon lose their flavour, but wood pigeons may be hung for a few days.

Turkeys.—A good turkey will be recognised by the whiteness of its flesh and its smooth black legs. The wattles should be a bright red, the breast full and the neck long. Beware of those with long hairs and flesh of a violet hue. A moderate-sized bird should be chosen. A hen is preferable for boiling on account of the whiteness of the flesh, and the cock is usually chosen for roasting.

If freshly killed it should be kept for at least three or four days before cooking or it will neither be white nor tender. It should be hung up to bleed.

Norfolk turkeys are considered the best.

Game.—It is rather more difficult to choose game than it is to choose poultry, as the birds are usually sold unplucked, but still some of the same signs will hold good. The young birds are known by their smooth and pliable legs and short rounded spurs. The feet should be supple and moist and easily broken. The feathers also help to indicate the age of the bird, as when young there are soft and downy ones under the wing and on the breast. The plumage of the young bird is even and soft, the long feathers of the wings are pointed, while in the older bird these become round and the colours are usually brighter.

The condition of the bird can be judged by turning back the feathers of the breast and seeing if it feels plump and hard; it should also weigh heavy for its size.

As regards the time for keeping game, it is impossible to lay down any definite rules. To begin with it depends very much upon individual taste, those who have it seldom as a rule liking it higher than those who are constantly having it. Then old birds can be hung for a longer time than young ones, and again the weather must be taken into consideration; close muggy days will not be so good for keeping purposes as those which are dry and cold.

Game should be hung unplucked and undrawn and in a current of air if possible. It must be remembered that if it is required to taste high when cooked, it should smell almost offensively so beforehand.

Water birds should always be eaten fresh, as their flesh, being of an oily nature, very soon becomes sour.

Hares and Rabbits.—When young the claws are long and pointed, the cleft in the jaws is very narrow, the teeth are small and white, and the ears can easily be torn. The small nut under the paw should also be well developed. When the animal is old the claws become rounded and rough, the cleft in the jaw deepens, the front teeth are long and yellow, and the ears become tough and dry, and the little nut under the paw disappears.

Rabbits, like poultry, should be used fresh. Choose one that is plump and short-necked, and the flesh should be stiff without any discoloration. Wild rabbits are generally preferred to tame ones, as they are considered to have a better flavour. The flesh of the tame rabbit is white and more delicate. A rabbit should be paunched before it is hung up.

Hares, on the contrary, require to be well hung —at least a week—and should not be paunched until about to be used.

CALENDAR OF POULTRY AND GAME IN SEASON

The following will be found useful for ready reference :—

January. — Capons, capercailzie, chickens, ducks, fowls, geese, hares, larks, landrails, partridges, pheasants, pigeons, pintail, plover, pullets, snipe, turkeys, wild-fowl, widgeon, woodcock.

February. — Capons, capercailzie, chickens, ducks, fowls, geese, hares, larks, landrails, partridges, pheasants, pigeons, pintail, plover, ptarmigan, pullets, prairie-hen, rabbits, snipe, turkeys, teal, wild-fowl, widgeon, woodcock.

March.—Capons, capercailzie, chickens, ducks, fowls, geese, guinea-fowls, hares, landrails, ortolans (partridges, pheasants, and plover until middle of month), prairie-hens, ptarmigan, pigeons, pullets, quail, rabbits, ruffs and reeves, snipe (until 15th), teal, turkeys, widgeon, wild-fowl, woodcock.

April.—Capons, chickens, ducks, ducklings, fowls, guinea-fowls, goslings, hares, leverets, ortolans, prairie-hens, pigeons, ptarmigan, quail, rabbit, ruffs and reeves.

May.—Capons, chickens, ducks, ducklings, fowls, guinea-fowls, goslings, green geese, hares, leverets, ortolans, pigeons, ptarmigan, pullets, quail, rabbits, ruffs and reeves.

June.—Capons, chickens, ducks, ducklings, fowls, guinea-fowls, goslings, green geese, hares, hazel hens, leverets, ortolans, pigeons, pullets, quails, rabbits, ruffs and reeves, turkey poults, wheatears.

July.—Capons, chickens, ducks, ducklings, fowls, green geese, goslings, hares, leverets, ortolans, pigeons, plover, pullets, quail, rabbits, ruffs and reeves, turkey poults, wheatears.

August.—Capercailzie, capons, chickens, wild and tame ducks, ducklings, fowls, geese, goslings, grouse (on 12th), hares, larks, leverets, pigeons, plover, pullets, quails, rabbits, snipe, teal, turkey poults, woodcock, wheatears.

September.—Capercailzie, capons, chickens, wild and tame ducks, fowls, geese, grouse, hares, larks, leverets, moor-game, partridges, pheasants, pigeons, plovers, pullets, rabbits, snipe, turkeys, turkey poults, teal, widgeon, woodcock, wheatears.

October.—Black game, capercailzie, capons, chickens, wild ducks, fowls, geese, grouse, hares, larks, partridges, pheasants, pigeons, pintails, plover, ptarmigan, pullets, rabbits, snipe, turkeys, turkey poults, teal, widgeon, woodcock.

November.—Black game, capercailzie, capons, chickens, wild and tame ducks, fowls, geese, grouse, hares, larks, landrails, partridges, pheasants, pigeons, pintails, plover, ptarmigan, pullets, rabbits, snipe, turkeys, turkey poults, teal, widgeon, woodcock.

December.—Black game, capercailzie (until 20th), capons, chickens, ducks, fowls, geese, grouse (until 18th), hares, landrails, larks, partridges, pheasants, pintail, plover, ptarmigan, rabbits, snipe, teal, turkeys, turkey poults, widgeon, woodcock.

THE CHOOSING OF FRUIT AND VEGETABLES

Although it does not require much experience to tell when fruit and vegetables are fresh, it does require some attention and care to see that one is served with the proper article.

Vegetables are never so good as when procured fresh from a garden, and when one is not the happy possessor of a piece of ground it is sometimes possible to make an arrangement with a gardener or farmer to send a supply two or three times weekly, if not daily.

If vegetables and fruit have to be bought from a shop personal choice is always preferable to a written order. The greengrocer or fruiterer is naturally anxious to get rid of his stock, and it is not to be wondered at if he tries to dispose of the articles he has had longest before selling those which are fresh.

The careful housewife will, however, insist upon getting what is really fresh and will accept nothing that is doubtful.

Salads and other green vegetables especially are only good when newly gathered; if they have been lying packed one on top of the other for any length of time they become unwholesome, and this is often the cause of green vegetables disagreeing with people who have a weak digestion.

Cauliflowers should be close and very white, and those of a medium size are best; avoid those that have a greenish colour.

Brussels Sprouts and Cabbages should be close and firm with plenty of heart. Young cabbages are the most delicate in flavour.

Cucumbers and Vegetable Marrows should also be firm, and those of a medium size and straight in form are to be preferred to the twisted and overgrown specimens.

Tomatoes must not be over-ripe. The home-grown red tomatoes are best for salads and for eating raw, while the foreign ones, which are cheaper, are excellent for cooking purposes.

Peas and Beans are best when they are young, especially if they are to be served separately as vegetables to accompany meat. The older ones can be served in soups and stews.

Celery should be chosen of a medium size, and the stalks must be very stiff and close together. The whiter it is the better.

Root Vegetables, unlike green vegetables, may be kept for some time without suffering in any way; they must, however, be firm and not withered or shrunken. Some kinds, such as potatoes, carrots, turnips, and parsnips can even be stored for winter use (see p. 102). Potatoes, for instance, can often be bought very cheaply by the sack in the summer, and there may be a distinct advantage in laying in a store at this season. There must, of course, be the proper accommodation for keeping them, and the greatest care must be taken to see that they are sound and good when bought.

It is always best to buy the vegetables that are in season; they are then at their cheapest and best. The early and forced varieties rarely have the same flavour as those of maturer growth and should not be bought by the thrifty housewife for the ordinary bill of fare.

The same care must be taken in the choice of fruit, and only that which is perfectly sound should be accepted. When it is to be eaten raw it ought to be fully ripe without being over-much so.

CALENDAR OF FRUIT IN SEASON

January.—Almonds, apples, bananas, chestnuts, figs, grapes, lemons, medlars, nuts, oranges, pears, pines, Spanish nuts, walnuts, &c.

February.—Almonds, apples, bananas, chestnuts, figs, grapes, lemons, medlars, nuts, oranges, peaches, pears, pines, rhubarb (forced), Spanish nuts, walnuts, &c.

March.—Almonds, apples, bananas, chestnuts, figs, grapes, lemons, melons, nuts, oranges, peaches, pears, pines, rhubarb (forced), Spanish nuts, walnuts, &c.

April.—Almonds, apples, bananas, dried fruits, figs, grapes, nuts, oranges, pines, rhubarb, &c.

May.—Almonds, apples, apricots (forced), bananas, cherries (forced), dried fruits, figs, grapes, green gooseberries, melons, oranges, pears, pines, rhubarb, &c.

June.—Almonds, apples, apricots, bananas, cherries, currants, figs, gooseberries, grapes, melons, nectarines, peaches, pears, pines, raspberries, rhubarb, strawberries, &c.

July.—Almonds, apricots, bananas, cherries, currants, damsons, figs, gooseberries, grapes, melons, nectarines, oranges, peaches, pears, pineapples, plums, raspberries, strawberries, &c.

August.—Almonds, apricots, bananas, cherries, cobnuts, currants, damsons, figs, filberts, grapes, greengages, medlars, melons, mulberries, nectarines, oranges, peaches, pears, pines, plums, raspberries, strawberries, walnuts, &c.

September.—Almonds, apples, apricots, bananas, cherries, cobnuts, damsons, figs, filberts, grapes, greengages, melons, medlars, mulberries, nectarines, oranges, peaches, pears, pines, plums, quinces, walnuts, &c.

October.—Almonds, apples, apricots, bananas, cobnuts, cranberries, cocoanuts, damsons, figs, filberts, grapes, medlars, melons, nectarines, oranges, peaches, pears, pines, quinces, walnuts, &c.

November.—Almonds, apples, bananas, chestnuts, cocoanuts, cranberries, figs, filberts, grapes, melons, nuts (various), pears, pines, pomegranates, plums (Californian), quinces, walnuts, &c.

December.—Almonds, apples, bananas, chestnuts, cocoanuts, cranberries, figs, filberts, grapes, melons, nuts (various), oranges, pears, pines, plums (Californian), pomegranates, rhubarb (forced), walnuts, &c.

CALENDAR OF VEGETABLES IN SEASON.

January. — Artichokes, beetroot, broccoli, Brussels sprouts, cabbage, cardoons, carrots, celery, chervil, cress, cucumbers, endive, leeks, lettuce, onions, parsnips, potatoes, salsify, savoys, spinach, tomatoes, turnips.

February.—Artichokes, beetroot, broccoli, Brussels sprouts, cabbage, celery, chervil, cress, cucumbers, endive, greens, leeks, lettuce, mushrooms, potatoes, onions, parsnips, salsify, Scotch kale, savoys, sorrel, spinach, tomatoes, turnips.

March.—Artichokes, asparagus, beetroot, broccoli, Brussels sprouts, cabbage, cardoons, carrots, cauliflower, celery, chervil, cucumber, endive, greens, horse-radish, leeks, lettuce, mushrooms, onions, parsnips, new potatoes, radishes, savoys, spinach, sea and Scotch kale, turnips, tomatoes, watercress.

April.—Artichokes, asparagus, beetroot, cabbage, cauliflower, celery, cucumber, endive, eschalots, leeks, lettuce, mushrooms, spring onions, parsnips, new potatoes, radishes, sea-kale, spinach, sprouts, tomatoes, turnips.

May.—Artichokes, asparagus, beans, beetroot, cabbage, new carrots, cauliflower, chervil, cucumbers, endive, lettuce, leeks, mushrooms, mustard and cress, peas, new potatoes, spring onions, radishes, sea-kale, spinach, turnips, watercress.

June.—Artichokes, asparagus, beans, beetroot, cabbage, new carrots, cucumbers, endive,

greens, leeks, lettuce, mushrooms, parsnips, peas, new potatoes, spring onions, radishes, sea-kale, spinach, tomatoes, turnips, vegetable marrow, watercress.

July.—Artichokes, asparagus, beans, beetroot, broad beans, cabbage, carrots, cauliflower, chervil, cress, cucumber, endive, leeks, lettuce, mushrooms, spring onions, peas, new potatoes, scarlet runners, spinach, tomatoes, turnips, vegetable marrow, watercress.

August.—Artichokes, beans, beetroot, cabbage, carrots, cauliflower, celery, cress, cucumbers, endive, leeks, lettuce, mushrooms, peas, potatoes, salsify, scarlet runners, spinach, tomatoes, turnips, vegetable marrow, watercress.

September.—Artichokes, beans, beetroot, cabbage, carrots, cauliflower, celery, cress, cucumber, endive, leeks, lettuce, mushrooms, parsnips, peas, salsify, scarlet runners, spinach, sprouts, tomatoes, turnips, vegetable marrow, watercress.

October.—Artichokes, beetroot, cabbage, carrots, cauliflower, celery, cucumber, greens, leeks, lettuce, mushrooms, parsnips, savoys, scarlet runners, Spanish onions, spinach, sprouts, tomatoes, turnips, vegetable marrow, watercress.

November. — Artichokes, beetroot, Brussels sprouts, carrots, celery, cress, cucumber, greens, leeks, lettuce, parsnips, savoys, Spanish onions, spinach, tomatoes, turnip tops, watercress.

December.—Artichokes, beetroot, broccoli, Brussels sprouts, cabbage, carrots, cauliflower, celery, cucumber, greens, leeks, parsnips, salsify, savoys, Scotch and sea-kale, Spanish onions, tomatoes, turnip tops, vegetable marrow, watercress.

IMPERIAL WEIGHTS AND MEASURES

Avoirdupois Weight

16 drachms (dr.) . .	make 1 ounce (oz.).
16 ounces	,, 1 pound (lb.).
28 pounds	,, 1 quarter (qr.).
4 quarters	,, 1 hundredweight (cwt.).
20 hundredweights .	,, 1 ton.

14 pounds	make 1 stone.
8 stones	,, 1 hundredweight.
112 pounds	,, 1 hundredweight.

Liquid Measure of Capacity

4 gills	make 1 pint (pt.).
2 pints	,, 1 quart (qrt.).
4 quarts	,, 1 gallon (gal.).

Dry Measure of Capacity

2 gallons	make 1 peck (pk.).
4 pecks	,, 1 bushel (bush.).
8 bushels	,, 1 quarter (qr.).

THE TABLE

A GOOD housewife will not rest content with the fact that the meals in her house are well cooked. She will also see to it that they are well served, knowing that dainty table equipment and skilful service does much to enhance the enjoyment of the fare provided.

This article deals with all the many important subjects bearing upon table service, including the fittings and arrangement of the pantry and its contents ; the choice of silver, china, cutlery, and glass ; the arrangement of a menu, with order of courses ; valuable hints are also given in regard to the choice of wines, and the rules which govern waiting at table in every refined and well-ordered house.

THE PANTRY

Where more than one servant is kept a small pantry is a very necessary apartment in a house, as it enables the maid who has charge of the table arrangements to do all her washing up without interfering with the work of the cook or getting in her way.

In large establishments the pantry would be the special sanctum of the butler. In it he would keep all the silver, glass, and china that came under his care, as well as the supply of wine that was required for immediate use. There would also be a small table or desk at which he could write his orders and make up his books.

In smaller houses the pantry need not be a spacious apartment, but even a small place conveniently fitted up will be found a great convenience, not only to the table-maid but also to the ladies of the house, as it is a place where they can do any washing of tea dishes or fine china, preparing of dessert, cutting bread and butter for afternoon tea, and the arranging of flowers, &c., without having to enter the cook's domain.

A pantry should be fitted with a small sink with hot and cold water - supply. At the side of the sink there should be a good-sized draining-board on which wet dishes can be placed, above the sink a plate-rack in which to drain plates, while a small cupboard fitted underneath would be a useful receptacle for plate powder, silver brushes, furniture polish, ammonia, soap powder, and other indispensable articles for cleaning purposes. Another necessary fitting is a dresser. It should be provided with two or three drawers in which glass cloths, dusters, leathers, and furniture sheets could be kept, one drawer being reserved for the maid's private use. The lower part of the dresser should be fitted with cupboards divided off into separate portions. One part might be reserved for clean-

ing utensils, another for larger dishes, and a third as a small store for sugar, jam, butter, &c. Then above the dresser there should be a nice high narrow cupboard, with sliding glass doors if possible, for holding china, glass, cruets, sugar basins, jam dishes, &c. If this is large enough one portion of it might hold a reserve supply of china and glass and be kept locked.

Other useful fittings would be a small pulley or rail for drying towels and a rack for holding two or three brushes.

If room permits there might be a good solid table in the pantry and also a chair on which the maid could sit down while doing her silver cleaning and other work of the kind.

The floor should be covered with cork carpet or linoleum and the walls papered with a good washing paper or coated with a light-coloured ripolin or distemper, which could easily be renewed when dirty.

The pantry should contain all that the table-maid requires for cleaning purposes, and the sink must be supplied with one or two tubs and other necessary appliances for washing up.

It is a good plan also to hang up somewhere in the pantry a list of all glass, china, &c. ; this list should be checked periodically by the mistress and servant together.

Cleanliness and order in the pantry are very important. Each time the sink is used it should be scrubbed out with hot water and then thoroughly rinsed with cold. The dresser and table should be scrubbed once a week and the floor washed when necessary. No dirty towels or dish cloths should be seen lying about, and a pride should be taken in the neat arrangement of the cupboards. (For " Washing Up," see p. 76.)

SILVER AND CUTLERY

Choice of Silver.—There are few families, except perhaps the very wealthy, who care to use solid table silver every day, for even if they

129

are fortunate enough to possess a set it is carefully guarded under lock and key and only brought out on special occasions, and with the exception perhaps of a few small articles, such as salt and mustard spoons, pepperettes, butter-knives, sugar-tongs, electro-plate is made to do duty for ordinary use.

Although silver costs about three times as much as electro-plate, it must be remembered that it will last for years without requiring any repair, and can even be handed down from generation to generation.

Solid silver is sold by weight and fluctuates a little in price, but the current price for table silver is about the following :—table-spoons and forks from £4, 12s. per dozen, dessert-spoons and forks from £2, 15s. per dozen, and tea-spoons from 30s. per dozen.

Solid silver is one of the things which can often be bought very well second-hand, and in most large towns reliable shops are to be found where it can be obtained at fairly moderate prices.

Electro-Plate.—A good quality should always be bought, as the plating soon wears off the cheaper makes. Good electro-plate ought to last from twenty to thirty years without requiring any renewing. For those who have only a small amount to spend on silver and who are not fortunate enough to have it given to them as a present when they start housekeeping, it is better to purchase a little of a good quality rather than full sets of an inferior kind. There are several regulation patterns such as Old English, King's, Bead or Thread, and Rat Tail, so that additions can always be made by degrees, as the best plated goods are sold by the single article when required. The above patterns are all simple and will easily be kept in order ; in fact, heavily ornamented patterns are rarely seen nowadays.

The price of electro-plate varies, but, roughly speaking, good electro-plate of a quality that will last for years can be had at the following prices :—table-spoons and forks from 25s. per dozen, dessert-spoons and forks from 19s. 6d. per dozen, and tea-spoons from 9s. per dozen.

When electro-plate begins to look shabby it can be replated for about the following charges:—table-spoons and forks from 17s. 6d. per dozen ; dessert-spoons and forks from 13s. per dozen, and tea-spoons from 7s. per dozen. (For the Cleaning of Silver, see p. 74.)

Choice of Cutlery.—As in the case of electro-plate, so with cutlery, a low-priced article is the

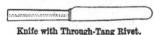

Knife with Through-Tang Rivet.

reverse of economical ; not only will the handles of cheap knives be badly fixed, but the blades will be made of a soft steel which never takes a proper edge. It is a wise policy, therefore, to buy knives the blades of which are made of the best Sheffield steel, and to see that they are fixed to the handles with what is called the through-tang rivet, which never comes undone.

There is a choice of materials for the handles, the cheapest of which are bone and horn ; then comes ivorine and ivoride, which is the nearest approach to real ivory that can possibly be made ; and, lastly, fine African ivory and sterling silver-plated handles.

Real ivory and sterling silver are rather expensive articles, and most people have to content themselves with one of the cheaper materials. The following will be a fair price to pay for really good articles :—

Best white Bone Handles with Through-Tang :—Table-knives from 13s. 6d. per dozen, dessert-knives from 12s. per dozen, joint or game carvers from 5s. per pair, steel 1s. 9d.

Imitation Ivory Handles :—Table-knives from 17s. 6d. per dozen, dessert-knives from 14s. per dozen, joint or game carvers from 6s. per pair, steel 2s. 4d.

African Ivory Handles :—Table-knives from 38s. per dozen, dessert-knives from 30s. per dozen, joint or game carvers from 12s. 6d. per pair, steel 4s. 3d.

Knives will cost about 2s. 6d. per dozen less without the tang fastening. New blades can always be fitted to good ivory handles at a reasonable charge. (For the Care and Cleaning of Knives, see p. 76.)

CHINA AND GLASS

Choice of China.—Now that both china and glass can be bought at such moderate prices and in such artistic shapes and pretty colours, there is no excuse for any one to have what is chipped and ugly on their tables. Although some of the china dealers of to-day make specialities of tea and dinner services of the most gaudy colouring and in the most impossible patterns, and ornament them with a liberal supply of gilt, there are other manufacturers who reproduce the most tasteful designs of Wedgwood, Spode, and the famous old Crown Derby Wares.

The choice of china is very much a matter of taste and circumstances, and space will not permit of giving many details regarding designs and price, as these are so numerous and varied. Before selecting it is advisable to send for the catalogues of some of the largest firms and to visit their show-rooms. Many valuable ideas may be gleaned in this way.

The frugal housewife whose means are limited and who will in all probability have to leave her china in the hands of inexperienced servants, will do well to buy the strong make of stoneware or semi-porcelain for every-day use and to choose a style which can be renewed when pieces are broken.

Such patterns as the willow, delf, rose-bud,

white fluted, and white with a gilt or coloured band are always stocked. Strong colouring should always be avoided whether for tea, breakfast, or dinner services, and it must be remembered that the price will be influenced very much by the amount of good gilt and also upon the novelty of the design and shape.

A Dinner Service.—When choosing a dinner service it is better to select one in which the centre of the dishes and plates is white, as food always looks more appetising when served on a light surface. Choose also a porcelain that will wear well and that will not chip and crack with the heat. China can either be bought in large or small sets for six or twelve persons, or single pieces can be bought in quite a number of different patterns by paying at a little higher rate. A nice set of what is called the " cottage " size can be bought from a guinea upwards consisting of the following pieces, while a medium set will cost from about £1, 14s. 6d. upwards—

Cottage Set (52 *pieces*) :—Twelve meat plates, twelve pudding or pie plates, twelve cheese plates, two covered dishes, six meat dishes, two sauce tureens.

Medium Set (81 *pieces*) :—Twenty-four meat plates, twenty-four pie plates, twelve soup plates, seven dishes, two covered dishes, two sauce tureens, one soup tureen, one fish drainer.

It must be remembered that in houses where there are a number of people or where small dinner-parties are given, the number of plates must not be too limited.

Tea and Breakfast Sets.—A small tea and breakfast service in plain ware can be bought for 6s. or 7s. and upwards, and in china from 16s. to 17s. and upwards. They would consist of the following pieces :—

Tea Set (40 *pieces*) :—Twelve tea-cups and saucers, twelve tea plates, two cake plates, one slop basin, one cream jug.

Breakfast Set for Six (29 *pieces*) :—Six cups and saucers, six plates, two cake plates, one slop basin, one sugar basin, one milk jug, six egg cups.

Choice of Glass.—Not a little of the handsome appearance of a well-set dinner-table may be ascribed to its array of shining well-kept and well-polished glass. The table glass should always be of as good a quality as possible, and the design should be characterised by its refined simplicity. Too much design and ornamentation is a mistake, as it tends to rob the glass of that bright transparency which forms the great charm of its appearance. But here, again, unless the glass is always under the care of a reliable servant, it is best to buy it of not too fine a quality and of a design that can be easily replaced. Very thin glass is no doubt appreciated by those who like dainty articles, but it requires the utmost care in the washing and drying. When cut glass cannot be afforded, plain thinnish glass or plain glass with a little engraving looks the best. Very good plain tumblers can be had from 4d.

each or with a little engraving from 6s. 6d. per dozen, while a cut glass tumbler will cost from about 1s. upwards.

Wine-glasses are made in various sizes to suit the different wines for which they are used ; the form changes with fashion, but they should always match the tumblers in quality and design.

Coloured wine-glasses were at one time much in vogue, but people of taste now appreciate the fact that the white wine-glasses of tasteful design are infinitely preferable.

Decanters also should be carefully chosen with due regard to their design. More ornamentation in the way of cutting or engraving is allowable in the case of all kinds of decanters.

HOME DINNERS

No matter how simple a meal may be, it should be put neatly upon the table and made attractive to the eye. There are certain table refinements which are within the reach of the very humblest ; they may not be essentials, but they are beyond doubt among the ameliorating influences of life which help to cultivate the mind and improve the manners. The every-day dinner should be as carefully prepared as the more formal meal when visitors are expected. The decoration of the table may be simpler, the number of courses fewer, and the dishes less expensive, but so far as the appointments are concerned they should receive the same attention.

Under these conditions if paterfamilias should take it into his head to bring in a friend to dinner without any previous notification of his intention of so doing, no disturbance will be caused by the arrival of the unexpected guest—rather will he be looked upon as a welcome addition to the family party.

The dinner-hour must be chosen with due regard to the needs and employments of the various members of the household, and, if possible, let it be at an hour when it does not require to be hurried over. It should be made a time of relaxation, when there can be pleasant and cheerful conversation, and worries and care are, for the moment at least, laid aside. It is a well-known fact that a cheerful frame of mind is a valuable aid to digestion.

Having fixed upon an hour see that the meal is punctually attended and punctually served. The very best cooking will be spoiled if the dinner has to be kept back owing to the unpunctuality of some member of the family, while, on the other hand, the cook who cannot send up a dinner to time should remember that a meal that has to be waited for often fails to be appreciated. Regularity is also good from a health point of view, and for those who are delicate it is all the more important.

The dishes given may be as simple and inexpensive as possible, but let them be well cooked and nicely served.

Then the arrangement is an important consideration—we do not all possess beautiful china and glass, and the choicest silver and damask, but it is possible to have even the simplest things spotlessly clean and bright and to have them arranged with order and taste.

And, again, no table should be considered properly laid unless decorated with some flowers or ferns. Some people may consider this an extravagance, but a small quantity is all that is required, and if flowers are scarce or too expensive, any plant which looks fresh and healthy or even some pretty foliage can take their place.

The dining-room itself ought to be in order and free from dust, and there should be a tidy fireplace and a bright fire burning in the grate if the weather is cold. Also pay attention to the ventilation of the room, as a stuffy atmosphere tends to spoil the appetite; so if the room has been occupied beforehand, let the windows be thrown open for a few minutes at least before the meal is served.

The clean cloth, the bright silver and glass, the tidy and pleasant room with the tasteful floral decoration will all add to the enjoyment of the meal. It may not be every one who bestows direct attention upon these details, but they affect the mind none the less. There is something elevating in beauty and order, whereas an untidy table is just as degrading as a slovenly dress. Let us make the home dinner as attractive as possible, and the simplest meal will then give satisfaction.

SETTING THE TABLE

The Informal Dinner.—Before the actual laying of the cloth there are certain preliminaries in the pantry, or in the kitchen if there is no pantry, which should be attended to. The cruets, for instance, will require attention. The salt-cellars should be filled with fine salt free from lumps, the surface made perfectly smooth, and a clean bright spoon laid across the top. The mustard-pots should be filled with well-made mustard. When fresh mustard is required, mix it first in a small cup and never in the pot itself. It must be mixed with a little water and beaten until perfectly smooth, and be of a consistency that will not run off the side of the plate. A pinch of salt should always be added. If French mustard is preferred, mix the dry mustard with vinegar instead of water, or half vinegar and half water. Tarragon vinegar is best. The pepperettes should also be well filled with white pepper, black being unsuitable for table use. Large cruets are not used now as a rule, but if bottles of any kind are put on the table, they should be clean and bright and the stands themselves kept in good order.

Next consider the number of people to be laid for, and count out the glasses required and rub them up, and fill the water-bottles with fresh water. Collect the necessary knives and examine the steel parts to see that they are free from tarnish. The bread too that is required should be put on the platter or small pieces put in a bread-basket. All these articles should be put on a tray and carried to the dining-room as soon as the table-cloth and sideboard-cloth have been laid.

Then in the dining-room itself see that the room is in order and well ventilated and the fireplace tidy before beginning to lay the cloth.

A dining-room table is usually made with leaves which can be taken out and put in as required according to the number of persons to be seated. An oval or round table is considered more sociable than a square or oblong one and will accommodate more people, but the shape is of little importance as long as the table is of a suitable height and size for individual needs.

An under-covering or " silence cloth " should first be laid on the table to prevent hot dishes spoiling the polish of the wood, to give the table-cloth a smoother and better appearance, and also to deaden the sound when silver, dishes, &c., are laid down. This can either be an old woollen table-cloth of some light colour, a piece of blanket or serge, or a piece of cotton felting or interlining sold for the purpose. This silence cloth should be about six inches larger than the table all round, and to keep it in position it may either be tied to the four legs by means of tapes, or hemmed and drawn up beneath the edges with a running string.

The table-cloth itself must be laid on perfectly even and as smoothly as possible, the centre of the cloth in the centre of the table, and the sides hanging gracefully with the creases in a straight line. As the appearance of the table will depend very much on the kind of table-cloth used, an effort should be made to have this as clean and unruffled as possible.

Next lay a carving-cloth at one or both ends of the table or wherever there is carving or serving to be done. This cloth may either be square or oblong—very pretty cloths with hem-stitched or fringed edges are sold for the purpose, but, failing these, an ordinary serviette of a large size will do very well.

Spread the sideboard also with a cloth and the dinner-waggon or butler's tray if required. In small houses and flats it is sometimes more convenient to have the latter placed just outside the dining-room door.

Now put the flowers or any other decoration on the table (see p. 253), as this is more easily arranged before the glasses, &c., are placed on the table.

In the allowance of space a good rule to go by is to allow twenty inches at least for each person's accommodation, but if the table is large a little more room does not matter. It is a good plan to place round the serviettes before laying the rest of the cover, as this will give an idea of the amount of space available. The fancy and artistic folding of serviettes is quite out of fashion for the moment and is only to be seen in hotels and restaurants. When clean they should be simply folded, and after they have been used put into rings.

The silver required must next be taken from the sideboard and everything must be carried to the table on a tray and not in the hands. Put a table-knife at the right-hand side and a fork at the left for each person, leaving room for a plate to be placed between, and place a small dessert-spoon and fork horizontally across the top, the handle of the spoon to the right-hand side and that of the fork to the left. If fish is to be served, place a fish-knife and fork outside the other knife and fork, as they will be required first ; if soup, a table-spoon on the right-hand side, and if cheese, a small knife at the right-hand side next the plate. Everything must be placed evenly and about an inch up from the edge of the table.

Next put down the spoons and carving-knives and forks that are required for serving the different dishes, and small cruets and water-bottles at a convenient distance down the table. It is no longer the custom to put dinner-mats on the table, but those made of asbestos may be placed under the cloth when there is danger of very hot dishes spoiling the table.

The glasses and bottles of water should be placed on the table almost last—a tumbler at the right-hand side of each person and a wine-glass for each kind of wine that is to be served. The bread may either be put round, a piece to each person, or left in the bread-basket to be handed.

The sideboard should be arranged as carefully as the table, and everything that is required for after use placed upon it, such as a few extra knives, forks, and spoons, extra bread, a basket for receiving dirty knives and silver, and a crumb brush and tray. See also that the chairs are put in their places before bringing in the first course and announcing that the meal is ready.

A Dinner-Party.—*Service à la Russe.*—A dinner-party ranks highest among entertainments, and time and thought are required if it is to be made a success. There are prescribed rules for the sending out of the invitations, the arranging of the guests, and the manner of serving the dinner (see Etiquette). The most popular way of serving a dinner at present is *à la Russe.* By this mode all the carving and serving is done from the side-table and none of the dishes are placed on the dining-table itself. It is certainly a much more luxurious and pleasant method than the old-fashioned style of having all the helping done by the host and hostess, who by this means are left free to attend to their guests and enter more fully into the conversation. It means, however, a more elaborate service as far

as waiting is concerned and one which cannot be carried out where there is only one table-maid. On the other hand, a dinner of this kind is more economical as regards food. When served from the side the quantity can be more exactly calculated and smaller joints can be supplied, whereas if the dishes are put on the table they must be handsome ones and there must be more than sufficient to go round. When dinner à la Russe is found too troublesome, a compromise between the two styles is very often adopted, some of the dishes, such as soup and joints, being served from the table and entremets handed round in the same manner as the entrées.

A dinner-party is looked upon by many people as a very difficult form of entertainment, and they will hesitate to give one for fear of its not being a success.

Certainly when one possesses a handsome dinner service, good silver and glass and well-trained servants it is a comparatively easy matter, but these are conditions which cannot always be fulfilled. But still this should not debar the housewife of more modest means from the pleasure of giving a little dinner-party to her friends, as a simple dinner well planned is very often more enjoyable than a very formal affair. There is no occasion to have things elaborate and costly, and if we as a nation were a little less pretentious in our tastes, pleasant social intercourse would be less rare. An invitation to a dinner is always considered a greater compliment than one to an "At Home." It is an indication of a wish for greater intimacy, for dinner-parties serve to place us in closer touch with our friends than is the case with almost any other social gathering.

If dinner à la Russe is decided on preparations should be commenced in good time so that there need be no cause for a hurry and bustle at the last minute. If special dishes, glass and silver are to be used for the occasion they should be looked out early in the day and made clean and ready for the table.

The setting of the table is very much the same as for the more simple meal, only no carving-cloths will be required and no spoons and forks for serving the different dishes.

Some possessors of polished oak and mahogany tables have adopted the fashion of replacing the large table-cloth with small mats of fine damask and rich lace laid before each guest and below the various dishes, but this is by no means a prevailing fashion. Another custom is to have small tables at which four or six persons can be seated instead of one large table, as this is considered a little more sociable and conducive of conversation.

As regards decoration the tendency is to have it as light as possible, but to have the damask of the whitest and finest that can be afforded. (For Table Decoration, see p. 253.)

The covers must not consist of too many

knives and forks—it is always better to put down others as the meal proceeds than to crowd the table in any way—but they must always be arranged so that the diner commences with those on the outside. The necessary glasses must be put at the right-hand side, with the highest one placed farthest away to avoid its being knocked over. The number of glasses will depend upon the wines to be served—three (sherry, claret, and champagne) is a very usual number, and small tumblers should be provided for non-wine-drinkers. The serviettes should be simply doubled and a small roll or some bread sticks laid to each guest. When name cards are used they must be clearly written and placed beside each cover in such a way as to avoid all confusion later. A menu card should be allowed for each two or three people. The fruit may or may not be placed on the table from the beginning; this is entirely a matter of taste, but small bon-bon dishes containing salted almonds or sweets are generally placed at intervals down the table or arranged amongst the decorations.

A good deal will depend on the lighting of the room, and as the table will be the chief attraction for the time being, the light ought to be centred on that while the rest of the room may be in shadow. If there is a large centre-light it should have a shade corresponding in colour to the flowers used or else forming a pleasing contrast. The pleasantest light is perhaps from shaded candles or small electric lights placed at intervals down the table. If candles are used they should be lighted at least fifteen minutes before dinner commences in order to ensure steady burning.

The sideboard will also require careful preparation. All wine decanters and extra glasses should be placed well to the back, and the dessert plates, finger bowls and doyleys, extra knives and forks and the like laid neatly in the front. When the fruit is not placed on the table that also must find a place on the sideboard until required. Champagne, hock, and other wines that are not decanted should be placed underneath on the floor.

The carving-table is another important item in the *diner à la Russe*. It must be furnished with a good light, and everything in the way of knives, forks, and spoons must be placed in readiness for the carver during the different courses of the dinner.

The temperature of the room must also be thought of; it must be well aired and still warm and comfortable. It must be remembered that the ladies will be in light attire and the room must not strike chilly. Many a good dinner has been spoilt by inattention to this point. If windows have to be opened a little way it is generally possible by a careful adjustment of screens to prevent the draught from beating down upon the persons seated.

Chairs must be put in position, and the first course, hors d'œuvres or soup, brought to the room before the meal is announced.

A word might be said here about the drawing-room fire; it ought to be one of the maid's duties to attend to this and to see that it is not allowed to burn too low. A bright fire ought to await the guests when they return from dinner.

WAITING AT TABLE

General Directions for Waiting at Dinner.—If a dinner is to be a success the waiting must be above reproach. Perhaps nothing tends so much to spoil the good effect of a meal as inferior service; then, no matter how excellent the cooking, nor how pretty and dainty the table, the result will not be satisfactory. If there are long pauses between the courses, if the waitress is clumsy and noisy in her movements and inattentive to the needs of the company, the finest dinner will be marred.

Even if the meal be but a simple homely one with one maid in attendance a mistress should make a point of having the service as perfect as it is possible, as intelligent and proficient waiting at once stamps the orderly and well-regulated household.

The maid who waits at table should be neatly dressed in a well-brushed black frock and spotless apron, collar and cuffs, and neat cap; or a clean and tidy print gown may take the place of the stuff dress at an early dinner or luncheon in small households when the maid has housework to do after the meal is served. Her hair must be neatly done without any untidy ends flying about, and she ought to pay particular attention to her hands and nails to keep them clean and in good order. If the lighting of fires and cleaning of stoves is part of her work she ought to be careful to wear gloves for the purpose, as it is almost impossible to remove black-lead from the hands when once it has sunk into the skin. She ought also to keep the skins of lemons to rub on her hands, as this helps to remove any stains.

A good waitress must be quick and light in her movements and at the same time quiet and gentle. Although it is of paramount importance to have the courses served quickly one after the other there must be no appearance of hurry; there is a happy medium between long waits and rushing people through, scarcely leaving them time to finish what is on their plates. The service should be carried on as noiselessly as possible; there must be no clatter of dishes nor rattling of knives and forks. The waitress must have all her wits about her and be ever on the alert to see what is wanted, and ready to give her whole attention to the work in hand. Forethought is another very necessary quality—she ought to consider beforehand what will be required for the meal so that there need be no unnecessary moving about or leaving the room when once the meal is served.

She must try to cultivate a pleasant and gracious manner, being thoughtful for the comfort of those she is serving and ready to forestall their wants. She must not take notice of any conversation that is going on, nor let a joke or funny story distract her thoughts. Should any of the company happen to be a little peculiar in manner and perhaps depart from the orderly rules of behaviour, the waitress must not appear to observe it, and if at any time an accident should occur, such as the spilling of a glass of wine or water, she must be ready to put the matter right without showing any signs of annoyance.

When the meal is ready, the chairs in their places and everything in order, the maid ought to see that doors leading into all kitchen and back premises are shut; then when the first course is placed upon the table the dinner may be announced. This may be done either by sounding a gong, ringing a bell, or by going to the drawing-room and saying in a clear voice, " Dinner is served " or " Dinner is on the table, Madam." The drawing-room door should then be left open, and the maid, returning to the dining-room, should take up her position there.

When the courses are served from the table, as is frequently the case at the ordinary family dinner, the waitress should stand on the left-hand side of the one who serves and commence by removing the cover if one is in use. At present the tendency is to abolish dish covers, although in many houses, especially where old-fashioned customs prevail, they are still to be seen. A cover must be taken off and turned up quickly to prevent any drops of steam from falling on the table-cloth.

A waitress should accustom herself to carry two things at a time, one in each hand, as for instance a plate of soup in one hand and a plate of croûtons in the other, a plate of meat in the right hand and a vegetable or sauce in the left, or a plate of meat in each hand. Vegetable and sauces are not placed upon the table when a maid is in constant attendance; they are kept on the sideboard and handed—an attentive servant will see at once when they are required. If the maid leaves the room, she usually puts them down on the table after she has passed them round.

When a dish is handed round it must be held steadily and firmly on a finger napkin and at a convenient height, so that the person seated may find no difficulty in helping himself. A table-spoon or fork and spoon, according to what is required, must be placed in the dish in readiness.

Except at the formal dinner it is customary also to ask if a little more meat or pudding, &c., is desired before the plate is removed.

Do not remove a soup tureen nor any dish being served until every one at the table has finished that particular course.

Soiled plates must be removed at once when finished with; they should never be allowed to remain in front of the person who has used them. They must be removed quietly, and care must be taken not to drop the knife or silver. A plate may be taken in each hand and they should be carried at once to the sideboard, the knives and silver placed in the box or basket placed there for the purpose, and the plates piled without noise one on the top of the other or put into a plate-carrier. A tray or basket must never be carried round the table to receive the knives and silver from the plates, although the reverse is the case with the dishes from which meat, &c., has been served. A carving-knife and fork should never be removed on the dish, as being large and heavy they would be very liable to fall, but a small tray for the purpose should be brought to the table to receive them. The dishes themselves must be removed carefully in order that no grease or gravy be spilt.

Before sweets and dessert, remove on a small tray all cruets and salt-cellars and any knives, forks, spoons, and glasses that will not be required. Also take away the carving cloth if one has been used. All crumbs should then be very carefully removed from the left-hand side of each person seated with a brush or crumb scoop on to a small tray or silver waiter.

A waitress must never reach across a person seated to put down or remove anything from the table, but should walk quietly to the right or left-hand side as required.

If any extra knives or silver are required they should be put down on the table in their proper place with the empty plate before the serving of a course—they must never be offered on a tray.

If more bread is asked for small pieces should be handed in a bread-basket or on a plate. If any small condiment is wanted it should be handed on a small tray or silver salver.

When dinner is served in the old-fashioned way it is quite possible for one maid who is quick and clever to wait upon six or even eight people, although of course the service can be better performed when there are two in attendance, or if some assistance can be given by dishes being brought from the kitchen to the dining-room door and soiled plates carried away.

If two maids are in attendance, the head servant passes round the fish and the second follows with the sauce and other accompaniments; the head passes the meat and the second the vegetables, and so on. The principal servant should never leave the room; the younger maid should inform the cook as soon as a course has been served and prepare her to send up the next at once. The younger maid should also do the carrying of the dishes to and from the room. When a maid is single-handed and is obliged to be absent for a short time a member of the family usually rings the bell at the end of each course.

Novices in the art of waiting have sometimes

a little difficulty in knowing at what side a dish or plate, &c., should be handed or removed. To these the following hints may be useful :—

(1) When there is no choice to be made, the plate with its contents should be put down at the right-hand side of the person seated.

(2) When there is a choice, as for instance two different sweets or two different kinds of fish, hand these at the left-hand side.

(3) When a dish has to be offered, as in the case of a side dish or vegetable, carry it to the left-hand side. It is a good rule to remember that everything that is offered (except wine) must be carried to the left-hand side.

(4) Soiled plates should be removed from the right-hand side.

(5) Clean and empty plates are put down at the right-hand side.

(6) Wine is offered from the right-hand side as the glasses are naturally standing in that position.

Precedence in Serving.—At a family dinner the lady of the house should be served first unless she is carving, then the daughters of the house according to age, and the governess, if there is one present, and lastly the master of the house and the sons according to age.

If only one or two guests are present serve them first, commencing with the ladies and the principal guest. At a formal dinner-party, where there are a number of guests, commence with the lady on the right-hand side of the host (the principal guest) and continue straight round the table irrespective of sex. It is not then the custom to serve the ladies before the gentlemen. If there are several maids in attendance the two sides of the table may be served simultaneously, commencing with the lady seated next the host on each side. In the case of small tables, the one where the principal guests are seated should be served first.

Hired Cooks and Waitresses.—When the staff of servants is not sufficiently experienced and a large and important party is to be given it is sometimes necessary to hire outside assistance. Both cooks and waitresses can be hired at the principal catering establishments ; or very often they can be heard of through private recommendation, which is even better. The usual fee for such assistance is from 5s. an evening for a waitress, and from 10s. 6d. a dinner for a cook.

DRAWING UP A MENU

It requires some skill and experience to make a good bill of fare ; any miscellaneous collection of good dishes does not necessarily produce a first-class menu.

There are several points to bear in mind when arranging the dishes for a dinner :—

(1) Dishes that are in season should be chosen. Although many articles, such as vegetables,

fruit, and fish, can be had out of their proper season, it must be remembered that an exorbitant price will likely be asked for them, and even at that they will in all probability be wanting in flavour.

(2) There must be variety in flavour, and the dishes must follow each other in such a way as will please the palate. An insipid dish must not directly follow one that is very tasty, and if two or three different entrées are served the most savoury one should come last. The same flavouring must not be repeated in two consecutive dishes.

(3) There must be variety in the method of cooking and in the character of the different dishes. It would not do for fried cutlets to follow fried fish, nor for two braised dishes or two grills to come together, and so on. A simple dish should be followed by one a little more elaborate or *vice versâ*.

(4) There must be variety in colour and decoration. The dishes must be pleasing to the eye as well as to the palate, there should be no sameness, and an element of refinement rather than ostentation.

(5) The names of the dishes should be written on the menu cards either in French or in English, French is perhaps the more fashionable, but this is entirely a question of choice. The names of standard dishes should never be altered, although more liberty may be taken with the names of made-up dishes.

(6) And, lastly, the powers of the cook and the capabilities of the kitchen-range must be borne in mind. If the cook is single-handed do not attempt too much and do not give her a number of dishes that cannot be finished off until the last minute. Of course it will always be possible to have a certain number of dishes sent in from a caterer, but this will add considerably to the expense, and in the end there is nothing better than good cooking well done at home. An important point is to give the cook plenty of notice and explicit directions as to what will be required.

The different courses of a complete menu will comprise the following :—hors d'œuvres, potage, poisson, entrées, relevé, sorbet, rôti, entremets, dessert, café.

Hors d'Œuvres.—These consist of small appetising morsels usually served cold, such as oysters, olives, anchovies, caviare, smoked salmon, small salads, thin slices of sausage, &c. They may either be served plain or made up in some more elaborate style. Small plain biscuits or thin brown bread and butter may accompany the plain hors d'œuvres.

Potage (Soup).—Either one or two soups may be served. If only one it is preferable to have it clear or of a very light character, especially if there are a number of courses to follow. If there are two soups one may be thick and the other clear.

Poisson (Fish).—This may either be plainly boiled with a sauce or dressed in a more elaborate fashion, or there may be one dish of each.

Entrées.—These may come either before or after the relevé; in fact, they can be served between any of the courses or omitted altogether. They consist of various kinds of made dishes and ought to be served very daintily. If more than one is served one might be brown and the other white, or one might be hot and the other cold.

Relevé (or Remove).—This consists of a solid joint either roasted, boiled, or braised, and a garnish generally gives the characteristic name. One vegetable besides potatoes is usually served with the remove.

Sorbet.—A half-frozen water ice which is served in cups immediately after the roast.

Rôti.—Roast game or poultry usually served with salad and chip potatoes.

Entremets.—These may be divided into three classes—(1) *dressed vegetables* (légumes); (2) *sweet entremets*, both hot and cold; (3) *savouries*, which precede the dessert and are usually hot.

Dessert.—Fruits of various kinds and *petits fours* or other fancy biscuits.

Coffee.—This must be black—cream being served separately.

In a small dinner some of these courses would be omitted. The number of dishes depends entirely upon the style of the dinner; it may consist of three or four or of eleven or twelve. For instance, the hors d'œuvres and sorbet are seldom given at a small dinner, and either the relevé or the rôti would be omitted. One sweet might follow the last meat course to be followed by a cheese dish or other savoury. Ices may either be served in place of a cold sweet, or they may form a separate course after the savoury.

HINTS ON SERVING THE DIFFERENT COURSES

Hors d'Œuvres.—These are frequently placed on the plate before dinner is announced—especially in the case of oysters—or a choice of several kinds is offered on a small tray.

Soup.—If the soup is served from the side and the dinner consists of numerous courses, three-quarters of a ladleful will be sufficient to give as a helping. If there are two different soups, the waitress should take a plate of each and offer a choice; if only one she should take a plate of soup in one hand and a plate of croûtons or pulled bread in the other. Parmesan cheese may also be served with clear soup.

Fish.—The waitress should take a portion of fish in the right hand and the sauce or other accompaniment in the left. If there is a choice she should take a portion of each kind and the accompaniments would be offered by a second waitress.

Entrées.—A hot or cold plate as required must first be put down to each person, and it must be seen that they have the necessary knives and forks. The entrée must then be handed with a spoon and fork in readiness in the dish. Entrées are always handed, no matter how simple the dinner.

Joints and Game.—Unless these have been carved beforehand, the head waitress must be able to help them neatly from the side and serve them out in small portions, which must be handed round followed by their various accompaniments.

Salad.—A small salad plate should be put to the left of each guest before the salad is carried round. The salad itself should be mixed at the side or in the kitchen and handed in the bowl with the salad spoon and fork in readiness. If not partaken of the special plate should be removed.

Sweets and other Entremets are usually handed in the same way as entrées, a hot or cold plate with necessary fork or spoon and fork being put before each guest previously. In the case of any sweet requiring cutting, such as tart, this would be served out in portions from the side.

Cheese.—It is not customary to serve plain cheese at a formal dinner, but when it is wished it is usually handed in a dish with different divisions containing cheese in small pieces, butter, and one or two different kinds of biscuits. A small plate and knife would be put down to each guest before the dish is handed.

Dessert.—The table should be cleared of crumbs and all unnecessary glasses, &c., before dessert is served. Unless the fruit has not been on the table during the dinner it should now be put down, and a dessert plate with a doyley and finger bowl, along with a fruit knife and fork, should be placed before each guest. If ices are served in this course they should be served first and the ice plates removed before the fruit is handed. Each kind of fruit must be offered in turn and then replaced on the table.

It is not usual to offer a second helping of any of the courses at a formal dinner. (For the Serving of Wine, see p. 248.)

CARVING AND SERVING

Although at the present time the formal dinner is always served à la Russe, when all carving and serving is done at the side-table or in the kitchen, the art of carving is still required at family repasts.

Every lady ought to know how to carve; in fact, it would be a good thing if even the young people in the house took turns in performing this duty; they would not then feel at a loss when they came to have homes of their own or when called upon to take the place of their parents.

The art of carving can only be learnt by practice; some instruction may no doubt be given in a book, and a beginner may also learn from watching an expert carver, but proficiency can only come by actually doing the work oneself.

To begin with there must be some knowledge of the anatomy of the various joints, of the relative position of bones, joints, muscles, and fat, and also which are the choicest portions. The most satisfactory way of learning this is to take the chance when opportunity occurs of studying the various pieces of meat off the table. In the case of game or poultry, for instance, the bird might be cut up in its raw state for a *fricassée* or stew and a point made of examining the different joints.

Carving does not require much physical strength; in fact, any undue effort or exhibition of exertion only shows want of skill or bad implements : the really clever carver is able to cut up the most difficult joints with perfect ease.

One must first of all learn to carve neatly without splashing the gravy over the cloth or pieces of meat beyond the dish, and then to cut straight and uniform slices so that the joint may not be made to look untidy and jagged, but inviting enough to tempt one to desire another helping, or, if large enough to appear at another meal, it may do so wearing a presentable appearance. A number of cut surfaces only allow the escape of juice and tend to make the joint flavourless. Bad carving is always wasteful, but the good carver will cut in such a way as to make every portion inviting and full of flavour.

Both the butcher and the cook can do much to facilitate the work of the carver—in the case of a loin of mutton or veal, for instance, neat carving would be impossible unless the butcher had performed his part of well jointing between the ribs. The cook, too, should see that all skewers, pieces of string, &c., are removed. The size of the dish on which the joint is served is also important. It must be large enough not only to hold the joint when whole, but also to allow room for several cut portions when they are detached. Some people prefer to have a separate dish for the cut portions, and these can, if liked, be handed round. It is a mistake to put a garnish on any meat which requires carving at table, and the less gravy there is the easier it will be for the one who is serving. An extra supply can always be served separately in a sauce-boat. The dish must always be placed near enough the carver to allow of her reaching it without any difficulty, and the chair on which she is seated ought to be high enough to allow her to have perfect control over her work without the necessity of standing. Some will find it easier to be raised on a firm cushion.

The sharpness of the knife is another very important matter. It must always be sharpened before dinner and never at the table, where the performance is most trying to people's nerves. It should have a handle that can be grasped easily and a long thin blade of a size adapted to the article to be served. A carving-knife should never be used for anything but its one legitimate purpose. There are different kinds of knives sold for the purpose, as, for instance, a meat carver, a slicer, a breakfast carver, a game knife, and game scissors ; but if means are limited and only one general carver can be afforded, choose one made of the best steel one and a half inches wide at its broadest part and from eight to ten inches long.

The carving fork should have two long prongs and a good guard to protect the fingers. The hand should be held over the handle of the fork with the palm downwards and the first finger extended. Insert the fork deep enough into the meat to enable you to hold it firmly in position. The knife also should generally be held firmly and then applied lightly. There will be less gravy squeezed out if the pressure on the meat is not too heavy. Both knife and fork must be held in a natural manner and not grasped as if they were weapons ; the cutting must be sharp and clean, never jagged like a saw. All meat should be cut across the grain with the exception of saddle of mutton.

The carver must try to make a fair distribution of the different cuts and bear in mind individual likes and dislikes. As a rule, one small slice is sufficient to serve to a lady and two small or one large to a gentleman, but the quantity must be regulated somewhat by the number of courses in the dinner. If there is only one joint on the table and there are ladies and gentlemen present, she should try to regulate the helpings so that a smaller portion is served to the ladies. If there is more than one dish to choose from the portions should be made equal and rather small in size.

Never ask a guest before beginning to carve to make a choice between two different dishes, but help the dishes first and then make the inquiry, otherwise they might feel that it was being cut into solely for them.

The following notes on the carving of some of the principal joints indicate the *general* method adopted, but these rules need not be hard and fast, and clever carvers very soon acquire their own style.

BEEF

Sirloin of Beef.—This joint should be placed with the back bone or thickest end at the left-hand side of the dish. Although it is usual to carve the undercut first, as this is one of the primest cuts when hot, the joint is served with this piece underneath and the carver raises it and turns it over. The undercut should be cut across in fairly thick slices C to D and a small portion of fat served with each. The upper part should be cut in long slices parallel with the ribs A to B. The slices should be as thin as possible

Sirloin of Beef.

without being ragged, and the point of the knife should be inserted to loosen the slices from the bone.

Ribs of Beef.—This joint should be carved in the same way as the upper part of the sirloin. There is no undercut.

Round of Beef or Rolled Ribs.—A thin-bladed and very sharp knife is required for this. First cut rather a thick slice off the outside to make the top surface even and then continue cutting thin slices right across the joint.

Ox Tongue.—As the centre is the choicest portion, the tongue should be cut through three or four inches from the top and thin slices cut from both ends. A small piece of the fat which lies near the root might be served with each portion.

MUTTON AND LAMB

Leg of Mutton.—Place this joint on the dish with the thickest part lying towards the outside of the dish and the small end to the left. The carving is not difficult and it is always done in the same way. Insert the fork in the thickest part and raise the joint slightly towards you. Then cut several slices of medium thickness through the thickest part and right down to the bone B to A. Next slip the knife along underneath

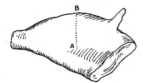

Leg of Mutton.

the slices and detach them from the rest. Some prefer a piece from the upper end and others one nearer the knuckle, as the meat is usually better done towards the thin end, and one of the tastiest morsels lies quite close to the knuckle or lower joint. A small piece of fat which lies underneath the thick end should be served with each portion. When the thick side of the meat is finished, slices should be cut from the other side in the same way.

Loin of Mutton and Lamb.—This cut must be thoroughly well jointed by the butcher or it will be found most difficult to carve. It will be well also to examine it before cooking, and, if necessary, joint any part that has been forgotten. Place the joint on the dish with the thick part towards the outside. Insert the

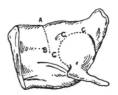

Forequarter of Lamb.

knife between the bones and cut right through, separating all the cutlets in the same manner. If there is a kidney a piece of it should be served with each portion.

Saddle of Mutton should be placed on the dish with the tail end to the left. Insert the fork firmly in the middle and carve across the ribs in long slices running parallel with the backbone. Then slip the knife under and detach the slices from the ribs. If too long they may be cut across in two or three pieces. A small piece of crisp fat from the lower part of the ribs may be served with each portion.

Shoulder of Mutton.—This is one of the most difficult joints to carve. Serve with the skin side uppermost on the dish. Insert the fork in the fleshy part and raise the joint slightly from the dish. Take as many slices as possible from

Shoulder of Mutton.

the side A and B to C, cutting in each case right through to the bone. The meat lying on each side of the blade-bone on the upper side of the joint should next be cut, carving the whole length of the meat from the knuckle end.

Then turn the joint and take slices off the under-side. The under-part is the juiciest and most delicate part, and is frequently cut before the upper portion.

Forequarter of Lamb.—This is another somewhat troublesome joint to carve. The first point to attend to is to raise the shoulder from the ribs and breast. Insert the fork in the most fleshy part of the shoulder and with the knife cut round as shown by dotted line C. Raise up the shoulder on the fork and cut it away without removing too much of the meat from underneath. The shoulder portion should be carved in the same manner as a shoulder of mutton, but unless the whole joint is required for one meal it is usual to have this put aside on

Loin of Pork.

a separate dish and served cold. Cut the under portion across, separating the ribs from the breast. Divide the ribs one from the other, A to B, and cut the breast in slices. A small portion of each may be served to each person.

VEAL

Fillet of Veal.—This should be carved in thin even slices in the same way as a round of beef. If there is stuffing a small quantity should be served with each portion.

Loin of Veal.—Carve in the same way as loin of mutton unless the cutlets are very large, when they may be cut in slices like ribs of beef.

Knuckle of Veal.—Carve in the same way as a leg of mutton.

PORK

Leg of Pork.—Carve in the same way as a leg of mutton, serving a piece of the crisp fat and a small quantity of stuffing, if there is any, to each person.

Loin of Pork.—Carve in slices from A to B, separating the cutlets between the bones in the same way as the loin of mutton.

Sucking Pig.—This is generally sent to table cut in half down the centre and with the head cut off with one piece laid at each side. First cut off the four legs from the carcase and then separate the ribs into small cutlets. It is all good, and it is just a matter of choice which part is served.

Ham.—If the ham is sent to table whole, the thickest part should be placed towards the outer side of the dish. Take a very sharp knife and make an incision through the thickest part and right down to the bone. Continue cutting in very thin slices towards both ends of the ham and serve a fair amount of fat with each portion.

A more economical way of carving a ham is to commence at the knuckle end and cut off thin slices working towards the thicker part. When the bone begins to look unsightly it can be sawn off.

GAME AND POULTRY

Fowl (Roast or Boiled).—The fowl should be placed on the dish with the legs to the left-hand

side. Insert the fork deeply across the breast-bone so that it takes a firm hold. First remove the wing on the side nearest you by cutting through the skin and shaving off a thin slice of the breast towards the wing joint. Then with the point of the knife sever the joint from the carcase. Next remove the leg on the same side by making a downward cut between the thigh and the body. Bend the leg over and sever the joint with the point of the knife. Now cut the meat from the breast in thin slices and the whole length of the bird B to A. The fork should never be moved from its original position, and the necessary carving should be finished before beginning to serve.

If the family is small and the whole fowl is not required the second side may be left, and if the bare piece of carcase is cut away and the half fowl served bone downwards on a dish with a nice garnish of parsley or salad, it will make quite a nice-looking dish. If, however, the whole fowl is required, remove the wish-bone from the neck in front of the breast-bone by inserting the point of the knife at the end. Then turn the bird round and carve the second side in exactly the same way as the first, and

Roast Fowl.

finally turn the carcase over and remove the oyster, a small dark portion which lies near the centre of the side bones. The wing and the breast are considered the finest parts.

Turkey.—This is carved in very much the same way as a fowl, only if it is large and the whole is not required it is usual to commence with the breast and to cut slices from that before removing the legs and wings. When the legs are cut off they should be divided in two at the joint and then cut in slices, as they make too large portions by themselves. If the bird is stuffed a small quantity of the force-meat should be served with each portion.

Goose.—Serve the bird with the neck at the left-hand side of the dish. As the breast is the best part it is usual to carve this first and not to use the legs and wings the first day unless they are required. Insert the fork in the centre over the ridge of the breast-bone and cut the breast in thin parallel slices, commencing at the wing and continuing until the breast-bone is reached. Then slip the knife under and detach them from the bone. Remove the legs and wings in the same way as from a fowl. If there is sage and onion farce inquire of each one if a small helping is agreeable, or hand it round separately.

Roast Duck.—Carve in the same way as roast goose.

Pigeon.—The usual plan to adopt is to cut the bird right through the middle into two equal parts. If these are too large they may be cut through again into quarters.

Partridge and Grouse should be carved in the same way as pigeon, a piece of toast being served with each portion.

Small birds, such as snipe, landrail, ortolan, are usually served whole or may be cut in two for ladies.

FISH

A silver or plated fish knife and fork or fish carvers ought to be used for serving fish. A steel knife should never be used or the flavour of the fish will be spoiled. Care should be taken not to break the flakes more than is necessary and to serve as little bone as possible.

Cod or Salmon.—The fish should be placed on the dish with the thick part of the back towards the further side. Carve in fairly thick slices right through to the centre bone, then slip the knife underneath and detach them. When the top part is finished remove the bone and cut through the lower portion in the same manner.

Turbot and Brill are both served in the same way. First cut through the thickest part of the fish right down to the back bone. Commence at the head end and continue to the tail. Then cut slices across from the centre towards the sides of the fish and detach them from the bone. Part of the fins and a little of the gelatinous skin should be served with each portion.

Sole.—Cut through the whole length of the thick part and then raise the fillet from each side. Then remove the bone and separate the other side into two fillets.

Plaice.—If large carve in the same way as a turbot; if small according to directions given for sole.

Small fish are either served whole or cut in two pieces.

SERVING OF WINES

In former times it was considered the correct thing to serve a different kind of wine with each course, and the choice was very complicated, but nowadays the number has been much reduced, and it is quite usual to serve only one or two kinds throughout the whole meal.

When wine is offered it must be good of its kind; poor cooking is bad enough, but cheap wine is even worse, being at times almost poisonous. People with limited means should not give champagne or sparkling hock, which in a cheap form are very deleterious, but let them rather be content in offering some other wine less expensive and yet good of its kind, such as claret, sherry, or some light white wine.

When one is in doubt as to what wine to buy or what brand to get, the best plan is to consult a reliable wine-dealer, as it is impossible for an amateur to know all the different brands and their distinctive qualities.

For a simple informal dinner it is very customary to give a good claret or burgundy and a good sherry or some light white wine. For a formal dinner champagne or hock is usually given either alone or with other wines.

If a variety of wines is given the following is the usual order in which they are served:—

Sherry with soup, champagne with the first entrée and throughout the meal; sherry and claret at dessert, and liqueurs with the ices and after coffee. Sometimes a white Rhine wine, chablis, or sauterne is offered with fish or with oysters when they commence the meal.

At luncheon one wine is usually sufficient, such as claret, burgundy, or hock. Champagne is rarely given. Whisky and soda may be offered if gentlemen are present.

At supper sherry, claret and hock, or champagne may be offered, or one wine only.

Claret should always be decanted when used for dessert—at other times it is a question of taste. Both claret and burgundy should be warmed to the temperature of the room. The best way to do this is to allow them to stand in a warm dining-room some hours before they are required; or if wanted in a hurry to stand the bottle in a pail of warm water for a short time. These wines will not keep long after the bottle has been opened.

Sherry and port should always be decanted, and this should be done carefully and some time before the wine is required, so as to allow any sediment to sink to the foot of the decanter.

Port and Madeira are little used, especially at large dinners, although they may be served with dessert or with a cheese course at the end of a dinner. A fine Madeira sometimes takes the place of sherry at the soup course.

Champagne is generally served from the bottle. A serviette should be wrapped round the bottle, or held beneath the neck after the wine has been poured out to prevent the drops falling on the cloth. It ought to be very cold, and in hot weather it is customary to stand the bottles in ice for two hours before using. Metal pails are sold for the purpose, and these are filled with a mixture of broken ice and salt. A dry champagne is the favourite, the sweet brands being little used, except sometimes for ladies. Hock and Moselle are not decanted; they should be drunk at a temperature of about 40° Fahr.

Decanters of wine are not put on the table at a formal dinner until dessert is served, when claret and sherry can be placed in front of the host.

To open champagne or other sparkling wines, first cut the wire with a pair of champagne nippers and then cut the strings. Hold the bottle in a slanting position and remove the cork slowly and carefully. The bottle must be held on the slant until the wine has been poured out. When drawing ordinary bottles care must be taken not to break the cork; the corkscrew should be screwed into the middle of the cork as straight as possible. A lever corkscrew is best.

Wine should always be poured out at the right-hand side of the person seated, and poured out very carefully. When handing champagne at a dinner it is usual to ask in the first instance if it is desired, but when handing it later the glass should be refilled without any comment.

Liqueurs are always served in small liqueur glasses on a silver tray or liqueur stand and handed at the left-hand side.

Mineral waters and lemonade should be at hand at all meals, as so many do not take wine. Barley water too is a favourite and fashionable drink, especially among ladies, and is often served at luncheon.

Brandy or whisky and soda may be in readiness at informal meals where men are present. These spirits should always be decanted.

When stout or ale is taken the bottle should be opened at the sideboard and then poured out carefully and slowly, holding the bottle at an angle so that the glass may be filled with ale and not froth. It should then be handed on a silver waiter. If it is draught ale it should be poured out briskly and then slowly from a jug in order to give it a head.

BREAKFAST

The service of the breakfast-table does not alter much, and whether the meal be simple or elaborate the mode of laying the table remains very much the same. Although there are no hard-and-fast rules as in the case of the formal dinner, as much daintiness should be observed in the setting of the breakfast-table.

In large houses this meal is usually set in the morning-room and not in the dining-room and at an hour to suit the habits of the household. In all cases it must be served early enough to permit of those who have special work to perform to take their meal quietly and without hurry. This is especially necessary in the case of children having to go off to school. The seeds of indigestion have often been sewn even in childhood by having to swallow this meal in a hurry.

Both table and sideboard must be covered with a cloth, sometimes a plainer one than that used for dinner; any decoration must be of the very simplest—a pretty plant or fern, or a few flowers in vases will be all that are required.

The usual plan is to place the tea or coffee or both at one end of the table in front of the hostess along with the necessary accompaniments of sugar and milk, the required number of cups and saucers and a jug or kettle of hot water. Everything must be within easy reach for serving, and hot articles should be placed on silver or china stands.

At the other end would be placed any dishes that were being served and the necessary plates. If there is a choice of dishes cold dishes such as ham, tongue, or cold pie are usually placed on the sideboard and served from there. When boiled eggs are served they are put on an egg-stand or in a folded serviette or lined basket to keep them warm. Butter and jam or marmalade should also find a place on the breakfast-table, the former neatly rolled or made up in pats in the butter dishes, and the latter tidily served in jam dishes or fancy pots.

Different kinds of bread would also be served according to taste, such as rolls and scones (white or brown), toast, oatcakes, cut white and brown bread, &c. These must be served on bread plates with doyleys underneath. If a loaf of bread is required as well it is usually placed on the bread platter on the sideboard and cut as required.

Fruit either stewed or raw is also becoming a recognised addition to the breakfast-table, the kind varying according to the season of the year.

When cereal foods, such as porridge, grape-nuts, quaker oats, bread and milk, &c., are wanted, they must be daintily served—some of the pretty bowls or fire-proof dishes now sold are very suitable for the purpose.

The other appointments of the table will depend on the number of persons and the special dishes being served. A small plate and knife and serviette must be put to each place and the necessary knives, forks, and spoons for the different dishes. Provision must also be made for any dish that is to be served, not forgetting such things as cruets, butter knives, jam spoons, &c.

A table-heater is a most useful article to have for the breakfast - table, especially in houses

The "Heatorboil."

where the meal is a prolonged one. By this means dishes can be kept warm, and if the heater has a sliding top, as in the "Heatorboil," as shown in illustration, it can be utilised for boiling eggs or a little water as well.

As a rule, there is no waiting done at breakfast, so that it is all the more important that the table be set carefully and that nothing is forgotten.

Variety of Food.—Perhaps there is no meal at which variety is more necessary than at breakfast, but in many middle-class houses it is made a most monotonous and uninteresting repast. This may be due partly to the early hour at which the meal is served, but it is also the result of want of thought or resourcefulness on the part of the cook or housewife. Elaborate dishes are not required; in fact, they would be out of place; what is wanted is simple tasty dishes nicely served—always remembering that what pleases the eye helps also to please the palate. It is well as far as possible to choose for breakfast such dishes as can either be prepared the night before or will take little time to get ready in the morning.

Besides such well-known favourites as ham, eggs, bacon, fried fish, fried sausages, &c., the dishes detailed below, recipes for which will be found in the Guide to Cookery (pp. 116 to 235), might be quoted:—

Cod's roe, fish cakes, fish curry, fish cutlets, steamed fish pudding, scalloped fish, smoked haddock balls, herring au gratin, pickled herring, fish pies (various), tripe with tomatoes, grilled kidneys, sheep's tongues, brawn, jellied veal, calf's liver, calves' brains, calves' feet, galantine of veal, cold meat shape, meat scallops, glazed beef roll, chicken and spaghetti, potted fish and meat, rissoles and croquettes, cold pie, various egg dishes and omelets, stewed mushrooms, nut rissoles.

If more suggestions as to what to give are required, the housewife would do well to supply herself with the little volume entitled " Breakfast Dishes," published by T. C. and E. C. Jack.

Tea and Coffee.—It is very important that the tea and coffee for breakfast should be well made and served very hot, and the few hints given below for the use of the novice in the art of tea and coffee-making may not be out of place.

Tea.—Half fill the teapot with boiling water, let it stand a minute or two until thoroughly hot, then empty it. Put in the requisite quantity of tea (the old rule of a level teaspoon for each person and one over is a good one, but for a number a smaller proportion may be allowed), and pour on, gently enough, boiling water to half fill the teapot. Take the teapot to the kettle, and never the kettle to the teapot. Cover with a cosy or let it stand in a warm place to infuse for three minutes, then fill up the teapot and pour out the tea. Tea is never good if allowed to stand too long, and the use of a tea-cosy is to be deprecated if it is employed to keep tea hot for a long time until it becomes black and bitter. If the tea has to be kept hot for any length of time, it should be poured off the leaves into another teapot, or some teapots are fitted

with an inner case which contains the leaves, and which can be removed when the tea has infused sufficiently.

When sugar and milk or cream are used, they should be put into the teacup before the tea. The addition of milk makes the tea more wholesome, that of sugar less so.

Coffee.—To get good coffee is often one of the difficulties of the housekeeper, and yet it need not be so. The making of it is very simple. It just requires some nicety and care.

Coffee to be good should be freshly roasted and freshly ground. When this cannot be done at home, it should be bought in very small quantities and kept in a tin box with a tight-fitting lid.

If pure coffee is wanted chicory must not be used. Chicory imparts a slight bitterness to the coffee and darkens the colour, and some people prefer coffee with it. The usual proportions are two ounces chicory to one pound coffee. The water, as for tea, must be freshly boiled. It is also important to have the coffee-pot very clean.

There are many different kinds of cafetières, and some of them are more complicated than others, but for ordinary purposes the simple tin or china cafetière with percolator answers very well and requires no spirit-lamp.

First fill the cafetière with boiling water, let it stand until thoroughly heated, and pour the water away. Then put in the required amount of coffee—the quantity will vary according to the taste of the consumer; but a very good proportion is one table-spoonful coffee to each half-pint of boiling water. Pour the boiling water gently and gradually over the coffee, and let it filter slowly through. Keep the pot standing in a warm place, and serve as hot as possible. Coffee to be good must be hot. If there is no percolator attached to the coffee-pot, it is a good plan to have an iron ring made to fit the top of the coffee-pot inside. To this ring sew a muslin bag, and fit the bag into the pot. Pour some boiling water through it, and when it is well warmed pour the water away. Put the coffee into the bag and proceed as before.

Coffee can also be made in a jug. Heat the jug thoroughly with boiling water and pour the water away. Put the coffee into the jug, and stand it on the top of the stove for a few minutes until the coffee is hot. Then pour the proper quantity of boiling water over it and stir with a spoon. Cover the jug with a lid or thickly folded cloth, and let it stand by the side of the stove for fifteen minutes. Have the jug or pot in which the coffee has to be served made very hot. Stretch a piece of muslin over it and strain the coffee through.

When milk is served with coffee it should be scalded but not quite boiled. The proportions are equal quantities of strong coffee and milk, or two-thirds milk to one-third of coffee. A little cream may be added.

LUNCHEONS

There are several different kinds of luncheons, and the manner of serving them is more varied and less formal than that of the late dinner.

First there is the simple meal of two or three courses, which serves as the dinner of the children of the family and also that of the servants.

Then there is the still simpler meal partaken of by those who look forward to a more substantial meal in the evening and consisting of some egg or vegetable dish, or perhaps some made-up meat dish, cold meat, or the remains of dinner of the night before, along with a little fruit, cheese, and perhaps a cup of coffee.

And, lastly, there is the rather more formal luncheon, very similar to the late dinner, but with fewer courses and simpler ceremony.

The mid-day dinner has already been described under "Home Dinners," and requires no further comment.

The luncheon proper is a more or less informal meal according to the style of the house and customs of the family. As a rule all the dishes are served from the table, the waitress only passing the plates and handing any vegetable. The plates would also be changed by the maid in attendance, but any other service is generally performed by members of the family themselves, unless there is a good staff of servants.

A more formal luncheon would be served à la Russe, but this is only suited to large establishments, as one or two maids would require to be in constant attendance. The decorations should be very simple and menu and name cards are not necessary. Long luncheons consisting of many courses are not liked, and the dishes should be lighter than for a dinner.

When soup is on the menu it is frequently served in cups instead of soup plates, and small racks of toast should be supplied as well as bread.

Entrées of different kinds frequently take the place of more substantial joints which require carving, and the sweets should be simple in character, or some novelty in the way of pastry or French gâteaux might be offered. Dessert may be omitted if it makes the service too long, but a few little dishes of bon-bons or salted almonds may be placed on the table as at dinner.

The table is not cleared at dessert, and fruit plates are used without finger glasses. Black coffee is usually handed at the table after the last course has been served.

AFTERNOON TEA

This can scarcely be called a meal, but rather a light refreshment taken in the afternoon to break the fast between luncheon and late dinner. It is usually served in the drawing-room between four and five o'clock, and although unceremonious in character, it is one of the most social and popular events of the day, and the taste and refinement of the hostess are readily recognised in the manner in which it is served. Everything should be as dainty and attractive as possible.

The tea itself should be of the best that can be afforded and must be well made (see p. 250). The question as to what special tea to use is entirely a matter of taste—China tea is much appreciated by many people, and it is light and refreshing, but it is an acquired taste and not liked by every one, so that when tea is to be offered to a mixed company whose individual tastes are not known, it is safer to use a good blended tea with no pronounced flavour.

The beauty and delicacy of the china is also important, and it is usual to have small thin cups and saucers of some dainty design with teaspoons of a suitable size. All the silver must be very bright. Plates are not as a rule required, unless cream cakes or other similar dainties are being offered—when used they must be quite small in size.

The hostess should try to study novelty and variety in the cakes or bread offered, and nothing of a large or clumsy nature must be seen. Plain bread, either brown or white, should be buttered and sliced very thinly and cut in any shape desired, or, for a change, it may be made up in little rolls. Scones and tea-cakes are best hot buttered and served in a muffin dish or in a folded doyley. Different kinds of small sandwiches might also be served (see p. 187), and there must always be a nice choice of cakes. Petits-fours and other fancy biscuits of various sorts are also favourites, as they are dry and not likely to soil the gloves.

All the bread plates should be covered with pretty doyleys or lace-edged papers; the latter is better for placing under any cake that has to be cut. The tea should be prepared in the pantry or kitchen. If the tray is not of silver cover it with a dainty white tray-cloth, then arrange the cups and saucers, sugar basin, slop-basin and cream jug on it, and have the plates of bread and butter and cake in readiness. When all is ready and a good kettle of water boiling, prepare the table in the drawing-room—this may or may not be covered with a cloth according to its kind, but if one is used it must be as dainty as possible—there is nothing prettier than the all-white cloth, embroidered or trimmed with lace, but if colour is introduced it must tone with the colour of the teacups. Small serviettes to match are sometimes used, but this is not a universal custom.

The table is generally low and should be placed beside the hostess. The plates of cake may be placed on a cake-stand or on another small table close at hand. Infuse the tea and fill up the hot-water jug or kettle last of all and carry all to the drawing-room at the hour appointed. Tea-cosies are no longer fashionable, although many people still prefer to use them.

When guests are expected the table is sometimes prepared beforehand, leaving only the tea and water to be carried in when it is required. If more visitors should arrive after the tea has been served, the waitress must see that there is a sufficient number of cups and bring more if necessary without requiring to be told. Fresh tea should also be made and more bread cut if needed.

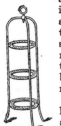

Cake-Stand.

Tea is usually poured out by the hostess or by a grown-up daughter, and the cups are passed by any gentlemen visitors or by the young people of the house. Servants do not as a rule remain in the room, but are only rung for when anything extra is required.

AFTERNOON "AT HOMES"

When a number of guests are expected the tea itself is sometimes served in a back drawing-room. A good-sized table spread with a pretty cloth should be placed in one corner, and upon it should be arranged the tea things with plates of bread and butter cakes and other dainties. The tea in this case should be poured out by one of the daughters of the house or by a lady friend, leaving the hostess free to receive and entertain her guests in the drawing-room proper.

At very large "At Homes" tea is frequently served in the dining-room, but this is a more formal affair. Visitors are shown into the room on arrival and waited on by servants before they enter the drawing-room. Gentlemen visitors often assist in handing round the refreshments. The table should be made into a sort of buffet, and, if space is limited, it should be moved to one end of the room. It must be covered with a fine damask cloth and the serving should be done from the back. Both tea and coffee are frequently served on these occasions and rows of cups and saucers should be in readiness. The jugs of cream and milk and bowls of sugar might be placed on the side of the table next the guests, allowing them to help themselves. There should be an abundant supply of all kinds of dainties, and one or two large cakes on high stands would help to give an ornamental appearance. The table must be prettily decorated with a few flowers or plants and everything made as attractive as possible.

In summer it is very usual to offer fruit, strawberries especially, and these are best served in small quantities on little plates. Ices too are sometimes served.

If there is sufficient space in the dining-room there might be two or three little tables and some chairs dotted about the room for the convenience of those who do not care to take their refreshment standing.

SUPPER

The Family Supper.—In houses where early dinner is the rule, supper of a more or less substantial kind is the concluding meal of the day. This is generally quite an informal meal, and the arrangement of it depends entirely upon individual requirements. As a rule, all the dishes are placed on the table and there is little or no waiting. The table is laid in very much the same way as for luncheon, and as the articles required depend entirely upon the kind of food provided, it is impossible to give any definite rules. If coffee is served, it is either placed at one end of the table and served by the hostess as at breakfast, or it is served by one of the daughters of the house.

The Formal Supper.—This may be served in several ways, and the arrangement chosen depends very much upon the wishes of the hostess. Many people consider it inhospitable not to provide a substantial meal to which their guests can sit down and be waited on by the servants of the house. In this case one large or several small tables are laid and the service is very much the same as for *Diner à la Russe*.

As a rule the dishes are cold, although hot soup and perhaps one hot entrée are frequently served. Such dishes as the following would all be suitable for the bill of fare :—

Cold meats of different kinds, such as game, poultry, ham, tongue, galantine and meat pies, dishes with aspic and mayonnaise, and various salads—jellies, creams, and all kinds of fancy sweets and plenty of fruit in season.

Buffet Supper.—When there are a number of guests and space is limited, a "stand up" supper is very often given. The different dishes are placed on the table, the ladies sit round the room, and the gentlemen wait on them and help themselves. Waitresses may also be in attendance. Only such dishes as can be easily eaten must be served, such as sandwiches, patties, aspic and mayonnaise dishes, and perhaps cold meats neatly sliced, followed by jellies, creams, various other sweets, and perhaps ices. Cooling drinks and light wines should also be offered.

This is a less expensive mode of serving the meal and one most frequently adopted by the housewife of moderate means.

Another way is to arrange a sort of buffet and to serve refreshments at any time throughout the evening without having a fixed hour for the meal. It will be the duty of the host and hostess to let this be understood by their guests and to see that every one is taken into supper in the course of the evening.

When only cold and light refreshments are given at an evening party it is very usual to offer a cup of hot soup or coffee to the guests just before they leave.

TABLE DECORATIONS

The floral decoration of the table is now a universal custom. Large sums of money are often spent upon the flowers and vases for a smart dinner-party, and hostesses will vie with each other as to whose table will present the most novel and effective appearance. But unless means are unlimited it is impossible to follow every passing fashion, and it is a good thing for most of us that floral decoration does not depend upon costly vases and expensive flowers; in fact, in most cases the simpler the arrangement the more charming the result.

Even although we are not all the happy possessors of a garden, flowers are brought into our towns in such lavish quantities nowadays, not to speak of those from our own market-gardens, that they have been brought within the means of the poorest. It is seldom one cannot get a bunch of some sort of bloom for a few coppers or even the modest penny, and when we consider the joy and comfort they bring we are amply compensated for the outlay. The delight a few flowers can give is unlimited.

What a difference between a table that is tastefully decorated with a few flowers and one on which a huge cruet-stand takes the central position. A table without a plant or flower is a desolate affair. There is no occasion to have a great display; more taste can often be shown in the arrangement of a few blooms than in an exuberant show. Flowers should not be crowded; they should have room to stand out individually. The Japanese, who are so artistic, consider one choice bloom quite sufficient to put in a vase. The main thing is to make the table pretty and attractive, and at the same time to think of something novel.

The foliage sprays should be inserted first, and the flowers then placed in carefully, so as to face whatever direction is required. If some flowers have a tendency to twist about, this can be remedied by pushing a piece of thin wire up the inside of the stem and allowing it to project half an inch. This projection can usually be inserted into a piece of foliage or stem, and the flower thus retained in the desired position.

Needless to say, the flowers must be fresh and the water should be changed every day.

The arrangement of flowers is very much a matter of skill and taste and the following paragraphs are only suggestive. The tendency at present is to keep the floral decoration low, tall-growing flowers, when they are used, being put in slender glasses or arranged in such a way that they do not obstruct the view. From the conversational point of view this is a great advantage, as it is never pleasant to be forced to look around ornaments in order to talk to some one on the opposite side of the table. Harmony of colour with the surroundings and a sense of proportion as to height, size, and shape of vases —a lightness of touch in the grouping together, with a quick eye for possibilities in the blending of shades, are all necessary to ensure success.

The quantity must depend upon the size of the table; a large table will stand some display of abundance, but now that small tables are fashionable, even for private houses, a very light form of decoration is all that is necessary.

Choice and Colour of the Flowers.—Flowers are now to be had in such variety and at every season of the year that their choice is very much a matter of individual taste, limited only by the resources at one's command. Flowers typical of the season are as a rule more pleasing than exotics and forced productions. Those with a strong scent should be avoided, especially if they are to be used in large quantities and in a heated room. When selecting a little thought must be given to the general tone of decoration. The colour of the room must be taken into consideration, unless the walls are cream or of some pale shade which will not clash with any of the brighter colours. Pleasing effects of colour are the first consideration. A mixture of colours rarely looks well; one or at most two colours with green is quite sufficient, although there may of course be graduations in shade of the prevailing colour.

Colour schemes are now the fashion, the flowers, candle shades, dinner ware, bon-bons, &c., being of corresponding hues. Some hostesses even aim at having the flowers, &c., to match the gown they are going to wear.

Foliage and Plants.—Plenty of foliage should be used, that of the flower itself wherever possible, and the teaching of nature followed if perfection is to be attained. The leaves themselves should not lie in the water, but should be stripped off the stalk, as they only crowd the vase and prevent the flowers getting sufficient water.

Asparagus, springeri, maidenhair, and smilax are among the choicest and best-known foliage plants, but there are many people, especially in the country, who may find these too costly for ordinary use or difficult to procure; to these it may be suggested that there are many trailing plants to be had for little or nothing, which could be employed in a similar way, such as the small-leaved gold or silver ivy, creeping jenny, canary creeper, periwinkle, and traveller's joy. To keep them from drooping the ends can be inserted in button-holders filled with wet sand and hidden among the leaves. Trailing plants can have silver wire inserted among the stems if it is wished to keep them in a special position. The tops of asparagus can often take the place of the more expensive fern; while more use might be made of carrot-leaves and those of the wild geranium, the latter sometimes being found in delightful shades of a red-brown colour. Convolvulus trails, with thick clusters of scarlet berries lasting for months after the leaves have withered, are a splendid addition to our winter decorations.

Vases.—Almost any kind of vase can be used as long as it suits the style of flower and does not clash in colour. As a rule, white and green crystal ones are the most adaptable. Tall-stalked flowers, such as chrysanthemums, lilies, lilac, daffodils, &c., look best in high glass, whilst short-stemmed flowers, such as violets, primroses, snowdrops, forget-me-nots, &c., should be arranged in low vases. Roses look especially well grouped in a bowl or single blooms set in slender glasses. Most people pick up quaint vases at different times, especially on a holiday, when they can often be found both pretty and cheap. It is astonishing, too, what can be done in case of necessity; an old meat or fruit tin packed with wet silver sand and hidden by moss can be made to do duty inside a basket quite as effectively as a proper zinc lining, while small baskets with the little china or glass drinking vessels used for birds or even a penny mustard tin are equally useful; similarly, all sorts of glass jars for potted pastes come in handy, so do cups without handles, especially the Japanese blue ones, also small china ash trays and saucers; indeed, any one at all resourceful need never be at a loss. If high glasses are used they should be slender and so arranged that they leave the line of vision clear. For corners all kinds of specimen glasses, upright or globular, cups, saucers, or pots filled with ferns, miniature trees or shrubs may be employed; a variation of the latter can be obtained by planting in tiny tubs (doll's washing-tubs painted dark brown serve the purpose), pips of oranges, lemons, grape fruit, apples, &c., which make excellent little trees; while rambles in woods and lanes will reward a search by giving us tiny oak, holly, and other trees to adorn our tables: these are especially desirable now that Japanese dwarf trees are the fashion.

Wild Flowers.—Those who live in the country often overlook or despise the decorative possibilities of the flowers around them; yet what can be more lovely than a large vase of golden buttercups loosely arranged. It is true the petals soon drop, but then how easy to renew them. Then, again, what a delightful effect is produced by a bowl filled with half-open buds of the deep pink wild-rose with pieces of sweetbriar among it. We do not half appreciate the artistic possibilities of the wild anemone with its delicate green leaf, or of the snowdrop, crab-apple blossom, wild hyacinth, the meadow crane's-bill with its charming lavender shade, meadow-sweet, poppies, corn-flower, and a host of others too numerous to mention, along with grasses and leaves of all kinds.

Table Decorations in Spring.—For spring there is nothing more easy to grow than bulbs of all kinds; they can be grown in bowls of cocoa-nut fibre in sitting-rooms; the lovely blooms are in this way always available for decoration and they last long. Daffodils, pheasant's eye, narcissus, tulips, and hyacinths of all colours following one another give a glorious variety with the added interest of being grown by oneself. A pretty picture is made of a low dark-green bowl filled with crocuses ranging from white through the shades of mauve to dark purple, or massed with the golden kind the bowl is particularly striking. Lily of the valley can also be grown in the same manner; but in growing bulbs it should always be borne in mind that a hot room is fatal for good results. As the season advances we get a bewildering choice of flowers, among which violets take a first place for their sweetness; a favourite combination is that of dark violets with the lavender-coloured parma-violets. Pansies and violas associate well with almost any light green foliage, but nothing is so suitable as their own foliage when that can be procured bright and fresh and of good colour. Violets, however, do not make a good show at night. A well-grown bowl of lily of the valley with smaller ones of violets looks charming. Violets can also be used with the lavender shades of iris. Another sweet spring decoration is that of lilac in blending shades, but the stalks of this flower and other woody kinds must be split up to allow them to get plenty of water, otherwise they soon droop. A large bowl of crimson peonies makes a very handsome centre-piece, and, being so showy, does not require more than ferns round it.

What an important niche is filled in our decorations by the little salmon pink anemone which appears in the late spring. Sold in small bundles of unopened flowers, it looks insignificant to those who do not know its value, but if kept for a few days a lovely show is made by the gradual unfolding of the buds to their full size, its colour alone making it valuable, coming as it does at a time when most of our flowers are white or yellow; as the blooms last well, its purchase is always a safe investment. The larger kind, though more showy, do not blend so well with other colours.

Table Decorations in Summer.—Summer brings us the rose, the queen of flowers, in all its many forms and shades, but as a queen it must reign alone, no other flower being permissible near it. You may have all one colour, or various shades as from pink to crimson, but do not mix all colours together; it is a fatal mistake. What is more perfect than an old silver or china bowl filled with rich crimson roses; or a few long-stalked pink ones in branched glass or other vases, small corner bowls holding each a rose with perfect foliage, the stems kept in place by leaden clips covered with moss? Rambler roses are more difficult to deal with, but if the dusters of bloom are not too heavy, and you get the right kind of vase to suit them, they make a perfect picture. All the larger lilies make a splendid show in tall vases, but many people find the scent too powerful in a room. Carnations rank next the rose, combining as they do both beauty of colour and fragrance. A simple but effective decoration can be made by arranging short trails of the dwarf nasturtium in a slender but broad-rimmed vase and allowing the ends to fall over, a few leaves and half-opening flowers being arranged in small bowls or saucers.

Sweet peas are both beautiful and plentiful; also particularly useful in schemes of colour with their many shades of pink and mauve, but theirs is a fragile loveliness, for should the weather be hot they droop almost as soon as picked; they look best in slender vases loosely arranged. The dainty colourings of gladioli are very charming, though the form is somewhat stiff; the defect can in this and many other cases be lightened by sprays of gypsophila. Pink or mauve ivy geraniums go well with some shades of gladioli as a combination. A delightful table decoration for a hot day is formed by large marguerites, blue Canterbury bells, and wild oats; the sense of coolness imparted by those in a white-papered room must be felt to be understood Harebells and dog daisies give the same effect.

The soft yet brilliant shades of the Shirley poppies make another welcome addition to our list of summer favourites; arranged in a tall tapering glass with sprays of the feathery white statice or gypsophila they look charmingly graceful, the various shades of white, yellow and orange or reds and pinks, blending beautifully together. Many people think they drop quickly, but they should be chosen as much in bud as possible, as every bud opens and then they will be found to last nearly a week.

Charming combinations can be worked in cream and lavender, in white and dark violet, in yellow and cream, and in mauve and white. Large fine blooms of fancy pansies are always admired on a table, and when well arranged no combination can be more attractive.

Table Decorations in Autumn and Winter.—As the autumn comes along we get the asters and dahlias in all their varied colourings; the single dahlias are the best for table ornamentation, though a bowl of the crimson or yellow double ones makes a rich feast of colour. The loose petalled asters are the most effective, and pink and white or mauve and white combine well together. The Michaelmas daisies have been much improved of recent years, and many varieties can now be obtained. There are two kinds of white Michaelmas daisies which are invaluable for putting among flowers; the blooms are very small and feathery. Now we get the lovely tones of the virginian creeper, so charming for adorning our tables, but it is

necessary to wire it, as the leaves so soon drop off; a few trails should hang from vases as well as be used in draping.

In the country many richly-shaded leaves of all sorts, also berries, can now be gathered, the leaves pressed and put aside for winter use. Hips and haws are well known, as are also the rowan berries. Trails of virginian creeper, a vase of bronze, yellow chrysanthemums, and smaller vases (of copper, if possible) filled with yellow marguerites make a charming picture, especially if the surroundings are of a brown tone.

For those who live in the country there is the possibility of making use of the rich hues of the crab-apple. A few discreetly selected small branches well laden with fruit, the stems clipped together with the soft leaden supports so cheap to buy, placed in a large green pot as if growing, the pot being half filled with moss, would make a novel decoration, while tiny specimen baskets, each containing one or two of the brilliantly coloured Quarantine apples, and the basket handles tied with a bow of green ribbon, might be placed round. This decoration would be suitable for a harvest home.

Winter gives us the ever-popular chrysanthemum, now grown in such quantities that it is brought within the reach of the most modest purse. Chrysanthemums always look best in tall jars or vases and require plenty of water; in fact, they should be left in a pail of water up to their heads every night. These flowers bring us to Christmas when holly reigns supreme, helped out by Christmas roses and forced scarlet tulips, the fragile-looking white of the Christmas roses making a delicate contrast to the prickly and brilliant holly.

Decorations for Special Occasions.—A few suggestions may be given for special occasions.

For Christmas the centre vase might be filled with large white or yellow chrysanthemums; round the base should be placed the small-leaved golden variegated holly, a well-berried piece of dark holly put at intervals; at the four corners horseshoes made of the leaves of the variegated sort, "A Merry Xmas," or similar motto formed of the berries running round or across as preferred, one corner of the horseshoe being tied with a bow of crimson ribbon. Fancy pots or baskets filled with ferns and scarlet tulips and tied with green ribbon could be used, or bowls of Christmas roses could take their place. The menu cards might have a robin or other seasonable device painted on them.

For Primrose Day.—Fill three round or long vessels with wet silver sand, put in the flowers one by one, separate the vessels with pots of light maidenhair, put the whole on a tin or zinc tray and bank up with moss. Smilax should be arranged round and draped along the sides, with small pots of maidenhair at the corners tied with bows of red ribbon, and a primrose button-hole put to each guest.

For a Wedding.—The place of honour being occupied by the wedding cake, pink and white roses, carnations, sweet peas, lily of the valley, and white heather are the most usual decorations. A pretty touch can be given by having tiny horseshoes for each guest ; these can be made of lily of the valley or forget-me-nots, with a small bunch of white heather at the side tied with pink or white ribbon.

SERVING OF FRUIT

Fresh fruit should find a place on every table ; it is always wholesome and beautiful, and much taste can be shown in the manner in which it is arranged. When fruit is served at a dinner-party it may either be placed on the table at the beginning and remain throughout the meal, or it may be put down when the guests are ready to partake of it. The first method is to be recommended as far as the decorative appearance of the table is concerned, although the fruit itself suffers from being exposed to the heat of the room for so long. The softer fruits especially suffer from the hot atmosphere and the odours of savoury dishes. Perhaps the best plan to adopt is to put down the harder and drier fruits, such as nuts, oranges, and apples, and to reserve the daintier and finer ones to be brought in fresh and cool when they are required, either in their natural state or *en salade.*

When arranging fruit it must be carefully looked over and any that is blemished put aside. Oranges and apples, pears and other fruit of the kind should be wiped with a damp cloth and polished. Grapes should be lightly brushed with a soft brush, peaches and plums very lightly rubbed, and all berries carefully picked and washed if necessary.

Fruit may be arranged in a variety of ways. Each dish may contain either a different kind of fruit, or else a miscellaneous assortment artistically grouped. If the table is large, a handsome centre-piece of mixed fruits sometimes looks well. Many pretty designs for fruit dishes are now sold, and these may either match the fruit plates or form a pleasing contrast. Rustic baskets of different shapes can also be made to look very pretty and artistic. Green leaves should always cover the dishes on which the fruit is served. For the larger fruits vine-leaves are the most suitable, while currant-leaves can be used for the smaller kinds. In winter when fresh leaves are scarce gold and silver paper leaves can often be employed with good effect, especially for dried fruits, dates, figs, Carlsbad plums, crystallised fruits, and such-like.

One important point to remember is that when arranging a dish of mixed fruits the lighter kinds must always be put on the top. Apart from this, there are no fixed rules for the arrangement of fruit, but an eye for colour and artistic taste are as necessary here as in floral decorations.

The following is a specimen of a Dinner Menu, written in both French and English :—

MENU	MENU
Melon Glacé	Iced Melon
Consommé aux Quenelles	Clear Soup with Quenelles
Turbot. Sauce aux Crevettes	Turbot with Shrimp Sauce
Crèmes de Bœuf aux Champignons	Beef Creams with Mushrooms
Gigot d'Agneau. Sauce Menthe	Lamb with Mint Sauce
Sorbet au Rhum	Rum Sorbet
Faisans Rôtis. Salade d'Orange	Roast Pheasants with Orange Salad
Nid de Marrons à la Crème	Nest of Chestnuts with Cream
Gelée au Vin Rouge	Port Wine Jelly
Pailles au Parmesan	Cheese Straws
Glacés aux Fraises	Strawberry Ices
Dessert.	Dessert.

HOUSEHOLD LINEN

A GOOD housewife will take great care of her household linen, and it will be her pleasure to see that it is kept in beautiful order.

In beginning housekeeping the quantity and quality of the linen that is bought must depend upon individual taste and means, the size of the household to be provided for, and the room there is for keeping it.

As a rule, it is a wise plan to buy just what is necessary to start with and to add to the stock as time goes on and the necessity for more arises. The space in modern houses is often somewhat limited, and if surplus linen has to be stored away in boxes in a cellar, it will probably be attacked by mildew and become unfit for use. Whatever is bought should be good of its kind, not necessarily of the finest quality, as this would be unsuitable in many cases, and the price paid will naturally depend upon the means at disposal ; but an inferior quality should never be bought. Even a little extra outlay at the beginning in order to obtain first-rate material will be amply repaid in the ultimate satisfaction afforded. Cheap linen may look very well when new, when it has dressing in it and a certain amount of gloss, but after the first washing it will be found limp and thin and without any body.

The material for household linen can always be bought by the yard and made up at home, but now that good ready-made articles can be had at such moderate prices, there is really nothing to be gained by taking this extra trouble. If hand work is still preferred to machine work, it can always be ordered or asked for specially. Of course, it is important to go to a first-class shop where the goods can be trusted. In this chapter useful information is given in regard to standard qualities and prices.

BED LINEN

Sheets.—*Material.*—Until within recent years linen was always considered the correct material for sheeting, and it would have been thought a breach of etiquette to provide a guest with anything but the finest and whitest of linen sheets. But now, owing to the many improvements made in its manufacture, cotton has to a large extent taken the place of linen. Linen is, however, still preferred by many people ; it is so fine and smooth to the touch, and delightfully cool in summer. One must of course be prepared to pay a good price for linen ; but it will be found very durable, and it keeps its colour better than cotton. Good linen is fine and even in texture. It should be bought fairly heavy, otherwise it will curl up and soon look shabby and crushed.

It is not wise to let delicate and rheumatic people sleep in linen sheets, as linen carries off the heat of the body and is very apt to give cold.

Cotton, on the other hand, is much warmer than linen, and for this reason it is often liked better. Besides, it is possible now to buy it of such fine quality and with such a nice soft finish, that even the most fastidious can scarcely object to it. The difference in price, too, is a consideration with people of moderate means.

Cotton sheets can be had in two kinds, twilled and plain. At the present time the plain calico seems to be the favourite and the kind most generally asked for, but this of course is a matter of taste, and the price of both is very much the same.

Both linen and cotton sheets can be had with either plain or hem-stitched hems at the ends ; the latter add very little, if anything, to the price, and they certainly add to the dainty appearance of the bed.

It is always well to have the top hem a little wider than the one at the bottom, or to have some other distinction, in order to prevent the foot of the sheet being placed near the face.

For servants' use a well-woven twilled calico is best. The unbleached material used to be bought for the purpose, but it is now seldom asked for, and the white certainly looks nicer.

A very usual plan when providing sheets for a household is to buy linen for the best beds, fine cotton for ordinary use, and a heavier twill for the servants. As some people object to linen sheets, it is well to keep one or two pairs of fine cotton in reserve for the use of guests.

Size and Price.—Sheets must always be bought of a right size for the bed for which they are intended. They must be long enough and wide enough to permit of their being tucked in

151

all round the mattress. An extra length, about three-quarters of a yard, must be allowed if the under-sheet has to cover the bolster as well. In breadth a sheet should at least be 72 inches wide for a single bed, and 90 inches for a double bed, and from 2 to 3½ yards long.

As regards quality taste varies so much that individual preference and the means at command can alone decide the choice. The following prices may, however, be a guide to those who have little knowledge of what ought to be paid. Only thoroughly recommended prices are quoted.

Cotton Hem-stitched Sheets.

Single-bed size—8s. 6d. to 15s 6d. per pair.
Double-bed size—12s. to 23s. 6d. per pair.

The difference in price depends upon the fineness of the material, and also upon the length.

Hem-stitched Linen Sheets (Irish).

Single-bed sheets—18s. 9d., 23s. 6d. to £3, 3s. per pair.
Double-bed sheets—25s. 9d., 30s. to £4, 4s. per pair.

For servants' use a very good twilled calico sheet with plain hem, can be bought at 6s. 6d. per pair, and a rather better quality at 8s. per pair.

The more expensive sheets have very often a pretty embroidered piece for turning over at the top.

The Jaeger or Sanitary Sheet.—This is a special kind of sheet made of pure wool, and of a thin texture that can easily be washed. The Jaeger sheets are used principally for children and delicate people, and especially for those troubled with rheumatism. The price varies from 19s. 6d. to 30s. for a single-bed sheet, and from 33s. 6d. to 60s. for a double-bed sheet. They can be had either of a fine white cashmere or in the natural wool or camel-hair shade. Pillow-cases can also be obtained in the same material.

Sheet-Shams.—These are fancy articles, and not by any means a necessity for any one starting housekeeping. They are strips of linen hem-stitched, and generally very prettily embroidered, which are slipped in under the bed-clothes and turned back over the cover to resemble a sheet, and they give to a bed a dainty appearance during the day.

Mattress Covers.—Every mattress should be covered with a cotton slip to keep it clean, and this need only be removed once or twice a year to be washed. Unbleached calico or thin holland is usually sold for the purpose.

Pillow and Bolster-Slips.—*Material.*—These can be either of cotton or of linen, to match the sheets with which they are used, although linen pillow-slips are very often used with cotton sheets. Lovers of ease always prefer linen pillow-slips to cotton ones, as they are cooler for the head and smoother and softer to lie on.

Any one troubled with headaches or sleeplessness should always use them, as they check the flow of blood to the head, and almost act as a cold-water bandage.

Pillow-slips can be bought ready made in different sizes. They look very pretty hem-stitched, and they can also be had with dainty frills ; but it must be borne in mind that these latter are not so durable, and that the washing of them will cost more than that of the plainer kinds. They can be had either fitted with tapes or with buttons and button-holes. Upon the whole, the latter method of fastening is to be preferred, as it is more conducive to neatness.

The newest method of fastening is with a double set of button-holes and small bone studs, which can easily be slipped out when the pillow-slips are sent to the washing. It is a good plan to sew these studs on to a length of tape—the proper distance apart—and this will prevent them from getting lost.

Bolster-slips are not always used, the under-sheet being rolled round the bolster and made to act as a cover. However, some people prefer the separate cover, and it is certainly the more comfortable arrangement, especially for indifferent sleepers, as the cushions can be moved about at will and arranged to suit one's special comfort.

Bolster-slips can also be bought ready made, but it is almost better to have them prepared to order, and to suit the special shape of bolster. They look better when they are drawn in at the ends and not button-holed, or sometimes they are made with a shaped piece at each end, which gives the bolster a more handsome appearance.

The newest shape of bolster-slip is made about half a yard longer than the bolster on each side. The ends, which are left open, are either hem-stitched or embroidered, and the extra length is allowed to hang over the sides of the bed.

Both bolsters and pillows should also have an under-cover of calico to preserve the tick, and also to prevent the stripes of the latter showing through the outer case. An old pillow-slip or bolster-slip will answer the purpose very well, and they should be removed once or twice a year to be washed. These inner slips are usually sewn on, but if fastened with tapes or buttons, the open end should be put into the outer case first, to prevent both fastenings coming together.

Size and Price.—Pillow-slips must be bought to fit the pillows for which they are intended, and as these vary somewhat in size, it is important to take careful measurements. If too tight the softness of the pillow is destroyed, and on the other hand if they are too large they look clumsy.

Very good hem-stitched pillow-cases can be bought for 2s. 6d.—fastened neatly at the ends with hand-made button-holes and well finished—and upwards to 8s. each, and even more. With frills they will cost from 3s. 6d. upwards. Plain white calico slips can be had from 8d. to 2s. each, and with frills from 2s. 6d. upwards.

Pillow-Shams.—These are dainty ornamental covers, which are laid over the pillows during the day and removed at night. They are generally made of fine linen or muslin, embroidered prettily with initials and some other design, and finished round the edges with lace or cambric frills. Sometimes a large bow of ribbon will ornament the centre. They help to make a bed look pretty, and when carefully folded at night they will keep clean for quite a long time.

Quantity Required.—*Allowances.*—The careful housewife should see that the linen cupboard is always kept well stocked with sufficient linen to meet all emergencies. If each bed has its own special linen, then three pairs of sheets, six pillow-slips, and two or three bolster-slips will be a very moderate supply for each, in order that the linen cupboard may never be left without a pair of sheets to fall back upon. If, however, the linen is used generally, and the cost of washing has to be considered, six pairs of sheets, twelve pillow-cases, and half-a-dozen bolster-slips might do service for three beds. This, however, is a minimum supply, and if frequent change is indulged in, double the number would not be too many.

Ideas vary much as to how often bed-linen ought to be changed, and to have a liberal allowance is certainly a luxury. When the expense and trouble of washing has not to be thought of, sheets may be changed as often as three times a week, and pillow-slips every day ; but this amount is beyond the means of the ordinary household, both as regards the supply of linen required and the somewhat heavy washing bill entailed. Once a week is considered a very good allowance, while once a fortnight should be the minimum of change. To keep sheets in use longer than this is not healthy. Some people prefer to change one sheet each week, always putting the top sheet down, while others prefer to have all clean at once. One pillow-slip a week at least should be allowed for each person, and a bolster-slip if used should be changed once a fortnight.

If the supply of bed-linen is limited, housekeepers should arrange that all the beds are not changed the same week, but in rotation. If there is a number of beds, it will be as well to make a note in a small book of the dates when each have been changed.

Servants too should be allowed one clean sheet a week, or a pair a fortnight, and one clean pillow-slip each week.

BED-COVERS OR COUNTERPANES

Dainty bed-covers add not a little to the attractive appearance of a bedroom, and they should always be kept as fresh and clean as possible. A little care expended in selecting new bed-covers will be amply rewarded in the additional wear to be had out of a well-selected article, which as a rule will combine the qualities of both decorativeness and durability.

Bed-covers are to be had in various styles, but the all-white coverlet is always a good investment, as it washes easily and looks well on any bed.

The tendency now is to have them of a very light make, and some of the newest styles are in white cotton or linen embroidered and hem-stitched, or a pretty white embroidered muslin. The finer and open-work ones are usually mounted on a sateen slip of a colour to match the bedroom, and these slips are fastened to the cover by means of small buttons and button-holes, which are easily undone when the upper part requires washing.

A very pretty embroidered cotton quilt can be bought for 12s. 6d. for a small bed, and 18s 6d. for a double-bed size and upwards. An embroidered and hem-stitched linen cover will cost from 23s. 6d. for a small, and 31s. 6d. for a double-bed size, while several pounds may be paid for one with a very elaborate design of drawn-thread work and lace.

A white embroidered muslin cover, which is very dainty and particularly suitable for summer use, can be obtained for 16s. 6d. small size, and 18s. 9d. large size, and upwards. An under-slip of sateen for these covers costs 10s. 6d. or 12s. 6d., according to size, and any colour can be chosen.

Coloured bed-spreads are also greatly used, made of printed cotton or taffeta. To obtain one of a good quality, it will be necessary to pay from 12s. 9d. upwards. They should be chosen to suit the curtains, or the prevailing colour in the room for which they are intended. For winter use, and especially if fires are burned in the bedroom, these coloured quilts are perhaps more practical than the all white, and especially where washing is a consideration.

Stronger counterpanes in colour suitable for servants' use are sold for 4s. or 5s., and it is quite possible too to get these with a nice design and of a pretty shade. There is no occasion to have something ugly because it is cheaper than the finer qualities, and a maid is more likely to take a pride in keeping her room in order if some encouragement is given to her to make it pretty.

Although somewhat out of date, the thick white Marcella and honeycomb quilts will always be useful for hard wear, as they stand frequent washing without any harm, and with care will last for years.

The bed-spread or cover must be large enough to cover the bed and hang well over the sides. If no valance is used, a little extra width will be required.

One bed-cover at least will be required for

each bed, and two or three extra ones to allow for washing. It is a good plan to have a change of quilts in summer and winter.

TOILET COVERS AND DUCHESSE SETS

No toilet table is complete without its toilet cover and doyleys, and the bedroom would indeed have a neglected appearance where their use was dispensed with. A daintily dressed toilet-table adds materially to the cleanly and cheerful aspect of a room, and besides nothing is more calculated to show off a good piece of furniture than this time-honoured essential to the toilet-table equipment, whilst on the other hand the appearance of shabby furniture can be considerably improved upon by the use of clean and dainty toilet sets. The variety in these is almost endless, and choice must depend upon individual taste.

The all-white covers, such as the Marcella and Honeycomb, can be bought ready made in various sizes from 1s. and 1s. 9d. each, and upwards. They will stand any amount of hard wear and frequent washing; in fact, the material will scarcely wear out. When the fringes become shabby, they should be cut off, and the ends of the cover hemmed and trimmed with a little edging if desired. The same material is also to be had by the yard, known as " Toileting." The required length can then be bought, neatly hemmed at the ends and trimmed with crochet edging or other suitable embroidery.

Of course, from an artistic point of view, the above covers are not pretty; they are strong and clean-looking, but there is nothing distinctive about them. The daintiest covers are those made to suit the room. A pretty cretonne edged with lace and insertion, or a dainty muslin with a frill of the same material, and coloured sateen underneath, or again, a nicely embroidered linen or some fancy material worked in colours, can all be made to look very nice and give a homelike appearance to the room.

Instead of the all-over toilet cover, a Duchesse set of mats is frequently used, and this permits of some of the wood of the toilet-table being seen. Needless to say, these should only be used where the table or chest has a good surface. If the wood is shabby, it is much better to have it entirely covered.

Duchesse sets can also be had in strong white Marcella material, and will cost from 1s. per set and upwards. The prettiest ones, however, are in fine linen or damask and lace, or drawn-thread work. The price of these will vary according to the amount of work in them and the quality of the lace. A simple hem-stitched set can be procured for 1s. 6d., while linen and lace will cost from 2s. 6d. and upwards to almost any price. But these are things which are frequently made at home, as small odds and ends of linen, muslin,

lace, &c., can be so easily utilised for the purpose.

For the changing of toilet covers no regular rule can be laid down; if the table is standing near the open window and in a dusty situation, the cover may look dirty at the end of a week, whereas in a clean place it may retain its fresh appearance for a month and even longer—therefore the only rule to go by is to change when necessary.

Two toilet covers or sets will be required for each room, unless they are used generally for the different bedrooms, when one each and two or three over to allow for washing will be sufficient.

TOWELS

Bedroom Towels. — *General Remarks and Material.*—For ordinary use the linen huckaback are the most suitable, while linen, damask or diaper will serve the purpose when a fine towel is required. The latter make very nice face towels, as they are so fine and soft. Towels can be bought ready made, either hemmed, hem-stitched, or with fringes. Those with fringes are scarcely to be recommended, as they so soon become shabby and untidy-looking. If they are chosen, it is wise to overcast the ends before putting the towels in use, as this will prevent any fraying out, unless this has already been done, which is sometimes the case with the more expensive towels. When the fringes become shabby they should be cut off, and the ends of the towels neatly hemmed.

Towelling can also be bought by the yard, fifteen yards being of fair allowance for twelve towels. But there is really little to be gained by doing this, as the ready-made towels have generally some kind of border, and the others would not have the same finished appearance.

The ends of towels are sometimes made ornamental by having a border worked across them, very often in Russian cross-stitch, in blue and white, red and white, or simply all white; or a monogram or initials may be worked in one corner, or any other effective design. The ends, too, are sometimes trimmed with hand-made lace—that of a strong make, such as a crochet or knitted edging, being the most appropriate. These little additions are considered by some people to greatly improve the appearance of a towel, and to make a pretty finish for those destined for the guest-room; but for practical purposes the perfectly plain towel is to be preferred.

Turkish towels are generally used for the bath. They are made of cotton, with a raised fluffy surface, and are very soft in texture. They can be had either all white or a mixture of red and white. Those of a large size are called bath sheets. When a very rough towel is wanted to produce friction after a bath, the brown linen towelling should be asked for.

Unbleached huckaback towels of a stouter make should be bought for servants' use, and these can generally be had with a coloured border, which would serve as a distinguishing mark where there are several maids. If something cheaper is desired, then the cotton honeycomb towels should be bought, and these too are made with some colour introduced.

Size and Price.—Very good pure linen huckaback towels, grass bleached and of a soft finish, can be bought for 14s. per dozen, and with a damask border in a heavier make for 21s. per dozen.

Damask and diaper towels will cost from 15s. to 35s. per dozen.

Turkish bath towels (Christie's) are also sold at from 15s. to 35s. per dozen, according to size and quality, while a bath sheet can be obtained for 3s. 9d., 5s., 6s. 6d. or 8s. 6d.

The rough crown linen towels are 2s. each and upwards.

The unbleached huckaback for servants' use will be about 8s. 6d. or 12s. per dozen, while the white honeycomb are only 6d. each and upwards. A very suitable bath towel is also to be had for 10d. or 1s.

When buying towels it is well to compare the sizes, as often by paying a shilling or two more per dozen a few extra inches in length can be obtained, and as the larger towel will not cost more in the washing, this is a point worth considering.

An ordinary towel should be at least 40 inches long and 24 inches wide ; anything less than this is very inadequate for the purpose, while an inch or two larger would be a distinct advantage. Bath towels especially are better if of a larger size, while for a bath sheet double the above proportions would not be too much.

Quantity Required—Allowances.—At least half-a-dozen bedroom towels and three bath towels should be allowed for each person. This will allow of two face towels and one bath towel being given out each week, the same number would be at the washing, and the other three would be in reserve. This is of course a very limited supply ; as many people like to have their towels changed more than once a week, the supply would then have to be increased accordingly.

Bath sheets may be had in addition to the above ; these need not be changed so frequently as the bath towels.

The usual allowance for servants is one face towel a week and a bath towel once a fortnight. Three face towels and two bath towels would be enough to allow for each maid.

BLANKETS

Choice.—In choosing blankets for the household it is advisable to select those of a first-rate and reliable quality. Good blankets will not only last longer than inferior ones, but they are warmer and lighter in make. Touch is the best guide to choice ; they should have a soft and silky feeling, with a nice woolly surface.

In England the Witney blankets have the finest finish, but the Yorkshire and Welsh are very good for hard wear.

The Scotch blankets are also famous, and one special feature of their manufacture is that they are generally all wool. They have a raised surface, although not so much so as a Witney blanket.

A blanket should be large enough to tuck in at both sides and at the bottom of the bed, but must not be so wide that it touches the floor. Where economy has to be considered, one pair might be chosen smaller, if the upper one is large enough to tuck in and keep all in position.

Before buying blankets it is very important to know the exact size of the beds for which they are required.

Quantity Required and Price.—Two pairs of upper blankets and one under-blanket is a very fair allowance for each bed. When an eiderdown quilt is used one upper blanket may be sufficient, but this is very much a question of individual needs, and it is always well to have one or two pairs of blankets in reserve.

A pair of very good single-bed blankets, guaranteed all pure wool, can be bought for 16s. per pair, while as much as 45s. can be paid for the same size in the finest and softest wool, with a pretty silk binding in sky-blue, rose-pink, or cream. For a double-bed blanket the price will range from 21s. to 75s. per pair. They can be supplied either all white or with blue or red lines, button-holed in the same colour.

For servants' use union blankets are generally bought. These are rather harder to the touch, as they are not all wool, but are woven with a certain amount of cotton. They are not so light in weight as an all-wool blanket, but are very suitable for hard wear. The price of these blankets will range from 8s. to 12s. 6d. per pair.

The under-blanket is generally a single blanket which can be bought new for 4s. and upwards, but except in the case of a new ménage, a worn or thin upper blanket can generally be used for the purpose.

Scarlet blankets when they are preferred can be bought for the same price as the white. Grey blankets are now little used, except those of a very hard make, which are sold for charity purposes.

The Scotch blankets are generally sold by weight. For instance, the well-known make called " Scotch Teviot " are made in weights from 5 lbs. to 10 lbs. 6 lbs. is a good single-bed size, and measures about 68 by 76 inches. 9 lbs. is a good double-bed size, and measures about 78 by 90 inches. An extra large size weighs 10 lbs., and measures 80 by 94 inches.

This range is sold according to quality—6 lbs. weight from 17s. 9d. to 25s. retail ; 9 lbs. weight from 21s. 9d. to 42s. retail.

The twilled blanket is also much used as binders or under-blankets. They resemble very much a serge material, but are very warm and durable. The prices are from 10s. to 18s. a pair (retail).

Note.—The above particulars and prices regarding Scotch blankets have been kindly supplied by Messrs. Charles Jenner & Co., Princes Street, Edinburgh.

Of course, it will be quite possible to buy blankets at a much lower price than the above, but nothing cheaper can be really recommended for comfort and good wear, unless it may be a lot slightly soiled which can sometimes be picked up at a sale.

Marking Blankets.—Blankets should always be carefully marked. This is best done in wool, worked in cross-stitch from a sample (see p. 406). The lettering should match in colour the button-holing on the blanket or any colour introduced in the weaving. If the blanket is all white, then the sewing might be done in some pretty contrasting colour. Cash's woven lettering can also be used for the purpose, or the name be written in ink on a piece of tape and sewn on to the blanket, but the first method looks best.

Care and Cleaning of Blankets.—Blankets that are not in use should be stored away in a blanket chest or on the shelves of the linen cupboard. If they are to be left for some time, precautions must be taken to prevent their being attacked by moths. Put camphor, naphtha balls, or Russia leather parings between the folds, and then sew the blankets into a piece of old sheeting or other cotton material, taking care that no holes are left where the moths could enter.

The washing or cleaning of blankets is another very important point. Some people consider that if they are cleaned once a year, generally at the annual spring cleaning, this should be sufficient; but one must be guided somewhat by circumstances. If the blankets are used in a room where a fire is frequently lighted, or in a smoky and foggy neighbourhood, twice a year will not be too often to have them attended to. Then again after a case of illness the blankets used on the bed should always be cleaned, and, if necessary, disinfected as well. Of course, unnecessary washing must be avoided, as it impoverishes the material, and there is always the danger of a certain amount of shrinking.

If washing is the mode of cleaning to be adopted, then great care must be taken in the choice of the laundry to which they are sent. Preference should be given to one where they are dried in the open air. If there is the slightest doubt as to their being well done at a laundry, then it is a much wiser plan to send blankets to a professional cleaner. The price for cleaning will vary from 1s. to 2s. per pair, according to size, which may mean a little extra expense as compared with washing, but it is cheap when one considers that the so-called washing often

spells "ruin" to a beautiful blanket. In the case of new blankets, it is always better to have them cleaned instead of washed, as the first time of washing is always more difficult. It must be remembered, too, that once a blanket becomes clotted and non-porous through bad washing, it ceases to be so healthy.

The length of time blankets keep clean depends upon the care that is taken of them. They should be protected by night as well as by day with a cover of some sort. So if the bed-cover is removed at night, which is the correct thing to do, there should be a thin cover underneath or an ordinary sheet to cover the blankets. Then again, when a bed is being turned down or made, the blankets must not be allowed to sweep the floor, but be laid over the backs of two chairs, and then handled carefully. It is a good plan to have the blankets well brushed from time to time, and hung in the open air for a few hours.

Upper blankets are always sold in pairs, but some people prefer to have them neatly cut in two, and the raw edges button-holed in wool to match the other end of the blanket.

Mending of Blankets.—When blankets begin to show signs of wear, they should be carefully darned with wool of the same colour, and when a hole appears it should be neatly patched with a piece of blanketing of a suitable texture. (For details, see under Needlework, p. 415.)

What to do with Old Blankets.—Old blankets can be utilised in many different ways. Large blankets can be cut down to make blankets for beds of a smaller size, or if not sufficiently good for the purpose they may be used as under-blankets. If very thin, the material might be doubled and button-holed together at the edges, and this would make a capital under-blanket. Then in houses where there are children small pieces of blankets will be found invaluable, either to cover them when they are asleep or for them to sit on. In cases of sickness, too, scraps of blanket are frequently required for fomentations and other purposes. Small pieces will also be required for patching other blankets; and very old pieces will always be found useful as floor-cloths or for cleaning purposes, such as the washing of paint, &c.

TABLE LINEN

It has often been said that the refinement of a household may be judged to some extent by its table appointments, and more particularly by the dainty freshness of the table napery. The soiled and crumpled table-cloth replete with holes is characteristic of the third-rate lodging-house and not of the well-ordered household.

If when buying table-cloths a little care is expended upon their selection, to keep them in good condition should be a comparatively simple matter; always providing, of course, that they are entrusted when soiled to a fairly capable laundress, and that the proverb " A stitch in time saves nine " is borne well in mind.

Double damask, bleached or unbleached, is the best material to buy. It wears well, and keeps its appearance to the end. There is nothing to be gained by buying inferior table linen; it may have a very fine glossy surface when new, but the first washing removes all this dressing and leaves only a poor limp material which wrinkles up and soils very readily.

The design to be chosen is entirely a matter of taste, and each season shows something new. It must be borne in mind, however, that the newest designs generally cost a little more money, so, where economy has to be considered, it is as well to ask for something of an earlier date, which may at the same time be just as pretty and effective. As a rule, a table-cloth with a small all-over pattern, such as spots, stars, diamonds or small sprigs, is cheaper than one with a large central design and border.

Table-cloths with some colour introduced, generally red or blue, are used by some people as luncheon or breakfast cloths, but the fashion is more German than English, and at present is not much in favour.

Then there is a fashion at present for using dinner sets—a centre and mats in place of a cloth ; but this can only be adopted by those who have a very finely polished table or a beautiful oak surface to show, and is not likely to become general.

For kitchen use the unbleached damask cloths answer the purpose very well, as they will not soil so quickly as the pure white cloths. They ought to be bought strong and good, although the quality need not be so fine as the other household cloths.

Table napkins, or serviettes, to be correct, should match the table-cloth with which they are to be used in quality and design. This, however, entails additional expenditure, as a much larger number will be required than when they are used generally with any cloth. For this reason it is a good plan to buy two table-cloths of one pattern, as it will then be found easier to regulate the supply of serviettes. In fact, in small households of moderate means it is just as well for everyday use to buy all the serviettes alike, and to choose a small unobtrusive pattern that can be used with any cloth. Then for special occasions there can be a set kept in reserve which matches the best table-cloth in pattern and quality.

Size and Price.—The size of the table-cloth is very important, as it will not look well unless it hangs at least half a yard over each end of the table and twelve inches at the sides. Careful measurements should therefore be taken of the tables for which the cloths are required before buying is thought of.

A very good double damask table-cloth in a small spot design can be bought at the following prices:—2 by 2 yards, 10s. ; 2 by 2½ yards, 12s. ; and 2 by 3 yards, 14s. ; and these are particularly suitable for breakfast or luncheon cloths. Those of a more elaborate design will cost from 14s. 6d. to 27s. 6d., 18s. to 35s. 6d., and 21s. 6d. to 42s. and upwards for the same sizes respectively, while larger sizes will cost still more in proportion. A large cloth of very fine quality cannot be bought under £4 or £5.

Other designs in fine quality damask, with hand-made lace insertion and hem-stitched borders, will cost from 50s. to £18 and upwards, according to size and the quality of the work.

Serviettes are made in different sizes—*i.e.* 22, 27, and 31 inches square ; the medium size is the most usual, although the smallest ones are frequently used for breakfast. Very good serviettes can be bought for 16s. 6d. per dozen for the medium size and 12s. 9d. for the small size, while as much as 45s. and 68s. can be given for the same size in an extra fine quality.

There are a number of small articles in the way of table linen, such as tray-cloths, afternoon tea-cloths, doyleys, carving-cloths, sideboard-cloths, table-cloths, &c., which will also be required in a household, but a list of these is scarcely necessary, as they must be bought to supply individual needs. These are the little things which are frequently given as presents to those starting house for the first time, while in an old-established ménage scraps of damask, linen, &c., can often be utilised for the purpose. In any case, they should never be bought in large quantities, as they can so often be picked up at a very moderate rate and at odd times as the use for them arises. Fashions too change so quickly, that it is better to have a small stock and renew it when necessary.

Quantity required.—*Allowances.*—This, again, depends very much upon the means of the household, and must be regulated according to individual circumstances and the special arrangement of meals. In houses where a large amount of entertaining is done the quantity will necessarily be increased.

A very moderate supply would be four table-cloths of average size for each meal, and three dozen serviettes, two cloths of extra quality and extra size, if necessary, for each meal, and two dozen serviettes to match.

It is always better to keep a cloth specially for dinner, and a different one for breakfast and luncheon or supper. In this case perhaps it will be sufficient to give out one of each kind in a week, although in many houses the dinner cloth will be changed as often as three times a week.

Serviettes should be changed at least twice a week, or fresh ones for dinner every day where it can be afforded. One table-cloth a week is the usual allowance for servants' use.

The table linen has so much to do with the success of a meal that it should never be allowed to become too dirty or crushed. If a table-cloth has to do duty for several days and look well all the time, great care must be taken of it. It should be folded carefully and always in the original creases, and each fold should be smoothed out with the hands. If it is kept in a drawer, it must be laid perfectly flat, but what is better still is to put it into a linen press, as shown in the accompanying diagram. When the cloth has been laid in between the boards, the tension should be screwed down as tightly as it will go without destroying the material, and if the table-cloth is allowed to remain several hours, it will come out looking as if it had been newly " done up." The screw of the press should be loosened when not in use. Failing a press, the cloth may be slowly mangled if it has become very much crushed.

Linen Press.

Another point about table-cloths is that they should never be put directly on the bare table. An old table-cloth or piece of felt should always be laid under it. This not only acts as a silence cloth, but it enables one to lay the cloth more smoothly. If a piece of felt has to be bought for the purpose, then white should be chosen, as then there will be no fear of staining should water or any other liquid be spilt.

Kitchen and Household Towels.—Besides the towels required for bedroom use, there is also a stock indispensable to kitchen and household purposes, such as :—

Roller Towels.	Lavatory Towels.
Glass Towels.	Pudding Cloths.
Tea Cloths.	Hearth Cloths.
Kitchen Towels.	Dusters.
Slop Cloths.	Oven Cloths.

&c.

All household cloths should be hemmed and marked with the name and purpose for which they are intended. If there are several servants in a house, it is a good plan to let each one have her own special set for which she is held responsible, and they ought to be instructed as to the legitimate use of each kind. In some household towels the name of its kind is woven into each one, such as "Glass Towel," " Tea Cloth," " Kitchen," &c., then to distinguish one maid's towels from another's they can be bought in various styles and colours, with a blue and white or red and white check, a blue or red border, or all white, and so on. If just a little difference is made, confusion will be avoided, and the blame of lost towels will not be likely to fall upon the wrong person.

Towels and dusters should be given out regularly once a week, and the last week's lot should always be accounted for. The number required depends entirely upon the amount of work to be done. It is a mistake to be niggardly in giving out supplies—it should be remembered that people have different ways of working, and as a rule it is not wise to limit a good worker, but to give what is asked for within reason.

The only point that must be insisted upon is that the towels and dusters are kept clean, taken care of, and never bundled away damp in dark corners.

Except in the case of a young ménage, it should not be necessary to buy all these towels new. The duster supply especially can generally be provided for by using up pieces of old soft material ; thin bedroom towels can be cut down to make lavatory towels or basin cloths, and old bath towels for drying floors and so on. (See also " What to do with Old Linen," p. 267.)

If new dusters must be bought, they can be procured ready made from 3d. each, or if the material alone is bought, there is nothing better than a cheap sateen. This can be cut up in convenient pieces, and a hem laid and machined round in a very short time. These will be found excellent for furniture, and they become softer each time they are washed.

Dish cloths again can be made of any old soft material, such as remnants of Turkish or other old towelling. It is a mistake to have them very close in texture, or they will too readily absorb grease. There is really nothing better than the knitted kind, made of strong unbleached knitting cotton worked with rather coarse needles. These wear well and can be washed and boiled over and over again.

Cloths known as " swabs " are very useful for house cleaning. They are made of a coarse open material, and are better and stronger than flannel for washing floors, tiles, and doorsteps, and they have the further advantage of leaving no fluff behind. The price is about 2d. each.

Dust Sheets.—Old sheets or bed-covers can generally be used, but where these are not available, thin unbleached calico or holland should be bought and sewn up into suitable sizes. It will cost from 4½d. to 6d. per yard. The number of dust-sheets required will depend entirely upon the amount of furniture to be covered.

House Flannel.—A linen cupboard should always contain a supply of this, but it must be given out with care. The remains of old blankets can often be utilised.

THE LINEN CUPBOARD

The durability of linen depends very much upon its being well kept. If it is treated with care, it will not only look better, but it will last longer. To keep it nicely, a linen cupboard or its equivalent is a necessity. In houses with good cupboard accommodation, and especially in the old-fashioned ones, a place specially fitted up for linen is generally provided. Sometimes even a small room can be reserved for the purpose, where, in addition to the linen proper, spare blankets, curtains, and other upholstery which is not in use can be comfortably stored away. The linen cupboard should be in a

Linen Cupboard.

dry and airy situation, and not against an outside wall, which is not always free from moisture. If linen is allowed to become damp it mildews and rots very quickly. It can frequently be arranged that the hot-water pipes going to the bath-room pass through the linen cupboard, and the inner wall is warmed by a kitchen flue, or that the shelving is fitted in close proximity to a hot-water tank. In this way the linen is kept well aired.

If no special cupboard is provided, and in modern houses, and especially in flats, this is frequently the case, then perhaps an ordinary cupboard can be utilised, or an old-fashioned wardrobe with shelves and drawers underneath. Failing this, it is sometimes possible to have shelving fitted up in some recess, and then a light wooden door made to keep it free from dust; or merely a door frame, the panels being filled in with some pretty cretonne or tapestry.

A linen cupboard should be well provided with shelves, and these should be wide enough to hold folded bed and table linen comfortably, with a little room to spare. The shelves are frequently made of simple spars of wood with spaces between, and this plan allows the air to circulate round the linen better than it would in the case of solid wood.

Arrangement.—The shelves of the linen cupboard should be covered with thin calico or with strong white paper, which can be renewed from time to time. Each kind of linen should have a shelf or a portion of a shelf devoted to itself; thus bed linen should be arranged in one place, table linen in another, towels in another, and so on. Linen sheets should be kept separate from cotton sheets, large sheets from small sheets, different sets of table-linen by themselves, each class of towel by itself, &c., and all of one kind together. Arrange the linen methodically in

neat piles, and in an order most convenient to yourself. Finer and better things which are not in common use should be wrapped up in muslin or pieces of old sheeting and labelled; otherwise they are liable to be pulled out by mistake and used in a hurry. The shelves of the linen cupboard must be kept carefully covered to prevent the dust falling on the linen. Some people have small rods fixed to the edges of the shelves, by which covers can be attached by means of rings or a casing, and these can then be folded back over the linen, or loose covers of thin holland fastened to the edges of the shelves with large drawing-pins will answer the purpose very well. The covers must be large enough to cover the linen well and to tuck in all round. Needless to say, they must be kept very clean and washed at regular intervals. The door of the linen cupboard must always be kept locked, or at least tightly closed.

Scenting the Linen.—The old-fashioned plan of putting lavender among the bed linen is a very dainty one. The dried lavender can either be bound up in bundles, or the flowers put into a muslin or thin silk bag, and laid between the folds of the sheets and pillow-cases. Instead of lavender, dried rose-leaves, heliotrope, verbena, or powdered oris-root can all be used. Any of these will give a delicate scent to the bed-linen.

Marking.—It is very important to have every article in the linen cupboard carefully and distinctly marked. Shopkeepers who supply the linen are generally very willing to do this in ink, free of charge. There are different methods of marking, and, of course, the most artistic is to have the name or monogram of the owner embroidered on the material. Linen drapers will generally undertake to do this on payment of the required fee—the simple initials will only cost a few pence, while more elaborate designs will, of course, be more costly. A pretty monogram may cost as much as 5s. or 7s. Those who have time and clever fingers will like to do it at home, and the process is not a difficult one.

Cash's lettering is another way of marking. A combination of any two letter combinations can be bought ready for 10d. per box of one gross, or any length name made to order in ten days, in Script, Old English, or Block style type, for 4s. 6d. per gross, 2s. 9d. per half gross. These can be embroidered in red, navy, black, blue, yellow, green or white, on fine tape, and are easily sewn on to the linen. They do very well, for such things as sheets, blankets and towels, but would not look well on table linen. There is always the danger, too, of their being picked off if the linen passes through the hands of dishonest people. If the washing of the linen is to be done in a public laundry, the simple ink marking is as good as any. The mark should be put in the top left-hand corner, as it is most convenient for folding. In addition to the name, it is a good plan when marking to put the number of articles in each set, and the date of purchase as well, thus—supposing the name to be Grant, and the number of articles six, one would put

6—Grant, 1910.

In the case of bed-linen some people put a mark to show for which room it is intended as well, and with table-linen when separate table-cloths are used, for luncheon and dinner, the word luncheon or dinner could be marked in accordingly. If the marking is to be done in ink at home, be careful to choose one of a reliable quality, as inferior kinds turn a bad colour, and sometimes burn a hole in the fabric. If there is any uncertainty as to the ink being satisfactory, it will be wise to test it first on a piece of rag; then submit the rag to all the processes of washing, boiling, and ironing, and see how the ink stands the treatment. If good, it should come out clear and black. A metal pen should never be used for marking, as the steel of the pen combined with the ink often forms an acid, which spoils the linen. A proper quill pen for the purpose is usually sold with each bottle of ink.

Small india-rubber stamps can be bought for marking linen, but the result is not elegant. These are more suitable for large institutions than for home use.

Kitchen towels and dusters must be marked as methodically as bed linen.

Inventory.—It is very important, too, that a list be made of every article the linen cupboard contains. This should be entered in a small book kept for the purpose, and space should be left for any notes or alterations. It is a good plan to put a note of the price and the date of purchase against each article, as this is useful for future reference. When new linen is bought, it must at once be added to the list, and any that is discarded should be struck off. The list will require revision from time to time, and the stock should be counted carefully and compared with the numbers in the book. If the linen is in charge of one of the maids of the household, the mistress should go over the list with her and check every item. A simple copy of the list, without any notes and comments, might also be fastened to the door of the linen cupboard by means of drawing-pins, as this can be easily referred to at a glance. Of course, some of these details may be simplified in very small houses, although at all times it is wiser to have housekeeping done in a methodical and business-like manner, and it really saves time and expense in the end.

Care of Soiled Linen.—To allow soiled linen to accumulate is a habit to be condemned. Both personal and bed linen is liable to have an unpleasant odour, and the sooner it can be washed the more sanitary and hygienic it will be for every one concerned. A weekly washing is strongly to be recommended, and under no circumstances should soiled linen remain unwashed longer than a fortnight. Meanwhile, it must be kept in a ventilated receptacle. A light basket is the usual thing, and nothing could be better. If possible, the soiled linen should be kept in a small room or closet that is not used for sleeping purposes—it is not a healthy custom to store it in a bedroom, but where this is unavoidable, there is all the more necessity to have it turned out and washed as soon as possible.

Sending out the Washing.—Before sending out a washing, great care must be taken to make an accurate list of all the articles. The list should be written in a book, and not on slips of paper, which are readily lost. In large households it is a good plan to make the list in duplicate, sending one copy to the laundry and reserving the other for reference on return of the washing. Some laundries supply their own books with a printed list of the different items, and all that is necessary is to date it and fill in the number of the different articles. Or special laundry books, such as Lett's, can be bought for a few pence. Everything that requires washing should first be collected together in a given place, and if there are different maids in the house each one should be responsible for the collecting of her own towels, &c. Then have the things divided into lots, according to their kind, and carefully counted. If the washing is a large one, it will be much easier if two can be engaged at the work; then one can do the counting, while the other enters the numbers in the book. It is always safer to count everything twice in case of any mistakes. It is always well too, in making the list, to put some notification of the kind of article sent—such as *linen* sheets, *cotton* sheets, *large* table-cloths, *kitchen* table-cloths, and not merely to classify them under the heading of *sheets* or table-cloths respectively.

The soiled linen must then be put into bags or packed in a basket ready to be sent away, and the written list must in all cases accompany it.

For directions for home washing, see "Guide to Laundry Work," p. 271.

Return of the Washing.—When the linen is returned from the washing, it must be most carefully checked, first as regards numbers, and then as regards the kind of washing it has received, and the mending that may be required. If there is any article missing, it should have a mark put against it in the book, and inquiry must at once be made about it, and when received a note must be made of the fact in the book. It is also important when checking to examine the linen to see that all has been well washed, and if there is anything faulty, it should be returned to the laundry with a note asking that it should be redone and returned in better condition. It is a good plan to keep a list of the laundry prices at hand, so as to compare them with those marked in the book. Anything requiring mending must be put aside until it can have attention, and the remainder aired if necessary, and then put away in its proper place on the shelves. The freshly washed articles should always be put at the foot of the pile already there, as this will ensure equal wear, everything being used in rotation. Regular use is also a protection from mildew.

Airing of Linen.—It is most important that all linen should be thoroughly dry before it is laid away. In many cases it is not necessary to air it when it comes from the laundry, as it arrives almost warm from the hot air closets, but where the least dampness is suspected it should have attention, or it will be liable to gather mildew. And then again, just before bed linen is used, it should be well aired, unless the linen cupboard happens to be a heated one. The sheets should be hung in front of a good hot fire, and turned and re-turned until they are warmed through and through. If linen is stored in a cold cupboard, it readily absorbs moisture, whilst a spell of wet weather, especially after frost, will render it quite damp, and when we consider what serious results may follow the sleeping in damp sheets, the slight extra trouble of airing the linen will not be objected to.

Mending of House Linen.—After the first few weeks of wear linen will require examination for repairs. Buttons and tapes soon begin to disappear, the ends of hems and seams come undone, and other stitches here and there will be required. Then later on more serious mending will be necessary—patching, darning, and adapting. The housewife need never be ashamed of linen that is well mended; on the contrary she should be proud of it, for it will serve to give eloquent testimony of her patience and thrift.

The proper time for patching and darning house linen is before sending it to the washing, and slight rents must have instant attention. If it is not convenient to mend bed linen and towels before washing, any holes or tears must at least be drawn together or roughly mended with a needle and cotton, or the hard treatment to which they will probably be subjected in the laundry will only tend to increase them tenfold. Table linen, however, must always be mended before it is done up, as it would be impossible to do it when starched and ironed without crushing it considerably. If a large patch or darn is required, it is even better to have the damask washed and rough dried in order to remove all the dressing before attempting the mending.

When sheets show signs of wear in the middle, it is a good plan to cut them in two lengthways, and to join the two outer edges together. The cut edges will then require to be hemmed. Or if a large sheet begins to wear in other parts, perhaps the best pieces can be taken to make a sheet for a smaller bed or cot. Always try to get as much as you can out of a sheet before putting it aside as old linen.

Note.—For directions for mending, see Needlework Section, p. 411.

What to do with old Linen.—No matter how much care is taken of house linen it will eventually wear out.

Old cotton sheets can always be used as dust-sheets, or if these are not required, the best pieces can be cut out and made into cloths for various household purposes, covers for the linen cupboard, covers for drawers, or for wrapping up fine linen or blankets, &c.

An old linen sheet is more valuable, and the remains should be put to some better use. The top and bottom which has not had very hard wear will likely be in good condition, and a strip can no doubt be cut off which, with a little hem-stitching and embroidery, will make quite dainty sheet-shams. Or small good portions might be made into pillow-shams, and smaller pieces still could be cut up into centres for doyleys and tray cloths, or the cover for a cosy, or perhaps even a complete toilet set for a bedroom. Any one with clever fingers and a little ingenuity can, with some embroidery and the addition of pretty lace and insertion, make many a dainty article out of small pieces of linen. Pieces of linen which are too worn to be worth any sewing should be carefully rolled up and laid aside, as they will no doubt be found invaluable in the case of sickness.

Old table-cloths, when they can no longer be darned or patched, can be cut down into tray cloths, sideboard cloths, carving cloths, &c., and also it is always well to keep a few old pieces of damask at hand for patching and mending.

Old towels can always be used up as household cloths ; in fact, the more thin and worn they are the more useful and valuable they will be for some purposes. A collection should always be made in view of any spring or special cleaning ; they will come in very handy for the drying of paint and woodwork, &c., and a plentiful supply will be a great boom.

Old pillow-cases make useful bags for keeping various patching materials, &c.

Old Blankets. (See p. 262.)

Replenishing the Linen Cupboard.—It is not wise to allow the linen supply to fall too low, as this will mean paying out a big sum sooner or later to bring it back to its normal condition. It is much better, when it can be managed, to add something new every year, even although it may only be a pair of good sheets, half-a-dozen towels, a fine table-cloth, or a few serviettes. In this way the supply is kept up at very little expense. It might just be mentioned here that household linen is one of the things that can often be very profitably bought at a sale. The large linen warehouses sell off their old stock, either because the patterns are not of the latest or because the materials are shop soiled, and as this in nowise detracts from the value of the article a great saving can be realised by buying what is necessary at these times.

The following lists with estimates have been compiled from information kindly supplied by Messrs. Waring & Gillow, Oxford Street, London, and will perhaps be a guide to those who have to stock their linen cupboard for the first time.

The quantities can, of course, be increased or decreased according to special requirements.

Estimate No. 1—£17 18s. 5d.

Description.	Price.		Amount.		
	s.	d.	£	s.	d.
3 double damask cloths, 2 by 2½ yards . . .	10	6	1	11	6
2 double damask cloths, 2 by 3 yards	12	9	1	5	6
1 dozen double damask dinner napkins . .	15	0		15	0
3 damask tray cloths . .	2	0		6	0
2 damask sideboard cloths	2	9		5	6
2 kitchen table cloths .	3	6		7	0
3 pair cotton sheets, 2¾ by 3½ yards	12	6	1	17	6
2 pair cotton sheets, 2 by 3½ yards	8	6		17	0
12 cotton pillow-cases .		10½		10	6
4 pair servants' cotton sheets, 2 by 3 yards	6	0	1	4	0
4 servants' pillow-cases .		8½		2	10
1 dozen linen bedroom towels	11	9		11	9
6 servants' towels . . .		8½		4	3
6 white Turkish bath towels	1	4½		8	3
½ dozen glass cloths . .	5	0		2	6
½ dozen tea and china cloths	5	0		2	6
½ dozen strong kitchen rubbers	6	6		3	3
½ dozen housemaids' cloths	6	6		3	3
1 dozen check dusters .	4	6		4	6
4 linen roller towels . .	1	4		5	4
2 pudding cloths . . .		4½			9
4 knife cloths		4½		1	6
2 pair double-bed blankets	18	6	1	17	0
2 under blankets . . .	3	9		7	6
1 pair single-bed blankets				12	0
1 under blanket . . .				2	9
2 large white toilet quilts	10	0	1	0	0
1 single-bed white toilet quilt	7	6		7	6
2 pair servants' blankets .	10	0	1	0	0
2 under blankets . . .	2	9		5	6
2 servants' coloured quilts	4	6		9	0
4 white toilet covers . .	1	3		5	0
2 servants' toilet covers .	1	0		2	0
			£17	18	5

Estimate No. 2—£31 16s. 2d.

Description.	Price.		Amount.		
	s.	d.	£	s.	d.
4 superior double damask cloths, 2 by 2½ yards (hand woven) . . .	15	0	3	0	0
2 superior double damask cloths, 2½ by 3 yards (hand woven) . . .	23	0	2	6	0
1½ dozen superior double damask napkins, 27 inches square (hand woven).	24	0	1	16	0
½ dozen damask fish napkins	6	0		3	0
4 damask carving napkins or tray cloths . . .	2	0		8	0
2 damask (or hem-stitched linen) sideboard cloths	3	6		7	0
2 kitchen table cloths, 2 by 2 yards	4	6		9	0
3 pair double-bed linen sheets, 2¾ by 3½ yards	27	6	4	2	6
3 pair single-bed linen sheets, 2 by 3½ yards	21	0	3	3	0
12 linen pillow-cases (hem-stitched)	2	0	1	4	0
4 pair servants' cotton sheets, 2 by 3 yards .	7	0	1	8	0
4 servants' cotton pillow-cases	1	0		4	0
1 dozen linen huckaback bedroom towels . .	14	0		14	0
1 dozen linen diaper bedroom towels (hem-stitched)	15	0		15	0
½ dozen servants' linen bedroom towels . .	10	0		5	0
6 large white Turkish bath towels	2	0		12	0
1 dozen glass cloths . .	6	6		6	6
1 dozen tea cloths . . .	6	6		6	6
1 dozen strong kitchen rubbers	8	0		8	0
½ dozen housemaids' cloths	6	6		3	3
1 dozen check dusters . .	4	6		4	6
1 dozen soft polishing dusters	3	6		3	6
6 linen roller towels . . .	1	6		9	0
3 pudding cloths . . .		6		1	6
½ dozen knife cloths . .	4	6		2	3
1 hearth-rug cover . . .	2	11		2	11
1 dozen sponge cloths, for lamps, &c.	2	0		2	0
2 pair double-bed fine wool blankets	25	0	2	10	0
2 under blankets . . .	5	0		10	0
1 pair single-bed fine wool blankets	16	6		16	6
1 under blanket				3	3
2 pair servants' blankets .	12	0	1	4	0
2 under blankets	2	9		5	6

Estimate No. 2—continued.

	s.	d.	£	s.	d.
2 fine white toilet quilts, for double beds . .	15	0	1	10	0
1 fine white toilet quilt, for single beds . . .	10	6		10	6
2 servants' coloured quilts .	5	6		11	0
4 white toilet covers . .	1	9		7	0
2 servants' toilet covers .	1	0		2	0
			£31	16	2

Estimate No. 3—£67 5s. 10d.

Description.	Price.		Amount.		
	s.	d.	£	s.	d.
4 fine double damask table cloths, 2½ by 2½ yards	25	0	5	0	0
3 fine double damask table-cloths, 2½ by 3 yards .	30	0	4	10	0
1 fine double damask table cloth, 2½ by 4 yards .	42	0	2	2	0
4 dozen fine double damask napkins, 27 by 27 ins.	30	0	6	0	0
1 dozen damask fish napkins	7	6		7	6
1 dozen damask pastry napkins	7	6		7	6
6 damask tray or carving napkins, 31 by 36 ins.	3	6	1	1	0
2 damask (or hem-stitched linen) sideboard cloths	7	6		15	0
3 kitchen table cloths, 2 by 2½ yards	5	6		16	6
2 dishing-up cloths, 1½ by 1½ yards	2	6		5	0
4 pair fine linen sheets for double beds, 3 by 3½ yards (hem-stitched) .	42	0	8	8	0
4 pair fine linen sheets for single beds, 2 by 3½ yards (hem-stitched) .	30	0	6	0	0
18 fine linen hem-stitched pillow-covers (square or oblong)	3	6	3	3	0
6 pair servants' superior cotton sheets, 2 by 3 yards	8	6	2	11	0
6 servants' superior cotton pillow-covers . . .	1	0		6	0
1 dozen strong linen huckaback towels	15	9		15	9
1 dozen fine linen huckaback towels (hem-stitched)	19	6		19	6
1 dozen fine soft linen diaper towels (hem-stitched)	21	0	1	1	0
1 dozen servants' strong linen huckaback towels	12	6		12	6

Estimate No. 3—continued.

	s.	d.	£	s.	d.
6 large white Turkish bath towels	3	0		18	0
6 extra large Turkish bath towels	3	6	1	1	0
2 white Turkish bath sheets	5	0		10	0
1 dozen glass cloths, fine quality	7	6		7	6
1 dozen tea or china cloths, fine quality . . .	7	6		7	6
1 dozen linen dusters . .	5	6		5	6
1 dozen soft polishing cloths or dusters	4	6		4	6
1 dozen housemaids' cloths (basin)	6	6		6	6
1 dozen strong large kitchen rubbers	8	6		8	6
1 dozen soft large kitchen rubbers	8	6		8	6
8 linen roller towels . . .	2	0		16	0
½ dozen pudding cloths. .	6	0		3	0
1 dozen knife cloths . .	4	6		4	6
2 hearth-rug covers . . .	2	11		5	10
1 dozen sponge cloths, for lamps, &c.	2	0		2	0
2 pair large double-bed blankets	30	0		0	0
2 under blankets	6	0		12	0
2 pair single-bed blankets .	18	6		17	0
2 under blankets . . .	4	3		8	6
3 pair servants' strong heavy blankets . . .	12	6	1	17	6
3 under blankets	3	3		9	9
3 fine white toilet quilts for double beds	21	0	3	3	0
3 fine white toilet quilts for single beds	15	0	2	5	0
4 servants' coloured quilts	5	6	1	2	0
6 fine white toilet covers .	2	6		15	0
4 servants' toilet covers .	1	6		6	0
			£67	5	10

Estimate No. 4—£177 3s. 1d.

Description.	Price.		Amount.		
	s.	d.	£	s.	d.
6 extra fine double damask table cloths, 2½ by 2½ yards	37	6	11	5	0
4 extra fine double damask table cloths, 2½ by 3 yards	45	0	9	0	0
4 extra fine double damask table cloths, 2½ by 4 yards	63	0	12	12	0
2 extra fine double damask table cloths, 2½ by 5 yards	84	0	8	8	0

Estimate No. 4—continued.

	s.	d.	£	s.	d.
1 extra fine double damask table cloth, 2½ by 6 yards	105	0	5	5	0
6 dozen extra fine double damask napkins, 27 by 27 inches	45	0	13	10	0
2 dozen extra fine double damask breakfast napkins, 22 by 22 inches .	30	0	3	0	0
dozen extra fine double damask tray or carving napkins, 31 by 36 ins.	63	0	3	3	0
2 dozen damask fish napkins (large and small) . .	7	6		15	0
2 dozen bread and pastry napkins	5	0		10	0
4 damask (or hem-stitched linen) sideboard cloths	10	6	2	2	0
3 afternoon tea cloths . .	15	0	2	5	0
4 strong damask cloths, for upper servants, 2 by 2 yards	6	6	1	6	0
4 kitchen table cloths, 2 by 2½ yards	7	6	1	10	0
4 extra strong dishing-up cloths, 1½ by 2 yards .	4	0		16	0
6 pair fine linen hem-stitched sheets, for double beds, 3 by 3½ yards	57	6	17	5	0
8 pair fine linen hem-stitched sheets, for single beds, 2 by 3½ yards	42	0	16	16	0
30 fine linen hem-stitched pillow-covers (square or oblong)	5	6	8	5	0
6 duchesse toilet covers .	5	0	1	10	0
8 pair strong cotton sheets, for servants, 2 by 3½ yards	10	6	4	4	0
12 strong linen pillow-covers, for servants .	2	0	1	4	0
2 dozen extra strong hem-stitched huckaback towels	21	0	2	2	0
2 dozen fine hem-stitched huckaback towels . .	25	0	2	10	0
2 dozen fine soft diaper bedroom towels, for ladies' use	25	0	2	10	0

Estimate No. 4—continued.

	s.	d.	£	s.
2 dozen linen huckaback towels, for servants .	14	0	1	8
1 dozen medium-size white Turkish bath towels .	30	0	1	10
½ dozen large-size white Turkish bath towels .	42	0	1	1
6 brown Turkish bath towels	2	6		15
6 large white Turkish bath sheets	7	6	2	5
1 dozen Turkish towels, for servants	12	6		12
2 dozen glass cloths . . .	8	6		17
2 dozen tea or china cloths (pantry)	10	0	1	0
1 dozen linen dusters (strong and fine) . .	5	6		5
1 dozen linen dusters (strong and fine), . .	8	0		8
1 dozen soft polishing cloths or dusters	4	6		4
1 dozen housemaids' cloths (basin)	8	6		8
2 dozen kitchen and scullery cloths, 1 yard square .	10	6	1	1
1 dozen kitchen china cloths, 1 yard square . . .	10	0		10
1 dozen linen roller towels .	30	0	1	10
½ dozen pudding cloths .	6	6		3
1 dozen knife cloths . . .	4	6		4
2 hearth-rug covers . . .	2	11		5
4 butlers' aprons	2	0		8
3 pair large double-bed superior Witney blankets	42	0	6	6
3 under blankets	6	6		19
4 pair single-bed superior Witney blankets . .	30	0	6	0
4 under blankets . . .	5	3	1	1
4 pair strong blankets, for servants	15	0	3	0
4 under blankets	2	9		11
4 fine white toilet quilts, for double beds	27	6	5	10
5 fine white toilet quilts, for single beds	21	0	5	5
5 coloured or white quilts, for servants	6	6	1	12
6 toilet covers, for servants	1	3		7
			£177	3

GUIDE TO LAUNDRY WORK

THE proper washing and "getting up" of linen is an art which remains practically unsolved by the average housewife, who, when she is obliged to do even the simplest laundry work at home, is content to get through her task in a most rough-and-ready fashion.

"What is worth doing at all is worth doing well" is a maxim which might be followed with advantage by the home laundress, who should make a point of acquiring a real practical knowledge of her work. The information contained in this chapter has been compiled as a result of many years' practical experience of laundry work in all its branches, and the amateur laundress should derive much help from a careful study of these pages.

Home-Washing.—Whether the washing should be done at home or not is a question which every housekeeper must decide for herself. There is a great diversity of opinion on the subject, and much to be said on both sides.

Given the necessary accommodation, a wash-house fitted with tubs, a plentiful supply of hot water, a good drying-green and convenient room for ironing, there is no doubt that home washing is more satisfactory and more economical than having the work sent out. It is more economical, not only from the money point of view, but in the wear and tear of the clothes the saving is unquestionable. Besides, there is the pleasure of wearing and using linen which we know has been washed and rinsed in clean water, and that has not come in contact with all and sundry garments. There is also the feeling that one can be a little more lavish with the supply when it is not necessary to reckon up the cost for the washing of each separate article. This is a very important point, when we consider that cleanliness in our garments and surroundings is one of the first laws of health, and a law which it would be false economy to break.

On the other hand, a housekeeper must consider whether there is the adequate convenience for doing such a large piece of work as the family washing, and also if there is sufficient help available for the labour to be undertaken satisfactorily.

In many houses, especially town houses, where space is valuable it would be impossible to carry out the work successfully, and certainly not without a great deal of discomfort. There are other economies to consider besides the saving of money; there is the economy of time, the economy of labour, and the economy of patience and temper as well.

The probable discomfort of a washing day deters many people from entertaining the idea of doing their washing at home, and it certainly requires some planning and knowledge of the necessary details to have the extra work going on, and to keep the wheels of the house running smoothly at the same time. If, however, the work is to be done at the expense of every one's comfort, then by all means leave it alone; any advantages to be gained would be dearly bought at such a price.

Now that public laundries are springing up all around us, and their methods for treating the clothes are improving year by year, there is no longer the *absolute* necessity for home washing.

Sometimes, although it is found impossible to do the whole washing at home, a part can be done quite easily, the heavier and more complicated articles being sent out. There is always more difficulty in undertaking the dressing of starched linen, especially such things as gentlemen's shirts, collars and cuffs, white petticoats, dresses, &c., and heavy articles like sheets and table-cloths. If these are sent away to be done, perhaps the rest will cause no difficulty.

If the decision is in favour of home washing, then it is very important that the process be planned with care, and then carried out methodically.

A REGULAR TIME FOR WASHING

In arranging your washing-day, of course take into consideration the circumstances of the household, but have it as early in the week as possible, and at a fixed hour. As a general rule Tuesday is the most suitable day, as this lets you have all necessary preparations made on Monday. Never let soiled clothes remain unwashed longer than a fortnight, and you must judge from the amount of work to be done if a weekly washing is advisable. Begin operations early in the day, as clothes dried in the morning air are always whitest and freshest.

LAUNDRY UTENSILS, THEIR CHOICE AND CARE

As all the utensils used in laundry work are subjected to a considerable amount of wear and tear, it is of the utmost importance to have them good and durable. A little additional outlay at the commencement in order to obtain first-class articles will be money well spent, the replacing of faulty goods will not be necessary, and much needless worry will be saved.

At its best laundry work is a somewhat arduous occupation, and although it is possible to produce excellent results with the most primitive implements, this requires the skilled worker. Under ordinary circumstances, in order to have the work well done and time and labour economised, the necessary implements must be provided.

The number of utensils required will depend very much upon individual circumstances. A large household with good laundry accommodation, and all the washing done at home, will naturally require more than a small household where the work has to be done in a kitchen and scullery, and perhaps only part of the washing undertaken. In the latter case the number of utensils should be reduced to a minimum through lack of space to accommodate them. Wherever possible, laundry utensils should be kept apart from those used for cooking purposes. In all cases it is better to buy just what is absolutely necessary to begin with, and to add as the need arises.

The following utensils will be required to do a complete washing conveniently :—

Tubs.—Two or three fitted tubs with hot and cold water, and one or two smaller movable tubs or zinc baths for small articles, are the most convenient for washing purposes. If fitted tubs are not provided, then larger zinc or wooden tubs will be necessary, and a stand or bench to place them on. It is very important to have the tub placed at the right height for the worker. All tubs must be kept very clean, and dirty soapy water must on no account be allowed to remain in them. They must be well scrubbed out after use to remove any dirty scum that may have collected on the sides. Then zinc or porcelain ones may be dried, but wooden ones should have a little cold water left in them to prevent them shrinking.

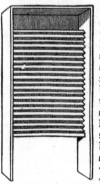

Washing-Board.

Washing-Board and Brush. —Both these will be found of great assistance. The board is useful in the washing of heavy articles, such as sheets, table-cloths, counterpanes, &c., and anything strong and dirty that will stand a fair amount of rubbing. A wooden board is preferable to one made of zinc. It should be well washed on both sides after use, and set up on end to dry. A brush with good bristles and not too hard is also useful in the washing of collars, cuffs, bands, or any very soiled parts which require extra attention. The brush should be well rinsed and set up to dry after use, and never used for any other purpose.

A Boiler.—This is generally a fitted arrangement with a small fireplace underneath. It must be kept very clean, and well washed and dried after use. If a greasy scum collects on the sides, a mixture of soft soap and shredded Brooke's soap should be applied with a wet flannel, or a little paraffin may be added to this mixture if something stronger is required. Clean cold water must always be put into the boiler before the fire is lighted, and the fire should be out before the boiler is emptied. Cinders from other fires do very well for burning in a boiler fire, or coke is very often substituted for coal. If no fitted boiler is provided, a large saucepan can be used and boiled on an ordinary fire or gas stove. A tin or enamelled one is best, and, if possible, it should be kept for laundry purposes only.

Mangle and Wringer.—A mangle is a large machine, with heavy wooden rollers used for smoothing household linen and the heavier articles of clothing. When in use the tension must be tight enough to press the clothes sufficiently, and loosened again when finished with. The rollers must be kept very clean and free from dust, and the working parts should be oiled occasionally. A *wringer* is a most useful machine and almost indispensable if any heavy washing is to be done. It is generally attached to a washing-tub, and the clothes are put through it while wet. The rollers are of india-rubber, and should be kept clean with soap and water, or if stained with any dyed material a little turpentine should be applied with a soft rag. As with the mangle, the tension must be tightened when in use and afterwards loosened. Nothing that is boiling hot should be passed through the wringer or the surface of the india-rubber will become roughened. With care the india-rubber ought to last a long time, and when it does wear out, the coating can be replaced and the wringer made as good as new. For small washings the wringer can almost take the place of the heavier and larger mangle.

Washing Machines.—Various machines are now made for home washing, and where there is a large number of things to be done they are certainly a great aid. A good machine carefully used will really wear the clothes less than the ordinary washing and rubbing in a tub. One of simple construction should be chosen, and the directions, which vary slightly with the different machines, will be given with each. Very often a wringer or small mangle is attached to the machine, and in this case the extra machinery would be unnecessary.

The "Sunrise" Patent Washing Machine can be thoroughly recommended. It is very simple

"Sunrise" Washing Machine.

in construction, absolutely efficient, and occupies very little space. The price too is only 35s., or with a rubber roller attached, 25s. extra.

Clothes-Ropes, Pins and Poles.—These are used when drying is done out of doors, and it is most important that they should be kept perfectly clean. Clothes are frequently seen with the mark of a dirty pin or rope upon them, and this happens through carelessness. The clothes-ropes should never be left outside when not in use. They not only get dirty, but will rot if exposed to the atmosphere. They should be rubbed over with a cloth, rolled up and put into a bag or basket where they will be under cover. The same care must be taken with the pins which fasten the clothes to the line. Do not let them lie on the ground, but see that they are quite clean, and put them away with the ropes. New clothes-ropes and pins should be soaked first in hot and then in cold water before use, as they are liable to mark the clothes. Clothes-poles, which are used for propping up the ropes, must be brought indoors when not in use, and kept in a clean place.

Clothes-Horse and Pulley.—These are necessary for drying and airing indoors. The horse, which is like a screen with bars, is placed round or near a fire, and the pulley is generally fixed to the roof of the kitchen or laundry, and can be pulled up and down as required.

The Ironing Table.—This must be of a good size, strong, and steady, and of a convenient height for working at. It should be covered first with felt or a double fold of thick blanket. The kind known as "charity" blankets, of a grey colour and rather a hard make, are very suitable for the purpose. The blanket should be large enough to come at least a few inches over the table all round. A clean sheet will then be required to place on the top of this, which should either be pinned at the four corners

or fastened to the table legs by means of tapes. Patches and seams should be avoided as far as possible, or put where they will not come in the way of the ironing. The heat of the iron must never be tested on the ironing sheet, as if once scorched it is almost sure to wear into holes when washed.

Never lay ironing blankets and sheets away damp, or they will probably mildew ; and never let them remain on the table longer than is necessary, as they get dusty. Shake them well, and fold evenly before laying away.

In addition to the ironing table, a smaller one for placing the work on will be found a great convenience if space permits.

Irons.—Those most generally used are called flat irons, and for all ordinary purposes they produce as good work as any other. They should be of different sizes and have comfortable handles. Numbers 5, 6, and 7 are useful sizes, and two, or better three, will be required for each worker. If any fine intricate work is to be done, one or two very small irons will be necessary. Flat irons are best heated on an ironing stove or on the top of a close range. Ironing stoves can be had in different sizes, they take up very little room, and where there is a large amount of work to be done, and consequently many irons to be heated, a proper stove will be found more

Flat Iron.

economical than keeping up a large kitchen fire for the sole purpose of heating irons. If a cooking stove is used for heating, the fire must be well made up, the hearth swept, and the top of the range wiped free from grease before the irons are put down. It is not such a good plan to heat irons in front of an open fire, as their surfaces are liable to get roughened and smoky. If it must be done, have the fire bright and free from smoke before placing the irons, and when fresh coal has to be added let it be put at the back of the fire, drawing forward the red cinders. A smoked iron is fatal to good ironing. Never put irons into a fire to heat or the surface will be roughened and the iron ruined for any fine work. Gas stoves are very convenient for heating one or two irons, but where a number are required it will be found an expensive method.

An iron must be well cleaned each time before using. Have a wooden box, and put at the foot of it some sand-paper, or ordinary thick brown paper with fine sand or bath-brick dust sprinkled on it. Rub the iron well on this first, and the slight roughness of the sand, &c., will clean it. Then have a piece of coarse cloth or sacking with a little grease on it. A piece of bees'-wax or candle-end shred down and put between the folds of the cloth will do. Rub the iron next on this to make it run smoothly, then finish off by dusting it with a duster to make it quite free from sand or brick-dust. Occasionally it is well to wash the irons thoroughly with hot water, soda, soap, and a brush, and then thoroughly dry. On no account must irons be black-leaded. Never allow them to cool flat on a stove when the fire is going out, as damp collects and rusts them, but either stand them up on end at the side of the stove or on the hearth-stone. Irons must be kept in a perfectly dry place. If you once allow them to get rusty, the rust eats into them, and their surface is never so smooth again. If they are to be laid away for some time, see that they are thoroughly dry, then grease them well, and wrap them in brown paper.

It is almost impossible to iron with perfectly new irons; they must be seasoned first. To do this heat them on a stove for several hours, then clean in the ordinary way, and let them cool. Repeat this process for several days, and the irons will be ready for use.

A very good invention is the new patent "Slip-On" Ironing Shield, which can be put

Iron Shield.

on to any flat iron, No. 4 to 7, after it has been well heated. This saves the trouble of so much cleaning, and the nickel-plated surface of the shield will iron the clothes without a mark, and produce a high gloss on the linen. The price is 1s.

Various special irons can now be had to replace the flat iron, such as box irons. These, as their name implies, are like a box, and are heated by means of a hot bolt placed inside. Charcoal or Dalli irons, which are heated with hot charcoal inside the iron. Gas irons, heated with gas, by means of an india-rubber tube attached to a gas jet. Asbestos irons, electric irons—heated by electricity, and also the spirit iron, which is heated with methylated spirits, and is most useful where no fire is obtainable, or for a lady's private use, and for travelling.

Polishing and Goffering Irons.—The polishing iron is like an ordinary iron with an oval surface of polished steel. It is used for polishing cuffs and collars or anything that requires a high gloss. Goffering irons are used for goffering

Polishing Iron. Goffering Iron.

frills, and it is well to have them in different sizes if both wide and narrow frills are to be done. They should be heated in a gas jet, with methylated spirits, or be placed under a flat iron on an ordinary stove. They must never be put into a fire.

Iron-Stand and Holder.—Each ironer must be

provided with an iron-stand, on which to rest the iron, and an iron-holder. Iron-stands are of different kinds, the simplest being a plain ring of iron, and others are of more elaborate design; but in any case they should stand high enough above the table to prevent the heat of the iron from scorching the ironing-sheet.

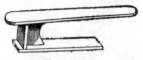

Sleeve Board.

Iron-holders should be made like kettle-holders, only more substantial. They should have several thick folds of flannel or two of felt inside, sewn together, and covered over with a clean cotton cover. A piece of kid put between the folds will help to keep the heat from the hands. The top cover must be strong. A piece of strong linen or ticking is suitable, but it must not be anything from which a dye will come off. For collars, cuffs, and shirts it is better to have the holder covered with white cotton. The holders must be made long enough to cover the length of the handle, and broad enough to come well round. When resting the iron, always take the holder off it. This not only keeps it cooler for the hand, but very often prevents it getting burnt when the iron is too hot to use. Iron-holders should be kept in a box or drawer where they will not get dusty.

Special irons which are provided with wooden handles will not require a holder.

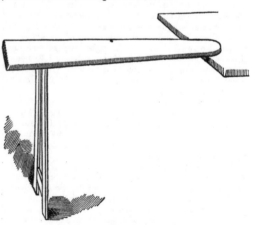

Skirt Board.

Shirt, Skirt, and Sleeve Boards.—These are all required in fitting out a laundry. The *shirt* board is used when ironing the fronts of shirts. One side at least must be covered with a double fold of white flannel, blanket, or felt stretched tightly over it, and either sewn or tacked on.

Above this place a cotton or linen cover, which can be made like a slip, to be easily removed when dirty and replaced by a clean one.

Sleeve boards, used when ironing the sleeves of dresses, &c., must be covered in the same way. Keep both shirt and sleeve boards covered up when not in use, to prevent their becoming soiled.

Skirt boards are used when ironing petticoats, dress skirts, children's frocks, &c. These being larger will do quite well if covered with grey blanket like the tables, only it should be tacked on, and then covered with a small sheet pinned firmly underneath. It is better to have a sheet that can be taken off after use, as it will keep cleaner.

Polishing Boards are like skirt boards, only they are left uncovered. They are used for polishing collars and cuffs.

Basins.—Tin enamelled basins are the most satisfactory for laundry purposes, and it will be found useful to have several and of different sizes. These serve for the making of starch, for holding water when sprinkling the clothes, and for the soaking and even washing of small articles, such as lace, handkerchiefs, &c.

Bags.—One or two bags for boiling clothes in will be found useful. They can be made of strong net or of cotton with a slit in the side to allow the water to enter, otherwise they will blow up like a balloon and float on the surface of the water.

Sundries.—A soap dish, a small enamelled saucepan and knife for making soap jelly, a wooden fork or stick for lifting clothes from the boiler, a clothes-basket, a can for water, a steel comb and small brush for fringes, one or two tea-spoons, one wooden spoon, one gill measure, three or four towels, and some soft rag for rubbers, one or two pieces of white felt for the ironing of lace and embroidery, and three or four jars for keeping stores will complete the oufit of a laundry, and the following will give an idea of the approximate cost.

PRICE LIST OF LAUNDRY UTENSILS

Flat irons, from 8d. to 2s. according to side.
Box iron with pair of heaters, 2s. to 3s. each.
Dalli iron (charcoal), 6s. each.
Spirit-heated ladies' iron, 6s. or 7s. each.
Gas iron, 3s. 9d. to 6s. each.
Polishing iron, 1s. 6d. to 2s. each.
Electric iron, from 17s.
Tubs—wooden with galvanised hoops, 2s. to 6s. according to size.
Tubs—galvanised zinc, 1s. 6d to 3s according to size.
Shirt board, 3s. to 5s.
Skirt board, 4s. 6d. to 6s.
Sleeve board, 1s. 6d. to 4s.
Washing board, 1s. 3d.
Large tin boiler, 3s. 6d.

Tin enamelled basins, 1s. 2d. to 2s.
Mangle, from £2.
Wringer, from 18s.
Washing machine, various prices according to make.
Clothes-ropes, 16 yards for 1s.
Clothes-poles or props, 8d. to 1s.
Clothes-horse, 3s. 6d. to 6s.
Goffering irons, 8d. to 11d. per pair.
Iron-stand, 4d. to 6d.
Soap-dish, 4d. to 8d.
Clothes-basket, 1s. 6d. to 3s.
Can for water, 2s. 6d. to 3s.
Steel comb, 4d.
White felt, about 1s. 2d. per yard, double width.
Laundry blankets (grey charity), 4s. or 5s.
Laundry sheeting, about 1s. 3d. per yard.

MATERIALS REQUIRED AND THEIR USE

Water.—For washing purposes it is necessary to have an abundant supply of pure and soft water. Cleaning is almost an impossibility when the water is of an earthy colour, and contains a quantity of mineral matter. Rain water, when it can be obtained free from impurities, is preferable to river or spring water, which is generally hardened by a certain amount of lime acquired in running through the ground. There are many chemical tests by which one can tell soft water from hard water, but for laundry purposes it is sufficient to know that the harder the water the greater is the quantity of soap needed to produce a lather. When hard water must unavoidably be used for washing, some softening substance, such as soda or borax, must be added.

Soap.—Good yellow soap is best. Cheap soaps are no economy, as they contain a large percentage of water and waste quickly. Many of them also contain soda to an extent hurtful to the clothes. Soap must never be allowed to lie in the water, and all ends, which are too small for washing with, should be saved to make soap jelly, or else shred down and put into the boiler when boiling the clothes.

Soda.—This has a softening effect upon water, and absorbs and removes grease, but if used in too large quantities it will be found destructive to clothes, and will give them a grey appearance. It will also make the hands rough and sore. Before soda is used it must be completely dissolved in boiling or very hot water, for were it to touch the linen undissolved, yellow marks would be left, in reality burns, and these would eventually wear into holes. Soda must not be used for coloured clothes nor for flannels, and for fine articles borax will be found safer as a water-softener. When washing and boiling the coarser clothes, one ounce of soda will be sufficient to soften one gallon of water.

Borax.—This also softens water, but not so powerfully as soda, and as it is perfectly harmless it may be used even for woollen and dyed articles. Boron, a substance found in borax, acts as a disinfectant. Allow one table-spoonful of prepared borax to one gallon of water. Borax is also used for stiffening and glossing linen, such as collars and cuffs. It may be bought either as a powder or in lump form; the former is the more convenient of the two.

Blue.—This is added to the water in which white clothes are rinsed to give them a good colour. There are a number of different blues both in solid and liquid form—indigo, ultra-marine, Prussian, and aniline; but the solid blues will, as a rule, be found handier, and the required quantity will be more easily judged. Having chosen the brand, keep to it, and then the question of quantity will be no difficulty. Blue which dissolves most readily and leaves least sediment after the water has stood some time is the best. Stone or solid blues should be firm and not gritty, and they ought to be kept in a dry place, as they readily absorb moisture. When a cake is required it should have the paper removed and be tied in a small bag or piece of flannel, when it will be ready to squeeze into the water. (See p. 278.)

Starch.—The stiffening and other qualities of starch vary according to the substance from which it is derived, so that it is a matter of great importance to choose a good kind.

Wheat and rice starches are those most commonly used. Rice starch is used as a substitute for wheat starch for all finer purposes.

Ammonia.—This is also used for the softening of water and will be found invaluable in the washing of flannel and knitted articles. It dissolves the grease and dirt in a wonderful way, and thus saves unnecessary rubbing. It must not, however, be used too freely, or it will impoverish the woolly fibre. Ammonia should be kept in a tightly corked bottle, as it is very volatile.

Turpentine.—Used in the making of cold-water starch, and also for the removal of certain stains. It should be kept in a tightly corked bottle.

Bees'-wax and White Wax.—The former is useful for the greasing of irons when candle-ends are not available, and the latter is sometimes put into hot-water starch.

Salts of Lemon—Salts of Sorrel.—These are useful for the removal of certain stains. As they are poisonous substances they ought to be labelled so, and kept in a safe place.

Chloride of Lime.—This is used for bleaching purposes, and also for the removal of very obstinate stains. It must be specially prepared. (See p. 277.)

Gum-Arabic.—This will take the place of starch in the stiffening of lace and silk.

Common Salt and Vinegar.—These are some-times required for the rinsing of coloured articles.

Methylated Spirits.—This is used in small quantities in the washing of silks.

PREPARATION FOR A WASHING

Sorting.—Without order and method much time will be wasted. After having collected all the clothes to be washed, arrange them in different lots according to the kind of article and the tubs available for steeping.

1. Table linen.
2. Bed and other household linen.
3. Body linen.
4. Laces, muslins, and finer articles.
5. Flannels and other woollen or knitted goods.
6. Pocket-handkerchiefs.
7. Coloured prints, muslins, and sateens.
8. Kitchen towels and very dirty articles.

When there is a scarcity of tubs one may be used for bed and body linen.

Pocket-handkerchiefs should always be kept apart from other articles until after the first washing.

As table linen might be discoloured by contact with greasy clothes, keep it also separate until after washing.

Mending.—Before washing, all holes or tears must at least be drawn together if not actually mended, as the friction of washing would tend to enlarge them.

All strings should be untied and undrawn, and any buttons unfastened.

Removal of Stains.—This is generally looked upon as very troublesome, but it will be found that the results fully repay the time and labour involved, indeed, it is absolutely necessary for the production of good work. The sooner stains are removed the better. Most stains can be easily eradicated when fresh, while they harden if allowed to remain. As soap combined with hot water makes most stains permanent, the removing process must take place before the actual washing begins. Different chemicals are employed for this, all more or less injurious to the fabric, so that after the application of any of them, the article must be immediately rinsed in clean warm water.

Rust or Iron-Mould.—Take a small basin of boiling water, dip the stained part into it, and then stretch tightly over the basin. Sprinkle with salts of sorrel, and rub it well into the stain; use a piece of rag or smooth stick to do this, as salts of sorrel is most poisonous and might be injurious to the fingers. Allow it to steam for a short time with the salts on it, when the stain should entirely disappear.

A solution of oxalic acid may be used in the same way. Rinse at once.

Ink.—When ink stains are fresh they may be removed by dipping the stained part in hot milk and letting them soak for some time, then wash out thoroughly. If the stain has been in for some time it will be more persistent, and the same method as for rust stains should be adopted. A black ink stain can also be removed by pouring some red ink over it, allowing it to dry, and then washing it out.

Wine and Fruit.—Spread the stained part over a basin, rub well with common salt, and pour boiling water through to avoid spreading the mark. If the stain is still persistent, try salts of sorrel.

If a fruit stain is left in for any length of time, it is most difficult to remove. It is sometimes better to let it wear out gradually; but if it must be removed, use oxalic acid well rubbed into the part or chloride of lime.

Tea and Coffee.—Spread the stained part over a basin, rub well with powdered borax, and pour boiling water through. If still persistent, use a weak solution of chloride of lime.

Paint.—When fresh, remove with turpentine well rubbed in. If it has become dry, mix a little ammonia with the turpentine. When the stain is on a fabric of which the colour is apt to be destroyed, moisten first with a little oil, and then remove with turpentine or ether.

Mildew.—This is a species of fungus of which there are several varieties. It often attacks and stains linen or cotton, and is caused by the material being laid away damp. It is one of the most obstinate stains to remove, and often impossible without injury to the fabric. Stretch the stained part over a hard firm surface, and rub off as much as will come with a piece of soft dry rag. Rub in a little salt, and try if the juice of a lemon will take it out. Failing this, make a paste of French chalk and water, spread it on the stained part, and let it dry slowly, if possible in the sun. Repeat the process if necessary, and then rinse well.

Use of Chloride of Lime and Sanitas.—Put ¼ lb. chloride of lime into a basin, and break it to a smooth paste with a little cold water, then add as much cold water as will fill a quart bottle, about 1½ pints; stir the lime well up, and let it stand covered over for a day or two, stirring it occasionally. Then let it settle; skim it well, and pour the clear liquid off the top. Strain this into a quart bottle, and keep it tightly corked.

To remove stains wet a rag with this solution and apply it to the part. When anything is very much stained all over, it is best to soak it in cold water with some of this preparation of chloride of lime added to it. Make the water smell just slightly with the lime. This will also serve for bleaching things when they have become a bad colour.

Sanitas is now frequently used for removing ink, fruit, and wine stains on white cotton goods.

When removing stains the simplest method should always be tried first before any of the stronger chemicals are resorted to.

Care of the Chemicals.—Most of the chemicals used for removing stains are poisonous, therefore they ought to be labelled as such and kept in a safe place.

Soaking.—Soak everything except flannels, woollen goods, and most coloured articles. Place each assortment in a tub, using large basins if more convenient for the smaller things, and cover all with cold or tepid water. Never use hot water for soaking purposes, as it tends to make dirt adhere to linen, whilst cold or tepid water loosens it, and so simplifies the process of washing. If the water is hard, either borax or soda may be added before the clothes are put in. For the coarser and dirtier things use soda in the proportion of one ounce of soda to a gallon of water. This must be previously dissolved in a little boiling water. (See p. 275.) For the finer articles use borax instead of soda in the proportion of one table-spoonful to one gallon of water. It is perfectly harmless, even colours not being affected by its use, but it has a marvellous power of softening water and of drawing out dirt. A little soap may be rubbed on the more soiled part of the clothes, or some melted soap added to the water.

Very dusty articles, such as window-blinds and curtains, should be soaked in plain cold water until some of the dust is got rid of, and the water should be changed several times.

Pocket-handkerchiefs should have a handful of salt added to the water in which they soak; it will make the washing of them easier.

Let the clothes soak for one night at least. If Monday is your washing day, they may be soaked from Saturday without harm.

Disinfecting.—This is not always necessary, but where there has been infectious illness, or even bad colds, it will be wise to put the infected clothing through some process which will destroy the disease germs. There are various methods of disinfecting, such as the use of soaking fluids, exposure to hot air, exposure to steam, and others, but for home purposes there is nothing safer nor more effective than Izol. It is non-poisonous, and is undoubtedly very powerful as a germ destroyer. Use it in the proportion of 2 ounces of Izol to 1 gallon of water. In this solution the clothes should be allowed to soak for at least twelve hours. After this the clothes may be treated in the ordinary way.

Sundry Preliminaries.—The boiler fire should be laid the night before the washing day, and the boiler itself dusted out and filled with clean cold water. It will then be ready for lighting the first thing in the morning. Cold-water starch, as it requires soaking, and soap jelly should also be prepared beforehand. (See pp. 281 and 287.) It should also be seen that all utensils are clean and ready for use the following day, and that all necessary materials are at hand. Early in the morning the fire should be lighted, and as soon as there is hot water the washing commenced.

THE WASHING OF LINEN AND WHITE CLOTHES

The linen having been soaked and all stains removed as far as possible, it is now ready for washing. The object in washing is to get rid of the dirt with as little wear and tear to the clothes as possible, and to keep them a good colour. This may be done either by hand or by machine, but whichever method is adopted the principles are the same, and it is as well to know how to wash by hand. Commence with the finest and cleanest articles, generally table linen, then proceed to the bed and body linen. Fine towels and sheets must be washed before the ordinary household linen, and all coarse and kitchen articles left to the last. First rub the clothes and wring them out of the steeping water. Rinse out the tub and half fill it with water as hot as the hand can bear, adding, if necessary, a little borax or ammonia to soften it, or soda when it is to be used for the coarser clothes. Do not put too many articles into the tub at one time, and press them well down under the water. Then soap as much of the article as can conveniently be rubbed, and wash one part of the material against the other, and not against the wrist or hand. The pressure of rubbing should come on the lower and fleshy part of the thumb. Work methodically over every part, paying particular attention to those that are most soiled, and dip the article from time to time into the water so as to get rid of the soap and the dirt. A washing-board, preferably a wooden one, will be found of great assistance in the washing of the heavier and coarser things, and such articles as collars and cuffs will be cleaned most easily by being brushed on the washing-board with a softish brush. The brush is also valuable for the washing of very soiled articles, such as kitchen towels and aprons. Large articles, such as sheets and table-cloths, should be folded for washing and then rubbed by the selvedge from end to end until the middle is reached, when it will be advisable to turn and begin at the other end. If the clothes are not clean after the first washing, take fresh hot water and repeat the process. Soap and rub in the same way in the second water as in the first, turning any article that is turnable on to the wrong side.

If the washing is to be done by a machine, it will be better to follow the directions given with each special make, as they vary somewhat in structure. Most of them are simple enough, and will be found invaluable in houses where a large washing has to be undertaken.

The above directions only apply to the washing of ordinary white clothes; special articles, such as muslins, lace, coloured articles, &c., will be treated under special headings.

Boiling.—The clothes should be well wrung out of the water in which they have been washed and left twisted, as this will prevent their floating in the boiler. Soap should then be rubbed on them, or added to the water in the boiler in the proportion of one pound of soap to four gallons of water. A little soda, borax, or ammonia may also he added if the water is hard and the clothes a bad colour. Tie together or put into bags all small articles, such as cuffs, collars and pocket-handkerchiefs; in fact, a careful laundress will put everything into bags; this prevents any soapy scum from settling on the clothes, and avoids the necessity of lifting each article separately from the boiler.

As the clothes must have sufficient room to toss about, do not put too many things into the boiler at one time. Bring the water slowly to the boil, and boil from fifteen to twenty minutes, pressing the things down occasionally with a stick to keep them under water. Do not allow the clothes to boil too long, or they will become a yellow colour, and they must on no account be boiled before washing. When the clothes have boiled sufficiently, lift them out into a tub, and, if time permits, cover them with the water in which they have been boiled, letting them cool in it. This whitens the clothes, and is almost as good as bleaching, but it cannot of course be done where washing and drying have to be accomplished in one day.

The water in the copper must never be allowed to become dirty, and more water and more soap must be added for each lot of clothes.

Bleaching.—When the clothes become a very bad colour, bleaching will very much improve them. Take the clothes from the boiler, let them cool slightly, and, with the soap still in them, spread them on a green for some hours, sprinkling them with water from a watering-can if they become dry. If the clothes are spread out boiling hot, they will scorch and discolour the grass.

Rinsing.—This is one of the most important operations in laundry work. The reason of clothes having a streaked appearance and bad colour is very often that the soap has not been rinsed out of them. Ironing reveals the faulty work, making unrinsed clothes look absolutely dirty and giving them an unpleasant smell. Use plenty of water for rinsing—first tepid, then cold. To use cold water to begin with would be to harden the soap into the tissues of the material, so that to remove it would be almost impossible. First remove the soap with tepid water, and then use a plentiful supply of cold until every trace of it is removed. Too much stress cannot be laid upon this point.

Blueing.—This improves the appearance of the clothes by bringing back some of the clear colour which they lose through wear and age, and counteracting the slightly yellow tinge they acquire in boiling. In preparing blue water see that the tub in which the water is placed is perfectly clean and free from dust and soap suds, and add sufficient blue to make it a sky-blue tint. It is impossible to lay down absolute rules as to quantity, as it depends both upon the kind of blue used and the texture of the articles undergoing operation. As a rule, body linen requires more blue than other articles, and table linen less. If there is any uncertainty as to the right shade, the water should be tested first on some small article or piece of rag. The aim must be to get the clothes of a clear uniform tint and not too blue. Do not prepare the blue water long before it is wanted, as a sediment will fall, and stir it well before immersing the clothes.

Wring the clothes out of the last rinsing water, open them out, and put a few at a time into the blue water, those requiring most blue first. Work them so as to let the water well through, then wring out as dry as possible. The solution will get weaker as it is used, so that more blue must be added when required, and this always when there are no clothes in the water.

Wringing.—Wringing is getting rid of the superfluous water in the clothes. This you may do either by hand or machine, but certain precautions are necessary, or the process will be destructive. In wringing by hand, twist the articles selvedge-wise, and be careful not to wrench them unduly, but to wring with a sustained pressure. The use of a machine causes less wear and tear and also saves time. Shake out the clothes and fold them evenly before putting them through the wringer, then work the machine slowly and carefully. If worked hurriedly the moisture will not be properly extracted. Pass the clothes through the machine once or twice that they may be wrung as dry as possible. Do not screw the wringer too tight; it both spoils the machine and is too great a strain on the linen. Hide away buttons in the folds of the fabric in order to protect them as well as the rollers; tapes should also be concealed, to prevent their being wrenched off.

After wringing, the clothes must be sorted, those requiring starching put to one side, and the others hung up to dry.

Drying.—Clothes are always fresher and whiter if they can be dried in the open air, morning air being best of all. But in towns this is not always possible, owing to the presence of smoke and other obstacles, and the absence of space. Still a fine bright day with a little wind blowing, a good green, and clean lines and pegs are luxuries for any laundress who has the success of her work at heart. The clothes-line must first be rubbed over with a clean duster, and the clothes pinned or pegged on to it with the wrong side out, if there is one. The direction of the wind should be considered, and the clothes hung so as to catch the breeze. Hang the articles well over the line to prevent straining, and so that they may not slip off and get soiled on the ground. Do not hang sheets and table-cloths by the corners, or they will be apt to tear. Neither should they be hung next the post nor near a wall or tree; a towel or something small can be put in these spaces. Nightdresses, shirts, and the like should be hung up by the bottom or by the shoulders. If by the former, only one side should be fastened to the line, and the other side left open to face the wind, which will blow through and freshen every part. Small articles, such as collars and cuffs, may be strung together on a piece of tape, and if there is any chance of smuts falling, it is a good plan to cover them with a piece of muslin or cambric. On no account must anything be fastened up by the tapes, as this is most liable to strain and injure the garment. Raise the rope well above the ground by means of a prop or pole, and allow the clothes to remain until sufficiently dry. When clothes are dried indoors they must either be hung on a clothes-horse near a fire, on pulleys swung to the ceiling in a heated atmosphere, or in steam closets fitted up for the purpose. If the drying is done before a fire, the clothes will require turning or moving from time to time, as the heat is not regular. Care must be taken not to place them too near the fire, as the linen will not only become discoloured by too close contact with the heat, but become so dry as to burst into a flame.

Damping and Folding.—Anything that has to be mangled or ironed must be damped and folded evenly first. It is a saving of time and trouble if these things can be taken down from drying while still slightly wet, for if allowed to become quite dry they must be sprinkled with water either by hand or with a small watering-can. Every part of the article must be evenly sprinkled, and at the same time not made too wet. When sprinkling by hand, hold the basin of water in the left hand, take up as much in the right as it will hold, and sprinkle it lightly over the material, letting the drops be as small as possible, and going over every part. Smooth out the things well, fold evenly, seeing that the selvedges in such things as towels, counterpanes, sheets, &c., meet exactly.

Avoid all unnecessary creases, but fold the clothes to a convenient size for passing through the mangle, and of an equal thickness, so that the pressure of the mangle may come on every part. Pack the clothes into a basket, placing all of one kind together; those requiring ironing underneath, and those requiring mangling only on the top. Cover them over, and let them lie for some time, over-night if possible, before ironing or mangling them.

Mangling.—Mangling is a process of smoothing clothes by passing them between heavy rollers, which are sometimes heated. All household linen, such as towels, sheets, pillow-cases, table-cloths, table-napkins, &c., and most body linen may be mangled. Mangling requires great care and attention in order not to stretch the articles nor strain them unduly. Take the damp and folded things and place them in the mangle perfectly straight. Do not put too many things in at one time, and keep smoothing them out as they are put in to prevent pleats and creases. Work the mangle steadily, not too quickly, and not by fits and starts.

It is better if two people can work together; then one can smooth and hold the linen as it passes through, and the other can turn the handle. Pass the linen through once or twice, and keep the tension tight enough to press the material sufficiently without straining the mangle unduly. Then fold up and lay to one side such articles as require ironing, and hang up to air those that are finished, such as sheets and some towels.

Airing.—Everything must be thoroughly aired either after ironing or mangling, and before it is laid away. The greatest care must be taken that no dampness is left in them before they are folded and laid away. Carelessness in this respect may lead to very grave results.

GENERAL DIRECTIONS FOR IRONING

There is no process in laundry work which requires greater or neater handling than that of ironing, and the proverb, " Practice makes Perfect," can perhaps be better applied to this than to any other branch of household work. Until it can be done with speed it cannot be done well. An iron cools so quickly that, unless it can be expeditiously handled, very little can be done with one, and constant changing not only makes it a very tiring process, but the clothes become so dry before they are finished that they never look well. A novice at the work is almost sure to meet with disappointment until a certain amount of experience has been gained.

The ironing table must be placed in a good light. Daylight is best, and the worker should stand in such a position that the light will strike upon the work. Cover the table according to directions given on p. 273, and have everything at hand that will be required before commencing to iron. Have on the table a basin of clean cold water, set on a plate to prevent its upsetting, and one or two pieces of clean rag or old handkerchief to use for rubbing or damping down the clothes. Place the iron-stand and holder at the right-hand side and the articles to be ironed at the left.

The clothes to be ironed must be slightly damp, but not too wet. Knowledge of the correct heat of an iron can only be learnt with practice, no written rules can be of much assistance. If too hot, it will scorch, and if not hot enough it will fail to give the necessary gloss, and may even soil the work. A learner should test the heat of an iron on a piece of rag kept on the table for the purpose. The heat of the iron will be regulated by the kind of material to be ironed, and also by the speed of the worker.

Where there is a large plain surface to be ironed, as in table linen, a hot and heavy iron can be used, but when it is something more intricate and the work cannot be done so quickly, a cooler iron must be taken. When ironing, lift the iron as little as possible, and do not thump it down. Ironing should not be a noisy proceeding. Iron quickly and at the same time press well. Prepare and smooth out the work with the left hand whilst ironing with the right. When any wrinkle is made in ironing, damp it over with a wet rag and iron again. Handle the things so as not to crush the parts already ironed. There is quite an art in the way the clothes are lifted and moved about. Iron until the material is quite dry, and air everything before it is laid away.

THE MAKING OF STARCH AND GENERAL DIRECTIONS FOR ITS USE

Clear or Hot-Water Starch.—It is somewhat difficult to give exact proportions for the making of this starch, so much depends upon the number of articles to be starched and the stiffness required. Individual taste must also be taken into consideration, some preferring the articles very stiff, and others the merest suspicion of starch.

For a moderate quantity, take say two table-spoonfuls of dry starch, put it into a clean basin, and add to it enough cold water to make a thick paste. Work this with the back of a wooden spoon until quite smooth and free from lumps. Have a kettle of fast-boiling water on the fire, take the basin of starch to it, and let a second person pour the boiling water slowly in. Keep stirring all the time until the starch turns clear and transparent, when it is said to be made. The kettle should not be taken from the fire, but kept fast boiling all the time. The water used ought to be soft and colourless. Should the starch not become clear, it will show that either the water in the kettle has not been boiling, or too much cold water has been used in the first mixing. The mistake can, however, be remedied by turning the starch into a clean lined saucepan, and stirring it over the fire until it boils and turns clear. In fact, some people prefer always to boil the starch, and say that it brings out its stiffening qualities to the best advantage.

If the starch is of a yellow hue, a little blue may be added to it. A little wax is frequently added to hot starch to make the articles starched iron more smoothly, but if the iron itself is waxed as before described (see p. 273) this is not necessary.

The starch should be stirred for a short time after mixing to prevent a skin forming on the top of it, and should be kept covered when not in use.

It may be used in its present condition for making articles very stiff, or can be diluted to suit laces and muslins. For diluting purposes the water need not necessarily be boiling. It is sometimes more convenient to use it cold, as it makes the starch of a more comfortable heat to use. Do not make more of this starch than will be required at one time. It will keep for a day or two, but is better when used fresh.

This starch is used for the stiffening of table linen, prints, muslins, embroidery, petticoats, dresses, &c.

Coloured starches are made in the same way as the above. As a rule they require mixing with some white starch. Used alone, the colour is too deep for ordinary purposes. For instance, for a pale yellow colour, mix in the proportion of $\frac{1}{4}$ of cream starch to $\frac{3}{4}$ of white, or for a deeper tint use half of each. The quantity must be regulated according to the shade required. Special care must be taken when breaking these coloured starches with cold water, as if any lumps are left before the boiling water is poured on they will show up afterwards as dark coloured spots.

If there is any fear of the starch not being perfectly smooth, it is safer to strain it.

There are other ingredients which may be used for tinting starch, as for example :—

For an écru shade, colour the starch with coffee. Have some very strong clear coffee, and use this for mixing the starch with instead of water, then pour on boiling water until it turns clear.

A duller shade, such as is seen in old laces, can be produced by using tea instead of coffee. If a delicate pink hue is wished, use a decoction of logwood.

Cold-Water Starch.—The usual proportions are :—

2 oz. cold-water starch (rice starch preferred).

3 gills of cold water.

1 tea-spoonful turpentine.

$\frac{1}{2}$ tea-spoonful powdered borax, or a piece the size of a small nut of rock borax.

These proportions may vary slightly according to the starch used.

Mix the starch with the cold water, using the fingers to work out the lumps. Cover the basin over, and let the starch soak over-night at least. It is much better if it can soak for several days ; even although it may turn slightly sour, it will be none the worse, in fact, almost better. The longer it can soak, the less apt it is to cake on to the linen.

Care must be taken to keep it very clean and free from dust.

When about to use it, mix it up again, add the turpentine, dissolve the borax in a little boiling water ; if it is rock borax, dissolve it in a saucepan over the fire and add it. If the borax is left undissolved, it will appear afterwards in shiny patches on the linen. Use the best quality

of turpentine, or it will smell strongly. The turpentine and borax are added to give a gloss and to make the iron run more smoothly.

The starch is then ready for use, but must be well mixed up from the foot of the basin. There is no harm in making more of this starch than is required, as it will keep from one week to another. It must be covered over, and when about to use it again, if the water on the top looks dirty, pour it off. The starch itself, which will have sunk to the foot of the basin, wipe free from dust, and add the same amount of clean water as before. Add also a little more borax and turpentine, about half as much as before.

This starch is used principally for the stiffening of collars, cuffs, shirts, and anything that is required particularly stiff.

BED, TABLE AND OTHER HOUSEHOLD LINEN

All bed and table linen should be washed according to general directions already given on pp. 278–80.

Bed Linen.—*Sheets* should be stretched well by two people while damp, folded very evenly in four, and then mangled. It is not necessary to iron them, but be particular to air them thoroughly, turning them occasionally so that they get dried right through. If there is any embroidery on the sheets, that must be ironed, pressing it out well on the wrong side ; or, if they are hem-stitched, iron the hems to give them a finished appearance.

Pillow and Bolster-cases may either be mangled and the tapes only ironed, or they may be ironed all over as well as being mangled. The latter method will of course make them smoother, and it really requires very little time to run over them quickly on both sides with a hot iron. This is specially necessary for fine linen pillow-cases.

Embroidered Pillow-cases or pillow-shams will look better if they are put through some very thin hot-water starch, put several times through the wringer, and then rolled up for some time in a towel before ironing. If there are frills, these should be ironed first, ironing them on the right side so as to give them a gloss, and go well into the gathers without making any wrinkles. Next iron the centre on the right side. If there is embroidery, keep off it as much as possible, just ir ning well round it—ironing it on the right side would press it down. If a pillow-case, put your hand inside and separate the two sides, as the starch always makes them stick a little, then turn over and iron the second side. Iron both sides free from wrinkles, and try to get a good gloss on the linen. Press out the embroidery well on the wrong side, and lastly crimp or goffer the frills (see pp. 284–85.) Air well, and it is finished.

Bed-Covers.—Thick heavy bed-covers only require to be stretched and folded evenly while damp, well mangled, and then thoroughly aired. Those of a lighter make are better to be put through some thin starch, or some ready-made starch may be added to the water in which they are rinsed. This will give them a slight stiffness, which will make them look better and keep their clean appearance longer. If a polish is wanted, they must be ironed as well as mangled. Any lace or embroidery must always be ironed, and fringes combed and brushed out.

Table Linen, Starching of.—Table linen will look better and keep its clean appearance longer if slightly starched. The amount of starch used depends upon individual taste and the quality of the damask. Many people object to the use of starch entirely on the ground that it rots the linen. If one had always the very best double damask to deal with the extra stiffening might certainly be dispensed with, as the material has sufficient body in itself to keep its appearance ; but when the ordinary thin damask is under treatment a little starch does no harm, in fact, it saves in the end, as a table-cloth that is made slightly stiff will keep clean double the time a perfectly limp one would do. Starch also preserves from stains, and it is only when it is made too thick, rendering the articles so stiff as to make them not only lose all their natural beauty, but also disagreeable to use, that it can be said to be hurtful.

Table linen should be starched while wet ; it would be too stiff if starched dry, and the starch would not penetrate through it so evenly. If there is a large quantity to starch, it will save time and much wringing if some very thick hot-water starch is made (p. 280) and added to the blue rinsing water ; or if there are only a few things, after wringing them, put them through some thin hot-water starch. Wring well after starching, putting the things through the wringer as smoothly as possible ; if wrung twisted they will have a streaky appearance when ironed. Table napkins and doyleys should be put through the starch before table-cloths, as they are required slightly stiffer.

Table-cloths.—After starching dry slightly, and then each one must be stretched by two people. Stretch it first one way and then the other, and shake it out well to get it a good shape and even at the sides. Fold it by doubling it, selvedge to selvedge, with the right side out. Let the single sides drop, and then pick them up, one on each side, to the double fold. The table-cloth will then be folded in four, and the right side will be inside. Spread the table-cloth out on a table and arrange it quite smoothly, making the folds and the hems at the ends quite even. Double it and mangle. Let it lie for some time rolled up in a cloth before ironing, or if there is difficulty in getting very hot irons, it will be as well to let it dry a little first, but be careful it does not get too dry, or it will not look well.

To iron a table-cloth spread it out smoothly on a table in the folds and with the two selvedges nearest the edge of the table. Keep it in the folds as much as possible. Iron first the upper part, turn that back, iron the next two parts, turn back again and iron the next two, and so on until the whole of the table-cloth has been ironed on both sides, then double the table-cloth and mark the fold down with the iron. Air well, and then either roll or fold. To get a good gloss on table linen, the hotter and heavier the irons are the better. Keep them well greased, and press heavily, ironing until almost dry. If the table-cloth is very large, it is better if two people can iron it at one time, otherwise it would get dry before it was all finished.

Table-Napkins.—Fold them double, selvedge to selvedge, perfectly evenly, and mangle several at one time, then let them lie rolled up in a towel for some time before ironing.

To iron them, take one at a time, shake out and stretch evenly, lay out very smoothly on the table with the right side uppermost and as square as possible. Iron the right side first, then the wrong, and back again on the right. Be careful not to stretch the edges out of shape, and iron until quite dry. They are ironed on both sides to avoid having one side rough and the other smooth, as sometimes happens. Give the hems an extra iron to dry them well.

Table-napkins can be folded either in three or in four, according to taste. To fold in four, fold in the same way as a table-cloth, only on the opposite side, bringing the right side outside instead of the wrong. Get the ends very even, press the folds well with an iron, and fold in four across, making a square again. Air well before laying them away. To fold in three, measure the sides (hems) first, and get them divided into three equal parts, press them down with an iron to keep them in place, then make the folds right across and iron them down, fold in three across to make a square again, and press with the iron once more. If there is a name, it must be on the outside when the table-napkin is folded ; if a monogram or raised initials, iron well on the wrong side to make the embroidery stand out.

Doyleys.—Starch in the same way as table-napkins, and let them lie rolled up for some time. If they have fringes, shake them well out against the edge of the table before beginning to iron. This opens out the fringes. To iron, spread out on the table, and brush out the fringe all round with a small brush, and comb it with a fine comb until it lies quite straight, then iron the centre of the doyley and the fringes on both sides, and brush and comb the fringe again until it is quite soft and free. The brushing and combing must be done carefully, so as not to draw out the threads, and always before the fringe is dried with the iron. Finish by trimming off any untidy ends with a pair of scissors. If liked, the fringes may be curled, using a blunt knife or a paper-knife, and curling them in the same way as an ostrich feather.

Doyleys with netted or tatted edges should be pinned out on a covered board or table, stretching each point well and putting in pins where required. Then iron the centres only (ironing would spoil the edges), and leave them pinned out until dry. After unpinning them, if the edges feel rather stiff and hard, pull them out with the fingers.

Doyleys with a full lace edge should have the lace ironed first, then the centre, and, lastly, the lace goffered round very evenly. (See p. 284.)

Tray Cloths and Sideboard Cloths.—These should be treated in the same way as other table linen. If they have fringes these should be brushed and combed out before they become dry. If they can be ironed on both sides, then do so ; but if they have a distinct right side, iron on the right side only, just pressing out any embroidery on the wrong side, and iron round the hems. If there is lace round the edges, iron it first before the centre, and do any goffering that is required last of all. There is no particular way of folding tray cloths and sideboard cloths ; just fold them to the size which is most suitable for laying away. Long sideboard cloths are better rolled than folded.

Other Household Linen

Bedroom Towels.—These should be folded evenly while damp and well mangled. Then run over them quickly with a hot iron on both sides, fold them in four lengthways, and air well. If there are fringes, these should be brushed and combed out before ironing ; and after ironing, combed out again to make them free and soft. If there are embroidered initials or monograms on the towels, press them out well on the wrong side.

Coarse Bath Towels and Turkish Towels.—These should neither be mangled nor ironed ; the rougher they are the better. Stretch them well, iron the plain piece at the ends, comb the fringes, and fold them evenly. Air them well.

Toilet Covers.—These should be put through thin starch when wet, wrung out, and hung up to dry slightly. Then fold them very evenly, double, and mangle well. Next iron on the right side to get a good gloss, and brush out any fringes. To fold them, double lengthways and press the fold down, and then either roll up or fold once or twice across. Do not make too many folds in a toilet cover, or it will not lie well.

Kitchen Towels, Dusters, &c.—These should just be folded evenly while damp, and then mangled. It is quite unnecessary to iron them, but air them well before laying away.

BODY LINEN

General Directions for the Doing Up of Body Linen.—All underclothing must be damp for ironing. Very thin cambric articles will be improved by being slightly starched, otherwise they will have a limp undressed appearance. If a little hot-water starch is put into the water in which they are blued it will be sufficient. All that is wanted is to give the cambric the slight stiffness of new material, and not enough to make it unpleasant to wear. Ordinary cotton will not require any starch ; it will be sufficiently crisp if ironed with a hot iron and slightly damp. All frills and embroidery are improved by being dipped in very thin hot-water starch, even although the whole garment is not being done. This should be done when the clothes are being damped and rolled up. Gather up the frill in the hand, dip it into some very thin starch, and then wring out in the hands or between the folds of a towel. The slight stiffness this will give will prevent the frilling curling up and otherwise looking limp.

First iron all embroidery or frills. Embroidery must be ironed on the wrong side over a piece of felt or double flannel, in addition to the ironing blanket, well pressed so as to raise the pattern, and the points pulled out and ironed until quite dry. Plain frills or frills with just a narrow lace edging must be ironed on the right side so as to give them a gloss ; care must be taken to iron well up into the gathers and without making wrinkles. All bands, hems, and double parts should be ironed on both sides to give them a more finished appearance. Always keep the neck or the top of the garment at your left-hand side, so that the iron may be more easily run well up into the gathers. If the cotton should get dry before it is all ironed, damp it down with a wet rubber. It will never look glossy if ironed too dry, but will have a rough appearance. Iron out all tapes. Never leave them twisted and curled up. Iron round buttons, not over them, or it will be apt to mark them. Sometimes seams and tucks are inclined to drag the articles and cause creases, especially when the clothes are new. They should then be well stretched out before applying the iron. New cotton is always more difficult to iron and make glossy than that which has been washed several times.

Crimping.—As a rule this is done on plain frills, or on plain frills with a narrow lace edging ; but embroidery can also be crimped, especially when it is put on only slightly full and not starched, in which case it would be unsuitable for goffering. Crimping can be done with an ordinary iron, using the back, side, or point according to the width of the frill. For a very narrow frill use the point ; for a wider one the back or side, as is found easiest. When the frill is very wide, it is sometimes easier to crimp half of it at one time, crimping first down near the drawings with the side of the iron, keeping the point close to the gathers, and then the upper part with the back of the iron. The iron must be cool enough for you to hold the fingers on it.

To crimp, keep the gathering of the frill at your left-hand side, and the frill itself lying straight across the table. Commence with the

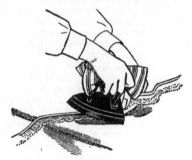

Crimping.

part nearest the edge of the table, drawing the frill towards you as it is crimped. Hold the iron with the right hand, run up part of the frill with the part of the iron with which you are going to crimp, put two or three fingers of the left hand under the frill and close to the iron, draw the iron quickly back, following with the fingers of the left hand, and crimping the frill underneath it. Only a small piece, an inch or an inch and a half, can be crimped at one time.

It requires a good deal of practice to do crimping quickly, and at the same time finely and evenly. The thicker the material, the firmer pull back must be given to the iron.

Special machines can now be had for crimping.

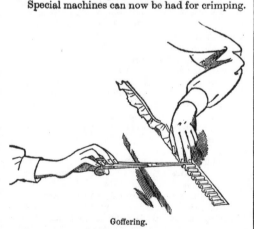

Goffering.

Goffering.—This is done with heated goffering tongs. A frill requires to be pretty full, and to be starched, in order to goffer well. For wide and full frills, use the large size of tongs ; and for narrow ones, the smaller pair. Have two pairs of tongs of exactly the same size in use at one time, so that one pair can be heating whilst you are using the other. Always test them on a piece of rag or paper first, and see that they are thoroughly clean and not too hot before you apply them to the frill.

Place the frill to be goffered lengthways on the table, with the drawings from you. Pin out straight as much of the frill as possible at one time, to keep it steady. Commence at the right-hand end of the frill and work towards the left. Hold the tongs in the right hand, putting the thumb in the lower hole, and the second or third finger in the upper ; put the tongs right up to the drawings of the frill, and then turn them half round, so that the hole with the thumb in it comes uppermost ; keep two or three fingers of the left hand close to the tongs to keep the goffering in position, and let them remain there until the tongs are loosened slightly and drawn gently out. Then go a little distance further back and do the same again, working from right to left, and being careful not to pull out what has been already done. In drawing out the tongs be careful to keep them as flat to the table as possible, and do not give them an upward jerk.

The distance the goffers are apart depends on the fulness of the frill. The fuller the frill the closer the goffers can be. Sometimes when a frill is only slightly drawn merely the mark of the tongs can be shown.

Always keep the goffering tongs on the straight of the frill, or with the thread of the material. Goffering should be regular, and an equal distance apart. This is sometimes rather difficult if the frill is not drawn evenly. If there are two frills to be goffered, do the upper first, then the under.

With practice, goffering can be done quite quickly. The more quickly it is done, the hotter the tongs can be used.

Folding and Airing.—Folding depends very much upon individual taste, and upon the shape of the garment to be folded. Shapes vary so much that it is difficult to lay down any hard-and-fast rules, only it is as well to have some general rules for guidance.

Always fold so as to crush the garment as little as possible, laying in pleats carefully where required. Iron down each fold or pleat as you make it to keep it in position. Fold garments so as to show as much of the embroidery as possible, always having the inside as tidy and smooth as the outside, and making each a convenient size. Keep all tapes to the inside.

All underclothing must be thoroughly aired before it is laid away. Although the things seem dry after ironing, there is always a certain amount of moisture which clings to them from the iron. The greatest care and attention should be paid to this, as want of thought may lead to the gravest results.

How to Iron and Fold a Chemise.—Have the chemise on the right side to begin with. First iron any trimming, frills, or embroidery, and also bands on both sides. Next fold the chemise down the centre of the back, keeping the neck at your left-hand side. Iron the back, first on

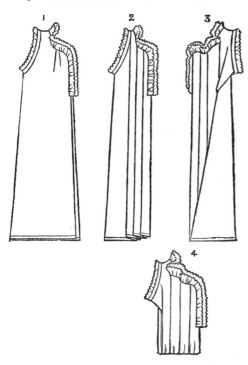

one side, and then turn over and iron on the other ; iron the hem at the foot on the wrong side, and when ironing up near the gathers at the neck, lift up slightly, so that the iron may run well up into the gathers, being careful not to crease the under side. Then open the chemise out and lay it on the table, so that the whole of the back is uppermost ; iron the front hem on the wrong side, and round the arm-holes and sleeves on the back. The back is then finished. Turn the chemise over and iron the front—first the bottom part straight across and the rest of it lengthways ; iron well up into the gathers and round the arm-holes and sleeves, and the chemise is finished. Any goffering or crimping must be done before folding, laying it out on the table, or double it so as not to crush. If there is only a little fulness at the corners of the embroidery, this can be goffered after folding.

A chemise may be folded in two different ways —the side fold or the front fold. For a plain chemise the side fold is best ; and for a more elaborately trimmed one the front fold. For the side fold, double the chemise, bringing the two side-seams and two shoulders together, with the back inside and the front out ; lay it on the table with the neck at the left-hand side, and the band down the opening of the front, turned uppermost (Fig. 1). Take hold of the neck and the bottom of the chemise, and stretch it so that it falls in pleats. Arrange these pleats evenly, two or three according to the fulness at the band, and iron them well down (Fig. 2). Turn the chemise over, see that the pleats are even on the other side, fold the chemise again lengthways, making it the same width all the way down, and turning in an extra piece at the foot if it is too wide there ; pleat the sleeves back a little so that the embroidery only shows over the sides (Fig. 3), and then fold from the bottom upwards in three or four, according to the size you wish it to be when finished (Fig. 4). Air well before laying it away.

For the front fold, first fold the chemise double so as to find the centre of the back, make a mark with the iron and open out again. Keep the back of the chemise uppermost on the table, and the neck at the left-hand side. Fold in two or three pleats from the side in towards the centre of the back and press them well down (Fig. 1). Then pleat the other side in towards the centre of the back in exactly the same way, making the chemise an equal width all the way down, and not too broad. Fold the sleeves so that the embroidery only shows over the sides (Fig. 2), and fold the chemise into three or four from the bottom upwards, press well, turn over and see that the front looks quite straight ; air well, and it is finished (Fig. 3).

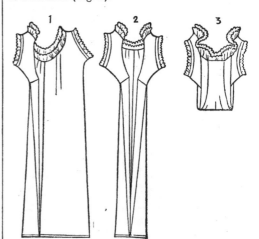

How to Iron and Fold a Pair of Drawers.—Iron any embroidery or trimming first, and the bands on both sides. When ironing the waistband, keep the band next you, and lying lengthways on the table, and iron the strings if there are any. Place the pair of drawers on the table front uppermost, with the waistband at the left-hand side. Commence with the leg nearest the edge of the table, smooth it out and iron straight across as far up and down as possible until the drawings interfere, then iron up into the draw-

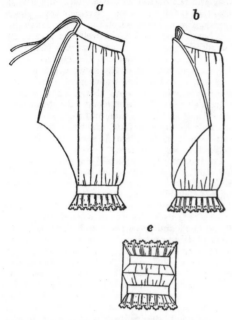

ings at the top, and if knickerbockers, iron down into the drawings at the foot, holding the iron with the left hand. Then iron the hem on the under part of the leg on the wrong side, and draw that leg over the table out of the way whilst the other leg is being ironed. Iron the second leg on the same side and in the same way. Next turn the pair of drawers over, still keeping the band at the left-hand side, and iron the other side of the legs in the same manner as the first, not forgetting to iron the hems of the front part on the wrong side. Goffer or crimp the frills if necessary, and the drawers are ready for folding.

To fold a pair of drawers, place the two legs evenly one on the top of the other, fold in the shaped piece so as to make them the same width all the way down, turn any strings inside to prevent their being pulled off, and fold the drawers from the top downwards in three or four. If there is any embroidery at the foot, separate the two pieces, doubling one leg back so far so as to show both pieces of embroidery. Crimp or goffer the trimming if necessary.

Knickerbockers require to be pleated to make them lie smoothly. Pleat one leg down, putting in two or three pleats according to the fulness between the bands, and not pleating the bands themselves, then iron the pleats well down. Place the other leg on the top of that one, and pleat it in the same way, keeping it exactly the same width, and having the same number of

pleats (Fig. *a*). Finish off the same as a pair of drawers (Figs. *b*, *c*).

How to Iron and Fold a Pair of Combinations.—Iron all embroidery and bands first, then place the combinations on the table with the neck at the left-hand side, and iron the upper part down as far as the waist, smoothing out each piece. Then fold the legs evenly by the side-seams, and iron them in the same way as a pair of drawers, first on one side, and then on the other, and the sleeves on both sides. Iron the front hems on the wrong side, do any goffering or crimping that is required, and they are ready for folding. Combinations require very careful handling, one part is so liable to be crushed while another is being ironed.

To fold a pair of combinations, fold them double first, bringing the sides of the bodice, the sides of the legs, and the two shoulders together. As the back is usually longer than the front, see that it lies smoothly underneath. It generally requires a pleat put in it just at the waist. If the combinations are very wide and like knickerbockers, put pleats in them, two or three according to the fulness, and continue one or two of them up the front of the bodice (Fig. 1). Then place the combinations on the table with the button-hole side uppermost, double over the shaped part of the leg by dotted line (Fig. 1), so as to make them the same width all the way up, then double them from the bottom upwards, so as to make the trimming at the foot come just

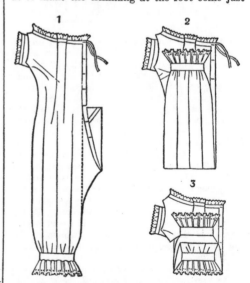

below the trimming at the neck (Fig. 2), turn over and double them again. Lastly, turn back and see that they look nicely arranged, doubling back the sleeves if necessary, and separating the legs so as to show both pieces of embroidery (Fig. 3).

How to Iron and Fold a Night-Dress.—A night-dress is ironed in very much the same way as a chemise. If there is a yoke, iron it after the embroidery and bands. Iron the skirt of the night-dress in the same way as a chemise, leaving the sleeves to the last. To iron the sleeves fold the night-dress double lengthways, keep the neck at the left-hand side and the sleeves towards the edge of the table, throw back the upper sleeve, and iron the under one on the top side ; then fold it back underneath, draw the other one forward, and iron it on the same side. Next turn the night-dress so that the neck is at the right-hand side, and iron the other two sides of the sleeves in the same way. This way of ironing the sleeves prevents any crushing of the night-dress. Crimp or goffer any frills that require it, and the night-dress is ready for folding.

A night-dress may be folded in two ways, like a chemise, by the side fold or the front fold, and the two sleeves must be made to lie nicely over the front.

FLANNELS AND WOOLLEN ARTICLES

The term flannels, when used in the following paragraphs, applies to woollen goods of all kinds, whether knitted, crocheted, woven, or flannel proper.

The washing of flannels is one of the simplest branches of laundry work. The rules are few and easy, but none the less important. Given the necessary requisites, a tub of hot water, some liquid soap, a little ammonia and a wringer, there is no excuse for the flannels not being soft and elastic after washing, but if the rules are disregarded, the result will in all probability be hard shrunken garments resembling cheap tweed.

Soap Jelly.—As this is used instead of a piece of soap, it ought to be prepared first of all.

Take as much soap as will be required, and cut it down in shreds with a knife. Put it into a saucepan, and just cover it with cold or hot water. Allow the soap to melt slowly over the fire until it is quite clear and without lumps. Let it melt slowly, as boiling wastes it. Do not fill the saucepan too full, as soap is very liable to boil over. The soap may be put into a jar instead of a saucepan, and melted in the oven.

Any ends of soap may be used up in this way. It is better to make soap jelly freshly each week, as it loses its strength if kept many days.

Remember that soap will taste very strongly anything with which it comes in contact, so that the knife and board on which it is cut, also the saucepan in which it is melted, ought to be kept for that purpose only.

Any good soap will do ; olive oil is excellent if it can be obtained, but, failing that, good yellow soap will serve the purpose.

Instead of soap jelly, Lux, or any other form of shredded soap, can be used, but care should be taken that it does not contain a quantity of soda.

General Directions.—The best plan is to wash flannels either before or after all the other clothes. The former is better if they can be dried outside, as they will then have the benefit of the morning air and sun. First shake the flannels, in order to get rid of any loose dust, and divide them into lots according to colour and kind—white articles and those that are least soiled by themselves, then other light-coloured articles, such as grey and drab. Stockings and socks should always form a lot by themselves, and also dark-coloured things, or those in which the colour is likely to run, as reds and crimsons. To wash the flannels prepare a tub half full of warm water, not too hot, but just comfortable for the hand to rest in. To be exact the temperature should be from 35° to 45° Centigrade. Then add enough ammonia to make the water smell slightly. The quantity will depend somewhat upon the strength of the ammonia ; from one to two table-spoonfuls in a tub of water will generally be found ample. This will soften the water, dissolve the grease in the flannels, and thus save some of the friction of washing. Commence with the whitest and cleanest articles, leaving the most soiled and those in which the colour is likely to run until the last.

Avoid rubbing flannels except any particularly soiled parts, or those of a coarse make, as rubbing inclines to shrink them ; but squeeze well and work up and down in the water, drawing them through the hands.

A little soap may be rubbed on any cotton bands. When the first garment is finished, squeeze it out in the hands, or, better still, put it through the wringer and proceed with the other articles in the same way. If not clean after the first washing, repeat the process, using less soap and ammonia in the second water. Garments that are turnable, as night-dresses, combinations, &c., should be washed on the right side in the first water and on the wrong side in the second, and then left on the wrong side until dry.

After the light-coloured flannels are done, the same lather may do for the darker ones ; only, if the water is dirty or if the lather has disappeared, take entirely fresh water, and use the second lather of the light things as the first of the darker. Never wash in dirty water, and never rub soap on to flannels. Do not commence too many flannels at one time, as the sooner they are finished and hung up to dry the better. It is specially necessary to hurry through the process in washing coloured flannels.

Rinsing.—When the flannels are quite clean, rinse them in plenty of warm water, two or three times if necessary, until they feel soft to the touch. Should any soap be left in them, they will not only be hard and sticky, but have an unpleasant smell when dried. Never rinse in too hot or cold water, as either of these would cause them to shrink suddenly, and feel hard like pasteboard. A little blue may be added to the last water in which white flannels are rinsed. When thoroughly rinsed, wring the flannels as dry as possible. This is best done through the machine, as it does not twist them. Any rough twisting would break the fibres of the wool. Shake them well to raise the " nap " or soft woolly substance on the surface of the material, pull into a good shape, and they are ready for drying.

Drying.—Flannels must on no account be allowed to lie about wet. This shrinks them more than anything. Whenever it is possible, they should be dried in the open air in a good wind and not too bright a sun. Failing this, dry them in a warm atmosphere, where they will dry quickly ; but at the same time they must not be put so close to an open fire or in such a hot place that they steam. This would be as bad as putting them into boiling water. Shake the flannels, and turn them once or twice while drying, pulling them into a good shape.

Mangling or Ironing.—For the coarser and thicker flannels it will be sufficient if they are mangled when nearly dry. Any bands or tapes must be ironed, and then the articles hung up again to finish drying. The finer kinds should be ironed when nearly dry with a rather cool iron. If they have become quite dry it will be necessary to spread a slightly damp cloth over them and iron over that, pressing heavily. Never iron flannels very wet or the hot iron will shrink them up, and on no account must the iron be too hot, especially in ironing coloured flannels. Should any scorching occur, dip the piece in warm water, squeeze it well, and rub gently, then wring out and re-dry, or rub with a silver coin and the scorch will disappear.

Reasons for Flannels Shrinking.—

1. Soap has been rubbed on them instead of soap jelly being used.
2. They have either been washed or rinsed in too hot or cold water.
3. They have been allowed to lie about wet, instead of being hung up to dry immediately.
4. They have been dried too slowly.
5. They have been dried so close to an open fire that they steamed.
6. They have been ironed while wet with a very hot iron.

Special Articles

New Flannels and Sanitary Underclothing.—These are better to be soaked for about half-an-hour before washing in warm water with ammonia in it, one table-spoonful to two gallons of water. Cover the tub over to prevent the heat escaping, and squeeze and wring them out of this before the water has time to get cold. This process draws out some of the sulphur which new flannels contain, and which would prevent the soap

making a lather, and it also helps to remove the grease. Then wash in the same way as flannels.

Stockings and Socks.—The comfort of stockings and socks, as well as their durability, depends very much upon their being well washed. The soles, heels, and toes require special attention. These should always be rubbed, using the washing-board and a little soap if necessary. Wash them first on the right side, then turn and wash on the wrong, giving them two waters. Fold them evenly by the seam at the back of the leg before wringing and drying. When nearly dry either mangle them or iron them on the wrong side, and leave them wrong side out ready for mending.

Red or Crimson Flannel.—This is rather troublesome to wash, and however careful one may be it is almost impossible to prevent the colour running. Ammonia should be omitted from the water in which it is washed, and vinegar should be added to the rinsing water in the proportion of four table-spoonfuls to one gallon of water. This helps to brighten the colour.

Blankets.—Always choose a fine day for washing blankets, as it is a mistake to dry them indoors. First shake them well, and then prepare water with soap jelly, the same as for flannels, and in the largest tub you have. Put the blankets in, one or two at a time, move them up and down in this, squeezing and pressing them against the sides ; then put them in a second tub of the same kind of water to repeat the process. In Scotland, instead of being washed with the hands, they are tramped with the bare feet. They may also be pounded with a dolly. Rinse well until free from soap, and then wring. If the wringer is used, let the rollers be as loose as possible. The colour of the blankets depends very much upon the cleanliness of the water they are washed in, so be particular to change it whenever necessary.

Shake the blankets well before hanging up to dry, and hang them quite straight and singly on the clothes-rope in a gentle wind. See that they are securely fastened and well raised above the ground. When dry, take them down, stretch them well, and rub all over with a piece of clean rough flannel so as to raise the pile, and then hang them near a fire for some time, as it is most important to have them thoroughly dry.

Shetland and other Shawls.—Wash in the same way as flannels, but handle more gently, especially the finer ones, squeezing them well, and being careful not to break the threads of wool. Rinse them in warm water, putting a little blue into the last rinsing water for white shawls, and for fine Shetland shawls a little hot-water starch, about one breakfast-cupful thick starch to half a gallon of water. Squeeze the water well out of the shawls, or put them through a wringer. Avoid twisting them in any way.

If there is no wringer, after squeezing out as much of the water as possible with the hands, beat well between the folds of a towel.

To dry a shawl, spread a sheet on the floor and pin it tightly at the corners ; pin out the shawl on this, stretching it well but not over much, pin out each point, and be careful to keep the shawl a good shape. Leave it till quite dry, then unpin carefully, shake it out, and air if necessary.

The Sulphur Bath.—White shawls and flannels which have become yellow may be whitened by putting them in a sulphur bath. Take a deep barrel, break up about one oz. of rock sulphur, and put it on an old plate or tin dish at the foot of it ; sprinkle over the sulphur a few drops of methylated spirits, and then set fire to it. When the methylated spirits has burnt out and the sulphur itself is burning, suspend the flannels or shawls across the fumes. This must be done just before they are dried. Twist them loosely round sticks, pinning them here and there to prevent their slipping down and catching fire, and place the sticks across the barrel ; or a wire cage may be used, suspended on the top of the barrel. Cover over with a blanket or something thick enough to keep in the fumes, and let them remain about twenty minutes. Turn the things once during the time, so that every part of them gets whitened. Great care must be taken to have the things raised sufficiently high above the sulphur to avoid all danger of their catching fire.

A Chamois Leather.—This may be washed and made to look equal to new if the following directions are carried out. Prepare a lather with water and soap, the same as for flannels, put the leather into this, and squeeze it gently between the hands. Repeat the process if not clean after the first water, and until the last soapy water looks quite clean. Do not rinse, but wring straight out of the soapy water. Hang up to dry, rubbing and pulling it out occasionally with the hands in order to keep it soft. It may be smoothed out last of all with a cool iron.

Eiderdown Quilts.—To wash a large eiderdown quilt is rather hard work, and unless a good wringer is available and ample drying accommodation, it should scarcely be attempted. But with these conveniences an eiderdown of moderate dimensions can be very easily tackled, and the results will be most satisfactory if the few needful rules are attended to. Before starting the actual washing shake the quilt, to free it from all loose dust, and if there are any holes, either mend them or draw them together with a needle and cotton. Then wash according to directions given for flannel washing, or when large treat as blankets. If the colour runs, use the water just tepid. Rinse in an abundant supply of warm water, adding a little salt or ammonia to the last to brighten the colour. There must on no account be any soap left in the quilt. Wring it carefully

through the machine, loosening the tension to the fullest extent if necessary. The drying requires special attention. Shake out the eiderdown ; it is better if two people can do this —and hang it up, out of doors if possible, in a good wind and not too much sun, or, failing that, in a warm atmosphere in the house. Whilst drying the quilt must be taken down from time to time and rubbed and shaken, to loosen the down and prevent it forming into clots. When dry, it should be quite as soft as when new.

Swansdown.—Wash gently in warm water, making a lather with soap jelly, and rinse in tepid water. Then hold it a little distance from the fire and shake till quite dry and fluffy.

Flannelette.—Wash in the same way as flannel, only it will take no harm if rinsed in cold water. White flannelette may even be boiled along with cotton articles. Dry and finish off like flannels.

Delaine.—When carefully washed, delaine should look equal to new. Wash it in exactly the same way as flannels, and be careful with the rinsing. Add ammonia in the proportion of one table-spoonful to one gallon of water to the last warm water. This will help to brighten the colour. Iron while slightly damp, and not so dry as for flannel. If it is lined, iron the lining first.

Velveteen.—Cotton velvets, especially the light-coloured ones, can be washed and be made to look quite well. Wash in the same way as flannel with a lather of soap and warm water, and rinse first in warm and then in cold water. When nearly dry iron on the wrong side with a moderately hot iron.

White Coque Feather Boas.—(See p. 318.)

MUSLINS, LACE, CURTAINS, AND NET

The Washing of Muslin.—Muslin requires very careful treatment, and especially coloured muslin if it is being washed for the first time. It must be treated more carefully than ordinary cotton, and not be pulled out of shape nor stretched, or it will have a drawn appearance. Being thin and open in texture it is easy to wash without any rough treatment. First soak the muslin in cold or tepid water to take out the dressing or stiffening ; then wring or squeeze out gently. Prepare a small tub or basin of warm water, and make a lather with melted soap in the same way as for flannels. Squeeze the muslin well in this, and work it up and down in the water. In the case of very soiled articles a little borax or ammonia may be added to soften the water and draw out the dirt. If not clean after the first washing, repeat the process in fresh soapy water, using rather less soap the second time. If washing is not sufficient to make the muslin a good colour, it should be boiled (see p. 278). Then rinse first in tepid and then in cold water, until every trace of soap has been removed. Pure white muslin may have a little blue added to the last rinsing water. If the muslin is *coloured*, and the colours are likely to run, soak it first in salt and water, allowing a handful of salt to a gallon of water. Let the water for the first washing be just tepid, and proceed as quickly as possible, putting salt again or a little ammonia in the final rinsing water. Coloured muslin must on no account be boiled.

Clear Starching and Ironing.—All muslin should be starched wet. If put into the starch dry, it never looks so clear. Prepare some clear starch (see p. 280), and thin it to the consistency required. This depends upon what the muslin is wanted for, and according to the degree of stiffness desired. It is impossible to give the exact quantities of starch necessary for clear starch, as different qualities and makes of starch require more water than others, but experience will soon teach this, and at first it will be just as well to test the stiffness of the starch on a small piece of muslin. Be sure to have the starch clear, put the muslins into it, putting in first those white articles which are wished stiffest. Let the starch soak well through, then wring well, putting them twice at least through the wringing machine. In starching coloured muslins do not let the starch be too hot, or it will destroy the colours ; and never put things through the wringer straight out of boiling hot starch as it ruins the india-rubber rollers. In thinning the starch, after it has been made clear with boiling water, cold water may be used, and that will make the starch a more comfortable heat to use.

After wringing the muslins shake them well, smooth out, and let them lie for some time rolled up in a towel before ironing. Muslin must be ironed wet. If allowed to get dry, it will have a rough appearance when ironed. Iron on the right side to give it a gloss, and the way of the thread as much as possible. When ironing a large piece of muslin, keep as much of it covered over at one time as you conveniently can, to prevent it becoming dry. Should the muslin dry before it is ironed, damp it down very evenly with a wet rubber or towel, not missing a piece, or it will not look smooth. *Embroidered muslin* should be ironed on the wrong side, to raise the pattern. *Spotted muslin* should also be ironed on the wrong side, unless the spots are pretty far apart, when it may look better ironed first on the right side to give the muslin a gloss, and afterwards ironed over on the wrong to press out the spots. In ironing coloured muslins do not use the iron too hot, as it is apt to destroy the colours.

Muslin trimmed with lace should have the lace ironed first and then the muslin itself. If the muslin feels too stiff after ironing, the fault can be remedied by putting it through water and then ironing again. Air muslin well after ironing or it will become limp.

Washing of Lace.—To " do up " lace nicely is by no means difficult, in fact, it is one of the most interesting and least fatiguing branches of laundry work and amply repays the trouble expended upon it. Care and attention to details is all that is required. The lace should first be carefully mended if necessary, and any tacking or drawing threads removed.

If very much soiled, soak it for several hours in a lather of warm water and soap, and allow one tea-spoonful of powdered borax to one quart of water. Then squeeze it out of the soaking water, and wash it in two or three warm lathers of soap and water. Do not rub it, but squeeze between the hands and press it well. Any rubbing or twisting would break the threads of the lace, especially if it were of a fine make. When clean, rinse well in tepid water and then in cold, and if time permits allow it to lie for some time in the cold water to clear it. Pure white lace may have the last rinsing water slightly tinged with blue.

If after repeated washings the lace still has a soiled look, it may either be bleached in the sun or boiled. To boil lace put it into a jar or jam pot, with cold water to cover it, and a little soap jelly ; stand the jar in a saucepan with boiling water to reach fully half-way up the jar, put the lid on the pan and boil for two or three hours. Care must be taken that the water in the pan does not boil away.

Stiffening of Lace.—There is great difference of opinion about the stiffening of lace, and many object to the use of starch on the ground that it makes the lace too stiff and tends to destroy it. As a rule, however, a little starch or other stiffening is an improvement to most laces, but the aim must be to get the lace of the same stiffness as when new and no stiffer. For the thicker and commoner laces use hot-water starch. (See p. 280.)

Take some clear starch and thin it down until it feels like slightly thickened water, or for heavy laces it may be a little thicker. Allow the lace to soak in this for some little time, and then squeeze out gently with the hands. Spread it out between the folds of a fine towel or old handkerchief, and either beat it between the hands to remove some of the starch or pass it carefully through the wringing machine. Avoid twisting the lace in any way.

Cream lace may be put through cream starch or through starch coloured with tea or coffee (see Coloured Starches, p. 281), instead of white starch.

In the case of very fine lace use gum water instead of starch. This can be used without any danger of its rotting the fabric, and the following are the directions for making it :—

Gum Water.—Take one ounce of gum-arabic and put it into a saucepan with one pint of boiling water. Dissolve slowly over the fire, stirring occasionally, then strain through muslin, and bottle ready for use. Allow one table-spoonful of this melted gum to half a pint of cold water. Soak the lace in it for half-an-hour, and proceed in the same way as with starched lace. To tint the lace use strained tea or coffee with the gum water instead of plain water.

After wringing pull the lace out gently with the fingers and roll it up with the wrong side inside. Wrap it in a towel and let it lie for an hour at least before ironing.

Ironing of Lace.—Take a piece of clean white felt or flannel of three or four thicknesses, and iron the lace over this on the wrong side and with a moderately hot iron. The points of the lace must be placed furthest from the edge of the table, and must be well ironed out. Do not unroll too much of the lace at one time, and iron until quite dry. If too stiff rub gently between the fingers to take out some of the starch, and iron again. Press well with the iron, and at the same time not too roughly, and use the point of the iron to raise the pattern of the lace. Keep the lace the same width all the way along, and air it well before laying it away. Very fine lace should be ironed with a piece of muslin over it, and never touched with the bare iron. Ironing too with regard to lace is frequently objected to, but if carefully done no trace of the iron should be seen, and the result should be most satisfactory.

White Silk Lace.—This may be washed in the same way as any other lace, but should never be boiled. After rinsing, steep for half-an-hour in half a pint of hot milk, to which one dessert-spoonful of gum water has been added. This will restore the colour. Then proceed as for other lace.

How to Iron a Muslin and Lace Handkerchief.—This must be put through the very thinnest starch or gum water, and wrung in the same careful way as lace.

Iron the lace first, pulling it out after ironing to keep it soft, and then iron it over again. Iron the centre part next. Turn over to the right side, and wet the muslin part over with a damp rubber (it is sure to have become dry while the lace was being ironed). Iron it with a rather cool iron until smooth and glossy. If necessary, press out the lace round the edges last of all, and the handkerchief is finished.

Black Lace.—First brush it well with a soft brush to get rid of as much dust as possible. If it is spotted or stained, wash it in tea with a very little soap jelly added, then rinse it in more tea, and finally let it soak for about half-an-hour in prepared tea. Add prepared gum (see p. 290) in the proportion of one table-spoonful to one pint of tea. If the lace is quite clean, and you merely wish to stiffen and renew its appearance, you may dispense with the washing, and simply soak it in the prepared tea. The gum-arabic in the tea gives the lace a slight stiffness. When doing up silk lace, add two tea-spoonfuls of methylated spirits to a half-pint of prepared tea to give a gloss to the silk in the lace.

After soaking, squeeze the lace out of the tea. Shake it well, and spread it out between the folds of a towel or cloth, and either beat it with the hands or pass it once or twice through the wringer, then pull it out with the fingers, and roll up in the same way as white lace.

To iron black lace take a sheet of kitchen paper, spread the lace out on the smoothest side of it with the points away from the edge of the table, cover over with more paper, and iron over that. Lift the upper pieces of paper occasionally to see that the lace lies smoothly underneath. Iron until quite dry, and hang up to air. Black lace must never be touched with the bare iron; there must always be something over it to prevent it getting glazed. Paper not only prevents the lace staining the ironing sheet, but it also imparts a slight stiffness to it.

Curtains.—First shake the curtains well, or hang them up and brush them down with a soft brush to get rid of the superfluous dust, then soak in warm water and borax—one table-spoon-ful to two gallons of water—for an hour or two. Squeeze them well in this, and then pass through the wringing machine.

Wash in warm water, making a lather with boiled soap. Work them up and down in this, squeezing and pulling them through the hands. If not clean after the first washing, repeat the process.

Rubbing of all kinds must be avoided, and it is always dangerous to wash curtains by machinery. Rinse them first in warm water, then in plenty of cold. Wring well and starch them. Pure white curtains may have a little blue either added to the rinsing water or mixed in with the starch. If two ounce of alum dissolved in one gallon of water be used for rinsing, it will prevent the curtains catching fire at any time. Starch curtains wet, and have the starch just a moderate degree of stiffness. For white curtains, use the ordinary white hot-water starch; for cream or écru, use starch coloured with tea or coffee, or cream starch. (See Coloured Starches, p. 281.)

Curtains ought to be dried quickly; they are always better to be stretched and pinned out on frames for the purpose, or on sheets spread on the floor. Allow them to remain until almost dry, take up and iron round the edges, pressing out all the points well, then hang up to air. If there is no convenience for having the curtains pinned out, partly dry them by hanging them at a safe distance from the fire, or in a warm room; then spread them out on a table, and iron all over. If curtains are lined, iron the linings first before stretching and pinning out to dry; and when ironing, iron from the middle towards the sides, so that if there is any fulness it may come to the edge where it will show least.

Plain and Spotted Net.—Wash in the same way

as lace, and put through thin hot-water starch. Iron plain net on the wrong side ; stretch and pull it out, and then iron again. It must not be too stiff, and should look clear. When held up to the light, the little holes in the net should not be filled with starch. Iron spotted net in the same way, only a piece of flannel may be put under it to make the spots stand out better.

A Gentleman's Evening Tie.—Care must be taken in washing these to keep them a good colour. They may be washed along with laces or fine muslins, but must not come in contact with anything dirty. After blueing, and while still wet, put them through clear starch of a moderate thickness, rather thicker than for ordinary muslins ; let the starch soak well through them, and then squeeze out with the hands. Shake them out well, put them between the folds of a towel, and pass them through the wringing machine. To prepare them for ironing pull them out well, and roll up from left to right, keeping the muslin the same width all the way along. If there are hems at the ends of the ties, notice which is the right side, and keep the right side inside when rolling. Cover each tie up as it is prepared, to prevent it becoming dry,

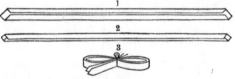

until all are finished, and it is time to iron them. To iron one of these ties, take a moderately hot iron, commence at the loose end of the roll, and iron carefully along from one end to the other, unrolling as required. Iron along several times until smooth and glossy, ironing on one side only. Turn over, and it is ready for folding. First turn down a small piece at the top of the tie, just sufficient to take in the rough edge of the material, and press it down with the iron. Next turn up a piece at the foot of the tie, rather larger than that at the top, and according to the width the points are to be (Fig. 1). Be careful to have both ends alike, and press down with the iron again. Fold down the top piece again, making the tie the same width all the way along. Measure the two points, and if they are exactly alike, iron along once more (Fig. 2). Fold loosely in four, and tie a thread round the centre to prevent it slipping (Fig. 3).

Chiffon.—Chiffon is washed in the same way as muslin, and after rinsing, put through very thin clear starch. Be careful not to twist it in any way, but enclose it in the folds of a towel, and either beat it between the hands until dry or put it through the wringing machine. Do not let chiffon lie too long before ironing, it dries so very quickly ; stretch it out to its proper shape, and iron it on the right side with a moderately

hot iron. If it is a large piece, do not expose too much of it to the air at one time, but keep the part you are not ironing covered over to prevent it becoming dry. Pull out occasionally whilst ironing to keep it soft, and iron over again. It must on no account be made stiff, but ought to fall softly, and just have sufficient stiffness to prevent it looking limp.

SILKS, PRINTS, AND FANCY ARTICLES

Washing of Silk.—There are many silks which can be washed quite easily and made to look equal to new, more especially the soft silks, such as Japanese, Tussore, Foulard, &c., but corded and glacé silks will not be successful, and it is wiser to have these dry-cleaned.

If a number of different silks have to undergo treatment, commence by dividing them into lots —white silks by themselves, light-coloured ones in another heap, and the darker and brighter-coloured ones in a third lot apart.

To wash *white silk* prepare a lather of tepid water and soap jelly. Squeeze the silk well in this, and work it up and down in the water. Take two or three different soapy waters if necessary until the silk is quite clean. Never use the water too hot, as it would make the silk yellow, and never rub soap on white silk for the same reason. If the pieces of silk are small, or if they are silk handkerchiefs, a basin will be quite large enough for washing in, and then less soap will be required. At the same time the basin must be large enough to enable one to work comfortably.

After washing, rinse the silk thoroughly, first in tepid, and then in plenty of cold water, letting the water from the tap rush on the silk, or letting it lie in clear cold water for a short time. It is most important to get the soap well out of the silk, or it will look thick and feel hard when ironed. Pure white silk should have a little blue added to the last rinsing water, to bring back its clear bluish colour.

Coloured Silks should be soaked for a short time before being washed in cold water with a little salt in it.

If the colour is inclined to run, this will prevent it doing so to a certain extent. Silks of different colours should be soaked separately. Wash the silks in the same way as white silks, still using the water tepid, as hot would be more apt to draw out the colours. If the colour comes out very much, hurry through the process as much as possible, and do not let the silk lie about between the different waters, especially where there is a mixture of colours in the silk, as one colour would run into the other. It is better to put the articles as quickly as possible from one water to the other.

A little salt should be added to the last rinsing water to help to fix the colour, or with blues, greens, pinks, and reds a little vinegar sometimes restores and brightens the colour.

To Put a Gloss on Silk.—After rinsing put the silk through cold water with methylated spirits in it, allowing one dessert-spoonful of the spirit to half-pint of cold water. There is no occasion to prepare a large quantity of this, but there must be sufficient to soak the silk thoroughly. Then squeeze well out.

Wringing and Ironing.—In wringing silk be most careful not to twist it in any way, as it will then have a drawn look and a washed appearance when finished. Squeeze the silk between the hands, then shake it out, fold it evenly, and place it between the folds of a towel or piece of muslin, and afterwards either beat it between the hands or pass it once or twice through the wringing machine. Be careful that there is no starch on the rollers when putting it through the wringer. The silk may lie for some time rolled up in a towel, but must not be allowed to get too dry before ironing, as to sprinkle it with water afterwards would give it a spotted appearance. If it should happen to get dry, it will have to be put into water again, or damped all over with a wet rubber. Before ironing, smooth the silk out well on the table, lay over it a piece of muslin or old handkerchief, and iron over with a moderately hot iron. When slightly dry, remove the covering, and iron with the bare iron, first on one side and then on the other, to give the silk a gloss. If the silk feels in the least hard after ironing, shake it and rub it between the hands, and then iron again. The silk when finished should be as smooth and soft as when new. Some silks look better without being glazed. These should never be touched with the iron, but have something between them and it. If a very hot iron is put on wet silk, it will stick to it and crinkle it up. That is the reason why the silk should be covered when the ironing is commenced.

In ironing coloured silks do not use the iron too hot or it will destroy the colours; and if the colour is coming out to any extent, spread a piece of clean cloth over the ironing sheet to prevent the silk staining it.

A Silk Slip.—Wash according to directions already given, and after rinsing put it through gum water in the proportion of two table-spoonfuls of the melted gum (see p. 290) to one quart of water. Add also a little methylated spirits to gum water, and let the silk soak in this for half-an-hour. This will give a gloss to the silk and also impart the slight stiffness which is found in new silk. Squeeze out with the hands, lay smoothly between the folds of a towel, and pass it through the wringing machine. Shake out and wrap again in a dry towel, and allow it to remain a few hours, if possible, before ironing. To iron the slip commence with the sleeves, ironing these on a sleeve-board if possible, but if this is not available iron first the upper and then the under half of the sleeve, then well up into the drawings at the top and at the wrist

if there are any. If the sleeve is gathered or pleated, a little management with the point of the iron will be required to prevent its being creased. It is somewhat difficult to give definite instructions, as shapes and styles vary so much. The easiest way must always be taken, and that which crushes the material least.

Next iron the bodice part. Place the neck at the left-hand side and commence with the piece lying nearest the edge of the table, and work gradually along until the other side is reached. Iron up into any gathers with the point of the iron, and smooth well round the armhole. If the silk becomes dry damp it over with a wet rubber, but do not sprinkle it. When the silk part is finished, press out any lace or embroidery on the wrong side and iron any tapes. If there are any lace frills these may be goffered (see p. 284). Then dry the silk slip thoroughly before laying it away.

Washing of Prints.—When prints are being washed for the first time, and there is danger of the colour running, it is well to soak them in cold water with salt in it beforehand. Allow a handful of salt to one gallon of water. Wash them in tepid water, making a lather with boiled soap the same as for flannels. In fact, the water in which flannels have been washed, if it continues clean enough, will be suitable for the washing of prints and coloured things. Give them at least two soapy waters, squeezing and rubbing them gently with the hands until they are quite clean. Pay particular attention to the most soiled parts. If there is the least fear of the colour running, do not rub soap on them. After they have been washed several times, and when the colour is ascertained to be fast, the prints may be washed by the ordinary method for white cotton articles. Some prints will even stand boiling, but do not attempt this unless it is quite certain there is no danger of their colour being destroyed. When clean, rinse the prints, first in tepid water and then in plenty of clear cold water. Add salt or ammonia, one table-spoonful to a gallon, to the last rinsing water when the colours are not fast. Vinegar is good for restoring blues, and ox-gall for dark colours. The strength of the colour depends very much upon the quality of the material. If the colours have been properly mixed before being used for printing, they will stand soap and water perfectly; if not, careful washing will not prevent them fading. When water becomes tinged with the colour of the material that has been washed in it, it must be poured away at once and not used for anything else. Goods of different colours which are not fast must be washed separately. After rinsing, wring them out, fold evenly, and pass them once or twice through the wringing machine. In all cases, when washing coloured articles, avoid the use of soda and washing powders.

Starching and Ironing.—When coloured things are only wished slightly stiff, they should be put through thin clear starch while they are still wet. Wring them again after starching, and then either roll up in a towel and let them lie some time before ironing, or hang them up to dry slightly. If wished very stiff, let them dry first, and then starch. Do not use the starch too hot or it will destroy the colours, and when ironing them do not use the iron too hot for the same reason.

Iron on the right side, except in cases where the pattern is raised or dull and a gloss would be unsuitable. When ironing any fancy article with sewed work, press out the sewed part on the wrong side over flannel.

How to Starch and Iron a Cotton Petticoat.—It is not necessary to starch the whole of the garment. It will generally be found sufficient if it is just starched about a quarter of a yard up from the foot, or to the top of any tucks or embroidery. The starching may be done before the petticoat is hung up to dry. Have a basin of clear starch, not very thick; dip the foot of the petticoat into this, squeeze the starch well through it, and then pass it once or twice through the wringing machine. In wringing put the band end through first.

Or the petticoat may be starched dry. Sprinkle it well with water down as far as the tucks or frills, and then dip the foot part into the starch in the same way as before. The petticoat being dry, the starch will not require to be quite so stiff. After starching and wringing, roll the petticoat up tightly with the starched part inside, and let it lie rolled up in a towel for some time before ironing. If the petticoat is made of rather thick material, it will be as well to hang it up to dry slightly before commencing to iron it.

To iron a petticoat or skirt of any kind well it is necessary to have a skirt-board. It will not only be better, but much more quickly done. Have the narrow end of the skirt-board at your left-hand side, and place it in a good light. Cover it with a small sheet kept for the purpose, and pin the sheet tightly underneath, so that there is no fear of it wrinkling up. If there is embroidery on the petticoat, put it on the board with the wrong side out to begin with, and the band of the petticoat towards the narrow end of the board. Iron the embroidery first, pressing it well out so as to raise the pattern. If there are two or more embroidered frills, commence with the lowest one; iron it first, then turn it back, and iron the second one, and so on. When the embroidery is finished, turn the petticoat on the right side. If there are frills on it, iron the plain piece under the frills first, then the frills themselves, except when they are made of embroidery, when they already have been ironed. Iron the plain top part of the petticoat last; let it be pretty damp, and iron it firmly, so as to get it smooth and glossy. If it has become in the least dry, damp it down with a wet rubber, or it will have a rough appearance when finished.

If there are full frills, goffer them before taking the petticoat off the board. If there is more than one, goffer the top one first, and then the lower. When finished, remove the petticoat from the board, iron the waist-band on both sides and the strings, fold the petticoat neatly and hang it up to air.

A Princess Petticoat.—Iron the bodice part of the petticoat as a slip-bodice before putting it on the board; then proceed as above.

A Dress Bodice.—This should not be starched too stiffly or it will be uncomfortable to wear. It is therefore better to starch it when wet, and then wring it well. If very thick, hang it up to dry slightly before ironing. If it is made of thin material, merely roll it up in a towel, and let it lie for a short time.

To iron, commence with the linings—first the neckband, then the sleeves, and lastly the bodice. When ironing the lining of the bodice keep the neck at the left-hand side; commence with the part nearest the edge of the table. When that is ironed, go on to the next piece, and so on until the other side is reached. Do not iron the linings too dry or it will be difficult to get the right side smooth afterwards. Iron all seams out flat. Do the right side of the bodice in the same order, trying to make each piece perfectly smooth. A sleeve-board may be found useful when ironing the sleeves. If there is any lace, iron it before beginning the right side of the bodice. Leave any goffering that is required till the end. Iron round the seam at the armhole to make it soft and comfortable for the arm. Air well, and fold as little as possible.

Holland.—Wash in the same way as white cotton articles. A little tea may be added to the last rinsing water to preserve the colour. Or rinse in water in which a little hay has been boiled. After wringing finish off in the same way as prints.

Chintz.—First shake the chintzes, or brush them with a soft brush, to remove all surface dust. Then soak them in a plentiful supply of cold water overnight. If they are very dusty it is a good plan to change the water once or twice during this time. Then wring out and proceed with the washing. Although the colours in chintzes, and especially the better ones, are almost invariably fast, it is wise to take every precaution against their running the first time they are washed. Wash chintzes in the same way as prints, punching and pounding them well in the soapy water. A little liquid ammonia may be added to the water if it requires softening. A second soapy water will generally be found necessary, and the process of squeezing and pounding should be repeated. When the chintzes appear to be quite clean, rinse them well in plenty of warm water, and then in cold water until it is free from soap. Then wring tightly, and next put them through rather thick starch, and hang outside to dry. When quite dry, starch a second time in hot-water starch, pounding and squeezing the starch well into the material. Pass through the wringer once or twice, then shake out and hang up indoors until dry enough for ironing. Take them down, and roll up in a cloth until they can be ironed. Or if there are straight pieces of material, these may be mangled first. Iron with hot and heavy irons, finishing off with the polishing iron. Each iron should be well rubbed on a little bees'-wax before it is used, as this will make it iron smoothly and help to give a gloss to the chintz. Finish off with the polishing iron (see p. 300) if a very high gloss is desired.

Note.—Instead of starch, size is sometimes used for the stiffening of chintz. Take a penny packet of size and dissolve it in half a gallon of boiling water. When lukewarm put in the chintz and let it soak one hour. Then wring out and hang up until sufficiently dry to iron.

TO WASH GLOVES

Cotton Gloves.—If very much soiled rub them with soap and let them soak in tepid water for several hours. Paraffin soap is good, especially if the gloves are soiled. Then rub well and squeeze out the dirty water. Wash again with hot water and soap until perfectly clean. Pay particular attention to the most soiled parts. It is sometimes a good plan to put them on the hands and brush them with a nail brush. Rinse in tepid water and then in cold, adding a little blue to the cold water for white gloves. Wring out and hang up to dry. They may be pressed with a moderately hot iron when nearly dry.

Silk Gloves.—Wash these in the same way as other silk articles—rinse and hang up to dry. When nearly dry press with an iron.

Chamois Leather and Doe-skin Gloves.—Wash and dry according to directions given for chamois leather (p. 289). Rub occasionally whilst drying and pull them into shape. The best way to dry them is to put them on wooden hands sold for the purpose.

Woollen Gloves.—Wash and dry in the same way as other woollen articles. Pull them out well whilst drying or put them on wooden hands.

COLLARS, CUFFS, AND SHIRTS

Importance of having them well Washed.—The above should be washed according to general directions already given (p. 278), and dried thoroughly. It cannot be too strongly impressed that unless the process of washing is well carried out, no amount of care in the starching and ironing will make the articles look well. It is a good plan when washing to give the articles a good brushing on the washing-board. Collars especially are so liable to be stained with the heat of the neck that, unless they are thoroughly

washed and rinsed, when they reach the stage of being ironed the iron will only show up the faulty work. A little extra trouble taken in the washing will save much future disappointment. Then again care must be taken in the drying. Dry in a clean place and dry thoroughly, or they will not take in the starch properly, and will be limp when finished.

All articles which are wanted very stiff should be starched in cold-water starch.

How to Starch Collars and Cuffs.—Before commencing the process have everything at hand that is likely to be required—a basin of cold water, a basin of cold-water starch (see p. 281), a plate, one or two clean towels, and a piece of clean soft rag to use as a rubber.

Mix the starch well up from the foot of the basin; put into it several of the collars and cuffs, or as many as the starch will cover easily at one time, and let the starch soak well through them. Squeeze them with the hands in the starch, and then wring as dry as possible and lay them on the plate, and do the others in the same way. They must not be put through the wringing machine, or too much of the starch would be taken out.

Take a collar or cuff at a time; rub it between the hands to get the starch well through the different folds of linen, draw out straight, and lay smoothly on the towel. Commence a few inches from the top of the towel, so that there is a dry piece to double over. Then proceed with the others in the same way; lay them close together on the towel, but do not put one on the top of the other.

Do not use the starch when it gets very low in the basin, but always have a plentiful supply to work with, so that it may not cake on the articles. When all are starched, put the basins of starch and water out of your way, and spread out the towel on the table to be ready for the collars and cuffs.

Roll up tightly and beat the bundle between the hands so as to bring the different folds of material together, and lay aside for an hour at least before ironing.

Method of Ironing Cuffs.—To carry out this process successfully it is absolutely necessary to have first a really hot iron and one which has been well dusted, the sides and top as well as the bottom, and then rubbed on a little bees'-wax or candle-end to make it run smoothly; and, secondly, a smoothly covered ironing table or ironing board without any objectionable wrinkles.

Do not take out more than one cuff or collar from the towel at one time, and keep the others well covered. If they get dry, they will not iron properly, and it is impossible to damp them over, as it would take out too much of the starch. Spread the cuff out on the table with the wrong side uppermost, and smooth away all wrinkles with a paper-knife. If there is any extra fulness on the wrong side, push it over to the edges, where it will not be seen. Iron once or twice across on the wrong side until slightly dry, then turn to the right. See that it is quite smooth before putting the iron down on it ; iron it well, and then go back again to the wrong side. Iron slowly at first, until the cuff gets pretty dry and smooth ; then iron more and more quickly backwards and forwards, until the cuff is quite dry and the surface glossy. Iron principally on the right side, as it is there that the most gloss is wished, but iron the wrong side smooth enough to prevent it feeling rough to the skin. Lift the cuff occasionally when ironing to let the steam escape, and dry the sheet underneath it with the iron before laying it down again.

When several cuffs have thus been ironed, they may be polished with the polishing iron (see p. 292), or if not, rounded into shape with the iron and placed near the fire to become thoroughly crisp and dry.

Collars.—These are ironed in very much the same way as cuffs, first on the wrong and then on the right side. When there are points to be turned down, be careful to iron them most on the wrong side of the collar, as that will be the side which will show most. When turning them down, make a mark first with the side of the iron, on the right side of the collar, then press down with the fingers. Do not iron down with the iron, as it is apt to cut the linen. Then turn the collar. When the whole collar is turned over, be careful to notice which is the right side before beginning to iron. Lift up any tabs there may be on the collars ; dry underneath them with the iron, and then iron down again.

Eton Collars.—Iron the band first, stretch it well, and iron on both sides until dry, being careful not to iron the collar itself so as to dry it. Then stand the band up, and make the collar lie flat on the table. Iron round it slowly—first on the wrong side, keeping the band well stretched to prevent any creases where they are joined. Do not iron too long on the wrong side, or the right will become so dry that it will be impossible to iron it smoothly. Turn and iron the right side until dry ; smooth and then turn with the fingers.

A Front.—Iron the neckband first on both sides until dry, or if there is a collar attached, finish it off before commencing the front. Iron the front on the right side only, and it is not necessary to iron the wrong ; and if there is any fulness, smooth it away towards the sides before commencing to iron. Stretch the neckband well when ironing towards the neck to prevent creases. Then work the iron quickly up and down the front to get a good gloss. (For Polishing of Collars, &c., see p. 292.)

A Gentleman's White Shirt.—Have the shirt perfectly dry, and keep it on the wrong side until it is about to be ironed. Commence with the cuffs ; place them evenly together, and gather them up in the left hand. With the right hand wet the cotton part just above the cuffs with cold water, as this will prevent the starch from spreading up the sleeve where it is not required. Then dip the cuffs into the starch, and squeeze the starch well through them. Starch right up to the top of the cuffs, but do not let the starch go any further. Wring out tightly, and rub with the hands in the same way as other cuffs.

Next starch the front. Place the two halves of it evenly together, and gather them up in the hands, commencing at the back of the neckband, and gathering down to the foot of the front. Wet carefully down the side of the front to prevent the starch spreading on to the body of the shirt, at the same time being careful that no drops of water fall on the front itself, which might cause blisters when ironing. Then dip the fronts and neckband into the starch and squeeze the starch well into them. A mere dip in and out again is not sufficient ; the starch must be forced through the different layers of linen. Wring out and rub between the hands. After starching spread the shirt on the table with the front uppermost and the neck nearest the edge of the table. Smooth out the front and give it a light rub over with a clean dry cloth or rubber. Fold it double, the neck towards the bottom of the shirt. Place the sleeves across the back, smoothing out the cuffs, and double the shirt again so that the sleeves are inside. As it is now folded, sprinkle it well with water on both sides, roll tightly up from one end to the other, and keep covered over until it has to be ironed. A shirt should lie for an hour at least before being ironed, but must not be allowed to become too dry.

To Iron a Shirt.—First turn the shirt on to the right side, and place it on the table with the front uppermost and the neck towards the edge of the table. Turn the yoke forwards, so that it lies flat on the top of the back of the shirt, and iron the yoke first on the right side, then turn it back, slip the iron inside, and iron it on the wrong. Next iron the neckband, first on the wrong and then on the right, ironing it until quite dry. Finish it off well, particularly at the button-holes, and be careful not to iron down on to the front of the shirt. When these are done, fold the shirt down the centre of the back, keeping the front apart from it. Iron the back on both sides, always keeping the neck at the left-hand side. Open out, so that the whole of the back lies uppermost on the table, and iron round the back of the armholes, and this finishes the back.

Next fold the shirt double lengthways with the front inside to prevent its becoming dry, and place it on the table with the sleeves lying out to right. Throw back the upper sleeve, and commence with the under one. Iron the cuff first on the wrong and then on the right, in the same way as other cuffs, then run the iron up inside the cuff and iron the thick part over the drawings. Iron also the wrong side of the hems at the opening of the sleeve, and turn the cuffs into shape. Smooth out the sleeve, and iron first on one side, ironing well into pleats or gathers at the top and bottom, and put a pleat into the sleeve itself if necessary. Turn down the shirt at the neck so that the other side of the sleeve can be ironed, but do not change the position of the shirt itself.

Then iron the second sleeve in exactly the same manner, the ironed sleeve being turned back and underneath the shirt out of the way. When both are finished, place the shirt on the table with the front uppermost and the neck at your left-hand side. Arrange the back in pleats, and press them down with the iron. Then iron the breast of the shirt; slip a shirt-board up in between the back and the front, without dis-

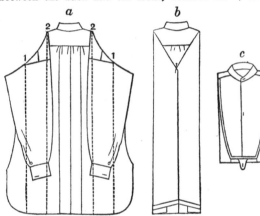

arranging the pleats down the back. Stretch the upper half of the breast on to the board first, drawing the other half as much out of the way as possible. Tuck the cotton part of the front underneath the board, so as to keep the breast firm. Smooth away all wrinkles on the breast with a paper-knife, pushing any fulness over towards the sides. Hold the neck firmly with the left hand, iron slowly up the centre, then gradually towards the sides. As it becomes smooth, iron up and down more quickly, lifting the breast occasionally to let the steam escape. Keep stretching it well with the left hand to prevent any wrinkles forming round the collar. Do the other side in the same way, and then hold both firmly together, and iron quickly and firmly up and down the breast to get a good gloss.

When the breast is finished, slip out the shirt-board and arrange the cotton part of the front smoothly on the top of the back, putting a pleat down the centre where required. Damp it over if it has become dry, and then iron it smoothly. If the shirt has to be polished with the polishing iron, do so now; but if not, fold it.

To Fold a Shirt.—First put a pin in the neck to keep the two sides together, then turn it over so that the back is uppermost and the neck at the left-hand side. Turn the sleeves down the sides of the back (Fig. a), noticing that both are turned in from exactly the same place on both sides. Turn over them a small piece from the sides by dotted line 1 (Fig. a); then turn over again from dotted line 2 (Fig. a), so that both sides meet down the centre of the back. Stretch them rather tightly, so that the front will have a curved look, and pin them firmly together (Fig. b). Hang up to air, and then fold so that the front only shows (Fig. c).

A Lady's Shirt.—After it is rinsed put it through rather thin clear starch and hang it up to dry. This gives a slight stiffness to the body part of the shirt. When quite dry starch the cuffs and collar in cold-water starch, being careful to wet previously just above the cuffs and below the collar with cold water to prevent these parts becoming stiff with the starch. If there is a plain band down the front, and this is liked stiff, dip it also in the cold-water starch. Rub the starch well in and then smooth the parts over with a clean rubber. Sprinkle the dry parts of the shirt with cold water and roll up tightly. Let it lie for an hour or two at least before ironing.

To iron the shirt, open it out and turn it on the right side. Commence with the collar, stretch it out, and iron first on the wrong and then on the right side. Next iron the yoke on both sides and then proceed to the sleeves. Iron these in the same way as the sleeves of a gentleman's shirt, or slip them on to a sleeve-board. Use a small iron for running up into the gathers at the top, and try to avoid creases. To iron the bodice place the shirt on the table with the neck at the left-hand side. Commence with the front lying nearest the edge of the table, smooth it out and iron it well. Next iron back and then the other front. Finish off by ironing the parts round the armholes, also the hems on the wrong sides and any strings. The cuffs may now be polished if wished, then turn them into shape and hang the shirt up to air.

To Fold the Shirt.—First pin the two sides together at the neck, and pleat the front if desired. Then lay the sleeves down the sides of the back the same as in a gentleman's shirt (Fig. a); fold them upwards again so that the cuffs show above the neck, and pin them into position. Fold over the sides so that they meet down the centre, and pin them together. Fold quite loosely; any pressing would crush the sleeves.

INFANTS' AND CHILDREN'S CLOTHING

Preliminary.—In washing infants' clothing it is always better to keep the articles separate, and not to mix them with other clothes. Special attention must be given to them, and in dressing they require very dainty handling.

The water used in washing must be changed as soon as it becomes in the least degree dirty.

Neither soda nor washing powders must on any account be used, as they are irritating to the skin.

Baby's Robes and Robe Skirts.—If time permits, allow these to soak for an hour or two in tepid water before washing. When about to wash, wring them out of the soaking water, and wash in water as hot as the hand can bear. It is best to wash these carefully with the hands. Being fine, they will not bear being rubbed on a board or with a brush. Rub soap on them, and pay particular attention to the most soiled parts. If the material is fine, use melted soap (see p. 287). Go methodically over every part; wash first on one side and then on the other, and give them a second soapy water if they are not clean after the first. Then boil if necessary, and afterwards rinse, blue, and wring (see p. 278). Give them throughout very careful treatment, as the least unnecessary strain is apt to tear them or cause holes.

After wringing, put through the thinnest possible starch and wring again. Then dry partially, roll up in a towel, and let them lie a short time before ironing, but not long enough to become dry.

To iron a robe skirt cover a skirt-board with a fine sheet, and put the skirt on it with the wrong side out. Iron any lace round the foot and embroidery on this side, pressing it well with the iron to make the pattern stand out. Then turn, and iron the rest of it on the right side. If any of the muslin part has been dried with the ironing on the wrong side, damp it down before ironing it on the right. If there are any tucks, iron them first, stretching them out well before ironing, and getting them quite free from creases. Iron the plain part of the skirt from the bottom upwards, and keep drawing it towards you as you go along. Do not let it stick to the ironing-sheet, but keep lifting it up from time to time. Should it get dry before the ironing is finished, wet the end of a towel and damp the muslin over lightly with it. The muslin must on no account be ironed dry, or it will have a rough appearance, instead of looking smooth and glossy.

The skirt of a *robe* is ironed in the same way. Iron the embroidery on the front of the bodice before turning the robe on to the right side. After turning, finish the skirt of the robe before doing the bodice. If the bodice has become dry, damp it down before ironing. Iron as much of it as possible on the board, using a small iron so as to get into the corners well. Any frills that cannot be done on the board may be left until the robe is taken off. The embroidered flaps or side-pieces on the front of some robes are better left until the end and ironed off the

board, the muslin part of them on the right side, and the embroidery on the wrong. Do the sleeves whichever way is found easiest. Sometimes they are wide enough to allow of the iron being slipped inside them, or they may be managed more easily by putting a roll of flannel inside and ironing over that. Goffer or crimp any frills that require it; iron out any strings, and then air well.

A Piquée Pelisse.—Wash according to general directions (see p. 278), and starch while wet in thin hot-water starch. Allow it to dry slightly before ironing.

Iron all embroidery first on the wrong side, over flannel, until it is quite dry. The piquée itself must be ironed on the right side to give it a gloss. Commence with the cape, iron it from one end to the other, and have the coat part of the pelisse turned back from under it so that the cape itself lies single on the table. Then iron the sleeves—lay out one at a time smoothly on the table, and iron first the upper and then the under part. Then lay the pelisse on the table with the neck at your left-hand side, turn the cape back, and iron the coat itself. Iron the piece nearest to you first, smooth out each piece as you go along, always keeping it lying the one way, and draw the coat towards you as you get it ironed. Press well with the iron to get a gloss. Double by the shoulders and sides, and finish off round the armholes; also iron the hems on the wrong side. Then finish by goffering any trimming that requires it; air well, and fold loosely.

Stays.—When washing these, place them on the washing-board and use a brush to brush them with. Being made of firm material, they will bear a good rubbing. Boil them if necessary, and after rinsing put them through thin hot-water starch. On no account make them stiff. Allow them to dry slightly, and iron first on one side and then on the other until quite dry. Stretch well while ironing, as the quilting is inclined to pucker. Hang up in a warm place to air before laying away.

Pinafores.—These should always be slightly starched; if left quite limp they will not keep their appearance any time, and will very soon soil. Muslin pinafores should be put through stiffer starch than those made of diaper and other fancy white material, and must always be starched wet. Diaper and other kinds of pinafores may be starched either wet or dry, and the starch should be quite thin. Pinafores made of muslin and other thin material should be wrung well and rolled in a towel for some time before ironing. Those made of thicker material may be slightly dried and then rolled up.

When ironing pinafores always commence with the embroidery, pulling it out well and ironing very carefully. The rest of the pinafore is as a rule very simple to iron. Always keep the top of the pinafore at the left-hand side, and iron the material single when possible. If the pinafore is joined up the back, iron it double—first the front and then the back, or iron it on a skirt-board. If there are tucks along the foot of the pinafore, stretch them out well when ironing to prevent them dragging. Iron as much as possible with the thread of the material. A small iron must be used for getting into all gathers. Always finish off well round arm-holes and iron out all strings, and run round hems on the wrong side. If there is a full drawn front on the pinafore it sometimes looks well crimped. Goffer or crimp all frills that require it, and fold neatly.

Knickerbockers.—After washing these, wring and let them dry slightly before ironing. On no account must the frills be starched, as the stiffness would irritate the tender skin of young children. Iron the frills first, then the waist-band on both sides. Keep the waist at the left-hand side when ironing the legs, and iron first the front and then the back of them. Iron whichever way crushes them least. There is such a variety of shapes that it is difficult to give definite rules. Iron well into gathers, and hems on the wrong side. Crimp the frills, and then fold neatly.

Flannel Binders, Pilches, and Barracoats.—Wash and dry these according to general directions given for washing and drying flannels (p. 287). They should, when possible, be dried in the open air ; it gives them a sweeter and fresher smell. When nearly dry, iron them all over with a cool iron to make them smooth and soft. Iron all strings and bindings, and be most particular to air well.

Knitted Socks and Bootees.—Wash these carefully in a lather of warm water and boiled soap, and rinse in warm water (see p. 287). If white, a little blue should be added to the last rinsing water. Pay great attention to the drying of these, as they are liable to shrink. Wooden blocks of different sizes are to be had for stretching them ; they are put on to these while still wet, and allowed to remain until dry. A simpler block may be cut out of a piece of cardboard the exact size and shape required, and in some ways this is even better than wood, as in this case pins can be put through the cardboard and the sock stretched in length as well as breadth. Failing to get either of these, pin the socks out to their proper shape on a covered table or board.

Knitted Jackets and Drawers.—For the washing of these, see p. 287. When drying them, see that they are pulled out to a proper shape before hanging up. If they are not very thick, it is almost better to pin them out on a covered table or floor, and allow them to remain there until dry.

Wincey and Serge Dresses.—These are both washed in the same way. Shake well before washing to free them from all superfluous dust.

Soak them in warm water with a little ammonia, and let them remain from twenty to thirty minutes. This softens them and makes them easier to wash. Wring them out and wash in the same way as flannels (see p. 287). Pay particular attention to the most soiled parts. Rinse thoroughly, adding a little blue to the last rinsing water for white or blue serge. Hang up to dry with the wrong side out, and if drying indoors turn and shake occasionally during the process. When nearly dry, iron with a cool iron. Wincey especially requires a good deal of pressure bestowed on it. Navy blue serge should be ironed on the wrong side only ; it would not look well to glaze it.

Smocks.—Smocking must never be pressed with the iron, but only steamed. Iron the rest of the garment first, leaving the smocking to do last. It takes two people to steam it. Let a moderately hot iron be held with the bottom upwards by one, while a second holds the smocking firmly on the top of it, and draws it slowly over the surface of the iron until it becomes quite dry. The heading round the top of the smocking should be ironed with a small iron, and if it is a starched material, afterwards goffered.

Boys' Sailor Suits.—These require very careful washing. They are as a rule made of drill or jean, materials which are both very hard to wash. Being of a firm texture, they will stand a good deal of rubbing and a brush on the washing-board. They may be boiled after washing if there is no fear of any colour in them running. After rinsing, starch while still wet. The starch must not be stiff, as the material itself is of a stiff nature. Wring well, and dry slightly before ironing. Be careful to choose a very clean place for drying, and dry with the wrong side out.

To iron the trousers turn them on the right side, smooth them out on the table, with the waist at your left-hand side and the front uppermost. Iron the fronts of the two legs first, but not too dry ; turn over and iron the back, then iron over the fronts again. Iron bands and hems on the wrong side, and press hard with the iron to get a good gloss.

In ironing the jacket, commence with the collar, and if this is of navy blue or scarlet, iron it on the wrong side only, or on the right with something laid over it ; it should not be glossed. Next iron the sleeves on the right side, first the upper and then the under half. In doing the jacket itself, keep the neck at the left-hand side, commence with the piece nearest to you, and iron from one end to the other, smoothing out each piece as it is reached. Then finish off at the shoulders, round armholes, and the inside of the jacket. Blue linen suits must not be polished with the iron, but either ironed entirely on the wrong side or ironed with something over the material.

Silk Dresses, Pinafores, and Veils.—For the washing of these, see p. 292. After a silk dress is wrung, starch any lace there may be on it in very thin starch, and hang it up to dry for a short time. Iron the lace first on the wrong side, then any linings or double parts on the wrong side. Next iron the sleeves with a small iron, first the upper and then the under part, ironing well into the gathers. If the dress is smocked, leave the smocking to the last (see p. 299). If there is a bodice, iron it before doing the skirt. Do the skirt either on the skirt-board or by laying it double on the table, and ironing first the front and then the back. If the silk is very wet in parts, iron with something over it to begin with, to prevent the iron sticking to and scorching it. When the silk is embroidered, press out the embroidery on the wrong side after the silk is ironed. It is not necessary to goffer the lace on a silk dress, as it looks better falling softly. Goffering would be out of place unless merely for a narrow frilling on the neck.

Silk Pinafores are ironed in the same way as others (see p. 298). The lace on them may be slightly starched, but do not goffer it.

Silk Veils should be pinned out on a covered table or board while still wet, and allowed to remain until dry. If they feel in the least degree stiff after they are removed, rub gently with the fingers to soften the silk again.

Blankets.—These being small may be washed in the same way as white flannels (see p. 287). Dry in the open air if possible, and then air before the fire.

POLISHING

When about to polish, have ready at hand a polishing board, a basin of cold water, a piece of soft rag, and a well-heated polishing iron. Let everything be particularly clean and free from dust.

To polish *cuffs*, take one at a time ; place it flat on the polishing board, dip the clean rag into the cold water, and then lightly wet the surface of the cuff. On no account must it be made too wet, or it will be apt to blister ; and be careful that no drops of water fall on it. Hold the cuff in position with the left hand, and run the polishing iron up and down it with the right.

There are different kinds of polishing irons ; the one like diagram on p. 274 is to be recommended. It is of a good weight, and has a rounded surface at the one end only. The opposite end is held up while in use, and the iron is swung backwards and forwards from the wrist, the rounded surface doing the polishing. Other kinds are to be had which are held flat while in use, and are worked quickly backwards and forwards on the surface to be polished.

Polishing at first gives the linen a streaky appearance, but it must be continued until the surface is evenly glossed all over. The iron must be changed when it cools. When all the cuffs are polished, turn them into shape. Polish *collars* in the same way, only be particular that you polish the proper side of those that are turned down, or have turned-down points. In polishing a *shirt*, slip up the polishing board without crushing either the front or the back. Polish the breast first, working the iron up and down the length of it, and not across. In all cases remember to wet the surface slightly before polishing. When the breast is finished, draw the board gently out, lay it across the shirt, place the cuffs on it, and polish them. Turn the cuffs into shape, and fold the shirt (see p. 297).

Different kinds of glazes are to be had for polishing linen, which are used instead of the polishing iron. They do not of course give such a high gloss, but by many people are preferred. Directions for using them are generally given with the different kinds. Some are added to the starch, while others are in a liquid form and are rubbed on the surface of the linen when ironing.

Polishing irons should be treated with great care. Their surface is made of polished steel, and if it once gets roughened it will not do such good work.

HOME PETS

THERE is scarcely a British home, from the mansion of the rich to the cottage of the poor, which does not boast of some pet, if it be only the humble domestic cat. The care of pets is a problem, therefore, which must present itself sooner or later to the average housewife. Dumb animals are often sadly neglected, not always willingly it is true, but most often from sheer ignorance of the best way to treat them both in illness and in health. The following notes upon the characteristics of our household pets with directions in regard to their diet and general hygiene, together with hints as to the best methods of treating the common ailments to which they are subject, are intended to give practical guidance to the housewife in all the most important problems in regard to the care and management of her pets with which from time to time she may be called upon to deal.

DOGS

The dog is the most companionable as well as the most faithful of our pets, and, properly trained, he may also become a most useful member of the household.

In purchasing a dog it should be remembered that some breeds are eminently suited for a hardy outdoor life, and for this reason would not thrive as household dogs in a town ; on the other hand, others make admirable indoor pets, provided of course that they have a certain amount of good daily exercise out of doors. " Lap dogs "—a designation which include all the tiny breeds of dogs which form ladies' pets —do not require so much exercise, although they are all the better for it.

Guard Dogs.—Some dogs are especially noted for their qualities as guardians of their master's house and property. Chief amongst these are the Mastiff, Bulldog, Great Dane, Retriever, Newfoundland, and Airedale Terrier. The Mastiff, Great Dane, and Newfoundland are best kept out of doors on account of their size, and for this reason are more suitable for country than for town life. The Bulldog makes a very good indoor dog. Of the smaller dogs, Fox Terriers, Irish Terriers, Skye Terriers, and Bull Terriers make splendid guard dogs.

Companionable Dogs.—The St. Bernard is a most faithful companion and very gentle with children. By reason of his size this dog should also be kept out of doors. The Collie is most companionable and sagacious. To keep in health it requires a very large amount of exercise, and is therefore best kept in the country. The Newfoundland is also companionable and fond of children. Deerhounds, Bloodhounds, Setters, Sheep Dogs are also faithful companions. They are best suited to an outdoor life.

Dogs to keep Indoors in Town.—In choosing a house dog for town it should be remembered that the small short-haired varieties are best on account of the less trouble entailed in keeping them clean. Long-haired dogs bring in mud from the street on their coats, and will often roll on the carpets and furniture in their attempt to get rid of it. Few people will take the trouble to brush the dog as he comes in from his walk, yet this should always be done if he has been in muddy or dusty roads.

The most useful dog for indoor town-life is undoubtedly the Fox Terrier. Sagacious, easily taught, faithful and companionable, he makes as a rule a good watch-dog, and his short coat is easily kept clean. The Irish Terrier is also a most useful dog for town, although he requires careful training on account of his fighting propensities. As has been said before, the Bulldog makes a very good indoor dog and guardian of the house. Skye Terriers and Aberdeen Terriers make capital little house dogs, only the coat of a Skye Terrier is rather a drawback as it requires very careful attention in regard to brushing, combing, and grooming generally. The Basset Hounds and Dachshunds are also excellent little indoor dogs. Spaniels are generally all-round useful dogs, and the Poodle is one of the most sagacious and teachable of our pets.

Pet Dogs.—Pugs, Pekingese, Pomeranians, Griffins, Yorkshire Terriers, King Charles Spaniels, Italian Greyhounds, Maltese Terriers are the principal dogs which rank as ladies' pets. These as a rule are pampered little individuals, accompanying their mistress in her drives and reclining on silken cushions in her boudoir and drawing-room, yet when properly trained and not allowed to become fractious and snappy (a result as a rule of over-feeding) they make charming little companions, with the most ingratiating ways.

Management of Dogs.—It must be remembered that the good qualities of a dog are enhanced by careful training and his faults cured in the same way. It is always better for this reason to rear our pets from puppyhood if we would obtain the most satisfactory results.

Strict cleanliness and judicious feeding are the two great essentials in the management of dogs. Dogs kept in the house should be washed once a fortnight if possible in summer, and once a month in winter. Outdoor dogs do not require such frequent washing. Plenty of warm water and good carbolic soap should be used when bathing a dog; the animal should be well immersed and the soap well rubbed over his coat, thoroughly rinsed off, and, last but not least, he should be well dried. All dogs should be carefully groomed daily. This is most essential with the long-haired varieties, such as Collies, Skye Terriers, &c. For these a strong broad-toothed dog-comb should be used as well as a brush.

Dog-Comb.

Dog-Brush.

Regular and careful grooming often does away with the necessity of such frequent bathing as would otherwise be needed.

Vermin.—If cleanliness in the way of washing and grooming is not strictly attended to, the animal will often be pestered with vermin as a result. Carbolic soap should be used in washing dogs which are afflicted in this manner. In very bad cases the dog should be rubbed all over with oil a few hours before the tub is given. This should be allowed to remain on until washed off in the tub.

The Kennel.—When a dog is kept in a kennel, he should be given fresh straw every week, and this straw should be shaken and turned over

Dog-Kennel.

every day and all soiled straw removed. In summer a piece of matting can be used instead of straw. Do not keep him chained up for a long time at a stretch if it can possibly be avoided. A dog should always have plenty of exercise; besides, the kennel will soon get foul if he is chained up all day.

Needless to say, the kennel must be kept clean, being washed out at frequent intervals. A dog-kennel should always be as roomy as possible, and it should never be allowed to rest right on the ground, on account of the danger of the dog catching cold from damp. The door of the kennel should, if possible, be at the side. When it is in the front the animal cannot get away from the rain and snow which in stormy weather blows through the opening. With the door at the side he can curl up in the corner away from the entrance, and so avoid it. For indoor dogs an old wine-case filled with straw makes an excellent bed. The tiny pets should be provided with little dog-baskets.

Feeding.—Many mistakes in regard to feeding are made by the average dog-owner; it is either a case of " killing with kindness " or semi-starvation through unsuitable food. The mistake first mentioned is the one most often committed, more especially in regard to the strictly house pets. Tit-bits of various kinds are given to them at all hours of the day, to say nothing of sugar, the excessive eating of which is most injurious. Pet dogs should never be allowed in the room at meal-time, particularly when they are versed in the art of " begging " or other similar blandishments, which make it hard to refuse them the tit-bits they covet. A dog should not be fed between meals. Two good meals a day are ample for most of our canine pets. To lap dogs, however, three smaller meals should be given daily. These may consist of meat, vegetables, and Spratt's dog biscuits, with a regular supply of bones. The latter are very good for the dog's teeth. Only large bones should be given—never bones of poultry or game. These are apt to injure a dog's stomach, as they are often swallowed whole. Meat should only be given at the chief meal. Animals which have little exercise should not be given large quantities of meat; it is a mistake, however, to exclude it altogether from a dog's diet. The biscuits can be given dry or soaked. They should always be broken up. The diet should be varied as much as possible—meat scraps from the table with vegetables make a good and suitable meal where one or two indoor dogs are kept, but the amount of meat should be regulated by the amount of exercise they get. Never allow food to be left lying about in the vessels; at meal times give only what is sufficient. Plenty of drinking water must always be at hand, and the drinking vessel must be kept scrupulously clean. Drinking-troughs should not be stood out in the sun in hot weather; the water should be kept in as cool a place as possible.

Above all things be guarded against the mistake of killing your pet with kindness, as is so often the case with strictly pet dogs, such as Pugs, Pomeranians, &c. The poor little animals have to pay in the long run for the indiscriminate pampering they receive at the hands of their mistresses. Their little lives are not only rendered miserable by ever-recurring disease, but in most cases they are materially shortened.

Exercise.—Never forget to let your pets have sufficient exercise. To keep them indoors all day long falls little short of actual cruelty. If you would have them keep strong and healthy, let them be your companions in your daily walks ; remember that exercise is almost as necessary to them as food. The dog should be trained early to follow well out of doors—this is all the more necessary in regard to dogs kept in towns—for the very real dangers of traffic are always present, and it is not safe to take a dog out in the crowded streets if he does not follow well or answer to his mistress's call.

When quite young a dog should always be taken out on a lead. All dogs when out of doors

Collar for Long-haired Dog.

must wear collars with the name and address of their owner inscribed thereon. The collars of long-haired dogs should be rounded in order to preserve their fur. When sending puppies or small dogs away long distances by train they

Dog's Travelling-Basket.

should be placed in a basket with plenty of room for ventilation allowed. Special baskets are sold for the purpose at moderate prices.

Puppies.—Puppies require very careful tending if that great ill of puppyhood, " distemper," is to be avoided. A puppy of a few weeks old when taken from the care of its mother should be fed at least six times a day. The last meal should be given to it late at night; after a late meal he is more likely to rest and refrain from disturbing the slumbers of the household by his yelping. Between six and eight weeks of age is the usual time for weaning puppies.

Milk thickened with meal is the best food after weaning. Later Spratt's puppy cakes soaked in milk may be added. The meals should be decreased as the puppy gets older, and at five months three meals daily will be

sufficient. When he is teething, bones and a very little meat should be added to his diet. Puppies at this time are apt to get destructive, tearing up whatever they come across. For this reason it is well to supply them with plenty of bones to gnaw at, and old boots, shoes, balls, anything which they can tear up and destroy at their will.

Care of the Mother.—The period of gestation is between eight and nine weeks, and during this time the animal should be well fed, and a small dose of olive oil occasionally administered. When the time approaches for the puppies to be born, a bed should be provided for her in some quiet, secluded place, which is warm, airy, and free from draught. The bed should consist of a roomy box or basket into which plenty of clean straw has been placed. Beyond the preparation of the bed, the animal can in most cases be left quite alone until the puppies are born. It is as well, however, especially in the case of a valuable dog, to arrange for the attendance of a skilled veterinary surgeon in the event of complications arising. After the puppies are born, fresh straw should be placed in the box, and the mother should be coaxed to take a little warm beef-tea. Then she should be left undisturbed as much as possible for a few hours. She should have three good meals a day while nursing, consisting of easily digestible food and a little raw meat at first.

Training Dogs.—A puppy should be trained early in the ways of obedience and cleanliness. If he contracts bad habits in his early life and these are left unchecked, it will become increasingly difficult to cure him as he grows older. He should be kept clean and given frequent baths, care being always taken to thoroughly dry him afterwards. He should be supplied with a nice warm bed and kept as free as possible from draughts. Violence and impatience are quite out of place in the training of puppies. By patience, firmness, and perseverance on the part of the owner a puppy will soon get to know who is master ; only firmness and perseverance on the part of the master or mistress are essential in order to achieve the desired result. The little creature must be first made to understand what is wanted and then made to do it. A too liberal use of the whip is inadvisable. A well-known authority on dogs has said that one good beating, if thoroughly deserved, will do good, inasmuch as it will not be forgotten by the little culprit, but to beat the dog on the smallest provocation will spoil his temper and often make him snappy and then ferocious in time. Such a method of training can only be productive of harm. Whilst some dogs are very fond of going into the water after stones, &c., others are afraid to do so. In these circumstances they should never be thrown in, as this will only increase their fear in this direction. Very often a dog may be persuaded to take to the water by seeing other dogs go in, more especially if these dogs are his daily companions ; but he should never be forced to do so.

Ailments.—A dog which is well housed, suitably fed, and well cared for hygienically should always keep-healthy. There are, however, certain ailments to which our canine pets are subject which will sometimes make their appearance in the best-regulated kennels. Unless the ailment is of a strictly minor order it is always better to at once call in a qualified vet. We owe it to our faithful companions and pets that they should have the best attention in sickness. It is as well, however, to be able to recognise the symptoms of the various canine ailments, so that the sufferers may be properly treated in the way of housing, feeding, warmth, &c. We shall therefore describe the symptoms of the chief ailments to which dogs are liable, together with the particular management and attention required to effect a speedy cure.

Administering Medicine.—Small dogs can be taken on the knee of the person who is administering the dose ; very large dogs, such as Mastiffs, usually require a man to handle them. Sometimes the pills or medicine may be mixed with food. When giving a pill, see that it is placed well on the back of the animal's tongue, closing its mouth quickly until the pill is swallowed.

Canker.—This appears in the form of acute inflammation of the ear. The dog will be seen to hold its head on one side as if in pain and to keep on scratching his ear. He must be prevented from doing this as much as possible, as the scratching will only increase the inflammation. The ear should be regularly treated with a good antiseptic solution. If taken in time, this treatment will often be sufficient to ward off a bad attack. Severe cases require special treatment, and a veterinary surgeon should at once be consulted. Very often ear inflammation occurs through accumulation of dust and dirt inside the ears of the dog, which he endeavours to dislodge by scratching. Those who have the welfare of their pets at heart can prevent this state of affairs by gently wiping the inside of the ear of the animal with a piece of soft rag, thus freeing it from all dust and dirt, whenever it is seen to scratch its ear or to be suffering from undue irritation.

Distemper.—Some people think that it is necessary for *all* dogs to have distemper. This is quite a fallacy. If a dog is well housed and kept free from all source of infection, it will seldom have it. Distemper is a most infectious disease and can be contracted from other animals or infected sources, such as bedding, &c.

Symptoms.—It is some time before the symptoms make their appearance, all that is noticeable at first being the fact that the animal is not well. The symptoms are similar to those of a cold—the appetite is poor, a watery discharge comes from nose and eyes, there is a rapid rise of temperature, the discharge from the eyes increases to such an extent that the eyelids often become almost glued together. In all bad cases of distemper it is best to seek the advice of an experienced veterinary surgeon, as many severe complications often ensue.

The patient should at once be isolated and kept in warm and comfortable surroundings. Very careful feeding upon light nourishing food is necessary : the diet should include plenty of milk and beef-tea. All the dog's surroundings should be thoroughly disinfected. Too much emphasis cannot be laid upon the necessity for cleanliness and warmth.

Eczema.—Eczema is often found in over-fed pets, more especially in older dogs. The skin eruption appears most often under the thighs and about the ears and back of the animal. Intense irritation is set up which is accelerated by the continual scratching, and painful sores often result. Careful dieting and regular exercise are necessary. The sores should be treated with boracic ointment. The animal should be kept very clean, and a tonic should be prescribed by a veterinary surgeon to improve the general condition of its health.

Fits.—These occur most frequently in puppies, and may be very slight, consisting merely of convulsive movements of the muscles, or else they may take the form of severe convulsions, with foaming at the mouth, rolling eyeballs, and all the other usual accompanying severe symptoms. Nothing can be done while the attack lasts. Dogs subject to fits should be kept on a very light diet, and aperient medicine should be regularly administered. Sometimes after an attack a dog will rush away at a tremendous speed foaming at the mouth, having altogether the appearance of a mad dog. He will hide himself and not return till the attack has quite passed over. This after-effect of an epileptic seizure may easily be mistaken for rabies, so in order to avoid the disastrous consequences of such a mistaken impression on the part of a stranger it is as well to tie him up until he has altogether recovered.

Hydrophobia.—As has been already pointed out, foaming at the mouth must not be taken to indicate hydrophobia. This dread disease has been stamped out in England, and it is very seldom that a case of hydrophobia is heard of. The surest indication of the disease is a complete change in the disposition of the animal. If, for instance, a good-tempered dog becomes suddenly snappy, ferocious or irritable, and it seems to frequently rub the sides of his mouth with his paw as if to dislodge something from it, it should be looked upon with suspicion, and kept tied up until it can be ascertained if there is any danger of its being attacked by this disease.

Mange is a highly contagious skin disease caused by an animal parasite. Sometimes the parasite takes up its abode on the surface of the skin. In this case a number of small red spots appear which form into sores, the hair falls off in quantities, and an unpleasant odour emanates from the skin. When the disease assumes this form it is known as sarcoptic mange. In follicular mange the parasite is to be found in the hair follicle. Though this form of mange is not so contagious as the sarcoptic form, it is more difficult to cure. Expert veterinary advice should at once be sought when either form of mange makes its appearance. The dog should be at once isolated. Give it a thorough bath and then apply the dressing prescribed to the entire surface of the animal's skin. This is usually composed of sulphur and slaked lime, or sulphur and train oil, the proportion of sulphur used being usually double that of the other ingredient. Allow the dressing to remain on for a few days, then wash it off. If necessary, the process should be repeated. In most cases of sarcoptic mange the destruction of the parasite will be effected after two or three applications of the dressing. The treatment for follicular mange is much more protracted, and the animal should always be sent away to the care of a veterinary surgeon until the cure is effected.

Rheumatism most frequently occurs in old dogs. It is sometimes brought on by confinement in damp and draughty kennels or sleeping on damp bedding, but most often by exposure to wet and cold. Most often it takes a chronic form, and is manifested in extreme stiffness of the joints, the animal having difficulty in walking. There are intervals of great pain and considerable stiffness and lameness, whilst at other times the dog will appear to be quite well. Sometimes the attacks are exceptionally severe. The affected parts should be carefully massaged with some good liniment every day, the dog should be given a warm and comfortable bed, and doses of iodide of potassium with salicylate of soda should be regularly administered.

St. Vitus' Dance.—This disease takes a somewhat similar form to that which it displays in human beings, its presence being indicated by the same twitching of the muscles. Warmth and careful dieting are essential. The patient should be prescribed for by a veterinary surgeon, and medicine regularly administered.

Worms.—A large number of dogs suffer from these internal parasites, as they often pick up the eggs of the various worms with their food and water. Tape-worms are the most frequently prevalent, although they are also infested with round-worms in several cases.

Treatment for Tape-Worms.—The infested dog should be starved for twenty-four hours, then a good vermicide should be administered. This treatment should be followed by a dose of castor oil or some other aperient within two or three hours.

Round-Worms most usually infect puppies, and fits may often be traced to their presence. Puppies should be kept without food for three hours before the vermicide is administered. No aperient is necessary unless the animal is an adult.

CATS

The Care of Cats.—Puss is one of the most common of our domestic pets, and perhaps it is for this reason that, with the exception of valuable animals which are bred for show purposes, she is often sadly neglected. Very few people think of feeding her regularly; one or perhaps two saucers of milk will be allowed her daily, and the rest of her food she is supposed to make up with mice or anything else she can forage for herself.

This is quite a wrong way of bringing up our feline pets: it is simply encouraging them to thieve whatever dainties they can get hold of. A cat who is left to hunt for her own food will not be too particular as to where she finds a meal, and the larder will suffer in consequence.

Properly trained, a cat will become a most docile animal, and a respecter of its master's property, but first of all she must be fed. Milk is not the sum total of all her requirements; she should have at least two good meals daily in addition to the milk allowance. The scraps from her master's table, including bits of meat, gravy, and plenty of green vegetables, will usually be sufficient; but the meals must be given regularly. Bread and milk in the morning, scraps left from the mid-day meal of the household, and another meal of scraps at night will be sufficient, whilst kittens require more frequent feeding. Cats should always have access to grass, which they eat with relish, as this is good for them medicinally. Drinking water should also always be within pussy's reach, as milk is not sufficient to quench her thirst. Cats are very fond of all kinds of fish, and their fancy in this direction should be indulged whenever possible.

The cat, more especially the common short-haired cat, is really one of the hardiest of our domestic pets. Persian and other long-haired cats require more care, and are apt to be more delicate than the ordinary short-haired varieties. A cat can easily be trained in habits of cleanliness, only the training must begin from kittenhood. When a cat is kept in a house where there is no garden, it should always be provided with a good-sized tin tray covered with earth; needless to say, the earth should be frequently changed. Cats are said to become very attached to the houses in which they are brought up, and they have often been known to run away and get lost after a household removal. An old-fashioned plan to prevent this is still often followed. As soon as pussy arrives in the new house, butter is rubbed well over her feet and legs. She will at once begin to lick off the butter, and by the time she has finished this engrossing occupation it is said that all idea of flight will have been abandoned. When a cat is expected to have kittens, a warmly-lined basket should be provided for her in a quiet place. In most cases it will be found necessary to get rid of some of the kittens, but one should always be left, as, apart from any questions of cruelty, it is bad for the mother to have all the young ones taken from her.

Different Kinds of Cats.—The most beautiful of our feline pets are undoubtedly the Persian and Angora varieties. Of these the blue Persians are perhaps the handsomest. Then there are black, white, and tabby Persians all with the beautiful long soft silky fur which is the chief characteristic of their breed. Persians require much more attention than our ordinary common cat, as they are more delicate of constitution; but they are such gentle and beautiful animals that any extra care expended upon them is abundantly repaid.

Other varieties of cats are the Manx, the Siamese, and the Abyssinian. The Manx cat has no tail, and in the colouring of its coat it resembles the British cat. The Siamese cat has a light-coloured body and a dark face, tail, and legs.

The ordinary cat keeps her own coat in good condition by cleaning it with her tongue. Long-haired cats, however, should be brushed and combed daily. During the moulting season this is more than ever necessary, for when long-haired cats moult, if they are not strictly attended to, they will often swallow quantities of hair which may accumulate in the stomach and kill them. The danger of this is obviated by regular and careful grooming.

Common Ailments.—Our ordinary cat is as a rule very hardy; nevertheless there are many ailments with which puss may be overtaken, and as it is said that some of the diseases which attack cats, notably consumption, may be communicated to human beings, the reason for the greatest care is all the more evident.

Colds.—These should not be neglected, as they may often develop into more serious ailments, They are usually indicated by fits of sneezing and catarrh. Keep the cat thoroughly warm and out of draughts, and give her warm milk to drink until the cold has run its course.

Diarrhœa.—Give a tea-spoonful of castor oil, and keep the patient on a very light diet for a day or two.

Distemper.—A veterinary surgeon should be consulted. In addition to administering the medicine he prescribes, pay great attention to diet, give plenty of fish and strengthening food. Isolate the animal, as the disease is infectious.

Puss is generally ailing and out of sorts before the actual symptoms appear. These usually manifest themselves in the form of sneezing and a watery discharge from the eyes and nose.

Fits.—These occur most frequently with kittens, especially when teething. Nothing can be done while the fit lasts, but a dose of castor oil should be administered when the convulsions are over. Be very careful how you lift up a cat in convulsions, always using a good thick cloth for the purpose. Place it at once in its basket out of harm's way. Get veterinary advice as to the general health of the little animal.

Other Diseases.—Cats are also liable to consumption, mange, canker of the ear, eczema, and other diseases. In all cases skilled advice should at once be sought.

CAGE BIRDS

No more cheery pet can be kept in a household than a little feathered songster if it is well tended and its cage kept bright and clean. To keep a bird and yet be wholly ignorant of the right method of caring for it is not only folly, but in many cases this ignorance amounts to actual cruelty. The sum of the requirements of our pet birds is very small, but they should be rigidly attended to. Cage birds suffer more almost than any other pet from the consequences of neglect. Their being kept in confinement produces a certain delicacy which is certainly not one of their characteristics when enjoying the freedom of their natural state.

Before keeping a canary or any other similar pet it must be borne in mind that no cage bird will thrive unless it has a roomy cage, plenty of good suitable food, and clean fresh water both for drinking and bathing purposes, and its cage and surroundings are kept thoroughly clean. Last but not least, the cage must be hung in a bright position, where the little songster may obtain plenty of bright light—not artificial light be it said; there is nothing more unhealthy, for instance, than for a bird to be placed near a gas-jet. Care must also be taken that the cage is well away from all draughts. Given strict attention to these first essentials and also a knowledge of the more common ailments to which our feathered pets are subject, the little captives will thrive and gladden the household with their bright song. They will come to know the hand that tends them, and with a little patience on the part of their keeper they may in time be tamed to almost as great a degree as any other household pet.

Canaries.—There are many varieties of canaries, chief amongst which are the Yorkshire, the Norwich, the Border, the Lizard, the Crest, the Belgian, and the German. Of the English birds the Yorkshire Canary is the most graceful, whilst the best songsters undoubtedly come from the Harz Mountains in Germany. As a rule, the latter are inclined to be delicate when brought over to England : where they are successfully reared, they undoubtedly make the best songsters. In regard to singing, amongst the English birds a mule is often a much better songster than a pure-bred canary, and mule birds are also usually fairly hardy.

Choosing a Canary.—In choosing a canary, care should be taken to go to none but a reputable bird-dealer. Many bird-dealers will send a bird to the customer's house on approval for a day or two in order that she may be able to judge its singing capacity. A reputable bird-dealer as a rule will be pleased to help the purchaser in every way in his power, and will give much valuable advice. In other cases it is always better for the purchaser to take some friend with her who thoroughly understands cage birds and their different points and qualities.

The prices of canaries vary to a great extent. As a rule, however, a very good bird may be had for from 10s. 6d. and upwards, and often 7s. 6d. will purchase a hardy little songster.

The Cage.—The cage should be as large and roomy as possible and furnished with at least three perches, one at each side near the food and water-troughs, and one higher up in the cage. The bottom of the cage should be fitted with a

Canary Cage.

sliding tray which can be taken out, cleaned, and covered with fresh sand daily. A little vessel for water and another one for food are placed at each side of the cage ; in most cages a little recess is built out on either side to hold these vessels with an opening in the cage bars through which the bird can reach its food. In others the food and water vessels are placed on stands inside the cage. A cage made of ordinary wood and wire is very suitable, and can be purchased for from 5s. and upwards. Brass cages are more expensive and more ornamental, but they become dangerous if the bars are not kept thoroughly dry, on account of the verdigris which forms upon them. Enamelled cages may also be had at all prices. In addition to the food and water vessels, a larger vessel should also be placed inside the cage in which the bird can take his daily bath. All vessels must be kept scrupulously clean and should be washed out daily. It is always as well to keep two complete sets of perches, so that while one set is being scrubbed with soap and water, the other set can be placed in the cage. Perches should never be returned to the cage before they are thoroughly dry.

Food and Water.—Canary seed is the chief food for canaries. The seed should be clean and free from grit. The food vessel should always be cleaned before placing the seed into it in the morning. A little fresh green food should also be given daily. Water-cress, groundsel, lettuce, or chickweed are all appreciated by our pets. In the winter, when green food is scarce, a small piece of apple should always be placed between the bars of the cage for the bird to peck at. By way of a delicacy a lump of sugar might also be placed between the bars of the cage : this dainty is much appreciated and serves to keep the bird's beak in good condition ; a piece of cuttle bone for the bird to peck at should also be placed between the bars.

The bottom of the cage should always be covered with good rough sand or gravel put in fresh every morning, to aid the canary in grinding its food. Fresh water should be given every morning for drinking and for the bath. In summer fresh water should be given twice daily. The water vessels should be kept scrupulously clean. For the bath an ordinary saucer or a glass vessel such as is used sometimes for packing potted meat would fulfil all requirements.

Breeding.—Much interest may be derived from the home-breeding and rearing of canaries. Care should be taken to select a hardy pair for mating, and they should be paired about the middle of March. It will be necessary also to buy a breeding-cage. This may be procured

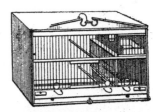

Breeding-Cage.

for a few shillings, and is divided into two compartments by a movable wire partition. The cock and the hen are put into separate compartments, and as soon as the cock is seen to feed the hen through the bars the partition is withdrawn and the cage thrown into one.

The breeding-cage is fitted with a nest-box, and nest-building material should be placed between the bars. As soon as the first egg is laid it should be taken away and a little china egg substituted, and so on with each egg until three have been laid, when they are returned to the nest and the hen sits upon them. Hard-boiled egg mashed up with bread-crumbs should be given daily during the hatching time, in addition to the seed, and plenty of good green food. When the little birds are old enough to leave the nest they may be placed in a separate compartment, where they will be fed by the cock. In addition to the egg, they may now have a little crushed seed, which they will learn to pick up for themselves. When they can feed themselves they may be placed in another cage.

Taming Canaries.—A canary will thrive much better if it can be so thoroughly tamed that it can be allowed to fly about the room for a certain time each day, and may be relied upon to return to its cage of its own accord. One person only should undertake the taming of the little captive in this respect, because it is necessary that the bird should get to know and care for the hand that tends him if any headway is to be made in the taming process. A great amount of patience is required to accomplish this—the bird should be taught to perch on its owner's finger, to feed from her hand. Then the cage-door can be opened and the bird allowed its liberty. At first it will require to be gently coaxed back to its cage by the display of some fresh green stuff or other dainty; but gradually it will return to it of its own accord. Care, of course, must be taken that no cats or other pets liable to harm the little wanderer are allowed in the room. A cat, if taught very young, may be trained to become quite friendly with a canary or any other bird, and to refrain from any attempt to harm it. Much more antagonistic pets than cats and canaries have been known to live together in harmony as a result of careful early training.

Birds in the Aviary.—Several birds of various kinds may be kept together in an aviary, and their rivalling notes will often make a most

Aviary.

delightful harmony. An aviary must on no account be overcrowded. If any of the inmates disagree, it is better to separate the offender from his companions and place him in a cage by himself. Strict cleanliness must, of course, be the rule.

Other Cage Birds.—Amongst other British birds which may be kept successfully as pets are the Bullfinch, Chaffinch, Goldfinch, and Linnet. The Goldfinch is a very fine songster,

and the Bullfinch may be trained to pipe tunes. The Chaffinch can also be trained as a songster, and the Linnet has a very pleasing note. All these birds are fed upon the same seeds as Canaries, and the general treatment is in most ways the same. The Goldfinch, however, needs plenty of hemp and maw-seed, and a Bullfinch needs a more varied diet than the other finches. In addition to a good seed mixture, he should be provided regularly with groundsel chickweed, a little egg occasionally, and meal-worms and other insects when they can be procured. The Chaffinch also requires insect food now and then.

The Soft Bills.—It is not as a rule advisable to keep birds which belong to the class known as "Soft Bills," although as songsters they are unrivalled. But to enable them to thrive in captivity they require the utmost experience and care on the part of those who tend them.

The Nightingale.—The Nightingale takes first place as a songster. It requires a large and roomy cage; the top and back should be of wood and the bars of osier. Shredded raw meat, chopped eggs, meal-worms, beetles, ants' eggs comprise its diet, the principal aim being to make its food partake as much as possible of the nature of that which it enjoys in its natural state.

The Skylark.—The Skylark, if properly tended, thrives well in captivity. Its cage should be a roomy one, and should always contain some green turf. Ants' eggs, meal-worms, meat, and one of the preparations sold as lark food should constitute its diet.

The Blackcap is another good songster, and has to be fed and treated in a very similar manner to the Nightingale.

The Thrush should have a very large roomy cage, which should be cleaned every morning. Its diet should consist of fig-dust moistened with milk and water to form a paste, shredded raw meat, worms, and snails. A stone should be placed in the cage to enable it to break the shells.

The Blackbird.—The Blackbird has a very soft clear note—the treatment of a blackbird in captivity is the same as that of a thrush. Starlings can also be managed in the same manner, as can Magpies, Jackdaws, and Jays. Large roomy cages are the first essentials for all these birds. It is useless to expect them to thrive in an unduly confined space. Strict cleanliness and attention to diet is also essential. On the whole, Canaries and Finches are the most suitable birds for home pets; and we would advocate that no one undertakes the care of birds of the soft-billed variety without having first served an apprenticeship, as it were, in the successful rearing of Canaries and Finches.

Parrots.—Of all the foreign birds which are imported to our shores parrots are perhaps the most popular as home pets. These birds possess the power of imitating human speech and afford an abundance of interest and amusement in this way. When purchasing a parrot, care should be taken that the bird is thoroughly acclimatised, as there is a great amount of mortality amongst them. Upon being brought over here it takes a person of the utmost experience to tend them and train them in accordance with the necessary change of diet and conditions. For this reason never purchase a parrot from any other but a recognised bird-dealer who can guarantee that it has spent at least a season in this country.

The Cage.—A parrot's cage should be large and roomy. In no case should it be less than

Parrot-Cage.

eighteen inches in diameter. The cage should be furnished with a swing which must be of sufficient height for the bird to be able to stand upon the perch without his head touching the swing. It is always advantageous to be able to allow a parrot to come out of his cage occasionally for exercise if he is sufficiently tame ; this can be done with safety if the flights of one wing are clipped. The cage should be placed out of doors on fine sunny days, and during summer it is good for parrots to be put out occasionally during a shower, as many birds object to bathing themselves. In very dry hot weather a little water might also be sprayed upon them once or twice a week, only care must be taken that they do not catch cold afterwards. A strong tinned wire cage may be had for from 12s. 6d.

Feeding.—The chief food for parrots is grain such as hemp, wheat, oats, Indian corn, sunflower seed, and canary seeds, and they also appreciate dainties such as fruit, green stuff, carrot, &c. Banana they are especially fond of. It is a good plan to give them a small piece of banana or other similar dainty every day, only they should not be furnished indiscriminately with scraps from the table. Parrots are also very fond of sop food such as bread and milk, and where, as in some cases, they object to water the sop will form a good substitute. Messrs. Spratt sell a very good parrot-seed mixture.

Water.—Parrots require very little water, but it is a mistake to think that water is harmful to them. The water-tin should not be left in the cage all day, but it should be filled with fresh water and offered to the bird at least twice daily. If a water-tin is left all day in the cage of a parrot who for some mistaken reason has been deprived of water for any length of time, he will drink too much of it and so become ill. To this fact may be ascribed the origin of the idea that water is harmful to parrots. A bath should be put ready for the parrot once a week. It should be taken away, however, if the bird shows no inclination to bathe. In warm weather it is a good plan to stand the cage out in the rain for a little.

Grit.—Grit of some kind is always necessary. Spratt's Parrot Grit Mixture is very good. A piece of cuttlefish bone should also be always put in the cage.

Feather-Eating.—The objectionable habit of feather-eating indulged in by some parrots is caused, according to a well-known authority, by skin irritation set up by parasites, improper diet, or want of occupation, more commonly by the latter. A parrot should be given twigs to gnaw to keep it well occupied, and it should not be kept in a little-frequented room, or the habit will certainly be brought on by ennui, as the parrot is a sociable bird and likes plenty of company. An empty reel of cotton is a favourite toy with " Polly," and it will sometimes keep him amused for an hour at a stretch.

Different Kinds of Parrots.—Amongst the chief varieties of parrots which are brought to our shores are the Grey Parrot, the Rose-breasted Cockatoo, Blue-fronted Amazon, Ringnecked Parrakeet, and the Blue and Yellow Macaw : of these the Grey Parrot is the best talker, although the Blue-fronted Amazon can in many cases be made to rival it in this respect. The Macaws are usually kept chained, having a parrotstand on which to perch, as they are too big to be kept in an ordinary cage.

Parrot-Stand.

Ailments of Cage Birds.—If birds are thoroughly well cared for they will seldom cause much anxiety in regard to health. If strict attention is paid to their diet, cleanliness, and general hygiene, and, above all, if they are kept free from draughts, they will be found as a rule to keep well and to give very little trouble. It is as well, however, that every one should know how to treat the more common ailments with which our feathered pets are afflicted, and the following brief notes should be useful in this connection.

Moulting cannot be exactly classed as an ailment, as all birds moult—that is to say, cast their feathers once a year, generally late in summer or early in autumn, but it is important that great care should be taken of our pets during the moulting season. They should be well fed and kept warm and free from draughts. A little maw-seed should be added to the usual food—a rusty nail or a little saffron placed in the drinking-water. Either will form an efficient tonic.

Nails and Beak.—Birds' nails should not be allowed to grow too long or they may get caught in the wires of the cage, and often injuries to the toes may be caused in this way. Take the bird in your hand and, holding it on its back, lift it up to the light, when you will be able to see the veins in the claws and thus avoid cutting as far as these. Cut with a sharp pair of scissors. Take good care to hold the bird firmly, so that it cannot wriggle whilst the nail-cutting is proceeding.

Colds.—Colds are nearly always the result of draughts. They often bring about loss of voice for a time. Put the cage in a warmer room which is at the same time free from draughts, and add a little hemp to its diet—a few drops of glycerine and whisky may be added to the water with advantage.

Asthma.—Where a cold results in asthma, the condition of the bird is most serious. The complaint is indicated by heavy breathing and wheezing. The bird should be kept in a warm, moist atmosphere and a cloth placed round its cage. Egg and bread-crumbs with maw-seed should form its diet. Asthma is one of the most fatal diseases that attack our pets—unless taken in time a cure is hopeless. It should be avoided by keeping the bird well out of draughts.

Diarrhœa.—This is often caused by unsuitable diet or too liberal a supply of green food. Give a tiny drop of castor oil in the beak. An egg diet consisting of the yoke of a hard-boiled egg mashed up with some biscuit is often effective, or scalded rape seed may be given instead.

Constipation is often caused through an insufficient supply of green food. Often drops of glycerine added to the drinking-water will be found effective, and the cause should be removed by at once increasing the supply of green food. A little apple should be given where no green food is available.

Egg-bound.—When a hen bird after sitting for some days on a nest does not lay, but appears instead generally out of sorts, she will be found to be egg-bound. She should be held over a jug of hot water, and then the vent should be anointed with a little olive oil. Two drops of olive or castor oil should also be given internally.

HOSEHOLD REPAIRS AND UPHOLSTERY

It is a source of great economy in a household when one of its members shows an aptitude for executing simple home repairs, and can also turn her hand to upholstery work and carpentry. Not only can the money, which would otherwise have to be expended in hiring workmen to do the various odd jobs, be saved, but the home upholsterer can add to the beauty of her surroundings by making pretty curtains and hangings, and fashioning dainty little articles of furniture at a comparatively small cost. Many useful hints in regard to home upholstery and repairs are given in this article, and the various methods of painting, papering, and distempering walls are fully described.

The Household Tool Chest. — It is always useful to have a certain number of simple tools ready at hand for doing the various odd jobs which are required from time to time in every home. Although small chests ready fitted with tools can be bought, this is not a plan to be recommended unless one is prepared to pay a high price, and even then it will be found that many of the tools supplied are never required.

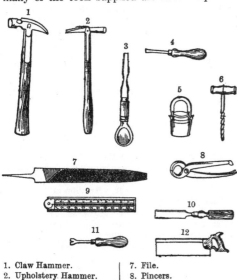

1. Claw Hammer.
2. Upholstery Hammer.
3. Screw-driver.
4. Brog or Bradawl.
5. Glue-pot.
6. Gimlet.
7. File.
8. Pincers.
9. Foot-rule.
10. Chisel.
11. Tack-lifter.
12. Saw.

It is much better to buy the few necessary tools of a first-class quality, and with care they will last for years.

The following will in most cases be found useful :—

2 Hammers—one strong and heavy and the other small and light for upholstery or light carpentry.

1 Screw-driver.
1 Saw.
1 Pair pincers.
1 Tack-lifter.
1 Foot-rule.
1 Chisel.

1 Gimlet.
1 Bradawl or Brog.
1 Glue-pot.
1 File.
A strong knife.

Also an assortment of tacks, nails, screws, hooks, &c., suitable for the purpose in hand, which can be bought as occasion arises. A nail-box should have different divisions in which the various kinds of nails can be kept separately.

Tools must be kept carefully or they will be unfit for good work. They must be protected from rust, and if they are not likely to be used for some time they should be rubbed over with a little grease.

To Prepare Glue. — Break some glue into small pieces and put it into the inner part of the glue-pot with cold water to cover it. Allow this to soak some time and then pour off any superfluous water. Then half fill the outer vessel with water, place the double pot at the side of the fire, and allow the glue to melt gradually, stirring occasionally with a stick. The glue must be applied with a brush or with a small pad made by tying a piece of flannel on to the end of a stick.

TO PAPER A ROOM

This is not a very difficult matter unless the room is a very lofty one. Like all other work it requires practice before it can be done very skilfully, and the amateur would be wise to try her 'prentice hand on an attic or small room before she attempts to paper one of more importance.

New wall-paper must never be put on the top of old, as this is most unhygienic. So the first step to take is to strip the wall of its old covering. Take a pail of hot water and a large white-wash brush and go over the wall with this, soaking the paper well. Allow the damp to soak in, and then scrape the paper off with an old knife or a piece of slate. If there are any holes in the plaster, fill these up with plaster of Paris made into a paste with water or size, or paste a piece of white paper over them. Next wash the wall over with a coating of weak size, and when this is dry the wall will be ready for papering.

Size is a jelly-like substance (8d. per lb.), generally used in the proportion of one pound to one gallon of water. This must be melted slowly over the fire and kept warm while in use.

Wall-papers are usually twenty-one inches wide, and are sold in lengths of twelve yards, so it will not be difficult to calculate the quantity required. If a patterned paper is chosen, an extra allowance must be made for matching the pattern on the various strips, but the amateur should choose either a plain or a striped paper in order to avoid this extra trouble of matching the pieces. Cheap wall-papers can be bought from 6d. to 1s. per piece, and, of course, there are many at a much higher price.

In addition to the paper, the following will be required: a pair of large scissors, a pail for paste, a paste brush, one or two soft dusters, or another dry brush for smoothing on the paper, and some good paste.

To make the paste :—

Take one pound of flour and mix it to a smooth paste with cold water ; then add more water until the mixture is of a creamy consistency. Boil this over the fire in a saucepan and add a little size or glue which will make the paste more tenacious. It is a good plan also to add a little alum (one and a half ounces), as this will prevent the paste from turning sour. The paste should be of the consistency of gruel when ready.

The paper must be cut in lengths according to the different parts of the room it has to cover, making it two inches longer than the actual measurements in every case. Then trim off the margins close to the pattern on one side and leave half an inch on the other. The pasting must either be done on a kitchen-table, or on newspapers spread on the floor. Paste one piece at a time, putting weights on one end of the paper if it is inclined to roll up. Be careful to paste all smoothly, and pay particular attention to the edges. Thin paper may be hung at once ; a thicker make should lie for two or three minutes to soften it, as it will then be less likely to tear in the lifting. When carrying the paper to the wall loop up the lower end of the paper with the two pasted sides together to prevent it from catching on anything. Then place one end to the top of the moulding or ceiling, and the left-hand edge to the corner line, cutting off any unevenness if necessary. When these two edges are well in position press the surface to the wall in every part with a duster or clean dry brush, first down the middle and then outwards to the sides. Avoid any rubbing which might spoil the colour of the paper. Unfold the lower part of the paper, and continue it right down to the top of the skirting-board length, where any surplus must be cut off. A few wrinkles and blisters may appear at first, but these will disappear when the paper dries and contracts. Place the next strip of paper so that its trimmed edge covers the margin of the first strip. It is always best to make two cut edges meet at the corners. Short pieces above doors and windows must be neatly fitted, and if there are any irregular parts to be covered use plenty of paste, as this will soften the paper and enable it to be moulded into any shape.

DISTEMPERING

This is painting with whitening and size mixed to a paste with water, and some colouring matter added. It is generally applied to plaster. When used in a natural white colour it is called white-washing.

To Prepare White-wash.—Take six pounds of whitening (cost about 3d.), put it into a clean pail, cover it with water ; let it stand twenty-four hours and pour the water off. This may be repeated several times if the wash is desired very white, but for ordinary purposes once is sufficient. Then add half a pound size dissolved in half a gallon of hot water and mix all to a creamy consistency. Add also one table-spoonful of powdered alum and enough washing blue to make it a natural white colour. Strain the wash and use when cold : it should be almost like a jelly and slightly sticky. It must be kept well mixed when in use. The above quantities will be sufficient to white-wash a small room or a good-sized ceiling.

Coloured Distemper is made by adding some colouring pigment to the above white-wash, such as yellow ochre for a cream tint, yellow ochre and black for stone colour, vermilion or Venetian red for pink, indigo for blue, and so on. These colours can be bought at any colour shop, and must be mixed smoothly with a little water before adding them to the wash. Add a very small quantity at a time, and then test the colour on a piece of paper. It must be remembered that the colour will look very much deeper in the pail than it will when dry on the wall.

Patent preparations can now be bought which will save the amateur the trouble of mixing the distemper, and these are quite inexpensive and easy to use. Full directions are given with each.

If the distemper is not to be used at once, a little water should be poured on the top to prevent a skin forming. It must always be well stirred up before use.

To Distemper a Wall.—The dust must first be brushed off and the wall then washed over with clean warm water and a brush. The water must be changed as soon as it becomes dirty. Then give the walls a coating of thin size and let them dry. If there are any cracks or holes, they must be filled up with plaster of Paris and whitening made into a paste with water and size, using one part plaster of Paris to three parts whitening.

For applying the wash use a good distemper brush, which will cost about 6s. Commence at the top of the wall and work downwards with even strokes backwards and forwards. Too much wash must not be taken up at one time or there will be splashing, and the work must be done as quickly and expeditiously as possible. The brush ought only to be put into the distemper half-way up its bristles, and then the surplus should be pressed out before applying

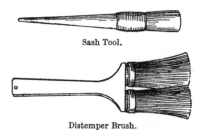

Sash Tool.

Distemper Brush.

the brush to the wall. Doors and windows should be kept shut while this work is being done to prevent the wash drying too quickly and looking patchy. When finished, a current of air may be allowed to pass through the room.

To White-wash a Ceiling.—This can only be done after considerable practice, and unless the ceiling is small and low the work should scarcely be attempted by a woman, as it means too much climbing about on steps and stretching of the arms and body. The ceiling must be prepared first, in the same way as a wall, by washing and then applying a coat of thin size. The white-wash should be put on in very even strokes along the length of the ceiling, the brush being worked evenly backwards and forwards. White-wash dries so quickly that unless it is applied quickly the work will have a patchy appearance.

PAINTING AND ENAMELLING WOOD

This work is very much simplified nowadays, as all colours can be bought ready prepared, and it is much better for the amateur not to attempt mixing the colours herself. Oil and colour men will supply any colour from about 6d. per pound, and sometimes they will lend a brush as well, only if painting is done to any great extent it is much better to possess one's own brushes. Brushes are expensive articles,

but good work cannot be done without them, and there is no economy in buying cheap ones. Fibre brushes, for instance, are sold at a much lower price than those made of bristles, but after they have been used a few times the fibres begin to drop out.

In order to obtain satisfactory results in painting, the article to be painted must be thoroughly clean and the surface smooth. Remove all dust, and wash the surface thoroughly with soap and water ; then allow the wood to dry, and fill up any holes with putty or cement. If there is any roughness this should be smoothed down with sand-paper. The professional painter will very often remove an old coating of paint before putting on another, especially if the former is blistered or broken in any way. This is done by the application of heat or some stripping fluid. It is work that can scarcely be undertaken by the home worker, and in many cases it is not necessary. When painting new wood a first coat of weak size will be necessary to prevent the paint soaking into the wood. The paint must be well stirred with a piece of stick before commencing and then applied with a brush with smooth, steady strokes. It must not be laid on too thickly, but well brushed in with the grain of the wood until no brush mark is visible. Two brushes are usually required, a small one for the intricate parts and a larger one for the wider surfaces. These brushes are called sash tools. The tips of the brushes only should be put into the paint. If two coats of paint are required the first must be allowed to become quite dry before the second is applied. New wood requires at least two coats, and sometimes a coat of varnish is put on the top.

Enamel Paints which are prepared with varnish are much used nowadays. They have a very smooth and glossy appearance when dry. They are used in the same way as other paints, and are especially useful in renovating plain wood furniture, water-cans, light wooden articles, &c.

When paint is not in use it should have a little water poured over the surface. This will keep it liquid and in good condition for future use.

CARE OF PAINT AND VARNISH BRUSHES

Before using a new brush it should be soaked in water for some hours. This swells the bristles and renders them less likely to fall out. Paint brushes that are in constant use should be kept in a tin with water or sufficient turpentine to cover the bristles. When they are finished with squeeze the paint well out on the edge of the paint pot, wipe the brushes with a rag, clean in turpentine, and then wash with plain soap and water and put aside to dry. Varnish brushes should be kept in the varnish while in use and then cleaned in the same way as paint brushes.

Old paint brushes can be cleaned by soaking

them over-night in strong soda-water and then washing them out thoroughly. The bridles of the brushes, whether of cord or metal, should not be allowed to soak in the water.

TO STAIN FLOORS

If it is a border round a room that requires staining, measure the distance from the wall all round and make a mark with chalk or a large-coloured pencil, always remembering to allow for an inch or two of staining to come under the carpet on all sides. Then knock down any nail heads with a hammer and fill up holes and crevices with a little putty, making the floor quite even. Sweep the floor over just before putting on the first coating of stain.

For a simple stain take two ounces of per-manganate of potash in crystals and dissolve it in one pint of boiling water. Apply this with a soft pad on the end of a stick, putting it on the way of the grain. Be careful not to soil the hands. Allow the first coating to dry, and then apply a second in the same way until the floor is dark enough. A floor that is stained for the first time will require more stain than one that is just being renewed. Leave the floor to dry, and then rub over with a flannel dipped in linseed oil. Leave again for a day and polish with bees'-wax and turpentine (see p. 65).

The above is a very simple and inexpensive staining, but it will be found satisfactory.

Ready-prepared stains of various kinds can also be bought from any colour merchants. They can be had in different shades, but walnut stain is perhaps the most suitable for a sitting-room. Some of these stains contain varnish, others require a coat of varnish put on the top. The former are on the whole the best to use. When putting on the stain apply it to one or two boards only at a time, as it dries very quickly and is apt to have a marked appearance, unless each small piece is finished before another is started. Be careful not to splash the skirting-board, and if an accident should occur wipe off the stain at once and wash the board. It is always better to use two brushes when applying the stain, a small one for painting near the skirting-board and a larger one for the other parts. After the staining is finished the floor should not be walked on for a day or two, and it should be kept as free from dust as possible. A plank supported on two footstools may be placed across the doorway.

TO ENAMEL A BATH

First thoroughly wash the bath with hot water, soap, and soda to get rid of all grease, and let it become quite dry. If there are any rough surfaces, rub them down with fine sand or glass-paper and brush away any dust this may make. Then take some good bath enamel and give the bath its first coating. White, cream, eau-de-nil, or flesh-coloured enamel may be used. Allow the enamel to become quite dry, and smooth it over again with the sand-paper if necessary. A second coating of the enamel must then be applied and allowed to dry as before. Two coatings are generally sufficient, but in some cases three may be necessary. It is very important to let one coating dry before putting on another, or the work will not be successful. Some enamel may take one or two days to dry. When finished fill the bath with cold water and allow it to remain two days. This will harden the paint and take away the smell.

TO MEND CHINA

Broken china that is to be used for liquids or to be frequently washed requires to be mended with rivets, and this can only be done by an expert. The rivets will cost 2d. each.

In the case of ornaments the pieces may often be united with cement, and with care will hold together for years. The cement may either be bought ready prepared or can be made at home. The following are two different methods of making it :—

(1) Take a little plaster of Paris and mix it to a creamy paste with beaten white of egg just before use.

(2) Take half an ounce gum acacia, dissolve it in water and strain. Add enough plaster of Paris to make a creamy paste just before use.

Both these cements must only be mixed in *very* small quantities as required.

China should be mended as soon as possible after it is broken ; if allowed to lie about the fine points or edges get rubbed or broken, and in consequence the joining will not be so close and will show more. Wash the broken pieces very carefully and then make them thoroughly dry and as warm as the hand can bear by putting them in the oven or near the fire. Use as little cement as possible—just enough to coat the two surfaces to be joined, and apply it with a match or fine piece of stick. Any surplus cement must be squeezed out and rubbed off at once. After pressing the two pieces together try to place the china in such a position that the weight of the pieces will tend to keep them together. If it is a plate, for instance, it might be propped up between two piles of books. Sometimes a binder is necessary, and an india-rubber band can be used with good effect. One piece must always be allowed to dry on before joining another, so if there are a number of fragments they might be joined in pairs one day and the next day two pairs put together, and so on until all is in shape.

BURST PIPES OR BOILER

Accidents of this kind usually occur after a frost if the water in the pipes has been allowed to freeze. The expanding of the water in freezing breaks the pipe, but it is only when the thaw comes that the water runs out.

When a leak occurs anywhere the stop-cock should at once be shut off so as to prevent more water from leaving the cistern. It is important, therefore, to know where the stop-cock is and also to see that it is kept in a turnable condition. Every second that is wasted may mean serious damage, and on no account must this special tap become so stiff that it cannot be moved.

Another plan is to flatten the pipe just at the break and thus check the flow of water. To do this slip a piece of wood or other resisting substance between the pipe and the wall and hammer the pipe sharply on to it. By this means the plaster of the wall need not be injured.

The accident of a burst pipe can generally be avoided by keeping the house warm enough. Where pipes are exposed to a very cold atmosphere it is a good plan to keep a gas jet or a small lamp burning on frosty nights.

An empty house, where there are no fires, is the one most likely to suffer. In this case it is safer to turn off the water-supply at the main and to empty the water out of the pipes if frosty weather is feared.

A more serious accident still is the bursting of a kitchen boiler. This is due to the boiler having run dry and the fire being kept on. If, on account of frost or any other reason, the hot water ceases to run, the kitchen fire should at once be put out.

GAS ESCAPES

An escape of gas may be caused by a break in the pipe—perhaps the result of a nail having been driven into it—by a badly-made joint having broken or given way, or because a screw-joint has become loose. The usual method of applying a lighted match or taper in order to find out the place of escape is a very risky one, and it is safer to avoid it altogether unless the escape is a very small one. If it is a big escape the safest plan is to turn off the gas at the meter and to allow a good current of air to pass through the room where the smell occurs. Then turn on the gas again for a few minutes, and you will no doubt be able to trace the hole quite readily by the smell or perhaps hear where it filters through the pipe.

A small hole can always be mended temporarily by patching it up with a good layer of soap or lard. Another way of stopping the escape is to flatten the pipe close to the faulty spot, but this may have the disadvantage of shutting off the gas from other parts of the house. If a pipe breaks in any part it may be temporarily mended by slipping in a piece of india-rubber tubing over the two ends and fastening it on with string.

The above are only temporary makeshifts, and the damaged pipe should be properly attended to at the earliest possible opportunity.

TO RE-MAKE A WOOL MATTRESS

When a wool mattress becomes slumpy it should be re-made; in fact, from a hygienic point of view this should be done every year.

Take the mattress into an unused room (one without a carpet is best) and spread it on a sheet on the floor. Take off the rounds of leather on the mattress, open one end and empty the wool on to the sheet. Then have the cover washed, starched and ironed. Pick the wool apart with the fingers or with a machine for the purpose. It is rather a tedious business to do it with the fingers, and sometimes it is possible to hire a machine from an upholsterer. The French housewife generally does this piece of work in her garden. When ready replace the wool in the case, keeping the mattress very even, and sew up as before. For sewing on the rounds of leather a long needle threaded with twine will be required.

TO RE-MAKE FEATHER PILLOWS

This should be done periodically when the covers become soiled. The simplest and tidiest method is to prepare the new or clean tick first by rubbing the inside over with bees'-wax or yellow soap, as this will prevent the points of the feathers from working through. Then make an opening in the old pillow the same size as that in the new tick and sew both openings together. Shake the feathers from one to the other, pin the seam before undoing the stitches, and the old case can be removed and the seam sewn up without any feathers flying about the room. Some people turn the feathers into a bath and wash and dry them before re-making the pillow, but this is rather a laborious and unpleasant operation. If the feathers require special cleaning it is better to send the pillows to a bedding manufacturer to have them properly re-made.

TO MAKE BLINDS

The simple blind on a roller is very easily made by the home worker. For material there is considerable choice in self-coloured or printed linens and hollands. If the blinds are being made for the front of the house, it is better to have them all alike, while for back or side-windows this is not so necessary.

When taking measurements take the length of the blind and six inches over to allow for a hem and a piece to go round the roller at the top. For the width measure the size of the roller less half an inch, so that the blind will be quarter of an inch narrower than the roller on both sides. Very often it is possible to buy the material the exact width required, as the rollers are generally made in regulation sizes, but, if not, allowance must be made for a one and three-quarter inch hem on each side.

It is very important to have a blind cut evenly; if badly cut it will pull up and down badly. Both top and bottom must be cut by the thread, and all hems must be measured exactly with a foot-rule or inch-tape, and a small pencil or chalk mark made where the hem has to come. The side hems must only be turned over once and then tacked down with herring-bone stitch (see p. 397). For the bottom hem mark a half-inch turning and a one and three-quarter inch hem. The latter will be wide enough to allow of a lath being slipped in, into which one end of the cord is fixed by making a hole through material and wood.

To fix the blind to the roller put a tack at each end on the raw edge of the material, turn the roller round until it is covered with the material, and then sew on with a needle and strong cotton. By this means the roller is quite covered and there is little danger of the blind tearing away.

It is not often that a blind is left perfectly plain as above; it is more usual to trim the edge with a piece of fringe or with some strong appliqué lace. When ornamentation of this kind is added, the blind itself must be cut shorter to allow for the width of the trimming. Sometimes a piece of lace insertion is let in as well just above the lath, or fancy-shaped medallions of the appliqué lace.

A MANTELPIECE DRAPERY

Perhaps the simplest way of hiding an ugly mantelpiece is the somewhat old-fashioned one of covering it with a cloth drapery of some sort. A plain board must first be made to fit on the top of the mantel-shelf, and this should extend

Drapery for Sitting-room Mantelpiece.

an inch or two beyond the edges all round. Underneath this shelf should run a thin iron rod fitted into eyes, and on this rod, curtains are run by means of rings. There is very considerable choice of materials for covering, such as serge, tapestry, silk, or velvet, but care must be taken to have it in keeping with the colour scheme of the room. A border of the material must first be made wide enough to cover the shelf and to hang down about a foot on the front and ends. If the material is light in texture it should be lined with sateen of the same colour to enable it to hang properly. A pretty fringe or gimp will be required to finish off the edge. It is always best to have this border separate from the board, as it can then be taken off and shaken when the room is cleaned. If made wide enough to tuck in between the shelf and the mantelpiece, there will be no danger of its slipping off. Underneath this border should hang curtains made of the same material and lined if necessary. These also should be edged with the same gimp or fringe along the foot and up the front edges. The curtains must be made wide enough to cover the entire fireplace, and if they are fixed to the rod by means of small rings they can be drawn backwards and forwards at pleasure. A more handsome effect can be produced by having the top border and edges of the curtains prettily embroidered.

Another Method of Draping a Mantelpiece.— A board must first be made as above with a one-inch strip of wood fastened underneath the front and sides. Cover this tightly with serge, sateen, or cloth of a colour to match the drapery and tack it underneath. The covering must be laid on very smoothly, the straight of the material running straight across the board. Commence tacking at the centre and work gradually towards the ends. If any wrinkles should appear they can generally be removed by damping the place and pressing with a hot iron. A valance is put on beneath this and fixed to the under-strip of wood. This can be of an ornamental character; a piece of pretty silk or wool tapestry, or some hand embroidery is the most suitable. A piece of buckram stiffening should first be put on; take the measurements carefully and make it two inches less in depth than the outer valance. Cover the buckram on both sides with thin sateen and tack it on to the strip of wood beneath the mantel-board. The top valance must also be lined with silk or sateen and finished along the edge with cord or fringe; fasten this on the top of the buckram background, and finish all neatly with an edging of gimp and studs or fancy nails. If curtains are required they can be fitted up in the same way as for the other mantelpiece border (see above).

When a bedroom mantelpiece requires covering, it is a good plan to make the drapery of some cotton material which can easily be washed, such as printed linen or cotton. The board might be tightly covered as above with a dark-coloured sateen and a buckram stiffening for the valance of the same colour below. The valance might then consist of a box-pleated flounce of the material about twelve inches in depth, and then curtains, if they are

Mantelpiece Drapery for a Bedroom—board covered with dark satin ; drapery made of chintz or printed linen with box-pleated valance ; curtains edged with a narrow gimp.

required, should be simply hemmed or finished with a narrow gimp which can be easily washed.

HOW TO LAY LINOLEUM

Except in the case of a large room it is not a very difficult matter to lay a floor with linoleum. If the room is very large and the linoleum thick, it will be better to have the work done by expert workmen ; in fact, in most cases when the linoleum is bought new the laying will be done free of charge. Still a few hints for the lighter pieces of work may be found useful.

First place the linoleum on the floor close to one of the skirting-boards. If it does not fit perfectly close any unevenness must be trimmed off with a knife. A very sharp hook-knife is the best for the purpose, as it will not slip out of position so easily as an ordinary knife. Fasten the linoleum in position with a few half-inch brads. If more than one width of material is required for covering, another strip must be joined to the first one, and if a patterned linoleum is being used care must be taken to match the pattern before cutting. When the edges are not exactly even, overlap one a little and trim off the surplus material with a knife. If the knife is held with the blade slanting towards the edge of the linoleum, this will give a slightly rounded edge which will fit all the more closely. Unless the edges of the joins are made to meet very exactly, water will soak through when washing is being done and cause the linoleum to shrink and rot. At the same time the two edges of a join must not be so tight that they require forcing down, as this would cause blisters. Fix the edges of the join with brads, driving

them in as close to the edge as possible without tearing the linoleum, and put them in pairs, one facing the other. If there is any likelihood of the floor being damp, tarred paper should be laid beneath the linoleum.

A BOOT CUPBOARD

A very neat and easily-made boot cupboard can be manufactured out of an empty orange-box, which can generally be procured from a grocer without any trouble. By setting the case on end the division in it will form the shelves.

First tighten all the joins by driving in a few small nails or strong tacks, and cover over the heads of these with a little putty. Then take a very hard brush and brush the wood well in order to remove all sawdust and splinters. Line the inside with some stout wall-paper, leather paper, or ordinary brown paper fixed on with strong paste or glue. Allow this to dry, and then cover the outside with some pretty chintz or self-coloured sateen, fixing it in position with small tacks or brads. Or, the wood on the outside may be smoothed over with glass paper and painted with two coats of Aspinal's enamel.

A curtain must then be made to cover the front. This may either be of chintz to match the outside or a self-coloured serge to match the paint or sateen with which the outside is covered. About a yard of material 50 inches wide will be required, and 2½ yards of ball fringe or other edging. Make a deep hem at the foot and sew the trimming all round with the exception of the top. Turn in the top to the required length, and fix it to the top of the cupboard with small brass-headed nails, arranging the material in box-pleats. Or, make a casing, draw up the curtain to the correct width with strong string or cord, and then fix it in position.

THE MAKING OF CURTAINS

The question of material for curtains in the various rooms has already been discussed under House Furnishing, the first section of this book, but a few hints for making may be useful for the novice who would like to make her own draperies.

Serge or Tapestry Curtains.—When measuring for a pair of curtains take the length from the curtain pole to the floor of the room plus six inches to allow for turnings, top heading, and a small amount for resting on the floor or looping up. When measuring for the fringe or other trimming take the length round the curtain with the exception of the top, plus half a yard to allow for turnings and easing on when sewing. Select material of from one and a half to two yards wide so as to avoid having a seam down the length of the curtains.

Commence by cutting the top and bottom of

the material perfectly even, because unless this is done the curtains will not hang well. Then lay a half-inch turning on the right side and along the bottom and two sides of the curtains. Tack or baste the fringe on to this turning, easing it on very slightly to prevent any dragging of the material, and stitch on with the machine. Two rows of stitching will likely be required to make the heading of the fringe lie flat, one along the outer and another along the inner edge. Some fringes have a double heading, between which the edges of the curtain can be slipped. In this case a turning on the material would not be required. If a fancy border or braiding is used instead of fringe this would be put on in the same way, easing it on *very* slightly

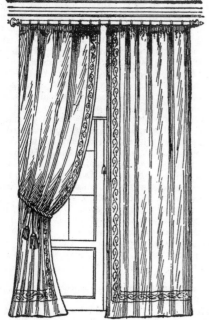

FIG. 1.—Serge or Tapestry Curtains—with fancy border stitched on, two rows of drawings at top with small heading, hooked on to curtain pole.

and then stitching it along the two edges. The trimming should be put an inch from the edge at the sides and from two to three inches from the edge at the foot, the turning on the material being made the necessary width. Care must be taken to turn the corners very neatly. Tacking before sewing is very important. When economy has to be studied one side only of the curtains need be trimmed, the side next the wall being left plain with its selvedge edge.

To finish the top of the curtains, turn over two inches of the material on the wrong side and make two rows of drawings a little way from the top and about half an inch apart.

Run a cord or piece of strong string through this and draw up the curtain to the width required. Tack a piece of upholstery tape over the drawings, arranging the fulness evenly, and then stitch along both edges with the machine. Finish off neatly with a needle and cotton and be careful to secure the ends of the drawing string. The upholstery tape should be the same colour as the curtains if possible, also the sewing cotton with which it is stitched.

Iron those parts of the curtain which require pressing, such as the edges and heading, and then sew curtain hooks on to the upholstery tape at intervals of about three inches apart or according to the number of rings on the curtain poles (fig. 1).

Curtains are sometimes lined if the material of which they are made is very thin or a specially heavy curtain is required. Self-coloured sateen to match the curtains or a special lining cashmere is very good for the purpose. The lining should be tacked on all round, leaving it a little full to prevent dragging, and then stitched in position at the same time as the fringe.

Linen or Cotton Curtains.—These are suitable for a bedroom, as they can so easily be washed. They can be made in a variety of ways. The simplest is to finish them off with a hem all round, a three or four-inch hem at the foot, and a one or one and a half inch hem at the sides. Or they may be trimmed with a cotton fringe or fancy edging in the same way as serge curtains.

If a fancy cretonne or printed linen is being used, a nice finish is a border or plain sateen in a pretty contrasting colour, or if the curtains are lined with sateen this might be brought

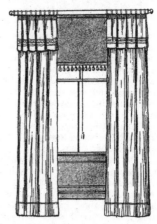

FIG. 2.—Plain Curtain with top turned over.

over to the right side to form a border. This would require to be carefully arranged and well tacked before any stitching is done.

The top of cotton curtains may be finished in the same way as those made of serge, or when they are light in weight, rings which can be slipped over a narrow brass rod might be used instead of hooks. If the curtains are made of some light-coloured material which requires frequent washing, they should be finished at the top in the same way as muslin or lace curtains, as they will iron more easily if the drawings can be undone.

A valance is sometimes used to finish the curtains at the top. The simplest way of making this is to allow an extra twelve inches when cutting the length of the curtains and to turn this piece over at the top before putting in the runnings. A fancy border stitched along this a few inches from the edge will make an appropriate finish (fig. 2). Another method of putting on the valance is to cut a separate piece

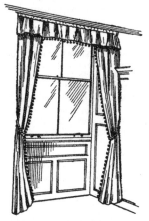

FIG. 3.—Chintz Curtains—edged all round with ball fringe. Drawn valance stretching across window, also edged with ball fringe.

and to arrange it right across the window (fig. 3). This may either be drawn or box-pleated. If drawn, allow half as much again as the width of the window for the length of the valance; if box-pleated, twice the width of the window will be required. A valance is usually made from twelve to fourteen inches deep and is finished along the foot with a ball fringe or trimming to match the curtain.

Instead of a valance a stiffly-shaped piece, called a pelmet, is sometimes used to cover the top of the curtains. This is a little more difficult to make, but still, unless the window is a very large one, it is within the scope of the home worker. A piece of stiff buckram, from eight to ten inches deep and the length of the width of the window, must first be cut, then covered very smoothly with a piece of the curtain material and lined at the back with self-coloured sateen. The edge may be finished

with ball fringe and a pretty gimp or other trimming to match the curtains.

Very careful measurements must be taken when cutting the buckram shape in order to get a straight edge, as any unevenness would be very noticeable. Instead of the straight pelmet, a shaped piece, as shown in fig. 4, might be made,

FIG. 4.—Top of Curtains covered with a shaped Pelmet.

but this is a little more troublesome to make and should only be attempted by an experienced worker.

Lace and Muslin Curtains should be finished on the top by turning them down about two and a half inches and stitching a broad tape along the line. A narrow tape should then be run through this casing and secured at one end. This can then be drawn up to the width required, and will be easily undone when the curtains require washing. Safety-pins with hooks attached should be used for fixing the curtains to the rings on the curtain pole.

Madras or plain muslin curtains should be made very full, as they will hang more gracefully. They must also be cut considerably longer than stuff curtains to allow for shrinkage in the washing. The edge can be finished with ball fringe, or sometimes a frill of the material is preferred. It is possible to buy the frilled material by the yard, or the frill can be made and sewn on to the curtain muslin. When cutting the frill allow double the length of the curtain to be trimmed for length and make the strips from four to five inches wide. Join the required number of strips together and make a narrow hem along one side. Turn down the other edge, draw it up with a strong cotton and sew it to the edge of the curtain, arranging the fulness evenly.

Casement Curtains.—In many of the modern houses casement curtains take the place of blinds. They should be made very simply of one of the special cloths sold for the purpose. Casement cloth is to be had in cotton, linen, silk, and woollen materials, and in a variety of colours and patterns. Cream colour is perhaps the most suitable. They may either be gathered into a heading and rings attached for running on a brass rod, or the rod may be passed through a casing at the top and the rings dispensed with. The former method is, however, better if the curtains are to be drawn backwards and forwards. These casement curtains are arranged in different ways and made different lengths according to the style of window under treatment. When the window is divided with a cross frame two pairs of curtains are used, one to cover the upper and the other the lower sash of the window. Or, again, they can be made the full length of the window, two or three pairs perhaps being required for a casement-shaped window. Some windows, again, have long casement curtains at the side and short ones as well to cover the windows. If the window-sill is broad the curtains should just touch it, but if narrow they might be brought a few inches below. The curtains can either be finished round the edges with a plain one and a half inch hem or with a hem-stitched border. They should always hang straight and never be looped up.

The woman who is clever with her needle can also make them look more artistic with some pretty embroidery, an open-work embroidery being particularly suitable for art-linen curtains. A little work of this kind will add very much to the charm of the curtains. Another pretty method of decorating casement curtains is by means of a stencil design. This is particularly suitable for little tussore or shantung silk curtains which are so much in fashion at present. It must be borne in mind, however, that stencil work will not wash well, and that it will mean dry cleaning each time the curtains require renewing, if the colours are to be preserved.

Stencil plates can be bought made of thin iron or zinc, and these can, of course, be used over

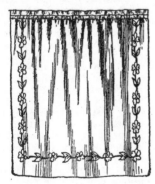

Small Casement Curtain with Stencil Design.

and over again, or a suitable design can first be drawn and then cut out of thin card-board or stiff manilla or wax paper. Various transfer designs can be used for the purpose: a con-

ventional pattern generally looks best. Spread a sheet of clean blotting-paper on a drawing-board, place the silk over this and the paper design on the top, and fix all very evenly in position with drawing-pins. Care must be taken to fix the stencil quite firmly. Stencil paint is then applied with a small brush, the choice of colours being a matter of taste. Allow the paint to dry, and then carefully remove the design. The pattern is sometimes outlined with a fine embroidery stitch to give it a more finished appearance. Stencil paints or dyes are sold in small tubes and must be diluted with water; the ordinary paints are not suitable for the work.

TO RE-UPHOLSTER A CHAIR

Small chairs are not very difficult to re-upholster, and an amateur might quite well attempt one that is simple in form.

Very often the cover of a chair becomes dirty or worn, and it has to be hidden out of sight for this reason and because it means considerable expense to have it sent away to be re-made. Loose covers are not much used nowadays, and, at the best, they soon get out of order and become shabby looking. Many pretty materials can, however, be bought for covering the seats of chairs. An oddment of good tapestry can often be picked up very cheaply at a sale, and nothing wears better or, what is better still, some very good art linen or serge worked with a pretty design can be used. The clever embroiderer will very soon transform an ugly set of chairs—chairs in a bedroom, for instance—and make them match the colour scheme of the room and look quite artistic.

The old cover must first be taken off the chair that is to be covered, as it is never a good plan to put a cover over anything that is dirty, a pair of pincers or a small tack-lifter being used to take out the small nails that fasten the cover. At the same time attention should be paid to the manner in which the covering has been fixed, as this will be a guide for attaching the fresh one. The old cover can then be used as a pattern for cutting out the fresh material. When using a patterned material be careful to centre the pattern when cutting the cover, otherwise it will look one-sided. If the stuffing of the chair has become flattened through long use, remove the under cover, which is generally made of linen or cotton, tease out the hair, and put a layer of fresh hair on the top in order to raise any hollow places. A layer of sheet wadding might also be put over the hair; it will make the top of the seat fuller and softer. Then cover this with a piece of fresh linen or calico. Next place the new cover on the top, centre the back and front, and fix them temporarily with small tacks. Do the same at the sides, and then tighten gradually all the way round, fixing the material in position with very small headless tacks. Always work from the centre of each side towards the corners. Trim off any superfluous material, and then cover the edges with a narrow gimp fastened on with brass-headed nails or coloured studs.

When the webbing supports of a chair give way, it will be necessary to take out the entire seat and to fix new webbing. This must be bought from an upholsterer's, and the best and strongest quality obtained. First remove the old webbing, fix on one end of the new on the old marks with small clout nails or strong tacks, then stretch well and nail down the second end before cutting. Nail on the other pieces in the same way, and when putting in the cross-way pieces, interlace them, as this will give greater strength and elasticity. A piece of new Hessian sacking should come next to cover the webbing, and then the hair for the seat should be teased out and replaced and the covers fixed on as above.

NOTES

NOTES

NOTES

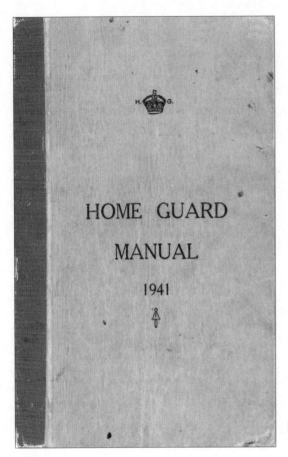

Home Guard Manual
1941

During the Second World War there was a call to arms that saw the founding of the Home Guard, a motley collection of men, poorly armed, many too old to fight. The Home Guard was untried in war, often without weapons or training, and they were Britain's last ditch defence against the Germans. But all was not lost and, over the period of a few months, this rag-tag group was armed, uniformed and trained using the *Home Guard Manual*. Taught basic fieldcraft, how to survive in the open, how to destroy tanks, ambush the invaders, use weapons of varying sorts, make boobytraps, read maps and send signals, the fledgling volunteer was turned into a veritable fighting machine.

0 7524 3887 5

£7.99

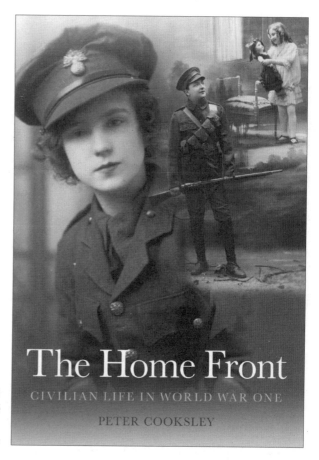

The Home Front:
Civilian Life in World War One

Peter Cooksley

The well-known history of the First World War is one of the trials and tribulations of men on the Western Front, but it is easy to forget this was the first truly global war that stretched out to touch civilians and soldiers alike. German submarines and their blockades saw rationing introduced across Britain, women went to work to replace men fighting in the trenches and the nation was shelled by battleships, bombed by Zeppelin and even attacked by plane. Here, for the first time, Peter Cooksley looks at the effects of the war on the civilian population and gives a new insight into what 'mummy and daddy did in the war', a propaganda slogan of the time.

0 7524 3688 0

£15.99

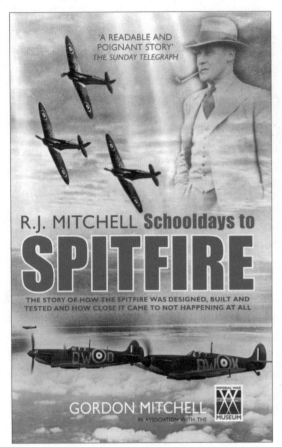

R.J. Mitchell:
Schooldays to Spitfire

Gordon Mitchell

The Spitfire began as a near disaster. The development of this famous aircraft took it from uncompromising beginnings to become the legendary last memorial to a great man – an elegant and highly effective weapon of war. The Spitfire would not have happened at all, however, without Mitchell's indomitable courage and determination in the face of severe physical and psychological adversity resulting from cancer. His contribution to the Battle of Britain, and thereafter to the achievement of final victory in 1945, was so great that our debt to him can never be repaid. This poignant story is written from a uniquely personal viewpoint by his son, Gordon Mitchell.

0 7524 3727 5

£12.99